D1490828

JUST JESUS

JUST JESUS
A Glimpse of the Three Volumes:

Volume 1 (chapters 1–51): Jesus goes to the Jordan to listen to John the Baptist. There he meets Peter, John, and Andrew. The news of John's imprisonment kindles his desire to do something for his people. Thus the spark: He must take over, and with a group of friends, he must awaken the spirit of the poor, telling them that God is on their side, fighting shoulder to shoulder with them. He forms his group in Capernaum, and through words and signs presents God's plan for humankind. Jesus gradually finds himself at the helm of a people hungry and thirsty for justice, who in turn see in God a Father, a Liberator, and a Friend.

Volume 2 (chapters 52–99): Jesus' activities in Capernaum and in the towns of Galilee, including his journeys to Jerusalem in the company of his twelve friends, where people meet them and follow them, prove that Jesus is a true leader of the people, a great prophet. His word becomes more and more intense as he criticizes the ambition and egoism of the rulers, while proclaiming the liberation of the poor. It is a liberation that will find realization in a new society that is communitarian and fraternal, where everyone is equal, where no one has more and others less. The conflicts among the ruling class — the priests, landowners, and officials — become more accentuated day by day. Jesus and his friends are fully aware of the calumny, the threats, the persecution, and the clandestine activities against them.

Volume 3 (chapters 100–144): Jesus' last journey to Jerusalem culminates in his arrest and death. The Romans as well as the religious authorities of the capital join hands to silence the threatening voice of the prophet. Jesus became prisoner, was tortured, and in his death experienced the weakness and helplessness of those who have fought for justice against the seemingly powerful and invincible rulers of this world. The God of life who does not allow the unjust to have the last word resurrected Jesus from the dead: this is the experience that Jesus' friends transmit to us. The first Christian community is built on this faith.

JUST JESUS

Volume 2:
The Message of a Better World

José Ignacio López Vigil
and
María López Vigil

Translated by
Trinidad Ongtangco-Regala

A Crossroad Book
The Crossroad Publishing Company
New York

The Crossroad Publishing Company
370 Lexington Avenue, New York, NY 10017

Copyright © 2000 by Crossroad Publishing Company

Originally published in Spanish as *Un tal Jesús*. First translated into English as *A Certain Jesus* by Claretian Publications, a division of Claretian Communications, Inc., U.P. P.O. Box 4, Diliman, 1101 Quezon City, Philippines; this edition has been adapted from the new Claretian edition, with biblical and liturgical references for pastoral use, copyright © 1998 by Claretian Publications.

All rights reserved. No part of this book may be reproduced, stored in a retrieval system, or transmitted, in any form or by any means, electronic, mechanical, photocopying, recording, or otherwise, without the written permission of The Crossroad Publishing Company.

Printed in the United States of America

Library of Congress Cataloging-in-Publication Data

López Vigil, José Ignacio.
    [Tal Jesús. English]
    Just Jesus : the scandalous gospel of Jesus of Nazareth, / by José Ignacio and María López Vigil.
    p. cm.
    Contents: v. 1. The people starving for love – v.2. The message for a better world – v. 3. The Passion book.
    ISBN 0-8245-1836-5 (v. 1 : alk. paper) – ISBN 0-8245-1849-7 (v. 2 : alk. paper) – ISBN 0-8245-1857-8 (v. 3 : alk. paper)
    1. Jesus Christ – Fiction. I. López Vigil, María. II. Title.
PQ6662.O664 T313 2000
863'.64 – dc21   99-050688

1 2 3 4 5 6 7 8 9 10   06 05 04 03 02 01 00

Contents

Foreword

I

Dorothy Day was the cofounder of the Catholic Worker. This was a house of hospitality in the poor area of New York City which was a haven for the outcasts of society. On any given day, one could find alcoholics, drug addicts, prostitutes, and petty thieves gathered around the table to share a big pot of soup and day-old bread. Adding water to the soup when unexpected visitors arrived (nearly every day) was a common occurrence. Dorothy herself had been arrested more times than anyone could remember. She was already in her seventies when she refused to take shelter in a mock nuclear attack and walked around the virtually abandoned streets to make a statement with her life that nuclear safety was an illusion, and the production of nuclear war material, sheer madness. Once she was introduced on a Catholic campus where she was to give a talk as "a living saint," to which she retorted, "you don't get rid of me that easily." A point well taken. There's something about elevating a person or a message to the spiritual that removes its bite. Peter Maurin, cofounder with Dorothy of the Catholic Worker, used to say that the gospels were dynamite but the church kept the dynamite wet so that it would never explode.

Every Good Friday within recent memory, in the City of Manila, the urban poor have enacted their own version of the suffering and death of Jesus. Carrying a large cross, banners, and cardboard replicas of their shanties, they do their own stations of the cross in front of government, business, and even church offices with the message that Jesus continues being crucified today in the urban poor, whose shanties are brutally demolished, they themselves seriously injured and often left "without a place to lay their head." Often enough, they meet a procession emanating from the church replete with members of mandated organizations and regular churchgoers. Though externally not radically different in appearance, they represent quite different messages: one, transcendent (Christ died for our sins); the other emphasizing the immanent (Christ has made a preference for the poor and continues to suffer when they are oppressed, beaten down, despised).

On Good Friday of 1980, Alex Garsales and Herman Moleta, two active lay leaders in basic Christian communities, took the parts of Jesus and an apostle in the passion play of Kabankalan, Negros Occidental, in the Philippines. Very much aware of the part that Jesus was exercising in the life of the community, Alex stated that more than a historical event was being commemorated in that celebration. As if to underline the truth of that statement, their bullet-riddled bodies were found in the cogon grass on Easter Monday.

What other country in the world has the number of martyrs that the Philippines has offered in the past twenty-five years, proving that the gospel has lost nothing of its bite, which caused the death of God among us two thousand years ago? A few years ago, I decided to make a calendar and recorded on the calendar all the men and women of faith who died (only those who died for justice, not those persecuted) because of what they believed in, that God continues to act in this world among the poor to bring about a kingdom of justice for all, and there were more than enough names for every day of the year.

This book, then, is for those who believe that the gospel has lost nothing of its bite and that it continues to disrupt and disturb our comfortable, cushioned Christianity. The Jesus presented here enters our lives as the great disturber, comforting the afflicted and afflicting the comfortable. May he continue to do so.

EDWARD M. GERLOCK*

II

Just Jesus is a work of art, at the same time a theological undertaking and a pastoral effort. One must insist on its worth, without looking at it as if it were just another book. This text is of great literary and dramatic quality, a proof of the seriousness and capability of the authors.

The content proves to be even more interesting. The theological backdrop presents relevant questions to us. This is not a new children's story about Jesus; nor is it written for entertainment; rather, it is a profound theological exposition.

---

*Edward M. Gerlock is a free-lance theologian, sociologist, and photographer. He is currently a part-time editor for Claretian Publications. He also ministers to the elderly.

We are accustomed to seeing the figure of Jesus from this side of his resurrection and ascension to heaven; we are used to seeing him in liturgical rituals, mythicized by painters, musicians, and other artists. *Just Jesus* focuses on him from another angle, prior to the resurrection, showing him as the historical Jesus, a human figure as seen by his contemporaries, his friends, his adversaries, and (this may be judged as more debatable) just as he saw himself from his human conscience.

These two perspectives on Jesus, however complementary, are radically different. To project onto Jesus of Palestine all we believe him to be, all we have thought of him as the Risen Jesus, is an error in historical perspective, confusing levels and bringing false and tragic consequences in understanding the entire phenomenon which is Jesus. If we reduce the total Jesus to the Palestinian Jesus, we cut off a very important part of that totality. Likewise, if we reduce the total Jesus to the Risen Jesus, we also amputate an important part of that same totality. The first amputation may discredit Jesus' divinity; the second, his humanity. Both are equally heretical and dangerous.

This book may seem to underemphasize the perspective of those who totally believe in the Risen Christ. The good thing is that this book will force them to go to the Palestinian Jesus, the historical Jesus, which is the real form Jesus adopted to preach the kingdom and to bring people to the Father. What might be disturbing to them is the tremendous demand of this earthly Jesus, who emptied his divinity in a concrete and historical way. These believers hide themselves not so much in the Risen Jesus, but in the ritualized and mythicized Jesus.

This book gets us totally into the scandal of Jesus according to his enemies — that Jesus, being a man, claimed to be the Son of God, the Messiah, greater than Moses, and so on. The Risen Jesus turns out to be less scandalous and more fitting if the intrinsic unity between the living Risen Jesus and the Crucified One is broken. For these people, reading *Just Jesus* can be of much help if they try to better understand this scandal rather than solely looking for reasons for their faith.

For those who do not quite know who this certain Jesus is, those who know him only through ideological manipulation passed down through the centuries, this book will also be very good. It will bring them back to a necessary initial experience, faithfully situating them side-by-side with the Palestinian Jesus in whom it was indeed difficult to see God in person. Will they remain there, focusing on the purely human aspect of the complex reality of Jesus? Is it not necessary to proclaim Jesus of Nazareth as the Risen One, as the God-chosen One? Does not the text underscore the difference between Jesus and his disciples?

This brings us back to what the gospels are meant to be. *Just Jesus* is written from the accounts of the gospels and, obviously, situated before the gospels. It is a fact that the gospels are not purely historical narratives; they are the expression of the memory and faith of the first communities, many of whom witnessed the experience of the Risen Christ more intensely than the memory of the Crucified One. The gospels are narratives in which the expression "Jesus is Lord" is very explicit, yet at the same time the concrete experience of what had been Jesus' historical life is not clearly stated.

Just Jesus is situated in the tangible experience of the historical life of Jesus. For this reason, an attempt must be made at a literary re-creation, just as the gospel stories strive at a theological re-creation. Both are based on historical data, used for example by Josephus (though he ignored many of the details transmitted more or less elaborately by the gospels). It is obvious that the theological re-creation proves to be more authoritative than the literary reconstruction this book presents. *Just Jesus* does not try to replace the gospels, but shows how these should be read, deepened, and lived.

An important point is the pastoral relevance of this book. It is, indeed, a pastoral work even if some theological problems may arise on account of the option taken by the authors in their approach to Jesus. It is certainly not a novelistic narrative of Jesus' life; it is a tool for evangelization — a proclamation of the good news not only for the poor but also for those who have heard it but need to be reimmersed in it. The book is certainly shocking, as it jolts the reader and recovers the vitality of the evangelical message, which has become somewhat mummified in translation.

For those very much steeped in traditional religiosity (with traditional and popular not being necessarily synonymous), the shock may be a bit violent. It could be a positive and necessary element to help place their faith on the level of Christian praxis. This should be done with care and vigor. For better assimilation the book may require a well-planned system of pedagogy and a sharing in community.

The style, the mood, and the contents of *Just Jesus* are derived and lived from the theology of liberation and from the preferential option for the poor. This is where some may stumble, not so much simple folk who may disagree with the form perhaps, but more so the educated and the

Sadducees who question more its content. They tend to see in *Just Jesus* a politicization of the faith and a revolutionary radicalism, a form of class struggle, the same way some view the theology of liberation. They confuse "class struggle" with the prophetic struggle against sin. I am aware, though, that neither in the theology of liberation nor in this book is everything prophetic struggle, even though the consoling call is addressed mainly to the poor.

In conclusion, *Just Jesus* is a great challenge and can be of practical benefit to a great number of people. Sometimes a direct reading of the Bible in ecclesial communities is sufficient to recapture the living word of God and to stimulate people to action. However, this is not always possible. A greater catechesis is needed which can be done through a discussion in community of books like *Just Jesus*.

IGNACIO ELLACURÍA, SJ*
Extract from the preface to the Spanish edition

III

For a number of years I had been toying with the idea of writing a life of Christ.

About ten years ago, a Jesuit friend of mine who has been working as a missioner in the mountain villages of Honduras urged me to get my hands on a copy of a book entitled *Un tal Jesús,* a creative retelling of the gospel story developed for the people of Latin America. My friend's enthusiasm proved to be more than justified. *Un tal Jesús* blends together Christology, contemporary New Testament studies, and liberation theology in a way that highlights, skillfully yet simply, both the immensely attractive humanness of Jesus and the overarching divine commitment to liberating human beings from every form of oppression.

This was the book, I soon realized, which I had secretly been wanting to write all along. "That's the way it actually was!" I kept exclaiming to myself as I made my way, chapter by chapter, through this version of the gospel story. For reasons I cannot altogether account for, I had the queer yet firm recollection of having been "there" before, as if, after two thousand years of lapsed memory, I had somehow awakened to the startling realization

---

*Ignacio Ellacuría, SJ, along with three other Jesuits, their housekeeper, and her daughter, were assassinated at their residence in El Salvador on November 16, 1989.

that I had been present to these scenes and events centuries ago. The work so excited me that it was all I could think or talk about for several months afterward. The first time I devoted a seminar to Un tal Jesús, the students did not want to see the course come to an end.

The theology of Un tal Jesús arises out of the experience of men and women fighting to surmount enormous poverty, economic exploitation, and political violence. The story "works" by drawing a parallel between the situation of injustice in many parts of Central and South America today and the life and time of Jesus. Jesus becomes a campesino whose awareness of himself as a prophet grows and develops, whose basic message is about the Kingdom of God being a kingdom of justice, whose humanity is never eclipsed by divinity, and whose good news is as much the attractiveness of his own personality and humanity as it is the message about God's Kingdom. He tells jokes and stories. He sings and dances. His hands are callused from hard word, and, like so many in South America, he even has a nickname, "Moreno" [in the original Spanish], "the dark one," because of the color of his skin.

There were two things which my students enjoyed about the book. First, they fell in love with the figure of Jesus. From week to week, they would remark about how human Jesus appeared there, so unlike the portrait of him they had grown up with. His story assumed a kind of naturalness, indeed, a believability, which drew them into the gospel. They would never again be able to read or hear many gospel passages the same way as before. Un tal Jesús had made the gospel story come alive without reducing it to the genre of religious fantasy. Jesus had feelings and emotions, as did his companions and his mother. He lived and breathed in this world. However prophetically he would react to the things he witnessed, Jesus never came across as mysterious, otherworldly, or serenely ascetical. Even the Jesus who was raised from the dead still remained a companion and friend; he had not suddenly become a distant, elevated supernatural being. The book helped some of them to relate to Jesus, really and earnestly, for the first time. For the first time, they heard a Jesus who laughed.

The second thing the students liked about the book was the way it deployed the theme of justice and God's "preferential love for the poor" throughout Jesus' ministry. For, just as the figure of Jesus as they knew it had seemed remote and unreal, so too his mission and work seemed un-connected with the pressing concerns of ordinary men and women. The Jesus they had been raised with was completely divorced from history, more a citizen of heaven than of the earth. He was a model of moral behavior, a teacher of high spiritual ideals and values, their point of contact with the unseen God, and the one who had rescued them in some inexplicable fashion from their sins. In fact, their understanding of salvation and redemption was so focused on the remission of sin and eternal life that the good news about Jesus himself amounted to little more than a pious curiosity or a soothing tale for world-weary souls; it had as much relevance as a statue of the Infant of Prague.

To put the matter bluntly, *Un tal Jesús* had given the story of Jesus back its guts. There really was something worth proclaiming and worth laboring to help men and women understand. There really was a "divine cause" which Jesus had taken upon his shoulders after being baptized at the Jordan. The gospel, fully lived, could make a difference to history, not merely in the private space of the individual's own spiritual development but in the public space of communities, politics, society, and culture. The matter of human sinfulness, which ultimately came to account theologically for why Jesus was crucified, was absolutely inseparable from the concrete misery, powerlessness, and injustice that had caused the prophetic voices of old to blaze out against the rich and powerful of the land; the same evils would have stirred the soul of Jesus.

Many people find it difficult to comprehend why the church, in talking about Jesus, makes so much of sin when forgiveness comes so easily. And the reason for their bewilderment is that the forgiveness of sins is not so much a matter of sacrament and ritual as it is a matter of doing justice and promoting reconciliation among men and women. The real work of redemption, in other words, involves throwing oneself, heart and soul, into confronting and transforming all the forces, structures, relationships, and institutions which rob human beings of their freedom and suck away their life. This task is something to which we can devote our lives, too, just as Jesus did. His story has compelling reason for being retold.

The reader comes away from *Un tal Jesús*, then, with two graces which have worked one over intellectually and morally. One discovers a new way of relating to "a certain person named Jesus," and one senses that the real purpose of Jesus' life was both more complex and more exciting than the claim that he came to take away the sins of the world generally sounds. Furthermore, these graces suggest two focal points for talking about Jesus today. Jesus was fully and attractively human, more so, perhaps, than any of us might ever hope to be; and God had chosen the side of those who counted as nothing in the eyes of the world: those chronically hungry, those who thirst for righteousness and justice, those whose basic rights had been violated, those burdened by poverty, guilt, and sin. What is there left for us to do, except to want to be with Jesus and to continue doing what he has begun?

WILLIAM REISER, SJ*

---

*Father William Reiser is a member of the Society of Jesus. He teaches theology at the College of the Holy Cross in Worcester, Massachusetts. He has written a number of books, including *An Unlikely Catechism* (Paulist Press), *Into the Needle's Eye* (Ave Maria Press), and *Renewing the Baptismal Promises* (Pueblo Publishing Co.). This section is an excerpt from the introduction to the book *Talking about Jesus Today: An Introduction to the Story behind Our Faith* (Paulist Press).

JUST JESUS

52

The Ten Drachmas

Peter: Get up, guys, it's daytime already! Hmmm. Hey, Philip, Thomas, Judas! C'mon, Nathanael, don't hide under that mat! And you, Jesus, stop pretending you're asleep — I know your old tricks already! Up, up, everybody, and double time!

James: Damn you, Peter, you never let anyone sleep! At night, you're even worse than a pig when you snore, and now you get up ahead of the cocks.

Peter: Stop grumbling, you red-haired whiner, and get up now!

Peter woke us up when it was hardly dawn, while there were still a few stars roaming the sky. Grudgingly, we lazily stretched our limbs, then headed for the fountain at the corner of the yard, so that we could freshen up. Although it was still early, Lazarus's inn at Bethany was already bustling with hundreds of pilgrims. As we left the yard, we passed through the inn's kitchen. There was Martha, Lazarus's sister.

Martha: Good morning, boys! So, did you sleep well last night?

Peter: Very well, madame. Now, we're a little bit hungry. Or better, we're starved.

Martha: Well, why don't you get yourselves a handful of dates from that barrel? That's precisely why they're there, to appease a grumbling stomach.

Lazarus entered carrying a pail of goat's milk.

Lazarus: Uff. That goat gives more milk than the late Ingrid, who fed all the children of Bethany. Here, take it, Martha. How are you, my friends? Do you want to try this milk? It's still warm and creamy! There's nothing better than goat's milk. God bless her teats!

Peter: And our bellies! Yeah, why don't you serve us some?

Martha: Serve them yourself, Lazarus. I gotta get the bread ready. It's getting late and I haven't kneaded the flour yet.

Lazarus filled a pot with milk and gave it to us. The fresh goat's milk passed from one mouth to another amid words of admiration. Meanwhile, Martha, with her striped sleeves rolled up, kneaded the dough, sinking her agile fingers into the flour. When the last of the thirteen guys raised the pot of milk, licking it with relish, Mary, Lazarus's other sister, appeared in the kitchen, with tears in her eyes.

Mary: Lazarus! Martha! You won't believe what just happened to me.

Lazarus: But is this the time for waking up, silly girl? Oh God of heaven, why did you give me such a sister? You overslept again, didn't you?

Mary: Oh no, Lazarus. I was awake at the first cock crow and I started to work. But you know how hard work brings bad luck. Oh!

Martha: What's happened, Mary? Tell us!

Mary: Martha, help me look for it. I can't find it anywhere. Oh!

Lazarus: What the hell are you missing?

Mary: One of my drachmas, one of my ten coins. I only have nine of them. I'm missing one of my coins.

In our town, the women would hang ten coins — a remembrance of the dowry given to them by their parents on their wedding day — from their ears or on the tip of their scarf in front. For all the women of Israel, those coins were of great value. Some, like Mary, from Bethany, never parted with them, even when sleeping.

Lazarus: Don't cry anymore, woman, you'll find it again. What a pain in the butt you are! When you're happy, you're like a whirlwind, and when you're sad, you're like an earthquake. I don't know which is worse.

Martha: Stop crying now, Mary. Later, we'll sweep that corner and you'll find that lost coin of yours. But first, let me finish with this flour. I've already put the yeast...

Mary: Oh my money! Oh my money!

When we left the inn, Mary was still weeping disconsolately over her lost drachma, while Martha was kneading the bread. We crossed the Mount of Olives and entered the great city of Jerusalem, which, as always, was bursting with people.

Peter: There are no more olives, fellas! Here goes the last one!

James: But there's still some wine to last us for a while! Well, unless this drunk, Matthew, finishes it off in just one gulp.

Matthew: Will you mind your own business and leave me in peace?

Nathanael: Let's buy some more olives or cheese.

Peter: Of course, Nata. C'mon, loosen up your pockets and give your share.

At noontime, we went inside a tavern in the fullers' street, to have lunch. The days in Jerusalem were passing rapidly, and we had a few days left before going back to Capernaum. We had little money left.

Peter: How 'bout you, Philip?

Philip: What d'ya mean?

Peter: Let go of your money. C'mon, don't turn your face aside. Don't you feel hungry at all?

Philip: Yes, but...

Matthew: But as always, you haven't got any coppers to share, is that right?

Philip: Well, the truth is, yesterday, there was a rogue who held me up in the street and took away the little money I had. Damn, if I could only grab him by the neck!

Jesus: Oh, a rogue, really, huh? What number did you bet on, Philip? C'mon, tell us the truth.

James: It's even worse than that, Jesus. Do you know what happened to this fat head? Seeing how stupid he was, they lured him into a doves competition in the square!

Nathanael: How is it possible, Philip? Even nursing children know it's all a hoax.

Philip: Well, they told me I was going to win a fortune.

James: And they stripped you naked of your money instead.

Nathanael: Don't you come to me and ask for even a single coin, do you hear? I don't feed stupid people like you.

Philip: What do I do now, Nata?

Matthew: Why don't you look for that coin Mary lost? At least you would have something for tomorrow's breakfast!

Philip: Hey, don't talk to me about that fool. Yesterday she made a big fuss about a rat, and now it's her coins. I don't know how that cross-eyed woman manages, but she's always in for trouble or involved in a mess.

Jesus: If I told you what she said last night, you wouldn't believe...

Peter: Who, Mary?

Jesus: Yeah, she was asking a lot of questions about us, and I was taken aback when she expressed her desire to do something for the Kingdom of God.

James: And you told her just to play the flute somewhere.

Jesus: No, I told her we hadn't thought of it, but it wasn't a bad idea, after all.

Peter: What was it that we hadn't thought about, Jesus?

Jesus: That Mary should come with us.

Peter: Are you out of your mind? You want women in our group?

Jesus: Why not, Peter? What's wrong with that?

Peter: No, no, no, this is going too far. Since when can a woman take part in men's affairs?

Jesus: Not one, but two, because Martha is also very enthusiastic about joining. There's no question about Lazarus. The three could help us a lot here in the South.

Peter: With Lazarus, there's no problem. But the women, no. The women's place is the kitchen. Damn it, that's where they belong.

Jesus: What do you say, James?

James: Well, Adam took his siesta at a bad time. We could have had one rib more and less problems. I don't want to have anything to do with women. What can those two dishwashers do?

Jesus: They can work for us; they can give us their opinion. In the Kingdom of God, everyone is needed.

James: Their opinion! Listen, Jesus, this crazy woman, Mary, what does she know that we don't know? And this chubby-cheeked Martha, what new things can she teach us? No, no, dark one, get back your senses, and forget it.

Jesus: And what do you say, Matthew? Don't you welcome the idea?

Matthew: All I can say is that with or without women, this group is going to fail. Yeah, and I say this not because I'm drunk. Open your eyes: we're a handful of good-for-nothing guys amid a multitude of people with problems. What the hell can we do?

Jesus: Look, I guess Martha could answer your question. Didn't you see her this morning? Didn't you see how she prepared bread?

Philip: How else, Jesus? As every woman knows: with water, flour, oil, and . . .

Jesus: And a bit of yeast. Martha knows how, with that piece of yeast, the whole dough rises, and she can teach us that.

James: And what has that got to do with us?

Jesus: We're like that yeast, James. God is like the woman who kneads the dough.

Philip: Therefore, God is the baker. I've never heard of this before.

Jesus: A male baker, no. A female baker, yes. The women's hands are made for the kitchen.

James: Watch your tongue, Jesus. As far as I know, God is a man!

Jesus: You've seen God? You know for sure God is male? How do you know it?

Nathanael: The Scriptures say that God is male.

Jesus: What I remember is that the Scriptures say that God created us in his own image. And he made us as man and woman. If man is God's image, then the woman ought to be too.

Peter: Okay, okay, what the Scriptures say is one thing, and Martha's legs are another!

Philip: And the other worse thing is Mary's tongue. Don't tell me God is also as scatter-brained as she.

Jesus: Listen, Philip: didn't you notice how desperate Mary was over her missing coin?

Philip: Right, Jesus. That woman is always restless.

Jesus: And so is God. This is where they are alike. God also despairs when a child of his gets lost. He looks for her everywhere. Just like Mary, who is not content with her nine drachmas. She loses one, and it's as if she had lost everything. She doesn't want to lose a single coin.

Peter: Hey, Jesus, has the wine gotten to your head?

We left the inn when we had consumed everything, the wine, the bread, and the olives. We went around the city four times and then returned to Bethany, at sunset. When we were near Lazarus's place, we began to hear the unmistakable voice of Mary. As we went inside, she welcomed us, dancing.

Mary: Hey, guys from Capernaum. Look! I've found my coin! Look at my missing drachma.

Jesus: Where did you find it, Mary?

Mary: Over there in the woodshed. I had to light some lamps and sweep the place well. And I found it! That's why I tell the good news to anyone who enters through that door!

Peter: Well, one doesn't have to go through any door to hear you. Your voice can be heard from Bethbasi!

Jesus: See what I mean, Peter? Look how happy she is. God also leaps with joy for the life of each of his children, he dances for us, like it was a feast day. That's also true of Mary.

We slept very late. It was quiet — only cricket sounds could be heard all over the yard of the Beautiful Palm Tree. The creamy light of the full moon of the Passover slipped through the cracks of every roof. I think that night everyone thought for the first time that we all slept in the huge lap of our mother God.

•

In Jesus' time (and even at present), in several Middle Eastern areas, women adorned themselves with coins. These were sewn to veils that covered their faces or hair, or they were embedded in various head ornaments, or the women simply wore them as necklaces or earrings. On several occasions, these coins were given to them as dowry by their parents on their wedding day. That is why they considered these coins as their most precious property. Some women would not part with them at any time, not even when sleeping. That Mary's ornament — the dowry — consisted only of ten drachmas was a sign of poverty. There were Middle Eastern headdresses in which hundreds of gold or silver coins were used. For an Israelite woman, losing a coin of the dowry brought great pain, largely because of its sentimental value. The woman of Israel had no role in public life, with respect to participation, decision making, and responsibilities. Her responsibilities at home were also secondary in nature. Her training restricted her role to domestic chores: she learned how to sew, how to weave, and how to cook. Generally, she was not taught how to read. On the farm and in similar situations, the woman worked side by side with the man in harvesting crops, selling them, and so on. Vis-à-vis her husband, her father, or her brother, her category became that of a servant. "The woman" — as a Jewish historian said in Jesus' time — "is, in every aspect, of a lesser category than man."

This discrimination against woman, this machismo in Jewish society, was justified in many ways. One was along moral lines, given this kind of thinking: the woman is weak and dangerous at the same time and, there-fore, must situate herself on the margin of public life, for she may provoke temptation, or man may abuse her, when overcome by his passions. When there is too much insistence on woman's debility, with respect to man, just as her ability to tempt is highlighted, likewise a radical inequality between the two sexes is established. Jesus, in his words, and much more in his attitude toward different types of women, had on several occasions shattered this idea and this false morality. That was how he came to accept women in his group: according to his vision of life, man is not a mere pawn of his sexual instincts but can have full control of the same. It is not merely an ascetic control of his instincts, or repression, but is something that is born out of a new scale of values: men and women are indeed brothers and sisters because they are equal in the eyes of God. The kingdom of justice is capable of touching man and woman in similar ways and, in so doing, of transforming their lives. Even one's looks can be purified (Matt. 5:28). In no other sphere of social life during his time did Jesus show his obviously radical attitude as in the manner by which he treated women.

In doing so, Jesus not only elevates the position of women, but also puts them on equal footing with men. This act gives us a new image of God. In the parable of the lost drachma and that of the yeast, Jesus presents two women as his protagonists in the analogies, and the endings appear surprising. In the story of the lost drachma, the parable simply means: God is like this. This is how God becomes happy and worried. Jesus compares God's feelings with those of a woman. It is a way of saying that God has no gender, that God is revealed through a man as well as through a woman. In the parable of the yeast, Jesus talks of what happens in the Kingdom of God: from the smallest — a bit of yeast — God makes something good. That is to say, by making use of a group of poor men and women, God will create a new history of humankind. In the parable, this process starts with a woman: the mediator of that transformation of the mass (dough) is a woman, Martha. The two parables are an indication of Jesus' enormous freedom as he speaks of the realities of the kingdom. The woman is part of the kingdom, just as the man is. If all this is characteristic of the gospel, then we can affirm that God is our Father and our Mother as well. In so doing, we not only find inspiration in Jesus, we also find basis for it in the Old Testament, where God's love is compared to that of a mother on several occasions (Isa. 49:14–15; 66:13).

In a number of countries there exists, side by side with a marked machismo in dealing with women, a profound love for the mother. For many men and women, to say that God is Father is either not to say anything or to give a more or less negative comparison, linking God to a paternal figure in some families or in others to a father who has abandoned his family or been guilty of violence. In contrast, to say that God is Mother may evoke, for many people, images of an immense affection, an absolute surrender, a great concern. All these are theological realities of the first order in our understanding of God.

(Matt. 13:33; Luke 13:21 and 15:8–10)

53

Beside the Sheep Gate

We left Lazarus's inn at Bethany before sunrise and took the road to Jeru-salem. We crossed the Cedron brook and proceeded until we came close to the walls surrounding the temple. At that time, through one of the gates to the north, called the Sheep Gate, passed herds of sheep for the Passover sacrifice.

Peter: Hey, what's that noise? They bellow a lot, more than sheep.

Philip: It's coming from there, from the pool.

Peter: Let's go find out what's going on there.

Very close to the Sheep Gate was the pond of Bethesda, meaning House of Mercy. It had two large pools surrounded by white columns and five entrance doors.

Praying Woman: Oh, most Almighty God, please make a miracle! Make a miracle! Lord of the heavens, send forth your angel! Send him soon, Lord!

Peter: Hey, James, what's with that woman? Is she crazy? Look, look how she dilates her eyes.

James: Don't be stupid, Peter. Can't you see she's blind?

Philip: Too many sick people around here! The ten plagues of Egypt have all gathered together here.

A Sick Woman: Hey, you stinking one, spit on the other side. Your filth turns me off.

A Sick Man: I will spit where I please, you crippled by the devil.

Another Sick Woman: Have pity on me, holy God, have pity on me, holy Lord, have pity!

Peter: Hey, Jesus, James, Philip, let's go inside!

While passing through one of the gates, we saw the pool of Bethesda. It was surrounded by dozens of sick men and women. The crippled, the blind, and the lame were milling around the edge of the pool. The air reeked intensely of urine, pus, and sweat. And the flies, inebriated perhaps by all that dirt, formed a black cloud over the sick.

11

James: What the hell is going on here? All the sick are looking into the pool, waiting for what?

Jesus: Hey, guy, come here. Tell me, why are there so many? Oh hell, he doesn't even care. Look, countryman, could you tell me what...? Uff!

Philip: It's impossible, Jesus. We won't find out, with this great commotion.

Peter: No one can stand the stench. Let's get out of here. There's too much shoving around, and we might end up being pushed into the water.

Then we went back to the gate. The old woman followed us there, her eyes turned toward heaven, as she called for a mysterious angel.

Praying Woman: Oh, most Almighty God, please make a miracle! And make it soon!

Philip: Guys, why don't we ask this woman?

James: I told you she's blind, Philip. She doesn't know what's happening before her.

Philip: She may not see, but she hears, and smells. She should be able to know everything through her sense of smell.

Praying Woman: Miracle, I want a miracle. Holy God, holy strong God, please make a miracle. Make it move, even a little. Make it move, make it move!

Philip: Hey, old woman, will you stop for a while? Please tell me, who's to move around here?

Praying Woman: Who're you? You've interrupted my praying!

Philip: Tell me, old woman, what miracle are you praying for?

Praying Woman: Come over, my son, and let me touch your face. You're not from here, are you?

Peter: No, and neither is this group. We're not from this place.

Praying Woman: Of course, that's why you ask. That's why you don't know I'm referring to the great miracle of the angel of God. They say he's coming down.

Philip: Who?

Praying Woman: I told you, the angel.

Peter: What's he coming down for, old woman?

Praying Woman: What else! To stir the water in the pool! Then whoever throws himself into the blessed water gets cured and cleansed of any disease forever and ever amen.

Jesus: So why do you stay here, by the gate, instead of immersing yourself in the water and having your eyes cured?

Praying Woman: Oh, my boy, you don't know how people shove each other just to get into the pool! They bite each other, pull each other's hair, scrambling like mad just to get into the pool first. And poor me, since I can't see anything, I just content myself sitting still here, and calling the angel, that he may hear my plea.

Philip: But you'll never get cured this way.

Praying Woman: That's true. But at least I keep my little business. Look, whenever anyone gets cured, and since I am the one who prays and prays here, we have agreed that I should be given a little tip for the effort, do you understand?

Jesus: And they have given you a lot of tips, old woman?

Praying Woman: Somehow I receive something, my son. But God and the angel forgive me — I think this dirty water doesn't cure. On the contrary, whoever plunges into it catches all the diseases. It's so filthy, one spits into the water, while another swallows what she spits. As for me, countrymen, I'd rather believe than question it. Miracle, miracle, miracle! Oh, most Almighty God, make a miracle! Lord of the heavens, send forth your angel soon! If you'll excuse me, I must continue praying so that God will listen to me. Touch the water, move the water, Lord!

We went near the pool again. The sick were fighting their way in, looking jealously at each other. Sometimes, one would plunge himself into the pool, imagining that the water had stirred, only to surface once again, drenched and sad, for not having been cured.

Philip: What do you think, fellows? Do you buy the story of the angel touching the water?

James: Why don't you prove it, Philip? Why don't you join in the uproar and get yourself soaked?

Peter: These people are crazy, believing the story of the angel.

James: If you make up a story about an archangel or a whole battalion of seraphim in heaven, they would believe it too. Hell, they're so gullible, they'd easily believe you. What a bunch of stupid fools!

Jesus: No, James, the people aren't stupid. The people suffer, which is different. When one is in suffering, one grabs even a burning nail, or an angel's plume.

Sick Woman: Hey, you, swine, I was here first, stay back!

A Sick Man: Damn it, you wretch, you do nothing but scream! May your two legs be crippled forever!

Sick Woman: Look who's cursing, why, you drag yourself around like a serpent!

Sick Man: Go to hell, you bitch!

We saw, a little way from this swarm of sick people, an old man lying on a stretcher. His skin sank deep on his bones. His hair was white as flour. His small eyes, resembling those of a mouse, moved continually from one side to another. As we passed by him, he grabbed Peter's tunic and stopped him.

Peter: Hey, what do you want, old man?

Sippho: Nothing. I just see you going around and I'm wondering what the hell you're looking for. You're not sick people.

James: We will be soon, if we stay here much longer.

Sippho: You don't like this, do you? Neither do I, damn it! Here, everyone thinks only of himself.

Philip: If you don't like it here, then why do you come?

Sippho: You're a funny guy. Why, I've got to think of myself too. There's no other choice.

Peter: Oh, look how they kick the hunchback.

Sippho: You know, guys, when they announce the coming of the angel, it's the end of it. People shove each other, bite and kick each other. What can we do? If there's only one bone for several dogs, then we've got to fight for it, to see who'll eat it. This little angel is our only hope. I, for one, don't believe in doctors anymore. They're a bunch of ignoramuses.

Jesus: How long have you been sick, old man?

Sippho: Make a guess and you'll be surprised.

Jesus: I don't know. Maybe ten years?

Sippho: Add ten more to it, and another ten, and you're still short by a few years. For thirty-eight years I've been like this, paralyzed. I've grown old waiting for that day when I could be healed. I've lost all my teeth already, but my hope has always been there. I've never lost it.

Jesus: So your faith is as great as that of our father, Abraham.

Sippho: Son, there's no other choice but to hope, even if one gets disillusioned with everything, with the angel, for example, who makes us fight one another. Here, no one helps anyone, there's no charity here. If you're not careful, they break your head so there will be one less in the line.

Sick Woman: Wretch! Get away from here or I'll split your head open!

Sick Man: And I'll break your bones for being a meddler! Here, take this, this will teach you a lesson.

Sippho: She's a quarrelsome bitch, and the man always takes her challenge. Huh! We spend the day grumbling against those up there, because they squeeze our necks. Know what? We're all starved to death here, but we keep on doing the same thing. One gets disillusioned, you know. Here, there's no mercy. I'm an old man and I have seen a lot of things happen before my eyes.

Jesus: But when you were young, did you do the same thing? Did you push people too?

Sippho: Of course, I couldn't do otherwise. But I'm old now. Do you think one of those young men will help me to the water? Never. Since I can only leap like a frog, I never get to be the first in the line. Since this angel won't come to me, I really don't know what to do.

Jesus: Do you want me to help you get close to the water?

Sippho: No, my son. Look, if you want to help me, then get me out of here. I don't think I'll ever get to see that angel. Angels are early birds and now it's very late. I better leave and take something for my stomach. The smell in the air simply whets my appetite.

Then Jesus went toward the old man and held him by the arms.

Sippho: Careful, young man, for my bones might break into pieces.
Jesus: Don't worry, old man. You may go away now. Come on, stand up.
Sippho: What did you say, my son?
Jesus: I said, stand up. Stand by yourself.

The old man cast a strange look at Jesus. Then he stretched his legs and discovered that he could stand. Meanwhile, the sick continued quarreling and shouting at each other by the pool. The old man looked at Jesus again, then seized his small bed, and without saying a word, left — running.

Sippho: Old woman, old woman, I've been cured! I'm cured!
Praying Woman: What do you say? Let's see. Let me touch your legs. You're Sippho, the cripple from the fruit vendors' barrio?
Sippho: I'm the one, old woman, I'm the one!
Praying Woman: The angel has come down! The angel of the Lord has come down to earth. Oh Holy God! It's a miracle, it's a miracle!
Sippho: Tomorrow, you'll receive your tip. That's a promise!

Praying Woman: Wait, Sippho, don't go away. Tell me, how did the angel look? Did you see him?

Sippho: Of course I did! He was a very strange angel. He was bearded and had brown skin. I'll tell you about this tomorrow. I'm coming back tomorrow, old woman, to bring you two denarii. Or even four! I'm cured! I'm cured!

After this, we immediately left the pool of Bethesda and disappeared among the multitude milling in the narrow streets of Jerusalem. Sippho, that sick and poor old man who for thirty-eight years had been waiting by the pool, spread the news that an angel had cured him through the entire city. The whole of Jerusalem knew that something strange had happened that morning by the Sheep Gate.

•

The Sheep Gate was located along the walls north of Jerusalem. The sheep to be sacrificed in the temple entered through this gate. Beside this gate was a pool. It was called by two names: Bethesda (House of Mercy) or Bezatha (The Pit). It had five doors for entrance and was divided into two by a row of columns. The ruins of this pool were found near a church dedicated to Saint Ann, Mary's mother. At present, there is hardly any water in the place.

In Jesus' time, Jerusalem was suffering from an acute water shortage. Water was bought and sold. In the city, there were two big pools or ponds: Siloam, outside the great walls, and Bethesda. The latter, which was near the temple, was where the sick gathered. Many of them were prevented from entering the temple precisely because of their illnesses. In this pool, they hoped to find God's mercy, which was denied to them by the religious laws, thus bringing them away from God's presence. The sick flocked to the pool for healing. Excavations have revealed that seventy years after Christ, votive offerings were still being made at the pool. Bethesda could therefore be compared to those Christian sanctuaries or sanctuaries of other religions where the sick went in search of miracles that would cure their illnesses. From these places sprang forth many false stories, and business thrived, as a consequence of people's gullibility.

Poverty, necessity, and desperation over illness can nurture egoism. When a person is forced to survive, more than to live, it is sometimes difficult to be generous with other people. A mechanism very common in human relations then shows itself: the powerful oppress the poor, who in turn (since this is the only form of treatment known to them) oppress those below them — a weaker companion, a wife, the children. A chain of servitude is thus created. One is made to believe that he or she is not a "somebody" if he or she has no one to oppress and take advantage of. The unjust structure of society only underlines and multiplies this model of relationship between the oppressor and the oppressed, the master and the slave. The oppressed majority of our society keep in their hearts a remnant of this oppression inflicted on them by the real exploiters. If complete liberation is to be attained for society and for all in it, then this dynamic among the poor must not be overlooked. But this does not mean forgetting that the same oppressed people, whose hearts are filled with more or less egoism, are the very ones whom God privileges with his love. God prefers the poor not because they are good, but simply and plainly because they are poor.

The episode at the pool of Bethesda is mentioned only in the gospel of John. Through his style, the evangelist is able to point out the special importance of some details: for example, the sick around the pool can not enter the temple.

Jesus approaches these neglected people who wait in vain for "miracles." The paralytic, who for thirty-eight years (forty years in biblical language would mean an entire life) was on the brink of death, was cured by Jesus so that he could walk on his own feet and decide his future. The miracle that Jesus made for Sippho is a sign that before God, the last — those who are rejected by the official religion — shall be the first.

(John 5:1–18)

54

The Prophet's Head

For several months, the prophet John saw the days and nights pass slowly in the dark and humid prison cell of the fortress of Machaerus, where King Herod had locked him up. That voice shouting in the desert, preparing the way of the liberation of Israel, was gradually fading away within the filthy walls of his cell. One day, the prison door was opened, and Matthew, one of the prophet's friends, came in. He came from Galilee, after seeing Jesus.

Matthew: John, John, I'm back! How are you?

John the Baptist: I told you I'd only die after you came back. I kept my word. Where is Thomas?

Matthew: In Jerusalem. He went there to celebrate the Passover with that guy Jesus, from Nazareth, and his group. He'll be back after the holidays.

Baptist: Tell me about Jesus. Did you see him? Did you give him my message?

Matthew: Yes, John. That's why I came — to tell you that . . .

Baptist: I can die peacefully?

Matthew: Don't say that, John. You won't die. Look, I brought you some medicines.

Baptist: Tell me what Jesus said. I want to know.

Matthew: Jesus wants you to know that in Galilee the people are beginning to open their eyes. The people are beginning to rise and move. That the poor are beginning to listen to the good news. That the Lord is on our side and that he expects you to be happy about this, John.

Baptist: Of course I am, Matthew. In a wedding, the groom remains with the bride. But the groom's best man, who is present, is also very happy. Now it's Jesus' turn. He has to grow while I fade away.

Jailer: Enough of that silly talk. Your time's up!

Matthew: I've got to go, John, but I'll be back soon, whenever possible.

18

Baptist: I'll be waiting for you. If you see Jesus again, tell him to grip the plow well, and not look back. If ever I get out of this hell, he, he can count on me.

Matthew: I'll tell him, John, I'll tell him.

Jailer: C'mon, you've been talking with your prophet for too long. Beat it!

Matthew and the jailer passed through the narrow stairs leading to the patio. John dropped himself on the dirty straw mat, and stared at the leaking roof. He fell asleep, recalling the brown face of Jesus, that peasant from Nazareth whom he had baptized just a few months before in the Jordan.

At that time, a celebration was held at the palace of Machaerus, because it was Herod's birthday. The luxurious halls of the palace were filled with the king's guests: Roman officials and captains, merchants from Jerusalem, desert chieftains of the Bedouin tribes . . . Everyone wanted to greet the tetrarch from Galilee.

A Man: May King Herod live one hundred years more!

A Woman: Good health to the sovereign of Galilee!

Herod: I welcome everyone to my house. Let's begin the party!

A Woman: Did you notice the huge bags under his eyes?

A Friend: They say the king has been experiencing terrible nightmares ever since he had the prophet imprisoned.

A Woman: Well, he'll be worse when he finds out what's been going on. They say that this John is never quiet, even in jail. He has revolutionized the other prisoners. He even incites the jailers.

A Friend: Really? I can't believe it.

Woman: You better believe it, my friend. I tell you, if the king does not watch out, this long-haired man will give us a hard time. Let's just hope that the king silences him soon.

Woman Friend: If the king can't decide, then the queen should push him into it.

In another part of the party, Herodias was speaking with Herod.

Herodias: What's with you, Herod, my love? You look worried since this morning. Or are you bored?

Herod: Leave me alone.

Herodias: Hmmm. What's wrong with you? Come, come . . . Why don't you have a shot of this liquor? It'll lift your spirits.

Herod: Herodias, do you think this noise will be heard down there?

Herodias: Down there? What are you talking about?

Herod: Down in the prison cell, where else?

Herodias: There you go again. Of course the noise will be heard. So what? Are you afraid of that scabby prophet? Of course he hears everything. And let him die of envy. That prophet! Wasn't he always involved in trouble? Well, this serves him right. Let him rot and eat his heart out.

Herod: Don't talk that way, Herodias. It could, it could bring bad luck.

Herodias: How I wish this damned prophet dead. I'm sick and tired of seeing you worrying about him all the time. Don't be stupid, Herod, either you forget about that good for nothing prophet or have his head cut off. You'd better decide.

Herod: I can't do that, Herodias. I can't.

Herodias, Herod's lover, was the wife of Philip, the step-brother of the king. She loathed John because he confronted Herod to his face with all his crimes and his adulterous affair with her.

Herodias: Salome! Salome! Come here, my dear!

Herod: What did you call your daughter for?

Herodias: Just a minute, you wait there.

Salome: Yes, mom.

Herodias: Look, child, the king is worried, and I thought that perhaps you could drive away his worries.

Salome: What do you want me to do, mamma?

Herodias: Dance for him the seven veils. You know what I mean.

The music was heard in the prison cells of the palace.

Jailer: Hey, you wretch, do you hear the noise coming from up there? It's our king's birthday!

Baptist: He's your king. I've got nothing to do with him.

Jailer: There's so much food, the most expensive wine, and music. There's a great splurging all over!

Baptist: Let them. They're all getting fat like swine for the day of the massacre.

Jailer: You've got such a sharp tongue. That's why you're locked up here. If only you could shut your mouth for once, then probably the king would set you free.

Baptist: If he did, then I'd shout all the more.

Jailer: Then you're doomed, my friend. Listen, I'm a cruel soldier, but not with people like you. I admire courageous men like you.

Baptist: I don't need your admiration. It's all silly talk. But you can do something. Go tell your soldier friends that we're all brothers and sisters and so none of us should lift a sword against another.

Jailer: You want me to say that and have my tongue cut off, huh?

Baptist: You wouldn't dare do that, would you? But there's something else you can do. You can set me free and let me talk to them.

Jailer: That's even worse. If I let you go, then they'll be after my head, instead of my tongue. No, no, I don't want to get involved in this mess. I'm a soldier and I have to obey orders. My chief commands me to keep close watch on you.

Baptist: You shouldn't follow the orders of an unjust man. Why don't you rebel, my friend?

Jailer: What are you telling me? Are you out of your mind? I'm a soldier, and I'm here to obey orders. The law is the law.

Baptist: The law of Herod is crime and violation. God's law is freedom. Open up this jail and set the prisoners free. Now's the time to rebel, friend.

Meanwhile, Salome was dancing.

Herod: Very good, Salome! How well you move your legs, young lady! Ha, ha! You make me drool over you. You deserve a reward. Ask me for anything — bracelets, silk, gold, silver, perfume — and you'll get it. You deserve half my kingdom.

At that moment, Herodias, who was reclining beside the king, looked at Salome and winked at her. Everything was planned before the dance.

Salome: My Lord: there's one dish missing on this table.

Herod: What? You want to eat more? I wouldn't want you to get fat, young lady, you're lovely as you are now! Ha, ha! Don't you think so? Tell me, what do you want? More sauce, chicken, a lamb's head?

Salome: No, I want the head of the prophet, John.

Herod: What?

Salome: I want the head of the prophet on a tray, for my gift.

Herod: But, but, do you know what you're saying, Salome?

Herodias: You heard her, Herod.

Herod: This is a trap. Damn you! I can't do that.

Herodias: You swore in front of many people, Herod. There are many witnesses. So the tetrarch of Galilee does not keep his word?

There was great silence in the hall, interrupted only by the clinking of glasses. The guests who were drunk did not know what was happening. Herod's lips were trembling when he gave the command.

Herod: Aquila, go down to the jail and comply with this young lady's request.

Aquila, who was one of the king's bodyguards, obeyed the order. John did not say a word. When they cut off his head, his eyes remained open, just as when he was in the river, staring at the horizon, awaiting the coming of the Messiah.

When Matthew and his friends learned about this, they took his body, which was hardened by the desert sun, and buried it. All Israel mourned the death of the prophet John, he who had prepared the way for the liberator of Israel.

•

The prison emerged as an institution in Israel about a thousand years before Christ. During most of this time some sections or portions inside the palace in Jerusalem served as a prison. In Jesus' time, the prisoners could be visited. They were usually put in chains, and their feet were put in shackles. John the Baptist languished for a number of months in the dungeon of the palace, which Herod had in Machaerus, near the Dead Sea.

Herod the Great, father of the Herod in this episode, did not have Jewish blood. He was the son of an Idumean and of a woman who was a descendant of a sheik. The customs of his court were influenced more by foreign and Hellenistic customs than by strict Jewish morals. Herod the Great maintained a harem and held orgies so extravagant that their fame spread to neighboring countries. He was fond of beast fights, the theater, and gymnastic games. The court of his son, Herod Antipas, the king of Galilee, during Jesus' time, adopted this style of life. In Machaerus — a fortress and a palace in one — a number of these parties were held. Herod's birthday was an annual celebration. Herod Antipas was a politically corrupt man. His personal ways were not exemplary either. Because of his greed for power, he married a daughter of Aretas IV, an Arab king. Later, when he traveled to Rome, he became a lover of Herodias, who was married to Philip, one of his step-brothers, leaving the daughter of Aretas out in the cold. This sparked a war between the Arab king and the Galilean king, from which Antipas apparently emerged the winner. Since then, Herod lived with Herodias, together with her daughter, Salome. The objection posed by John to this adulterous union and his criticisms of the crimes and abuses committed by the king earned for him the ire of Herodias, who, in the end, devised the death of the great prophet of the Jordan. Herod — superstitious and coward that he was — would never have decided by himself to have John murdered.

In the episode, before his death, John the Baptist incites to rebellion one of the soldiers he has befriended in jail. He dares him to make a decision to choose between an unjust law, ordering the killing of a brother, and the law of God, which is life and freedom. The most ancient Christian tradition has taught us that in cases like this, one must obey God, rather than men (Acts 5:27-29). This prophetic cry of subversion has reached us in our day, in the words delivered in his cathedral in San Salvador by Archbishop Oscar Romero, who was martyred for his courage. The archbishop proclaimed: "God's law must prevail over an order to kill one's brother. God's law says: Do not kill! No soldier is obliged to obey an order that is against the law of God."

John's death was, at that particular moment, the consequence of the king's drunkenness and of the calculated astuteness of his lover. But this is just an appearance. Although John was murdered, the result of his work was glorious. His death was the ultimate price of long fidelity. The prophet often has to pay with his life for his criticisms and his rebellion against authority. This consistency of purpose, up to the final consequences, is a sign of the true (or real) prophet. He is not an opportunist who goes with the tide when it suits him, who is courageous only because he hopes to be applauded, who says this now but sings another tune the next day, and who does all this well simply because he is a good actor. A prophet is one who follows one line and sticks to it, even if it costs his life. This is John the Baptist, from the time he enclosed himself in the monastery of the Essenes or his popular days in the Jordan up to that day when an unknown solder cut his head off in the dungeon. His was a life of fidelity for the cause of justice.

(Matt. 14:3-12; Mark 6:17-29)

55

An Eye for an Eye, a Tooth for a Tooth

All Jerusalem trembled upon learning of the death of John, the prophet of the desert, beheaded like a Paschal lamb in the prison cell of Machaerus. Many wept for him, as if they had lost a father and become orphaned. The news spread from house to house. Pontius Pilate, the Roman governor, ordered that security be tightened in the streets of the city to prevent any popular uprising. But the Zealots were not intimidated.

A *Zealot:* Comrades, the blood of the son of Zechariah must be avenged. Herod beheaded John. May the heads of all Herodians fall!

The revolutionary Zealots had their daggers hidden under their tunics. That night they went to the neighborhood of the silversmiths, near the tower of the Angle, where Herod Antipas had his palace and where the Herodians, followers of the king of Galilee, lived.

Herodian: Ahhh!
A *Zealot:* Less one. Let's go, hurry!

The following day, dawn greeted the people with the heads of four Herodians balancing between the arches of the aqueduct.

Woman: Damn! Now the soldiers will behead our children in retaliation!
Another Woman: May God protect my neighbor, Ruth. She has a son imprisoned in the Antonia Tower.

The retaliation of the Romans, instigated by the courtesans of King Herod, took place swiftly. At the first hour of the afternoon, when the sun was at its height, and the black and yellow flags waved atop the Antonia Tower, ten young Israelites and sympathizers of the Zealots were crucified at the Skull, the macabre hill where political prisoners were executed.

24

Man: Damn these Romans! They'll pay for this someday.

Another Man: Shut up, imbecile, or you'll be nailed up like these unfortunate ones.

In front of the ten who were condemned to death, a crier was yelling, calling out for others to hear him and be forewarned.

Soldier: This is how those who rebel against Rome will end up. Your sons will suffer the same fate if they continue to conspire against the imperial eagle. Long live the emperor and death to the rebels!

Man: Someday, you'll pay for this, sons of a bitch!

The ten crucified men remained agonizing that whole night. Their desperate cries and curses could be heard from the walls of the city. The victims' mothers were pulling their hair and scratching their faces beside the crosses, pleading clemency for their sons, in vain. Jerusalem could not sleep that night.

Zealot: Listen, Simon. We'll meet at Mark's house at nighttime. Tell Jesus of Nazareth and the rest of the group. Don't come together — you'll arouse suspicion. Hurry up.

Judas Iscariot and Simon, the freckled one, who had contacts with the Zealots of the capital, brought us the message. Barabbas's group had a plan, and they wanted to know if they could count on us.

Jesus: What's wrong with you, Philip? Are you afraid?

Philip: Afraid, no, but horrified. Uff! Whoever asked me to come with you to this city?

Jesus: He who doesn't risk himself accomplishes nothing, fat head. Right friends? Let's go and find out what they want from us.

When the sun hid itself behind Mount Zion, we left by twos, and, passing through different streets, came to the house of Mark, Peter's friend and a sympathizer of the movement, who lived near the Gate of the Ravine.

All lights were out so we wouldn't call attention to the soldiers, who were patrolling ceaselessly, even to the last nook of the city. Greetings were made in silence. Then we sat on the ground, and, amid shadows, Barabbas, the leader of the Zealots, began to speak.

Barabbas: A tooth for a tooth, comrades. Herod beheaded the prophet John in Machaerus, and we avenged his death by beheading four traitors.

We have hardly cleansed our daggers, and now we have to use them again. They have crucified ten of our best men.

A Zealot: May their blood spill on Pontius Pilate's head! God's curse be on him and Herod Antipas!

Barabbas: Pilate thinks we'll be scared. Well, he'll have to have all the wood in Phoenicia cut for crosses because we'll fight on until he's crucified every man in Israel!

Barabbas had been imprisoned before. Twice he had been trapped by the Romans, and twice he was able to escape, when he was about to be executed. He was still the object of a manhunt in Perea.

Barabbas: Okay, what now, Galileans? Can we count on all of you?

Philip: What for?

Barabbas: What else? To get rid of a dozen Romans and a number of treacherous Jews in our midst. We can't allow these henchmen to overcome us. So, what do you say? Can we count on you or not?

Jesus: Then what?

Barabbas: What did you say, Nazarene?

Jesus: I said, what happens next?

Jesus' inquiry somehow surprised us.

Jesus: I don't know, Barabbas. After hearing you speak, I'm reminded of the shepherd on top of the mountain who throws a stone, pushing another stone as it rolls down, and the two stones push down another pair, then four and then ten, until finally, no one can prevent the avalanche. The violence you're talking about is dangerous, like a stone thrown from the mountain top.

Barabbas: Enough of your stories, Jesus. It's they who are violent. Do you understand?

Jesus: Of course I do. Yes, they beat us, they destroy us, and they are the ones who sow death. But we shouldn't allow ourselves to be influenced by their thirst for blood. The height of all this is if they succeed in making us clones of their own image, people who know nothing but revenge.

Zealot: Okay, okay, fine, so what do you want now? Shall we just put our arms akimbo?

Jesus: He who crosses his arms plays along with them too. No, Moses didn't have his arms akimbo before the Pharaoh.

Barabbas: Moses said: "An eye for an eye, a tooth for a tooth."

Jesus: That's right, Barabbas. But whose eyes and teeth? Those of Herod's men whom you beheaded yesterday? Who were those men? Tell me. Were they the ones who killed the prophet John? Were they responsible for all the injustices in our midst? Or were they poor creatures, like you and me, who were simply dragged into fighting against us by powerful men?

Barabbas: Oh damn, why do you talk that way, you, of all people? Have you forgotten about the death of your father, Joseph?

Jesus: That's it, precisely, Barabbas. I suffered from the pain of seeing my father beaten like a dog, for having hidden a few countrymen, during the uprising in Sepphoris. I also felt in my flesh the desire for revenge. But no. Now I think this road will bring us nowhere.

Zealot: Is there another way, Nazarene? Our country needs a way out. And the only way we see is through the use of force.

Jesus: You from the movement want a people's rebellion. The way I see it, the people are still reticent about it. We still have blinders on our eyes. Don't you think we should do something first to make the blind see and the deaf hear? What do we gain from all this bloodshed if the people don't understand what's really happening?

Barabbas: We're the people's guide. They go where we lead them.

Jesus: Don't you think that would be nothing more than changing the yoke? The people ought to stand on their own two feet and learn to walk their own way. We must find our own way out, the only true way that will set us free.

Barabbas: You talk like a dreamer. But God is not as much of a dreamer as you. It is God who seeks revenge. In the name of God, we'll all end up with our enemies.

Jesus: You behead Herod's men in God's name. And they crucify us in the name of the same God. Tell me, how many gods are there, anyway?

Barabbas: There's only one, Jesus. The God of the poor. If you are with God, then you're with the poor. If you're with the poor, then you're with God.

Jesus: You're right, Barabbas. I too believe in the God of the poor, he who set our ancestors free from slavery in Egypt. He's the only real God. The rest are idols created by the Pharaohs, so they could continue abusing their slaves. But ...

The waning moonlight crept into the cracks of the house, shedding somber light on the serious faces of the Zealots.

Barabbas: But what?

Jesus: You must learn to love them too.

Zealot: Love them? Love who?

Jesus: The Romans. Herod's followers. Our enemies.

Barabbas: Is that meant to be a joke?

Jesus: Listen to me. And forgive me if I can't make myself clear. But I think God makes the sun rise everyday not only for the good but also for the bad people. We, who believe in the God of the poor, must be a little like him. We mustn't allow ourselves to fall into this trap called hatred.

Barabbas: I can hardly see your face in the dark, Nazarene. I don't know if it's really you talking to me, the one they say is the prophet of justice, or you're simply a crazy man pretending to be a prophet.

Jesus: Look, Barabbas, if we fight for justice, we'll have enemies, that's for sure. And we'll have to fight them, strip them of their wealth and power, as our ancestors did, while getting out of Egypt. Yeah, we'll have enemies, but we can't do what they're doing, we can't be dragged into this evil act of revenge.

Barabbas: Okay, once and for all, let's finish this off. All these are bedtime stories. Tell me if you're willing to kill.

Jesus: No, I'm not, Barabbas.

Zealot: And so they'll kill you, imbecile. Then everything will have gone to perdition.

Jesus: When do you win and when do you lose? Can you tell me?

Barabbas: To hell with you, Jesus of Nazareth. You're a crazy man, a real crazy man. Or probably you're a good for nothing coward. And the rest of you, do you also think the same way as he does? Are you as crazy as he is?

Peter was about to respond, but all of a sudden all of us froze.

Zealots: Soldiers! The soldiers are coming!

Another Zealot: The guards of Pilate! They've discovered us.

Another Zealot: Damn! We're all doomed.

Barabbas: Hurry! Flee through the garden.

Jesus: Peter, pass through that door.

Peter: What about you, Jesus?

Jesus: Go ahead. I can hold the soldiers back until you get away from here.

Peter: You're out of your mind, Jesus. They'll kill you.

Jesus: Go away, go away fast.

Peter: What'll you do?

Jesus: The same thing that David did to the Philistines.

The soldiers were already banging the door.

One Soldier: Hey, who's there?! Open the door!

Jesus: Go, go!

Barabbas's men ably leaped over the walls facing the other street. We slipped through the garden of Mark's house and disappeared in the shadows. Jesus was left alone. He was trembling with fear as he opened the door.

One Soldier: Why is there so much noise around here, huh?

Jesus: Agu, agu, agu! Ha, ha, ha, he he!

Another Soldier: Who's this creature? Hey, you, what are you doing here?

Jesus: Down with the soldiers, up with the captains, down with the centurions, up with the generals! Ha, ha, ha!

Jesus was beating the top of the door frame with his fingers and looked at the soldiers with a blank smile, as saliva dripped from his mouth over his beard.

One Soldier: Aren't you ashamed of yourself? You big stupid fool! Here, take this so you'll learn!

Jesus: Give it to me on the other cheek too! Ha, ha!

Another Soldier: This man's crazy. As if we hadn't enough of his type in Jerusalem! Let's get out of here.

Jesus: Ha, ha, he, he! Ufff! What we should free ourselves from...

It was still dark when the group met at Lazarus's inn, at Bethany. We were still talking when the cocks crowed. King David acted like a fool in order to save his skin. Jesus had used the same trick and saved all of us that day. At times, it became clear, it was better to be astute than to resort to violence.

•

Although the Zealots concentrated their activities in Galilean lands, the seat of the movement, they were also mobilized in Jerusalem. Pilgrimages during the holidays served as occasions for them to establish their links in the capital, where they also had groups of sympathizers. Among the revolutionaries influenced by the Zealot movement was the notorious group of assassins — terrorists armed with daggers — who found it more convenient to conduct their attacks at the height of the holiday celebrations. Zealots and assassins kidnapped important persons, assaulted landed properties and houses of the wealthy, and laid siege on the city's armory. They considered their struggle as a kind of "holy war." The jealous God who tolerates no other gods (money, the emperor, the unjust laws) gave them their name: Jealous, Zealots. The punishment for all political crimes against the Roman Empire was death on the cross.

Barabbas (an Aramaic name that means "son of the father") appears in the gospels only in the books of the passion, as a political rebel who killed a Roman soldier in an uprising. In this episode, he appears as one of the important leaders of the Zealots in Jerusalem. He would have likely heard of Jesus, because Jesus was then a popular man whom the city's poor people listened to, putting their hopes in him. Since the Zealot movement was of the people, it would have been natural for Barabbas to identify himself with Jesus and his group.

The so-called law of retaliation ("An eye for an eye..." [Exod. 21:23–25]) should not be interpreted simplistically as a law of revenge. There have been efforts to set up an opposition between the God who gave Israel this "savage" law and Jesus, who was all love and mercy. But such a duality is wrong. In the world of four thousand years ago the law of retaliation was one that respected life: by mandating a penalty that corresponded to the offense, it in fact sought to put a limit on revenge and stop violence. The ancient world, recipient of this law, was a bloodthirsty one, with people overpowering each other, by force, and not because it was a right. All this must be taken into account in order to understand the position taken by Jesus and the Zealots. The latter were not beasts thirsty for blood. They were faithful to an old legal tradition, which, in a sense, was valid in their time. Jesus came offering them another way, removing all barriers for a possible coexistence of all humankind, speaking no longer of restricted revenge, but of other values, like strength in weakness and love of enemies.

Jesus was not a Zealot. The Zealots were intolerably nationalistic people. They wanted Israel's freedom from the Roman yoke, but they remained in that yoke. Jesus was patriotic because he loved his country, but he was not nationalistic. His mission did not recognize barriers or discrimination. The Zealots were profoundly religious, but their God was exclusively chosen by the people of Israel, and his kingdom would take revenge on the pagan nations. This was never the God of Jesus. The Zealots ardently defended the strict compliance with the law. Jesus differed from them on this point, as he advocated total freedom before the law and authority, notwithstanding their Jewish character. Nevertheless, to set Jesus and the Zealots in absolute opposition is to overlook some significant realities: Jesus related with them without reservations — in all probability, some of his disciples were Zealots. Jesus shared with them many social concerns and expressed a common desire for the coming of the kingdom of justice, in a similar manner. Jesus' association with this popular movement can not be dismissed categorically. Perhaps what is most certain at this point is to affirm that what Jesus proposes is a lot more profound and goes beyond revolution as envisioned by the Zealots.

On the question of tactics, Jesus differed from the Zealots in his stand regarding violence. In his words, as well as in his attitude, Jesus questioned the use of violence as a means. This topic is too complicated to discuss in just a word or two, nor can it be affirmed simplistically that Jesus was a nonviolent man and that the gospel condemns violence in any form. One must first take into account that there is violence not only in the act of killing but also in a situation where one is not allowed to live. There are not only acts of violence but also structures and situations of violence. There are violent people, but it is even more dangerous to experience violent societies, where, because of injustice, many perish from hunger, unemployment, disease, and misery. Further, Jesus was violent when he faced the authorities. His words were intensely violent. This was especially the case when he figured in that massive act on the temple's esplanade. Nevertheless, Jesus killed no one; they killed him; he never encouraged people to use any form of violence, neither did he resort to armed resistance in order to save himself, when he could have very well done so. In this Jewish context, the violence advocated by the Zealots had no escape. It was doomed to fail, yet it was an excuse for the Romans to unleash their powerful repression against the people, as happened in the year 70 after Christ, when Jerusalem was devastated by the Romans in a war against the Zealot subversives.

It is evident that before such power of arms, the Christian principally offers the strength there is in weakness, hidden in the true Word and in the freedom given in the struggle, a strength rooted in not being attached to anything and therefore having nothing to lose. Certainly, if we respond to violence with violence, we shall end up being as violent as the one we are trying to fight. On the other hand, we must not forget that starting from the Fathers of the Church, St. Thomas, up to Paul VI, the church has defended the right to an armed insurrection in a situation of prolonged injustice and when all peaceful means to overcome it have been exhausted.

Bearing this in mind, Jesus speaks of loving one's enemies. Without taking this phrase in context, we run the risk of distorting it, transforming it into a sweet formula that is bereft of meaning. In the episode, Jesus utters that difficult phrase about loving one's enemy, basing it on his own experience. Perhaps only he who is tempted to hate his enemy can truly love. Only he who suffers from the hatred of his enemy by torture, humiliation, or death can forgive him. The one who preaches pardon and love by lip service has little authority to speak about it and is never convincing. The evangelical word about loving the enemy must be taken seriously. It can not be overused, nor must one abuse it. In a way, the gospel does not tell us that we should not have enemies, but in having them, we must be able to love them. That is to say that the gospel is not shunning conflict. It does not create conflict, neither does it encourage it. It accepts it and aims to direct it toward love.

In this episode, Jesus does not say that one has to offer the other cheek, but he himself gives it. He does it, getting his inspiration from what King David did in the land of the Philistines in order to escape from his enemies (1 Sam. 21:11–16). It is a prophetic gesture, and therefore it is a liberating one. Through the act, he saves his companions. It is a way of saying that if giving the other cheek is viewed as a form of passivity or resignation, then we are not being faithful to the gospel. However, if we consider nonviolence as a manner of looking for efficacy, a strategy, astuteness, then we are very close to understanding the meaning of nonviolence in the message of Jesus.

(Matt. 5:38–48; Luke 6:27–36)

56

The Wailing of the Wind

James: Hey, guys, better get to sleep early, because tomorrow you've got to rise at dawn.

Peter: Oh my feet! Long journeys like this are never my cup of tea.

Mary: Why don't you stay a couple of days more? There's room in the inn, especially now that people are beginning to return to their towns.

Peter: No, Mary, we've got to go back to Galilee. Do you know why? Because we've already run out of money. We haven't even got a copper coin.

Mary: Bah, that's no problem. My brother Lazarus has grown fond of you. If you can't pay now, you can do so later, on your next trip here. You're coming back, aren't you?

We were gathering the trinkets and things we bought during the feast of the Passover in Jerusalem while saying goodbye to Martha and Mary. It was already night when Lazarus, the innkeeper, came back, running.

Lazarus: Pshh! Is any of you carrying hot items back north?

Peter: Hot items? Are you crazy? They're very strict in the customs nowadays. Why do you ask?

Lazarus: Because you've got a visitor. A bigwig. One of the seventy magistrates from the Sanhedrin. He's there outside, with a couple of bodyguards, and he's asking about you. I thought you were carrying smuggled goods.

Mary: If they do, then they conceal them very well. They're not Galileans for nothing!

Lazarus: Most of you should go upstairs and hide, but somebody's got to go out there and face them.

James: I'll go and speak with them. Will you come with me, John?

My brother James and I went to see who was looking for us. There at the door of the Beautiful Palm was a tall man with a long white beard, waiting for us. He was wrapped in an elegant purple cloak and was accompanied by two Ethiopians with shaven heads and daggers at the waist.

James: Let's see now, what can we do for you, sir?

Nicodemus: I'd like to speak with your leader.

James: With our leader? Here no one is a leader of anyone. We're a group of friends.

Nicodemus: I'm referring to a man named Jesus of Nazareth, the man who accomplishes "things."

James: What "things"? Please make yourself clear.

Nicodemus: I came not to talk to you but with him. Please call him.

James and I went back to the inn.

Jesus: He wants to speak with me? What does he want?

James: I don't like the looks of him. He's an important Pharisee, you know. It's rather strange that he should come here at this time. There must be something else.

Mary: Don't be long, Jesus. You haven't finished your story yet.

Jesus went out to the garden where the mysterious visitor was waiting for him.

Nicodemus: Damn, finally I find you, Nazarene! I'd like to have a word with you, alone.

Jesus: That's all right. If you're looking for hot items, then you're wasting your time. The only thing I'm taking from Jerusalem is a hanky for my mom, because here they're very cheap.

Nicodemus: No, nothing of that sort, young man. Let me explain. Hey, you two, wait for me over there.

The two Ethiopians distanced themselves about a stone's throw.

Nicodemus: There must be some place here where we can talk.

Jesus: We'll be fine under that palm tree. Let's go!

From the kitchen stove, we saw Jesus heading for a corner of the garden. The clouds moved swiftly in the sky, pushed by the night winds moaning amid the trees.

Jesus: What is it?

Nicodemus: My name is Nicodemus, Jesus. I'm a magistrate in the Supreme Court of Justice. My father was the illustrious Jechonias, the senior treasurer of the temple.

Jesus: What does an important man like you want from me?

Nicodemus: I know you're quite puzzled by my visit, although you already have an idea as to why I'm here.

Jesus: I must have very little imagination, because, frankly speaking, I have no idea what you want from me.

Nicodemus: I don't need anything from you. As a matter of fact, I'm here to help you.

Jesus: To help me?

Nicodemus: Let's say it will be a mutual cooperation. A mutual benefit, do you understand?

Jesus: I don't get it. Please make yourself clear.

Nicodemus: Jesus, I know a lot about you. Look, what you did in the Bethesda pool has already spread throughout the city. Come on, don't put on that face. I've heard about the paralytic you made to walk, just like that. I have also heard about similar things that happened in Galilee: a madman, a leper . . . They even say that you brought a dead girl back to life at the height of the wake. These rumors have gone as far as the Sanhedrin.

Jesus: Uff, how fast news spreads in this country.

Nicodemus: As you can see, I have been following you. And I congratulate you, Jesus.

Jesus: I still don't understand where you came from and what you want from me.

Nicodemus: Oh, come on, don't deny it. Tricks must be performed well for them to become tricks, I know that. Don't tell me those were miracles. You don't have the face of a saint. That's okay, that's okay. You don't trust me, I understand. But let's get to the point. After all, I don't really care whether they're tricks of yours or God's miracles, or if it's the devil who's behind all this. It doesn't really matter. The people can't distinguish one from the other. They have been suffering enough and they need something to entertain them. You're a master in amusing the people. In other words, I have a business proposition, Jesus of Nazareth. We can be partners and share the profit equally. Or if you want, I can give you a fixed rate, say for example fifty denarii. Is it too small? Yeah, I know. How about seventy-five? Some more? I think that's too much for a peasant, since, after all, you'll just spend the money drinking in the taverns.

Anyway, you're a nice guy, so I'll raise it to a hundred denarii, and the deal is closed. Now, let me explain what I want you to do. Hey, what are you laughing at?

Jesus: Nothing. I just find it funny.

Nicodemus: Yeah, I know. You Galileans are known for your cunning. Fine. I think a hundred denarii is a salary good enough for a magician, but that's okay, name your price. How much do you want? Believe me, man, more than anyone else, I'm very much interested in your craft.

Jesus: Yeah, I see that, but I don't think I'm the right man for you, Nicodemus.

Nicodemus: How's that? Why? I can give you a lot of money, you know that, and I mean it.

Jesus: No, it's not that.

Nicodemus: Then what is it?

Jesus: Well, it's because you're very old.

Nicodemus: That's it, precisely, young man. They say that the devil is wise because he's old, and not because he's the devil. With my experience and with your ability, we can go very far.

Jesus: No, Nicodemus. I must tell you that I need young blood.

Nicodemus: Well, I may be old, and that's true, but my health isn't that bad. I'm still quite strong.

Jesus: Nicodemus: I need children.

Nicodemus: Children? Come on, Jesus, leave the children alone in school and let's talk about serious things.

Jesus: I'm serious, Nicodemus. I need children. If you want to get involved in this matter, then you would have to be born again. That's right, be a child again.

Nicodemus: They told me you joke a lot, Nazarene. Well, since you know a lot of tricks, maybe you can put me back in my mother's womb, that I may be born again. Anyway, let's get back to our deal. As I was saying, this has something to do . . .

Jesus: You've gotten old amassing a lot of wealth, Nicodemus. Your heart has grown calloused and you've become hard of hearing. That's why you don't understand. That's why you don't hear the wind blowing.

Nicodemus: Hey, I may be old but I'm not deaf. Of course I hear the wind. But I don't understand a word of yours. What are you trying to tell me? Aren't you interested in making money? Is that it? Oh, you young people are hopeless cases. You sing the same tune. Of course, money becomes the least of your worries, after all: "Daddy is just behind us!" Then, when the fruit becomes ripe, you realize that with money, you can buy almost anything in this life. However, if you're not ambitious at all, then I'll keep my money. That'll be the worse for you.

Jesus: No, don't keep your money. I didn't tell you to.

Nicodemus: Ah, you smart guy, I knew you would take the hook. I knew you would be interested in my proposition. Look, we could start with a presentation in a theater, or in the hippodrome, where we can take in more people, or, well, what's the matter with you? Are you shocked or something?

Jesus: Nicodemus, don't you hear the wind? It brings in the moanings of the suffering people, those who die calling the Lord for justice to prevail on earth. How can you keep your money and be so deaf to the wailings of the wind? Listen. It's like a woman crying while giving birth. She's bringing to light a new human, one who lives not for money but for others, because he or she would rather give than receive.

Nicodemus: Now I don't understand a thing you said.

Jesus: Of course, because if you want to understand, then you'll have to choose.

Nicodemus: Choose what?

Jesus: You can't serve two masters at the same time. Choose between God and money. If you choose God, you will hear the wailing of the wind and it will take you some place that you haven't imagined in your whole life. If you stick to your money, you'll be all alone by yourself.

Nicodemus: Really, I don't understand a thing you're saying.

Jesus: You ought to know. You're a learned man, with so many titles to boast of. Can't you understand what's going on? The people are claiming their right. We want to be free like the wind. We want to be happy. We want to live.

Nicodemus: Jesus of Nazareth, now I know what you are: a dreamer! But this world you're dreaming of will never come.

Jesus: It has already come, Nicodemus. God so loves the world that he has already done it. The Kingdom of God has already begun!

Nicodemus: Get down from your pedestal, young man, and be more realistic. Take this advice from an old man. Think of yourself in the first place and in the second place too. Then think of the deluge to come. Things are as they are and they will always be so.

Jesus: No, Nicodemus. Things can change, in fact, they are already changing. In Galilee, we have seen very poor people sharing what little they have with others. You wanted to see miracles, didn't you? Well, get down from your master's chair and go to our neighborhood. I assure you, Nicodemus, you'll learn how to make the greatest miracle of all, that of sharing what one has.

Nicodemus: Of course, you're a crazy man. There's no doubt about it. But hearing you speak . . .

Jesus: Look up, Nicodemus, don't you see it?

The full moon of the month of Nisan was as round as a coin, and spread its immaculately white light over the garden of the inn.

Jesus: Look at it. It's as bright as your money. But do you know what Moses did in the desert? He took the bronze coins and created a serpent to stand in the middle of the camping site. Those who looked at the serpent were cured from their snake bites. The snake from the money has bitten you, Nicodemus, and you've got the poison inside you. If you want to be cured . . .

Nicodemus remained silent as he stared at the moon. The handful of coins he had in his pocket became as heavy as a bundle. He felt he was older and wearier than before, as if his life had not been more than water flowing through his hands.

Nicodemus: Do you think there's still hope for old men like me?

Jesus: Of course there is. Water cleanses and the Spirit is renewed, if you wish.

The wind continued to blow among the trees. It came from very far, picked up the words of Jesus, and took them off to the far away mountains. When Nicodemus left the inn on his way to Jerusalem, the wind kept him company on his return journey.

•

Nicodemus's name is mentioned only in the gospel of John. He is one of the few persons belonging to the religious institution who maintained a friendly relationship with Jesus. He was a Pharisee of the Sanhedrin group. The Sanhedrin was the supreme council of the Jewish government. It also functioned as a court of justice composed of seventy members who were profoundly knowledgeable of the Scriptures, in order for them to be able to pass judgment. Specifically, the Sanhedrin members of the Pharisee party — like Nicodemus — had occupied the administrative positions of the council and they wielded great influence. The Sanhedrin members were highly privileged persons in society: masters of knowledge and of the power which gave them the authority to interpret the laws. Besides, they were generally rich. In the gospel of John, reference to the "chiefs of the Jews" pointed to men occupying religious-political posts of this type. A well-placed man like Nicodemus would have had vague intentions in approaching Jesus. In this episode, he appears interested in "lucrative" business. He wants to capitalize on Jesus' notoriety for his own benefit. Among the members of the Sanhedrin, such an attitude would not have been unusual. In Jesus' time, the Sanhedrin was a body with corrupt political, social, and economic power. To a man with this type of orientation, Jesus offers a basic alternative: God or money. To choose God is to be converted to the kingdom. To go for the money is to be excluded from God's plan.

In the dialogue between Jesus and this influential Pharisee, as told in the fourth gospel, John employs a series of theological themes: the water and the Spirit; what comes from above and what is of the earth; light and darkness... He likewise makes use of symbols: Moses' serpent, the wind... This tells us that he does not confine himself solely to a real conversation. Rather, he deals with a theological explanation. Jesus speaks of freedom (the wind blowing where it will) to this man dominated by the law, and he brings up the possibility of being born again, of starting a new life of conversion.

The idea of "a new person" as expounded in this chapter is basic in understanding the dialogue between Jesus and Nicodemus. This, in the end, is what the whole conversation is about: the transformation toward life, toward what is new, toward the future. The new human that Jesus proposes to Nicodemus in this account is one whose attitude of sharing gets first priority over personal benefit. He is a person for others. This is difficult, as it demands a youthfulness of heart. The theme of the new human is frequently found in the letters of Paul (Col. 3:9–11; Eph. 8:2–10 and 4:20–24).

The consequences of Christian baptism have been traditionally expressed in the terms Jesus used in dealing with Nicodemus: to be born again by water and Spirit. Water, which is the symbol of life, and Spirit (in Hebrew, spirit and wind are expressed by the same word: *ruah*), the symbol of freedom, are the marks of a Christian. A Christian must be that new person who will always choose life and defend freedom before any form of servitude. Baptism makes possible this new human whose disposition will be to choose the God of life in all commitments and all actions.

(John 3:1–21)

57

Five Loaves of Bread and Two Fish

When King Herod killed the prophet John in Machaerus, the people were filled with rage and fear. We were then in Jerusalem. After knowing what had happened, we hurriedly returned to Galilee by way of the mountains.

Nathanael: Ay, Philip, I can't stand it anymore. My feet are swollen!
Philip: Stop complaining, Nat. It won't take much longer.
Nathanael: What do you mean it won't take long? We haven't reached Magdala yet.
Philip: Man, I mean, it won't take long for us to be beheaded like John the Baptist. By then, we won't feel the pain anymore. Not even the corns on our feet.
Nathanael: If that's meant to be a joke, it's not funny.

Finally, after several hours on the road . . .

John: Hey, fellows, I can see Capernaum! Look over there!
Peter: Long live our Sea of Galilee!
Philip: And long live these thirteen crazy men who will dip themselves into it again!

After three days of walking on the road, we returned home. We were happy, in spite of the long journey. As always, Peter and I started to run the last mile, to see who arrived first.

John: Damn you, stone thrower, you won't be first this time!

When we got home, Peter's family, ours, and half of the neighborhood were all out to receive us and to find out how things were in Jerusalem.

A Neighbor: Hey, Peter, is it true what they say, that Pontius Pilate stole the temple's money again for his damned aqueduct?
Peter: Not only that! All the prisons are overcrowded. From the temple's atrium, you could hear the shouts of the tormentors in the Antonia Tower.

Another Neighbor: Swine!

John: Before we left, they crucified ten more Zealots, ten young men who were full of life and were ready to fight.

Zebedee: Yeah. They even took Linus and Manasses prisoners, including the son of old Sixto.

Salome: They were after the husband of your friend Chloe, and he had to hide in the lepers' caves. Gideon, the Sadducee, reported him.

John: What a traitor!

A Neighbor: A group of ironsmiths protested against the latest tax imposed on bronze, and presto — all of them ended up in jail.

Salome: And were all beaten!

Zebedee: It's been six days now, but they haven't been released yet.

Jesus: What about their families?

Zebedee: As you might expect, Jesus: they're all suffering from hunger. What else can they do? Before, it was the beggars and the farmers who lost their harvest. Now it's the prisoners' children. This leaves Capernaum in a pitiful state.

John: We've got to do something, Jesus. We can't just take it sitting down.

Philip: That's exactly my point. We went to Jerusalem, and now we're back from Jerusalem. Now what?

Peter: Since all thirteen of us are here, we can plan something.

Salome: Don't make trouble, Peter, if you want your head spared. Herod's policemen saw four men in the inn, and accusing them of conspiracy, arrested them.

Jesus: Let's stay outside the city, so as not to arouse suspicion. Yeah, tomorrow we can go and look for a quiet place where we can discuss this. Do you all agree?

Nathanael: Right, tomorrow morning will be fine. But if it's in the afternoon, better. I'm too dead tired to go even one more step. My kidneys are killing me!

The next day — in the afternoon — James asked old Gaspar to lend us his big boat. All thirteen rowed in the direction of Bethsaida. It was spring and the lake shore was teeming with flowers and the grass was very green.

John: Hey, you, Peter! Did you bring along some olives to fill up our bellies?

Peter: Here, grab some olives and bread.

Philip: Why are those men along the coast? Could anything be the matter?

John: They're probably drowning. The water is rough along those bends.

Man: Hey, you on the boat, come over here! Come on!

Nathanael: I guess we're gonna be the ones to drown. Look, Peter, those men making signs at us, aren't they the twins from the big house?

Peter: Exactly. How come they're here?

John: Gaspar must have told them we were coming this way, so they came ahead of us.

We rowed closer to shore, close enough to talk to the people on the banks.

A Woman: Peter! Isn't Jesus with you?

Peter: Yeah, he's here.

A Man: Things are bad in Capernaum. Haven't they told you about it yet?

A Woman: We're starving here. Our husbands were taken prisoner and we have nothing to feed our children.

A Man: We who are free can't find work and can't even earn a single, lousy denarius.

Peter: Well, what can we do? We're even worse off than you.

Another Man: C'mon, c'mon, why don't you fasten your boat here! C'mon!

John: Say, Jesus, wouldn't it be better to proceed to the other side? There are just too many people here.

Jesus: The people are desperate, John. They don't know what to do, nor where to go. They're like a flock without a shepherd.

There were several people waiting on the shore. Some came from Bethsaida. Others, from the hamlet of Dalmanutha. There were also a number coming from Capernaum.

A Man: You always claim that things are getting better, that we shall finally lift our heads, but look what happened, when the prophet John raised his head, they cut it off!

A Woman: Now we have no one to vouch for us. What hope is left for us, huh? We're doomed!

Jesus: Please don't say that. God won't abandon us. If we ask, God will give it to us. If we look for a way out, we'll find it. Didn't you know what

Bartholomew did the other day, when some relatives of his came to visit him at midnight?

A Man: Bartholomew? Who's Bartholomew?

Jesus: Hey, don't you remember that man who was shouting at the synagogue?

A Woman: Oh yeah, and what happened to that rascal?

Jesus: Well, he kept on asking, in order to feed his visitors. Poor man, he had no other choice.

Jesus, as always, ended up telling stories to be understood better. We all sat down, one by one. It was green all over the place.

Jesus: Well, the other night Bartholomew was visited by his relatives. He had nothing in the pot to offer to them, so he went to his neighbor: "Neighbor, open the door! Do you have leftover bread from dinner?" But this neighbor was already snoring, deep asleep. He went to another neighbor: "Neighbor, please!" Another neighbor shouted from his bed: "Will you leave me in peace! Can't you see we're all in bed now?" But Bartholomew continued knocking at every neighbor's door until finally a neighbor relented, got up, and gave him pieces of bread, just to get rid of him.

A Woman: And so?

Jesus: God's like that. If we knock at God's door, God will open it for us and help us out of our difficulties at that moment. Don't you think so?

When Jesus finished his story, a thin woman carrying a basket of figs on her head and wearing a soiled apron came near us.

Melanie: Please pardon my boldness, rashness, but I don't know, I think sometimes, things happen the other way around. Many times, it's God who knocks at our door. We're the ones sleeping very soundly. God comes and bangs on our door so that we can share our extra bread with those who have nothing.

Melanie's words surprised us all.

Melanie: Isn't it true what I'm saying, countrymen? Yeah, it's good to be asking the Lord, but as far as I know, no manna comes from heaven anymore. It used to, before, when our ancestors were walking through that desert. But now, miracles no longer happen.

Jesus: This woman's right. Listen, my friends: the situation is bad. There are several families suffering from hunger in Capernaum, in Bethsaida, and in all of Galilee. But if we had unity, if we put together the little we have, then things would go better, don't you agree?

John: I agree with you, Jesus, but it's just too late. Let's stop this and let's all go. Yeah, fellows, it's quite late, don't you see? Let's go back to Capernaum.

A Man: No, no, you can't leave now. We've got to settle the matter of the prisoners' wives and how the jobless are going to eat.

Peter: We'll talk about it some other time. It's getting dark and frankly...

A Woman: Good Lord, if we leave now, we'll surely pass out along the way!

Jesus: Hey, Philip, isn't there any place here where we can buy something?

Philip: We can buy a few pieces of bread at Dalmanutha, but we would need two hundred denarii to feed so many people!

Jesus: This is how it is, friends. You're hungry, and so are we. We brought along some olives, but they're not enough for everyone. Maybe some of you don't want to share the bread that you have under your tunic, so you can't bring it out!

John: Right on, Jesus, and look, here's a boy who has brought along some food.

Jesus: What've you got there, little boy?

Boy: Five loaves of barley bread and two fish.

Jesus: Listen, neighbors, why don't we do as Melanie said a while ago? Let's all think as one family and share what we have with everyone. Perhaps there'll be enough for all.

Man: Very well then. Hey, little boy, bring your five loaves of bread over here! I've got two or three more!

Jesus: Peter, take out your olives and put them here in the middle for everyone. Has anybody got anything else?

Another Man: We have a few pieces of salmon over here! Two from this little boy here, and probably a few more from others.

Melanie: Here's my basket of figs, countrymen. Whoever is hungry may eat them free of charge.

It was so simple. Those who brought bread shared it with everyone. Cheese and dates were likewise distributed to all. The women improvised a few bonfires and cooked fish. And so that night everyone ate, by the shore of the Sea of Galilee.

A Woman: Hey, if anyone cares for some more fish or bread, we still have some here. How about you, Peter?

Peter: No, I've eaten a lot. I'm more bloated than a hippopotamus!

Another Woman: Little boy, go and collect all the pieces of leftover bread. We can still make use of them!

John: And now men, everyone to the boat! We've got to go home!

A Man: Just a minute, guys, don't leave yet. We haven't settled the problem of the prisoners' wives yet. Oh, well, of course, I understand. All that we have to do is . . .

Melanie: Share what you have.

Jesus: Right. You share today and tomorrow too. In this way, there'll be food for everyone.

All thirteen of us got into Gaspar's boat and paddled our way to Capernaum in the middle of the night. While crossing the lake, I realized that a miracle, a great miracle, had taken place right before our eyes that afternoon.

•

About three kilometers from Capernaum, very near the Sea of Galilee, is Tabgha, where, according to ancient tradition, Jesus ate bread and fish together with a multitude of his countrymen. Tabgha is the Arabic contraction of the Greek name "Heptapegon," which means "Seven Fountains." The church that is presently visited in Tabgha is built over a church that used to exist there one thousand four hundred years ago. The Mosaic tiles on the floor of the so-called Church of Multiplication belong to the ancient church. They are of great artistic and archaeological value. One of these very ancient tiles represents a basket with five loaves of bread with two fish on the sides. Since ancient times, the bread and fish have been a Eucharistic symbol, in reference to the text in the gospel where what is essential in our celebration of the Eucharist takes place: a community sharing their faith, their hope, and their bread in the presence of Jesus.

In the episode, Jesus tells his countrymen the parable of a friend who asks for help in the middle of the night (Luke 11:5–8). Jesus wants to point out the trust we ought to have in the Lord, because he listens to the voice calling out to him for help. Sooner or later, he will open the door for us. On the other hand, Jesus presents to us a humorous story with a practical lesson. That tenacity in asking, that stubbornness, that Middle Eastern perseverance in knowing how to insist, that astuteness of one who has nothing in getting what he wants, all these are values one must understand in building the kingdom of justice.

Bread was the staple food in Jesus' times. It has been the staple in many parts of the world throughout history. Some uprisings and revolutions have been caused by a lack of it or by its increase in price, making it unaffordable for the poor. Lack of bread — which is tantamount to saying hunger — has, on many occasions, sparked rebellion among the poor. Through the writings of the period, we can more or less approximate the price of bread in Jesus' time. A daily portion for one person was equivalent to one-twelfth of a denarius, that is, one-twelfth of the daily wage. For the majority of jobs, it was common to earn one denarius a day. Bread was eaten in the form of flattened rolls, buns, a little thick perhaps, like what continues to be eaten in many Middle Eastern countries. An adult consumed at least three of these pieces for a meal.

God does not feed people directly. The most palpable proof of this is the prevailing hunger all over the world that is experienced by the majority of humankind, a hunger not willed by God. The hungry need not wait for the solution of their misery from heaven. The gospel gives us an alternative: sharing. It is not necessary to "buy" — as the disciples proposed. It is enough to "give," share in common what each has. Thus, there will be enough for everyone. This would be the greatest of all miracles. If everything is shared, "everyone will be satisfied" and there might even be an excess.

The mission of the Christian community in a world dominated by injustice and where the rule of money and accumulation of wealth prevails will always be love. It is not love expressed in words, in beautiful speeches, but in the act of sharing. God is generous and wants everyone to eat, live, and be happy. This desire of God can only be a reality through the generosity of the community. And this is the message that the community conveys and celebrates when they get together in the Eucharistic sharing of the bread.

(Matt. 14:13–21 and 15:32–39; Mark 6:30–44 and 8:1–10;
Luke 10–17; John 6:1–14)

58

In Front of the Synagogue
of Capernaum

It was Saturday. Like all Saturdays, we would get together in the synagogue of Capernaum. In the assembly were several of those who had eaten with us in Bethsaida, where we had shared the fish and the loaves of bread. The prisoners' relatives were also present, as well as a number of beggars. After the ritual prayers, Phanuel, one of the wealthiest proprietors in the city, stood up to render the Scripture reading.

Phanuel: "Then a small thing, like a grain, similar to frost, appeared in the desert. Moses told the sons of Israel: this is manna, the bread of God that nourishes us. This is what the Lord commands: that each one gets what he needs for him and his family to eat. The children of Israel thus obeyed. However, some got more than what they needed and so the others got little. So they divided it equally among themselves so that everybody would have only what they needed. Moses likewise said: no one is to keep the manna for the next day. But some did not obey him and they started to hoard food, which became infested with worms and became spoiled. Moses had commanded each one to get only what was necessary for his subsistence." This is the word of God in the sacred book of the law!

All: Amen! Amen!

Then Eliab, the rabbi, in his usual shrill voice, addressed himself to everyone in the synagogue.

Rabbi: Brothers and sisters, who among you wants to explain the text? Come on, feel free to comment on the holy word that we have just heard.

Amos: The one who read it ought to feel ashamed of himself!

Amos, one of the laborers on the property of Phanuel, had broken the silence.

Amos: I don't want to comment on anything. What I want is to shout at the face of this greedy man: comply with what you've just read! All of you, please listen and be the judge: Phanuel hasn't paid me a single cent for four months already. I work myself to death on his farm, and yet he never pays me. Thief!

Rabbi: You shut up and bring out your grudges somewhere else! This is not a tribunal, but the house of God!

Amos: If they don't listen to me in the tribunal, where do I go?

Rabbi: Shut up, I said! I repeat: Is there any brother of ours who would like to comment on the word of God?

Simeon: Yes, yes, rabbi, I'd like to comment on it.

All eyes turned to the hunchback, Simeon, a poor man living near the market.

Rabbi: What have you got to say?

Simeon: Well, actually, I've got nothing to say. Moses said it all. You heard him, didn't you? No one is to have more and no one is to have less. No one is to have excess bread, and no one is to be wanting it. That's the law of Moses. I'm a son of Moses. That man over there, Eleazir, is Moses' son too. Then why are his barns bursting with wheat and barley while I'm here dying of hunger?

Rabbi: You shut up too, silly man! What you're saying has nothing to do with the word of God. If you want to discuss politics, then go to the tavern.

Simeon: I'm not talking of politics, rabbi. All I'm saying is that my children haven't got even a piece of bread to eat.

Rabbi: Eat! Eat! That's all that you can think. Brothers and sisters, we are in the house of God. For a moment, let's forget all these material concerns and talk of matters of the spirit.

A Woman:: Of course, you can say that because you always have hot meals everyday! If you were starving like us, you would sell your spirit for a plate of lentils!

Rabbi: Get this scandalous woman out of the synagogue! I'll never allow anyone to desecrate this holy place! Let us talk of sacred things, the divine bread, the manna. As the reading says, manna fell from heaven over the Israelites.

Woman: But what falls on us are the beatings of the guards! My two sons have been imprisoned for a week and beaten like dogs! Do you know why? Because this swine of a Sadducee denounced him! Yes, Gideon, you did it and don't you turn your face, for everyone knows, you traitor!

Rabbi: What's going on here? What have you come here for, to pray or to pester your brothers in the community?

Amos: Brothers? How can this usurer be my brother when just yesterday he grabbed me by the neck and forced me to pay the damned interest? Stop playing dumb, Reuben, it's you I'm referring to!

Rabbi: Stop it! That's enough! You are in the house of God and you are here to pray!

Simeon: But rabbi, don't you understand what we're telling you? How can the lion and the sheep pray together? The lion prays for the sheep to fall asleep that he may eat him up. The sheep prays for the lion to sleep that he may cut off his mane.

Amos: Well said, Simeon! How can I pray together with Eleazir when I don't even have a handful of soil to cover my dead body? This place is too small for the two of us!

Another Man: Old Berechiah robs you of twenty and then bribes the judges, who rob you of twenty more! How can I pray with him under the same roof?

Another Man:: Yeah, this must be said loud and clear for everybody to hear! Look at his pious face. The wheat you keep in your barns could feed forty families in this town. Your wife's jewelry could repair all the houses in this town. So you've got to choose between them and us!

The noise heightened like a tide. Accusing fingers were raised and we spoke fearlessly, denouncing the abuses of the mighty people of Capernaum. Then Eliab, the rabbi, red with fury, took to the lectern and began to shout.

Rabbi: You are too much, damn it! You who have no respect for the word of God, you who only want to make politics! Yes, yes, I know what's happening here. Just like last time, at the wheat farm. An agitator filled all your heads with dreams. I know this man well. He's here with us. But let me say this for the last time: either you shut up or I'll drive you all out!

Jesus: That's not necessary, rabbi. We're leaving. One of us is excess baggage here.

Jesus stood up, gave a half-turn, and left the synagogue.

Rabbi: Damn you! It's all your fault! You have divided the community! You'll pay for this, rebel!

We, of the group, left too and followed Jesus. The farmers, Eleazir's laborers, Phanuel's unpaid workers, the prisoners' wives, and many others left the house of God in silence. Soon there were only a few left inside the synagogue. The rabbi was walking to and from the lectern, with clenched teeth and fists. Friends of the landowners as well as the usurers remained too. There were some who, for fear of the rabbi's reprisal, dared not leave. In one corner of the square outside, all of us surrounded Jesus.

Old Woman: Hey, you from Nazareth. Have we done something wrong by leaving the synagogue?

Jesus: No, don't worry, grandma. Even the prophet Jeremiah had to set his foot against the doors of the temple, to expose that the house of God had been converted into a den of thieves.

A Man:: So, what now, Jesus? What's gonna happen?

Jesus: The usual thing, neighbor. They throw stones at us and hide their hands. Then, when we protest, they'll accuse us of inciting trouble and sowing discord in the community. Meanwhile, they pretend to be like meek lambs, but don't be deceived by their guise, for deep inside them, they're wolves with sharp fangs. All they want is to snatch everything from you and get away with it.

A Woman:: What do we do now, Jesus?

Jesus: The opposite of what they're doing: share. God is asking this from us. That's exactly what Moses wrote: no one is to have more or less. This is the sign that the Kingdom of God has started with us. Listen, my friends: why was there enough bread for everyone yesterday? Because what we had, we shared with each one. This is the will of God. If we share our bread in this life, God will share eternal life with us. If we share the bread of the earth, God will give us bread that's even better, the bread from heaven, like that manna that fell into the desert.

A Man:: Tell me, where do we get this bread from heaven?

Jesus: Never mind that now, Simeon. First, you've got to share the bread of earth, don't you think so?

While Jesus was talking outside, Eleazir, the landowner, left the synagogue and headed for our group, threatening us with his fist.

Eleazir: Hear this well, all of you. We can't tolerate what you've done. With the rabbi's consent, I'm reporting all of you to the police, specially you, Nazarene, the leader of all this agitation!

A Woman:: It's obvious who got hurt the most!

Eleazir: You can laugh all you want, fools! Let's see how you laugh when the soldiers come and put you in prison, when they grab your sons, beat them at the pillar and crucify them on the Roman cross. Don't tell me I didn't warn you!

The silence that ensued was heavy with ill-boding. Eleazir's threats froze all the laughter on our lips, for they were serious. The Romans never spared anyone. Everyday, new crosses stood all over the country to drown the cry of protest coming from the poor of Israel.

A Man:: Well, companions, maybe we should stop this dialogue for now, what do you think?
Another Man:: Yeah, besides it's a little bit late, so goodbye everyone!
Amos: I must go too. I'll see you next time.

One by one, the people proceeded to their homes, just as they had left the synagogue moments before.

James: Cowards! They're all a bunch of cowards.
Jesus: Of course, James. We all feel scared at the moment of truth. No one likes to risk his life. But one must do it. We've got to share our bread, but we've also got to share our body and blood too. Many of us will break our bodies like we're breaking bread. A number of us will shed blood like we're spilling wine. When we've offered our lives for our country, then we'll be worthy of the Kingdom of God.
John: Well, those words are easily said, Jesus, but very hard to swallow.
A Boy: The soldiers are coming! Run, run, they're carrying lances and clubs!

Many scampered away when they heard the soldiers coming. We, too, started to look at each other with anxiety.

Peter: Well, Jesus, so, so...
Jesus: What's wrong, Peter? Do you want to go too? Go ahead. What about the rest of you?
Peter: Well, if we want to go — yes we do...Ufff. That's okay, Jesus, we'll stay with you. You're right. The truth simply gets stuck in one's throat, like a fishbone.
Jesus: Now we're thirteen. Anyone of us may falter. That's why we've got to support one another. May God give us the strength to share with everyone, even fear itself!

Peter: The soldiers are here, Jesus.

One Soldier: Hey, all of you, disperse, disperse! We want no trouble. C'mon, c'mon, on your feet. And you, stranger, watch your actions. We're aware of everything, do you hear? You and your group are blacklisted. Go now, go back to your homes.

Fortunately, the soldiers paid little attention to Eleazir's complaint. They let us go that time. All this happened on a Saturday, a rest day, right in front of the synagogue of Capernaum.

•

The ruins of Capernaum during the time of the gospels were not discovered until the end of the nineteenth century. About six hundred years after Jesus' death, Capernaum was destroyed, and all the local sites referred to in the gospels were gradually reduced to rubble. One of the tasks undertaken with great care after the discovery was the restoration of the synagogue. It was not the same synagogue that Jesus knew, but was built over the one which existed during his time. The present building belongs to that of the fourth century, very spacious, with thick columns and beautiful decorations on the walls. It is very near Peter's house.

During the worship rites celebrated every Saturday in the synagogue, which Jesus customarily attended in the company of his countrymen, an excerpt from the Scriptures was read and the members present commented on it. Neither the reading of the text nor commentary was the specific task of the rabbi. The women ordinarily never spoke publicly in the synagogue, although in this episode, their participation is understandable, considering the flow of discussion among the neighbors.

In the episode, the text read is taken from chapter 16 of the Book of Exodus. Manna or "bread from heaven" was the food the Israelites found in the desert in their long journey to the Promised Land. The norms given by God in gathering the manna aimed at preventing accumulation and inequality in the distribution of food so that everyone would have enough.

No matter how the Jewish worship in the synagogue differs from that of Christians, and how the former's Saturday worship cannot be equated with the Eucharistic celebration on Sunday, in this episode, a certain similarity is found, in order to focus on the basic theme of worship-justice.

The theme of Eucharist-justice is a problem as old as Christianity. Paul affirms that wherever a glaring inequality exists, then there can be no celebration of the Eucharist, but an act condemned by the Lord. His denunciation in this sense is strong (1 Cor. 11:17–34). During the first centuries of Christianity, an evangelical consciousness retained the relationship between the Eucharist and justice. Only those who shared their wealth with their brothers and sisters celebrated the Eucharist and broke bread. Furthermore, it was the bishop's obligation to watch out for those who gave offerings during the Mass. If these were oppressors of the poor, then the latter were prohibited from receiving anything from them (*Apost. Const.* 2.17.1–5; 3.8; 4.5–9). This was so strictly enforced that the *Didascalia* of the third century provides that if there is no other means to feed the poor but to receive money from the rich who commit injustice, then the community might as well die of hunger, rather than receive help from the oppressors (*Didasc.* 4.8.2). Mandates of this type proliferate in the writings of the Holy Fathers and churches from various places through the centuries. Another example of how radical this was is shown by the bishop of Milan, Saint Ambrose, who, having been informed of the massacre of thousands of persons, for which Emperor Theodosius was responsible, not only criticized the latter, but also threatened him with a letter that "the Bishop will not offer the Sacrifice of the Mass in his presence" (Epistle 51.13). At the start of the ninth century, the official church got rid of this practice and concentrated solely on the theme of Christ's real presence in the bread and how such a sublime mystery could be explained and understood. Thus, the other dimension of the Eucharist was lost.

The prophets of Israel are in this line also. At the very doorsteps of the temple of Jerusalem, a place much more "sacred" than the synagogue of a town of fishermen, prophet Jeremiah "scandalized" the religious people of his time and their own king by criticizing the false security of those who sought protection in cult, but were remiss with their obligation to be just (Jer. 7:1–15; 26:1–24). With this sense of freedom, characteristic of the great prophets, Jesus puts justice before worship, and in the sacred place he expounds on what is more sacred for God: the life of people, and justice among all. No one is to bring offerings to the altar if another person has something against him or her. The person must first be reconciled with the other (Matt. 5:23–24).

In the Eucharist, we believers celebrate the one whom they killed because he was faithful to God, and who became God by resurrecting from the dead. In the Eucharist, we celebrate this common faith, extending it through history by living this same faith. We celebrate a common hope that things will change toward life, equality, and community among people. We celebrate love that compels us to share, to risk our lives for this cause and to create our community. The celebration of the Eucharist — the word of the prophets as well as Jesus', the bread that is broken and shared — sustains this faith, this hope, and this love.

(John 6:22–71)

59

The Ghost by the Lake

It was a dark night over the great Sea of Galilee. The moon, a slice of orange hanging in the sky, hardly illumined our faces. There were six of us, including Peter, in his old green boat. The others were in the other boat manned by Andrew. Jesus was not with us that night. When the twelve of us got into the boats, he said he wasn't coming, and left in silence toward one of the dark streets coming from the wharf.

Peter: Fellows, this is strange. Why did he stay behind?

Thomas: Jesus is a...a...afraid of the water at n...n...night. Could th...this be the r...r...reason?

James: Nonsense, Thomas. It must be something more serious. Fear of the water, no. That's stupidity. Fear, yeah. Jesus is scared. I can see it in his eyes.

Peter: Fear of what, James? What's he scared of?

James: Things are getting worse, Peter. Jesus is being watched each day. The Pharisees hate him and are after him. Something smells rotten here.

Peter: What are you talking about? That can't be. Jesus is a very courageous man. He's shown it. How can you be so sure of what you're saying?

James: No one's certain of anything, Peter, anything. We're just talking. But you can't deny that he's acting strange today, and he's left us alone.

Thomas: Maybe he r...re...remained to pray. Jesus prays a lot.

Peter: But why would he pray there? No, Thomas, that doesn't explain it.

James: Could he have betrayed us? He might be joining the other group and hasn't the guts to tell us.

Peter: Why would he do such a thing? Jesus is upright. You're crazy. No, that can't be.

Philip: I've got something else in mind. Listen, fellows. I think Jesus is sick and tired of all this. He's tired of saying that the Kingdom of God is near, that it's coming, because it'll never come. He proclaimed himself a prophet, he's used up all his energy saying that things are heading for change. As you can see, things have remained the same. And then...

Peter: Then what? What do you mean by that, Philip?

Philip: That one of these days — today, for example — Jesus will say: "To hell with you, bitter world!" All these things about justice, the Kingdom of God, even the group, and everything, are baloney! Then he'll go away, passing over a dark road like he did tonight, and we'll never see him again, ever.

Peter: What're you saying? Where the hell did you get that crazy idea? Jesus would never do that to us! He's not what you think.

James: It's okay, Peter. He's not so. But why the hell didn't he join us tonight?

All words uttered during the conversation that night pierced through the heart like the cold wind inflating the sails, and stirred the tranquil waters of the lake. On the other boat, Andrew, Judas, Simon, and the rest were talking of the same thing, with the same words and asking the same questions. After a while, everyone remained silent. Only the increasing murmur of the wind could be heard.

Peter: Hell, will you say something, at least! I'd rather we have a storm than see all of you mum like you're dead!

Then, as if in response to Peter's cry, the wind began to jostle the two boats furiously. The clouds started flashing lightning bolts and thunder over the lake, previously darkened in the clouds' dark bosom.

Peter: Damn! I knew a storm was coming! Get a good hold of the sails, John!

Thomas: W...wh...what's all this?

Peter: What else, Thomas! You don't think there's gonna be a party, do you?

Thomas: Then we'll all d...d...drown?

James: Yeah, damn it! We'll all drown! And you'll be the first to drown if you don't shut your big mouth!

Andrew: Hey, Peter, let go of the sail a little! Peter!

Peter: Stay apart a little, dummy! We'll collide!

The waves, like gigantic mountains, broke over our heads; we were drenched again to the bones. The boat manned by Andrew was caught in a whirlwind and was getting close to ours, spinning furiously like a top.

Peter: Damn you, James! Release that sail some more! We'll get smashed!
James: Out of here, Thomas! Hold tight, John! Harder, c'mon, harder!

The keel was creaking like a soul in torment. The boats, lifted up by the waves, suddenly crashed down on the water's surface. While Philip and Nathanael were hastily bailing out the water that entered through the boat's sides, Thomas gave out a terrifying cry, spread his arms and fainted. He fell over the stern's ropes.

Thomas: Ayyy!
James: That's one head less! Hold tight, John! Careful now, careful!

James and I tried to control the sail. But then the wind caused the mast to crack, and it split right down the middle.

Peter: We're doomed! We'll all go down to the bottom of the lake! That's why Jesus left us all alone: he knew it! He abandoned us! We'll all die!

When our boat was almost filled with water on all sides, Andrew screamed louder than thunder.

Andrew: Hey, all of you, look over there! Look over there! Toward the shore!
Philip: It's a ghost! The ghost of the lake! It's heading toward us!
Peter: What's that, James? Do you see it too? And you, John?
James: Of course I do! It's coming here!
Philip: Go away, ghost, go away! Wait a minute, I know of a prayer against ghosts. Let me see, how does it go now? Ah, yes! "Ghost, I'm telling you, the Lord is with me! I'm telling you, Ghost, the Lord is with me!"
James: Don't be silly, Philip!

Walking over the stormy waters of the lake, a white and luminous figure was slowly heading toward our devastated boats. The moon suddenly extinguished its dying light. The sea was a huge dark mouth, all too willing to swallow us all up. Thomas, who had regained consciousness, trembled as he held on to that piece of mast that was left after the split. We were all terrified, and couldn't make out the mysterious shadow. All of a sudden, the ghost spoke.

Jesus: Don't be afraid! It's me! It's me!

Thomas: And w . . . w . . . who is this "me"?

Philip: Stay away, ghost, God will not leave me! Stay away. Ghost, God will not leave me! Go away, ghost, God will not leave me!

Jesus: Hey, guys, it's me! Don't be afraid.

James: Peter, that's Jesus' voice. It's him, it's him!

The waters of the sea grew calm. The wind ceased to blow when we recognized Jesus. Once again, our boats began to sway gently over the waves.

Peter: Jesus, if it's you, tell me to come where you are.

Jesus: Come, Peter, come.

When he heard the command, Peter jumped from the boat and started to walk over the lake to meet Jesus.

Peter: Look I can walk over the water! Look! Let's see, with one foot! Then with the other foot! Yippee! I'm the smartest guy in all of Capernaum and the whole of Galilee! Yippee! Look at this, guys!

Peter was doing some pirouettes over the waves as he approached Jesus, when, suddenly, lightning split open the sky's huge dome and the wind began to batter the waters in turmoil. Peter, terrified, began to sink slowly.

Peter: Give me a hand, Jesus! Jesus, save me, I'm drowning!

Jesus, walking calmly over the waves, went near Peter and held him by the hand.

Jesus: You man of little faith, Peter! Why were you afraid? Why did you get scared?

Peter: I got scared because I was drowning! I was drowning! I'm drowning, I'm drowning, I'm drown! . . .

Rufina: Peter, Peter, what's the matter? You'll wake up all the boys! Look at how you rolled yourself up into that mat; you rolled up like a snail! Wake up, man!

Peter: Ah, the mast, it was horrible. Ay Rufi, it's you. Pff! What a relief! He saved us, Rufi, he saved us!

Rufina: Take it easy, Peter. And stop screaming. Grandma Rufa is a light sleeper.

Peter: Ay, Rufi, what a relief. We're saved! Rufina, tonight I understood everything. He's the man.

Rufina: What on earth are you talking about?

Peter: Rufi, look, we were on the boat. Then a really terrifying storm came up. We were so afraid. We were alone. Our sail was broken, and our mast split into two. We all lost our faith. We were doomed, until he came.

Rufina: What the hell are you talking about?

Peter: I'm talking about Jesus, Rufi. When I was drowning, he held me by the hand, and saved me. The storm stopped. And the fear was gone too. We were saved.

Rufina: Beautiful, that was very beautiful. You were having a good time the whole evening, weren't you? And may I know, you rascal, at what time you got back, as I didn't hear you anymore?

Peter: But Rufi, don't you understand? That was a sign! Jesus is the man!

Rufina: What man, Peter? What's all this mystery about?

Peter: Listen to me, Rufi. Open your ears well and keep this to yourself only. I think Jesus is the Messiah.

Rufina: What the hell are you talking about? Are you okay?

Peter: I've never been so happy in my life! The storm is over, Rufi. And the fear is gone!

Rufina: Don't scream, damn! Look, forget about it, straighten the mat, and go back to sleep. Tomorrow you'll be yourself again.

Peter lay down on the mat. But he sat up again, as if pushed upward by a spring.

Peter: Rufina! What if this isn't a dream? What if it's something else?

Rufina: Of course it's something more than a dream. It's a nightmare.

Peter: No, Rufi. In all my life, I have never seen such a terrifying storm, such an agitated sea. In my life, I was never so scared, nor did I feel so secure when he took me by the hand. As if this wasn't a dream...Hey, Rufina, are you still there?

Rufina: Of course I'm here, but my eyes are getting heavy.

Peter: But are you sure? Don't you think it's at this moment that we're dreaming?

Rufina: Listen, Peter. You heard the first crowing. Forget all that crap and get some sleep. And let me get some too. I'm groggy.

Peter: Okay, but I'll continue telling you what happened tomorrow, and don't tell anyone. I think this isn't a dream. I think...

Rufina: Hmmm. Certainly you'll tell me tomorrow, tomorrow....

Peter closed his eyes and fell asleep again. Later, after many years, he told me everything. Then, he still couldn't tell me what happened that night. But he remembered it so vividly. It was as vivid and warm as Jesus' hand that held him so he would not drown in the troubled waters of the lake.

•

In the Sea of Galilee, because of its geographical characteristics, sudden storms are frequent and sometimes come with the strength of a real hurricane. The fishermen would ordinarily set sail even if it was still dark since the last hours of the night and the first hours of dawn were the best times to find schools of fish. In Galilee, as in any part of the world, the fisherman is an early bird.

Throughout the Bible, the dream appears as a space where God is revealed to people. In telling us about the dreams of those whom God used as instruments to make known his plans, the Scriptures are reflecting a preoccupation with dreams that was common in Israel and in the majority of the ancient countries. It was believed that God could reach out to people and vice-versa by way of dreams. In the Old Testament, dreams revealing to people God's wishes for them are significant (Gen. 28:10–22 and 37:5–11; Num. 12:6–8). We must not interpret them as superstitious or infantile. Even today, dreams provide us with some truth if we can discern their meaning, as the wise men of Israel advised (Sir. 34:1–8). We are not supposed to believe our dreams to the letter. Rather, we should open our hearts to the endless realities in life. Great experiences within us are as real as what is without. Or as real as a plate of food that we eat, although we are not able to express these experiences in exactly the same manner. The limits of our conscious and unconscious state are likewise difficult to define. It is also possible, by way of the unconscious, to discover some truths, to experience intensely some lasting feelings that include important decision making.

One must bear in mind that the evangelists used various styles in their writing. Thus, we find in the pages of the gospels historical narrations of the Old Testament, catechetical schemes, accounts based on the stories of the Old Testament, and symbolic accounts. This text about Jesus walking over the water contains a symbolic message. The sea, according to the Jewish mind, was a prison where the devil and the evil spirits, overpowered by God at the beginning of the world, had to go. Among them figured the powerful Leviathan, a monster very dangerous to people. This negative idea about the sea spans the entire Scripture up to the last biblical book. When the Book of Revelation describes how the world will be in the future, when the Kingdom of God has arrived, it does not mention the sea (Rev. 21:1). Naturally, God has power over all the spirits of the sea, and Leviathan is like a plaything for him (Job 40:25–32). Jesus possesses this power as well, since God gave it to him. He has given it not to a sage, nor to a theologian, nor to an exorcist, but to a lowly worker. This text, therefore, is the proclamation of Jesus as God's Messiah. This is exactly what Peter thought.

Like the rest of the disciples, Peter was beginning to see in Jesus the prophet who revived the people's hope (faith) in the God of Israel, in the Messiah whose coming had been proclaimed for many years. This was for him, as for all the rest, the result of a process: the process of knowing Jesus, understanding his message, and, above all, committing oneself to follow him. It is something we obtain not in baptism nor in times of prayer, nor in our community reflections with our brothers and sisters. It is a long process.

(Matt. 14:24–33; Mark 6:45–52; John 6:15–21)

60

Two by Two

Peter: Very well, all is said and done: we'll scatter ourselves, like ants spreading after a downpour, through all of Galilee!

It was during the first few days of summer that we decided to leave Capernaum and undertake the journey to other cities of our province, in order to announce the Kingdom of God. We were then just a handful of nobodies. But Jesus always countered that a little salt was enough to give flavor to the food. That a small lamp on top of a table could brighten up the entire house.

Philip: Just a minute, adventurers. Forget about the fun and teach me what to say. I can promote my wares, like combs and brushes, but not this job of delivering a divine speech. Well, the truth...

Jesus: Listen, Philip: it's very simple. Besides, you don't have to talk much. All we've got to do is gather the people and teach them how to share what they have. Remember what we did with the loaves of bread and the fish?

Philip: Yeah, but what if they don't want to get involved?

Peter: Well, shake the dust off your feet and go somewhere else. You can't force people to share if they don't want to.

Thomas: That's what I'm saying, that in the K...K...Kingdom of G...G...God, n...n...nobody enters by f...f...force.

Philip: We're the ones who'll be forced somewhere if the soldiers catch us gathering our countrymen and inciting them to rebellion...

Matthew: Don't worry about that, Philip. We'll bring you some soup in jail.

James: And if an old usurer cuts our throats, then we go straight to Abraham's lap.

Jesus: Well, we're all ready. James and Andrew will go to Bethsaida. Thomas and Matthew, to Chorazin. Philip and Nathanael, to Magdala.

Philip: And together we perish!

Jesus: John and Peter will go to Tiberias. Simon and Judas to Sepphoris. James and Thaddaeus, to Nain.

James: So when do we leave?

Jesus: On the first day of the week, each shepherd to his own flock!

Matthew: When do we see each other again?

Jesus: Well, within a month everyone must be back here in Capernaum. Okay?

We left by pairs for the neighboring towns. The truth is that in those times, each one of us imagined the Kingdom of God in his own way. No one had a clear idea of it, and our knees trembled a little at the thought of it. But we kept on encouraging one another in announcing the good news among our countrymen.

After a month, we all went back to Capernaum as agreed upon, and we met in Peter and Rufina's house as always.

Peter: Hey, comrades, help yourselves to some wine. We must thank the Lord for allowing us to return and still be in one piece!

James: That's very well said, stone thrower! After all those skirmishes, the group has become well known to the people and the authorities. They've got me and the skinny one blacklisted. They know us better than David knew Bathsheba. It was a miracle to be able to escape from that place.

Peter: So let's all have a toast to celebrate this. Hey, Matthew, what's wrong?

Matthew: Nothing.

Peter: Why don't you make a toast with us? Don't you love wine?

Matthew: If I take a shot, then I don't stop until I end up drinking the entire barrel. I know myself quite well.

James: And so? Have you changed after the trip? What happened?

Thomas: It so happened that one day, w...we w...were...

Matthew: That's enough, Thomas. It's just that I've lost the desire to drink much. I had the appetite for it before. But now, it's the opposite. That's it.

Thomas: No, it was because of s...s...something they told him: shoemaker, re...re...repair your shoes f...f...first. One day, in Tiberias, we were at the c...c...corner of the square. This M...M...Matthew was talking about unity and c...c...conversion. Then two men broke in:

A Man:: You don't know what you're talking about! You're drunker than Noah by the grapevine!

Another Man:: We'll listen to you when you have purged yourself of all that wine in your belly, rascal! Let's go, guys; this man doesn't even know where his mustache is!

Matthew: That happened one day. Then another. What a meddlesome bunch! They made me sick, you know!

Thomas: B...b...but they were right, Matthew. First take the plank out of your own eye, before you can take the speck out of anyone else's eye.

Jesus: So, you don't drink anymore, Matthew?

Matthew: Well, the truth is there are days when I can't bear it, and other times, I grab my two hands very tightly to control myself. Damn it! Give me a few days more, but it's something... Isn't it?

Peter: So this other shot is for Matthew, who has stopped drinking!

Matthew: Bah, to hell with all of you!

Jesus: And what was the mess you got yourselves into, skinny one, and you, James? C'mon on, tell us what happened.

James: Ha! Or better, what didn't happen. You all know Bethsaida, where Onesimus is, who thinks he's the pharaoh of Egypt because he owns the boats. But the fishermen are not dumb. They're alert. This is what happened, word for word:

James: Listen, countrymen, my grandfather always repeated that saying of the wise men: it is more difficult to break a three-threaded rope.

A Fisherman: Make yourself clear, my friend.

James: This means that when a poor creature fights for his rights alone, he's easily defeated. But if there are three of them, then it's more difficult. If there are thirty of them, that's much better indeed. Do you understand? It's necessary to braid a thick rope from among all the threads.

Another Fisherman: This red head's right. The ones up there are advantaged in many ways. But we're more than they. That's where our strength lies.

Another Fisherman: Trouble is, we're not united. Each one thinks only of himself.

James: God wants all of us to look in the same direction. Where there's a group pushing as one, God also lends a hand. This is what we've done in Capernaum.

A Fisherman: Things are a lot easier in your town. You're well organized and you defend one another. Here, it's old Onesimus who controls everything.

Another Fisherman: All boats and nets are owned by Onesimus. Therefore, he gets all the profit. While we, we've got nothing but our arms.

James: And so? What else do you need? Hear this, my friends: without your arms, those boats will not move, nor those nets be cast, is that right? Onesimus wouldn't earn a single cent.

A Fisherman: Yeah, of course, but what can we do with our arms?

James: Cross them. That's it. Cross them and tell that bloodsucker that no boat will be rowed nor will a single net be cast nor a hook thrown until the wages go up to two denarii!

And so it was. The following day, the wharf of Bethsaida was like a funeral parlor: everyone was silent with arms crossed. Onesimus, the patron, was fuming mad.

Patron: Two denarii! Two denarii! Are you out of your mind? Tell me: who's the instigator here? Yeah, I know, that red head from Capernaum and the skinny one. And that man called Jesus is behind all this. You damned agitators! I'll have your tongues cut off! I'll have them cut off!

James: And look, fellows, we're still here in one piece. But the best part of it is that we've won the battle! That scoundrel Onesimus had to increase the wages. The news spread like wild fire. We were told that the fishermen of Gennesareth are doing the same thing, with crossed arms and demanding two denarii.

Jesus: Let's give another toast for James and Andrew, who knew how to work in justice's name. They have their names written in heaven!

Matthew: As well as in the police blotter of Bethsaida!

Peter: Well, Philip, it's your turn now. Let's see, what have you and Nathanael done in Magdala? How did you fare in that place?

Philip: Badly, yes and very badly. Your enemy was Onesimus, while ours was God. Who can go against him?

Jesus: What do you mean?

Philip: Well, God no, but those strange ideas of the people about God, which turn out to be more difficult to scrape than scabies. Here's our story, beginning when we arrived in the city:

Philip: Over here, everyone! Listen, companions! I'm not here to sell my wares today. Look, I didn't even bring my cart. My bald friend and I are here to bring you the good news.

A Woman:: Well, do it quickly and let's see if it's better than the lipstick I bought from you last week!

Philip: Listen well, my friends! Unplug your ears. I mean, one ear of yours, so that what enters through one doesn't come out through the other. Today, the Kingdom of God has come to this city of Magdala! Yeah, that's right, just as it sounds, the Kingdom of God!

Another Woman: Look here, fat head, stop these stories. The only thing that has reached this place is the kingdom of worms!

Philip: How's that again?

Woman: You heard it. All the orchards of Magdala are infested with worms: all tomatoes, eggplants, everything is worm-infested. It's God's punishment, his sacred wrath! The worst thing is, if God doesn't cool it, even my melons will be damaged; the worms are on their way to my melons!

Philip: What are you talking about, ignorant woman? What has God to do with your melons?

Woman: Why, don't you know? Go and ask the rabbi to tell you! This worm epidemic is a punishment from heaven, for the many sins of this perverted city!

Another Woman: And tell him out loud, that God must be more enraged here than when he was in Sodom! Why? Because the devil runs loose here. All one can see here are taverns and drunkards and women who wink at you from every corner. That's why God must be taking his revenge.

Woman: We rightfully deserve it, don't you think so, stranger?

Philip: Ehem . . . Well, I think God is not as terrible as you imagine.

Woman: God sent us this misfortune and must be preparing something worse.

Philip: Oh no, woman, don't say that. God is good and doesn't like to pester people.

Women: I told you so! First the worms, and now some madmen have come!

Philip: Not even my horn could pacify them. They were all there, so obstinate with this punishing God. Pff, you know what, Jesus? If things must change, then one of the first to change should be this crazy idea that people have of God.

Peter: We had the same idea before, Philip. Or don't you remember anymore? Only a few months ago, we also viewed God as an executioner with his ax raised high. Now, that's a thing of the past. Now we see God like a father.

Philip: But Peter, you don't those Magdalenes. They're so stubborn. The more we explained to them . . .

Matthew: Well as they say, a stone gets a hole by the constant dripping of water. I'm talking from experience.

Jesus: Well said, Matthew. All of us start this way and gradually, God melts our hearts.

Philip: I hope so, Jesus, but the truth is, they're too much.

Jesus: But God's on their side. Damn! That's what matters more. What about a toast for God our Father who has wished to be revealed to the humble and be hidden from the arrogant! Look at all of us, Philip: there's no one among us learned or great. The Kingdom of God grows from below, as the trees do.

Philip: Well, brace yourself, Nat. We'll have to go back and visit our countrymen from Magdala, and their worms!

Jesus: That's exactly it, Philip. This thing's not finished in one day. Look, why did we have to go by pairs, like the asses when they pull the plow? Because the yoke can't be carried alone, but with another. One alone gets weary and disappointed. With someone along, the burden is lighter. There's still much terrain ahead.

James: But now is the right time, and we must take advantage. There's always work to be done. Everywhere the poor are lifting up their heads and strengthening their knees. The day of liberation is at hand!

Jesus: Many prophets wanted to see that day, but didn't live to see it. Many wanted to hear these things but heard not.

Peter: And many would have wanted to taste Rufina's soup, but couldn't, as she has it reserved for all of you! Yes, sir, a soup with two drops of oil can restore the life of a dead person! Hey, Rufi, why don't you serve the pot of soup, in celebration of the return of this group of crazy men!

That summer, we went from one town to another, through all of Galilee. And the Kingdom of God that came to us, for free, we also announced to our brothers and sisters. Free.

•

The sending of messengers by pairs was a deeply rooted custom in Israel. Messengers carried news — as there was no mail then — went on missions of assistance, or were sent to gather information, according to the specific situation. Generally, they left by pairs for two reasons: on the one hand, for protection, since the trips were long and much danger could arise; on the other hand, traveling in pairs had something to do with compliance with a norm found in the Book of Deuteronomy (Deut. 17:6 and 19:15). This norm in the beginning only applied to judicial processes. Later, it became applicable to other areas as well. According to this law, only the testimony of two witnesses could be given credit, and although only one would speak, the other ought to be present in order to confirm the testimony, thus giving it validity.

Reading in the gospel the instructions Jesus gave to his disciples, before sending them to announce the Kingdom of God, one observes how incomplete they were. Jesus was not a moralist. The gospel is not a collection of norms for every situation in life, as if it were enough to face life's reality with the application of formulas or slogans. The messengers of the gospel are not handed a set of instructions; they are given a spirit. Their whole life must be a sign of new values. They must proclaim them with the word, but above all, live them. In this episode, Jesus' disciples find themselves in situations not described in the gospel to the letter, but rather, the situations they face have to do with the spirit with which Jesus sends them. This is what the group is to learn eventually, as they are inspired by Jesus' word.

Like Jesus, the disciples addressed themselves to the poor as the privileged recipients of the good news of God. The gospel must be announced to them, the least ones, so they can start to live, knowing that as far as God is concerned, they are the first.

The liberation proclaimed in the gospel encompasses everything that is human, and all people, and consists necessarily of phases and mediations.

One stage is the organization of the poor. God does not want masses of men and women submerged in ignorance or in apathy, men and women who are passive and submissive. God wants a nation of free people. God came into history precisely to make of the oppressed Hebrews, enslaved by the Pharaoh, an organized and fighting nation. From servitude, God gave them passage to freedom. Liberation has, during one phase of the process, this period of awareness and organization, in which the poor bind themselves together by a common ideal and discover their dignity as children of God. A free person cannot imagine a punishing God who makes children suffer, who demands an accounting of every small sin in order to take revenge. People must be freed of this false image of God. A profound evangelization always bears as a consequence people's liberation from erroneous ideas about God and the relationship of God with people and history.

As Jesus has shown us in his life and in his words, there exists no conflict between action and prayer, between love for God and love for one's neighbor. We must not pose any opposition between the work of evangelization and that of promoting humankind, as if such a task of promotion were of a lesser category for a Christian by being "political." But the task of evangelization is sometimes taken as superior, more pure, for establishing our direct relationship with God. Such opposition is false, since there is a continuous relationship between evangelization and the promotion of humankind. To evangelize people is to proclaim the good news of people's dignity as the sons and daughters of God. In the name of this infinite dignity, human beings must be freed from hunger, from ignorance, from economic dependence. To promote people is to bring them to physical, intellectual, and political fulfillment. One must likewise be open to the reality of faith, since the religious dimension is essential to being human. There exists no contradiction. Both endeavors are profoundly related. Thus, the Latin American bishops who met at Puebla, Mexico, stated: "The situation of injustice makes us reflect on the great challenge faced by our pastoral people, to help them overcome situations that are less humane and to find themselves in more humane conditions. The profound social gaps, extreme poverty, and the violation of human rights in many parts are challenges to evangelization. Our mission to bring people close to God likewise implies the construction here of a more fraternal society" (Puebla final document, 90).

Jesus makes a toast to the Lord, gives God thanks for the return of his friends. The act of thanksgiving occupies a significant role in Jesus' manner of praying. The wise men of Israel claimed that in the world to come, only the act of thanksgiving would remain. It would no longer be necessary to ask for forgiveness or favors, nor to confess our sins. We would only be grateful to God. With his manner of praying, Jesus anticipates the world to come: the Kingdom of God.

(Matt. 10:5–15; 11:25–27; Mark 6:7–13; Luke 9:1–16; 10:17–24)

61

A Denarius for Each

Foreman: Ironsmith! Ironsmith anyone? I can shoe your five mules! Ironsmith!

Woman: Hey, you one-eyed man, how much will you charge to fix a barn door, huh?

One-Eyed Man: Lemme fix it first, then we talk about the fee.

Woman: No, tell me how much you charge first.

One-Eyed Man: Look, Madame Frissy, just let me do it, and I'll do it for free. Let's go!

Every morning, people looking for work gathered in front of the synagogue in Capernaum Square. Even before sunrise, some of them were already there, sitting on the steps or leaning against the wall, displaying their tools: the bricklayers with their trowel and plane, the carpenters with their hammers, and the farmers with their callused hands.

Daniel: Hey guys, why don't you work in my vineyard? There's so much to harvest! Yeah, all of you! A denarius at the end of the day! C'mon, hurry, and take advantage of the day's yield!

A group of men stood up and followed Daniel. Everyday, Jesus also roamed around the square, with his nails and hammer, hoping to find work.

Neighbor: Hey, Jesus, you look sleepy!

Jesus: I came late yesterday, so I didn't get any work. Let's see if I'm lucky today.

Neighbor: The early bird catches the worm. Look, just before you came, Daniel was hiring some men for his vineyard. It's harvest time and the harvest seems good.

Jesus: How much is he gonna pay them?

Neighbor: A denarius, as always. A denarius each, and Daniel means it. When he says he'll pay, he does it. Daniel is okay. He can be trusted.

Foreman: A bricklayer, for two days' work. I need a bricklayer to work for two days.

Jesus: Hey, I'm your man. Shall we go?

Foreman: Let's go! You receive one denarius today and another tomorrow. Okay?

Jesus: All right! See you, Simeon!

Neighbor: Goodbye, Jesus! I told you, the early bird catches the worm!

Neighbor: Jesus is lucky. He's hired at once.

Nato: You bet. I've been coming here for three days, but nothing. This is not the time for shearing the sheep, damn! Everyday I sharpen my shearing knife, but what for? One day I'll end up cutting my head off with it.

Neighbor: Is that what's bugging you?

Nato: I'm just sick and tired of doing the same thing: everyday I come home bringing nothing for my starving children. "It's only this piece of bread for today, son. Tomorrow, tomorrow, there'll be more." Tomorrow comes, and it's the same as today!

Neighbor: Times are hard, Nato, very hard.

Nato: I'm not coming home without a single denarius. I can't bear to see my children starving to death. Really, I can't!

At nine o'clock in the morning of the same day, Daniel came back to the square, when the sun's warm rays had spread all over the square.

Daniel: Hey, guys! I need more men to work in my vineyard. Anyone interested?

Neighbor: Let's go, Nato. This is a sure job. Your children will surely have something to eat with the money you'll bring home.

Nato: Let's go, Simeon!

Simeon, Nato, and a few more went to Daniel's vineyard. Soon, the square was again filled with men looking for jobs. At this moment, the children were playing and jostling each other all over the area.

Boy: I'm an ironsmith! Do you need horseshoes for your mules?

Another Boy:: I'm the mule!

Laborer: I'm a mule too, son.

Titus: Why do you say that?

Laborer: Because that's what I am, a mule, no more, no less. You're no less than a mule too. And so are the rest. We're all mules here, and the only thing we haven't got is the tail.

Titus: C'mon, there you go again.

Laborer: But it's the truth. I think we were born simply to engage in back-breaking work. Day in and day out, we do the same thing! Doesn't this get on your nerves, Titus, huh?

Titus: What can we do, man? Is there anything we can do?

Laborer: Nothing! It must have been written some place that the poor like us came into this world to do hard work and to have lots of children who will follow in our footsteps: that's right, to continue doing hard work and with empty bellies. Look at these children. They'll take our place here, when they're grown up, expecting to work, like mules, in order to live.

Wife: There's nothing yet, Samuel?

Samuel: Nothing, woman. There's nothing yet.

Wife: What shall we eat now?

Samuel: A piece of boiled stone, perhaps!

Old Woman: A little alms for the blind. Have pity on this poor blind woman!

Wife: Old woman, I haven't seen you around the square for sometime! What happened?

Old Woman: Oh, child, look at my skin. Those who see me say that my skin has become more yellow than an egg yolk.

Wife: But what happened?

Old Woman: I'm dying, child, of an illness that's sapping my life. Look at me: blind, lame, and now, this!

Wife: Oh, Grandma, I don't know what to say!

Old Woman: Child, you don't have to say anything. Really, if I could only write all about my misfortunes, I would come up with a book longer than Moses'!

Wife: Well, you should thank the Lord for having made you blind. At least you're spared seeing the ugly things around here. What the hell! If only the waters from the Sea of Galilee dried up, we would fill it up again with our tears!

Daniel: Hey guys, what's wrong with you? Hurry up and don't waste time! Come with me to my vineyard, for there's much work to be done! Let's go!

A group of men stood up and went with Daniel to his vineyard. At three o'clock in the afternoon, as the sun's rays penetrated through the walls of the square, several men remained squatting on the steps, still waiting for a chance to be hired for a job.

Samuel: I was told that Daniel is hiring half of Capernaum to work in his vineyard. I hope he'll come around again.

Another Laborer: His grapes are ready for harvest. If he doesn't get them picked fast, the rains will destroy them.

Samuel: That's nice! First you harvest them, then you bring them to the grape press, and then you have them fermented in the vats. And what for?

Laborer: What do you mean, what for? So we can have a good shot of wine to wet our throats, damn it! Isn't that enough?

Samuel: Just enough to wash our blues away. But after that, when the wine has come down from our heads, life goes on the same. Bah!

Laborer: And what do you want?

Samuel: What do I want?

Laborer: Yeah, you, what do you want?

Samuel: I just want to be happy, that's all.

Daniel came back again looking for more workers for his vineyard. There were men still waiting, as always, with crossed arms, and heads looking down at the ground.

Daniel: Hey, what're you doing here yawning and idling time away? I need men to work in my vineyard! Anyone coming with me? There's still a couple of hours to work! Let's go, let's go!

At five o'clock in the afternoon, Daniel went back to the square.

Daniel: Good Lord, there are still some of you looking at the clouds!

Man: There's no one to hire us. So, here we are, waiting for our luck to change.

Daniel: No luck will ever befall you here. Why don't you come with me to my vineyard? After all, the sun hasn't set yet!

When the moon's silhouette shone over Daniel's vineyard, and darkness was beginning to envelop the place . . .

Daniel: Guys, it's time for you to stop working. You may now collect your dues. Come, come, so that I can pay you.

Daniel called for his foreman.

Daniel: Cyrus, pay each one a denarius. See you another time, fellows!

One-Eyed Man: Just a minute, Daniel. How much did you say you were going to pay us?

Daniel: One denarius for each one. Anything wrong?

Nato: It's just that these four men just came an hour ago, while there are some of us here who have been working the whole day under the heat of the sun and . . .

Daniel: And so? Didn't I hire all of you for one denarius a day?

One-Eyed Man: Yeah, but it's unfair to pay us the same amount that you'll pay those who came last.

Daniel: Oh, really? And why is that?

Nato: Well, because . . .

Daniel: You've got children, haven't you? And you need money to feed them. That's why I'm paying you your denarius. This fellow who came last has got children too, and he needs a denarius to feed them. Where's the injustice there? Each one did what he could.

One-Eyed Man: But we worked longer on your farm!

Daniel: Or better, they waited longer than you did in the square. You can't complain, my friend. Tomorrow, when you're the last one to come, you'll be happy to receive one whole denarius. Everybody needs a denarius in order to live.

Jesus had come back from his work laying bricks and sat talking with some of the women and men of Capernaum, discussing what had happened at Daniel's vineyard.

Salome: My friend and neighbor, Leah, told me that today her husband and some men have been working in Daniel's vineyard. You know something, Jesus? Some were hired early in the morning.

Jesus: Yeah, I was there when Daniel came.

John: Hey, the dark one woke up early, isn't that a miracle?

Salome: Then, at nine o'clock he went back and took more men along. He did the same at twelve o'clock and at three o'clock. They say he was still looking for men as late as five o'clock, to work in his vineyard. But this rascal gave everyone one denarius each. Everybody received the same amount, do you understand? Whether he came early or worked for only an hour . . .

John: He's always like that. He says that everybody needs something in order to have something to eat. And everyone gets paid the same amount.

Salome: This Daniel is a crazy landlord!

Jesus: Why do you say that, Salome? On the contrary, he's the best landlord here in Capernaum. Do you know what I think? When God hires workers in this world, he does the same as Daniel.

John: I don't get you.

Jesus: Just as Daniel said: we need a denarius in order to live. A denarius of bread. And a denarius of hope, too. All of us are seated in the square, hoping to be happy.

Salome: Of course, that's what all of us want, but...

Jesus: But we become green with envy when some get up from here ahead of us, even if sooner or later, our turn will also come. Similarly, God will do as Daniel has done: he'll see to it that we are rightfully paid our salary. Everyone receives equal share, which is the best form of justice. Yeah, I'm certain that at the end, when the square is finally empty, we shall get the same denarius, enjoy the same happiness that we have long been waiting for.

The lights in the fishermen's village were slowly fading away, leaving the streets and the whole square empty and dark. Capernaum, tired and weary, went into a deep sleep, in anticipation of the light of a new day.

•

The parable of the workers in the vineyard has been generally interpreted as being about the stages in one's vocation (during youth, adulthood, and old age). However, it can be justifiably called the parable of the good master.

In this episode, the parable offers not only a moral lesson but facts about life. Jesus drew this story from the life of the poor, at a time when the specter of unemployment kept haunting them. In any town, the square is a place where people get together. The story took place in Capernaum and is about people looking for work. In those times, there was an abundance of casual workers who were hired by the hour, for a few days, at harvest time. This was more common in small towns, on the farms, than in Jerusalem. The workers did not have any security; they did not enjoy any rights like the laborers do at present, nor was there any labor union nor any specialized labor. Because of this, life for the poor was totally precarious. The Roman domination further aggravated the situation. In Galilean lands the imposition of taxes led to a situation that favored the concentration of

arable lands in the hands of a few. The forced selling of lands by small proprietors suddenly converted them into wage earners. A great number of
disorganized laborers seeking work wherever possible constituted cheap
labor. Not being hired to work for several days would constitute absolute
misery for a worker and his family. This situation is experienced by various
families in many countries today. And in this harsh condition of the poor
who live "day by day," Jesus becomes their companion.

Jesus, as a poor worker, shared this situation. It is important to point out
that he did manual work, that he was a laborer, not an office worker, educated, estranged from the daily reality of earning one's daily bread by the
sweat of one's brow. His callused hands could handle rough tools better
than learned documents. His origins also taught him to do whatever odd
job was given him. When the gospel tells us what his occupation was, we
must not refer to him solely as a carpenter. Mark (6:3) employs the Greek
word *tekton,* which originally meant "builder" and "artisan." It was used
in reference to the carpenter as well as to the ironsmith and the mason
(bricklayer). A man from a poor neighborhood, like Jesus, was by necessity a jack-of-all-trades. He had to learn masonry. On various occasions, he
spoke in detail about putting up a house, comparing it with building the
Kingdom of God (Matt. 7:24–27; Luke 14:28–30).

The grapevine is one of the most typical plants in Palestine and in all
the neighboring countries. Grape harvest begins toward the middle of September and may last up until mid-October. At any rate, it must be finished
before the autumn rains set in, because the cold nights may destroy the
fruit. Daniel had a good harvest and wanted to gather the fruit before it
was damaged.

A laborer in Jesus' time ordinarily received one denarius for a day's
work. In some cases, food was included in the day's wage. In small towns,
it was often paid in kind. The denarius was the official currency in Israel
during the Roman rule. It was a piece of silver, and on it was engraved the
face of the emperor who ruled the provinces from Rome. It was equivalent
to the drachma, also a piece of silver, which was officially used during the
time of the Greek domination, about two hundred years before the birth
of Jesus.

Daniel was a good master. Although some had to sweat it out for twelve
hours while others worked for less hours, he knew that everybody had a
family to care for. That is why he pays them the same wage. He does not
pay more than what is usual, yet he does not allow that anyone should

be wanting in necessities for the day. It does not matter if the last laborer was slack in the work or did not start early enough. Everyone must eat and feed their children. If he got paid only for an hour of work, then it would not be sufficient for his family's needs. Daniel was not arbitrary, unfair, or capricious. He was a good man. His heart understood the plight of a jobless laborer, disgusted over life's uncertainties. Such is Daniel, the good master. And such is God: this story outlines God's profile.

Beyond the strict justification of the single wage given to all, Jesus likewise expounds the theme of happiness in this episode. Deep inside us, behind all our actions as human beings, we are constantly pursuing one and the same goal: happiness. All the jobless men in the square and the neighbors of Capernaum were constantly in one way or another seeking their happiness. Well then, this happiness, as Jesus said, will come to all, and God will not fail in the promise of being the good master. The history of humanity, with all its injustice and sorrows, shall be saved by the love of a liberating God. The intimate history of every human being, replete with tears and difficulties, shall likewise be rescued. For God's plan is for us to be happy today and always. This is the certainty of our faith (Rom. 8:31–37).

Many people react indignantly and bitterly to this parable. Theirs is a commercialized mentality: equal pay for equal work; equal reward for equal effort. What comes out of this is unjust. God, however, is not a banker; neither is he an efficient capitalist. God has a heart. Gestures of generosity are bothersome to the wretched mind. Thus, this story will always scandalize the people who only think of merits that will "guarantee" heaven for themselves.

The first Christian community reiterated the gesture of the good master: each was given in accordance with his or her own needs, not with what was produced (Acts 2:44–45). True justice is more qualitative than quantitative; it seeks unity and not uniformity. It aims to develop each one as he or she is, in every way, so that each may live.

(Matt. 20:1–16)

62

The Yeast of the Pharisees

Eleazir: Well, I'm here. I have long wanted to talk to you.

Josaphat: Make yourself comfortable, Mr. Eleazir. This cushion has been waiting for you, ha, ha, ha!

Eleazir: And where is Abiel, the teacher? Hasn't he come yet?

Josaphat: He must be on his way now. You know him, when he prays, he forgets everything. Ha, ha, ha!

A few moments later, the scribe Abiel arrived at the house of his friend Josaphat, the Pharisee. There they met that morning with Eleazir, the powerful landlord of Capernaum. They wanted to talk about something that had been worrying them for quite some time.

Eleazir: We can't tolerate this. Ever since this man came to Capernaum, everything has become a mess. There's no respect for the law, for religion; there's no respect for anything. And it's all his fault. That mob he goes with is capable of anything. With this man around, stirring the people with his ideas, we're all in danger. Listen to me: that includes you too.

Abiel: Are you therefore proposing, Eleazir, that . . .

Eleazir: Yes, and with full force. Let there be formal charges against him before the Roman authorities. After all, aren't they here to maintain order and put troublemakers in jail? No one can beat him! What happened in the synagogue the other day topped it all.

Josaphat: Well, you saw it, Eleazir; the Romans came but they didn't do anything.

Abiel: Bah, the Romans don't take us seriously. They despise us. They let us do our own thing, as long as we don't bother them.

Josaphat: Besides, if we accuse him, they'll bring the case to King Herod. Herod's a superstitious man, and will wait at least a year before he orders him beheaded, like he did with John the Baptist. I think we'd all like to finish this case soon.

Eleazir: Well, why don't we pressure him to face the Romans directly?

Abiel: He won't do it. Let me tell you this, Eleazir: he is as wise as a serpent.

Eleazir: So?

Abiel: I've got another idea. Let's leave Herod and the Romans in peace. Maybe we don't need them.

Eleazir: What do you mean, master Abiel?

Abiel: Every human has a price. Jesus of Nazareth ought to have it too, don't you think so?

Eleazir: What do you intend to do?

Abiel: We'll throw him a good bait, and the fish will bite it. I'm sure he will.

A day after that discussion, the word was out about the meeting between the three powerful men. Word spread to the fishermen's district.

Peter: James, listen to me: Salome went to the wharf a while ago. According to her, Josaphat the Pharisee was looking for Jesus in your house this morning.

James: What did that sly old fox want?

Peter: To speak with Jesus about something important. Salome went to look for Jesus and found him at some big house nailing a door in place.

James: Hey, that gives me the creeps. There's always a rotten carcass where the vultures gather.

Jesus arrived in Josaphat's house before noon.

Jesus: Well, here I am, ready to listen to you.

Abiel: Nice of you to have come, Jesus. It'll be better that we go directly to the point.

Josaphat: It's about your future, Jesus. A man like you matters a lot. You can ease people's burdens with just a few well-chosen words. You're a man who can go very far.

Abiel: We know that your father died a few years ago, that you are an only son, and that your mother lives alone in Nazareth.

Jesus: I see you know a lot about me.

Abiel: What will become of your mother if you insist on the road you're taking? Whom will she turn to if anything happens to you?

Jesus: I thought we were going to talk about things clearly. What's my mother got to do with all this?

Josaphat: We want to help you, Jesus, and your mother too. Since you came to the city, you have never had a regular job. Maybe a few odd jobs here and there, then you always pass away your time in the taverns. This is really sad for a man like you.

Abiel: We could help you obtain something better. A sure job. You wouldn't have to wait in the square every morning waiting for nothing. We'll give you work. Not much work, ha, ha, but something easy and interesting. We've got connections, you know that.

Jesus: And what's the price for this favor? I guess you wouldn't do that for free.

Abiel: Look, Nazarene, let's get to the point. You have created a lot of trouble in Capernaum. Everyone knows this, even the Romans. It wouldn't be difficult to make them see that you're a menace to Rome. You know what happens next. They will cut off your tongue. But there's still time.

Josaphat: If you keep your mouth shut, we'll leave you in peace. And to prove to you that we know how to appreciate your worth, we'll in turn give you a good post, and you could earn plenty of money.

Abiel: Yes, of course we know that money is not everything, but in this job people would be at your beck and call. I'm sure that will encourage you. You are an ambitious man, and you don't settle for less. Look, Herod wants to revamp the administration in Galilee. He needs intelligent and capable people like you.

Josaphat: Think about it, Jesus. It would be good for you to accept it.

Jesus: And if I refuse . . .

Josaphat: Well, in that case your life might be in danger. And not only yours, but also those of your fishermen friends, poor fellows. They're still young and can defend themselves well, but your mother can't, and people could make things difficult for her.

Abiel: Try to understand, Jesus. Set aside all these idle dreams in your head. They're like clouds that appear at one moment and disappear in another. Put your two feet on the ground, young man, and stop looking at the clouds.

Jesus: No, I can't. I've been doing it since I was a little boy. We farmers can hardly read from books, and that's why we learned how to read what the clouds and the sky have to say.

Abiel: Talk to us clearly this time, Jesus.

Jesus: That's very clear. Like me, you also know how to read the clouds. If the sky becomes red like blood in the afternoon, that means we'll have fair weather, isn't that so? And if the clouds hide themselves and the south wind begins to blow, what would you say's gonna happen?

Josaphat: Ha, ha! That's a sign of warm weather.

Jesus: And you, Master Abiel, what happens if the clouds gather along the west?

Abiel: There's gonna be a storm.

Josaphat: Enough! Where are you leading us, anyway?

Jesus: Hypocrites! How come you know the signs from above, yet do not see those from below? Yes, there's going to be a storm from below! Hypocrites! Aren't you aware of what's happening around you? The people are awake, but you continue to sleep. You call one crazy and a dreamer if you can't buy him with your money. Hypocrites! The prophet John did not eat nor drink, and you accused him of being possessed by a demon. On the other hand, when I go to the tavern, you say I'm a drunkard and a glutton. You are like stupid children doing things at the wrong time: you don't dance at a wedding, neither do you cry at a wake. To think that you are the wise men and the priests of Israel! Hypocrites!

Abiel: Just a minute, Nazarene, listen . . .

But Jesus turned his back and began to leave the house.

Abiel: Imbecile! You'll regret this some day.

Jesus headed back toward the wharves and Peter's house, meeting some of his friends along the way.

Peter: What happened, Jesus? What did they want from you?

Jesus: The usual thing, Peter. They've been after us since that incident in the synagogue.

James: You've got to be careful, Jesus. These people are dangerous.

Jesus: They say we're the dangerous ones, and not they.

James: Oh yeah? So, they're afraid of us! Hell, I like that!

Philip: Well I don't. They also feared the prophet John, and see what happened to him.

Jesus: John had to end up that way. What was he? He wasn't a bit of bamboo jostled by the wind. No, he didn't bow before anyone.

Peter: Not even before King Herod himself, so to speak.

Jesus: That's why they cut him in two, like an upright tree. That was the only way to finish him off. He was also offered the good life of influence and money, but John never gave in to anything.

Peter: Okay, so what happened, Jesus? Why did they call you? To talk about the prophet John? Are they still afraid of a dead man?

Jesus: No, Peter, now we're the ones worrying them. They fear that people may open their eyes and realize that the religion that's taught them is nothing but a roll of human laws and precepts invented by the powerful. That's why they want to keep our mouth shut, by force or cunning, whichever works best.

Philip: What'll they do?

Jesus: They'll have to use force, Philip. They're violent men. All the privileges they're enjoying were obtained that way, at the expense of others. Now, they want to buy the Kingdom of God through the use of force.

James: Did they offer you money, Jesus?

Jesus: Yeah, and a good job. Anything, just anything if we shut up. You know what I'm thinking? From now on, we should keep an eye on the yeast of the Pharisees. A little of the old yeast is enough to spoil the whole dough. These people are rotten and can ruin everything.

James: They'll think of every scheme to use against us.

Jesus: Today they wanted to trap me. Tomorrow it could be Nathanael or Thomas or Judas or anyone of us.

Philip: Well, the way I see it, this matter of the Kingdom of God is becoming complicated.

Peter: People must be warned. These people have spies all over. With a couple of denarii, they pay a squealer and can ruin everything.

James: Damned owls! That's what they are, lurking in the dark!

Jesus: Our job will be done in broad daylight. We'll announce all our plans, and everything they do behind closed doors shall be revealed right from the steps of our houses. If they think we're intimidated, they're wrong. We'll never give up.

The powerful came together again to discuss whether their plan had worked and what alternatives they would have if it hadn't.

Eleazir: So, Master Josaphat, do you think you were able to scare him?

Josaphat: Scare him? That fellow is too proud to be scared! He's crazy. He thinks he's a prophet!

Abiel: The only thing he knows is to eat, get drunk, and hang around with his gang of rogues.

Eleazir: So what do we do now, Josaphat?

Josaphat: Bide time, Eleazir. The fish is caught by its mouth, as the lake people say. Well, this fish will also perish through his mouth. He's so imprudent and arrogant. If he doesn't shut up, then it'll be the worse for him. You'll see, friend, everything will just be a matter of time. Let's leave him alone. He's putting up his own cross, ha, ha, ha.

Eleazir, the rich landlord, and Josaphat, the Pharisee, a teacher and faithful follower of the law of Moses, continued talking. Meanwhile, the clouds, whirling about the west, promised a strong storm coming.

•

The social groups wielding economic, political, and religious powers in society were gradually banding themselves together against Jesus. In this episode, the first of these alliances has taken shape. On the one hand is Eleazir, the landlord. In Galilee, after Roman domination took hold, the agrarian structure became highly centralized in the hands of a few. These landowners were naturally opposed to any popular movement with social justice as its goal. Together with Eleazir are two Pharisees, teachers of the law. Although it was not always the case that the Pharisees came from the ruling class, a number of them belonged to the latter. They had religious powers: they "saved" and "condemned" according to their interpretation of the law. For this group, Jesus — who was associated with the "damned" and had no respect for the law — was extremely dangerous. He questioned everything about the mechanism of religion. These two powerful groups finally tried to involve the political and military elements of Rome, in order to picture Jesus as dangerous, because he awakened in the poor the hope of liberation. Bribery is one of the innumerable tactics of the powerful to counteract any resistance from the people. In general, before getting rid of a leader, first there is an effort to "buy him." Blackmail, a good job, money, or even threats are methods used to weaken commitment to a cause that demands sacrifices. Jesus, at this point in his life, was already very popular among his countrymen. He was a leader and, as such, must have been exposed to pressures of this type.

Jesus talked to his enemies of "the signs of the times," which they failed to read. Not so long ago, the great prophet, Pope John XXIII, frequently referred to what he called "signs of the times." He said we should be aware of what was going on around us in history in order to see the future and work for a better one for all. Just as Jesus awakened the people of Israel from their passivity, giving them hope through a community that shared and worked for the attainment of justice, in our times this kind of awakening is a sign of the times as well. Christian base communities are one element of this. From such a grounding, people's organizations multiply, mature, and grow. These are signs of the times. They shall determine the future.

For "decent" people of his period, Jesus was a notorious man, and his life was a real scandal for them. The gospel retained what was said of him: "one who ate a lot, a drunkard, and a friend of the prostitutes." On another occasion, he was called "a Samaritan" (John 8:48), which was a strong insult, equivalent to "bastard," a "son of a prostitute." The entire gospel gives testimony to the fact that Jesus was not antisocial, nor a shy man. His life had little to do with those of the monks and ascetics who inflicted self-punishment in order to free their spirits. Neither did he resemble the solemn and sober prophet John the Baptist. Jesus was a man from the town. His natural environment was the square, the street, and the barrio. His daily life was sanctified by people's joy, full of simplicity and without complication, the very way by which to reach out to God.

(Matt. 11:7–19; 16:1–12; Mark 8:11–21; Luke 7:24–35, 54–56)

63

A Millstone

In those days, King Herod, the tetrarch of Galilee, increased the taxes on wheat, wine, and oil in order to maintain his style of life in court and please the officials of the army. The people's protests were to no avail. The prison cells of Tiberias, where the king had his best palace, were bursting with nonconformist young men and rebellious Zealots.

Herod: Where have you put those men conspiring against me?

Jailer: Here they are, King Herod. Not one has escaped the vigilant eyes of your guards.

Herod: And neither will anyone get away from the ax of my executioner.

Jailer: This young man is the son of Abiathar, the Pharisee.

Herod: So?

Jailer: Abiathar is at the palace door with two talents of silver as ransom for his son. He's pleading clemency for his son.

Herod: Clemency? Did you say clemency? Ha, ha, ha! What's the charge against the boy?

Jailer: He and a group stole some weapons from the Arsenal of Saphir.

Herod: Really? He has hardly grown his beard and he's already stealing swords! That's conspiracy against his king! Ha! Cut his right hand off with that same sword. That will teach him a lesson.

Young Man: No, no, have pity on me, my king, have pity on me!

Herod: Take him and inform the executioner. And this stupid-looking guy here, what's his offense?

Another Young Man: I didn't do anything, my king. This is an injustice!

Jailer: Shut up! Is that the way to talk to your king?

Herod: What crime was committed by this imbecile?

Jailer: This guy gave us a hard time. He runs like a hare. Twice he escaped right under the noses of the guards.

Herod: Well, he won't escape the third time. Have his right foot cut off!

Young Man: No, no, no!

Jailer: This one's a spy, your majesty. They caught him last week going over the records of our sales and purchases. He belongs to the Zealot movement.

Herod: So you're a spy, huh? Gouge his eyes out with a nail and throw them to my dogs, and let them feast on their favorite food.

King Herod Antipas was ruthless, just like his father. It was better to die than be brought to the dungeons of his palace, where dozens of men and women rotted in dark prison cells. There was a rat-infested room, firmly shut, a dark and stinking dungeon where living cadavers and lice coexisted and rebels were thrown to die. There was a torture chamber guarded by four hangmen who were tasked to carry out the orders of the king.

Young Man: No, no, no, no, don't do this to me! You're a man like me! You can't do this to me!

They grabbed the boy, son of Abiathar, and pulled his right arm over a wooden wedge, where the blood of the previous victims flowed.

Young Man: For God's sake! For God's sake! Don't cut off my hand! No, no! I don't want this. Noooo!

Jailer: Damn it, cover his mouth and hold him tight!

Young Man: No, no, ohhh!

After a series of interrogations and torture, some prisoners went back to their homes, ruthlessly mutilated in those prison cells of Tiberias.

Mother: Oh my son, my son! What have they done to you? My son!

Abiathar: Beasts, beasts!

Abiathar's son tried to hide his right arm, which ended in a stump.

Adviser: Has your majesty been informed about the new prophet in Galilee? Prophets here grow like mushrooms.

Herod: Prophet? To whom are you referring, you crook?

Adviser: That man named Jesus, a tall, brown, and bearded fellow. A peasant from Nazareth, to be exact.

Herod: Why do you tell me this?

Adviser: Because the king must know what's happening in his kingdom. This Nazarene is everywhere. He's astute and organized. They say he wants to change everything, even religion. He's been going from town to town along the lake, with his group, two by two.

Herod: Tell me, what do they do?

Adviser: What everyone else is doing, conspiring against your excellency, telling the people to rise up against the king, not to pay taxes, and ...

Herod: Then why did you tell me he was a prophet? He's more of an agitator, like the rest.

Adviser: Yes and no. It seems this Jesus is a good magician. He makes miracles! His words seem like honey. People follow him and stick to him like flies. Some even say he could be the Messiah.

Herod: Ha! The Messiah! A good for nothing peasant becoming the Messiah! My prisons are already full of messiahs, and they still want more!

Adviser: They also say this Nazarene speaks with fire, just like the prophet Elijah.

Herod: That fire can be extinguished by filling his mouth with sand, until his belly explodes.

Adviser: He's said to be like King David who dances, laughs, and frequents taverns.

Herod: Let's see if he can still laugh when he's in shackles.

Adviser: They also say, well, they say a lot of things.

Herod: Are you insinuating something? Speak out clear, man. What else do they say of him?

Adviser: Just plain people's gossip, my king.

Herod: What else do they say about this fellow? Damn it!

Adviser: That he's John the Baptist, who has come back from the dead.

Herod: What a big lie! John is dead. I myself had him beheaded!

Adviser: They say John's spirit left his body through his neck when his head was cut off. Then he went back to Machaerus seven times looking for the door. And when he found it, he fled in haste and ...

Herod: And what? Finish it, man!

Adviser: And his spirit slipped into the Nazarene's body. This is true, your majesty, because this Nazarene speaks exactly like Zechariah's son.

Herod: You're a big liar! Why do you deceive me? Have you heard him speak?

Adviser: Personally no, my king, but they say ...

Herod: I'll have you beaten for being a liar!

Adviser: Take it easy, your majesty. You were the one who obliged me to inform you.

Herod: I want this man right away!

Adviser: Yes, my king.

Herod: I want to see his face, and I'll know what kind of a man this Jesus is. I've got acute senses, you know. If he's a fake, then I'll have his tongue pulled out. And if he's a prophet, I'll have him beheaded.

Adviser: What if he's the same John who resurr...

Herod: Shut up, rumor-monger! Shut up! You just want to scare me! And damn you, John the Baptist! Even in death you don't leave me in peace!

That same day, two men came to the house, asking for Jesus. They came from Tiberias.

Pharisee: Are you Jesus of Nazareth?

Jesus: Yes I am. But why do you speak in such a low voice? There's no one sick in this house.

Second Pharisee: There may not be right now, but perhaps there'll be a dead man soon. King Herod has been looking for you, Nazarene.

Jesus: Really? How come you know that?

Pharisee: We're from Tiberias. We're friends of the king's adviser.

Jesus: And what does this fox want with me?

Pharisee: He thinks you're the resurrected John the Baptist and you want to avenge John. Herod is a very superstitious man.

Second Pharisee: Just a piece of advice, young man. Go away from here. Hide in any village in the mountains, and don't tell anyone, not even your friends, where you are.

Jesus: There's something I don't understand here. You're friends of a palace adviser, yet you're helping me flee from the king. Why? Aren't you well paid by Herod?

Second Pharisee: No, no, it's not money, Nazarene. Last week, they cut off the right hand of a nephew of mine, the son of Abiathar the Pharisee. Tears rolled down my eyes when I saw that worm-infested wound of his, and I promised myself to help any Israelite escape from the claws of this assassin, whatever his ideas might be.

Jesus: I understand. What about you, why don't you say anything? Did you see the mutilated boy?

Pharisee: He's my son. I'm Abiathar, the Pharisee.

Jesus, enraged, clenched his fists and became teary-eyed.

Jesus: Criminal!

Pharisee: Get away from here, young man, if you don't want the same thing to happen to you, or it might even be worse.

Jesus: No, I'm not going away.

Second Pharisee: Believe us, young man. Your life is in danger. Don't you understand?

Jesus: Yes, I do, and I thank you for having informed me. But I'm not leaving. When you go back to Tiberias and see that fox in his den of gold and marble, tell him this on my behalf: that he can't stop me from doing what I'm doing now, tomorrow, and the day after tomorrow; that I'm not scared of him nor of his threats, because until now no prophet has ever died in Galilee. They only die in Jerusalem.

Pharisee: Don't be crazy, Nazarene, and listen to us.

At that moment, my brother James and I came back from the wharf. Even our neighbors peeped through the house to take a glimpse at our visitors.

John: Is there anything wrong, Jesus? What's the problem?

Jesus: Nothing. Herod is not satisfied with the blood that has been shed. He wants more. He wants to drink of the blood of all the children of Israel.

John: Scoundrel, that's what he is! Look what he's done with the taxes: he wants to drain all our pockets of the little money we have, for his mistresses' jewelry.

A Woman:: The king is an adulterer. He lives with his sister-in-law, his brother Philip's wife. What a vicious man.

Jesus: That would be the least, neighbor. He can do anything he pleases with his life, but not with his neighbor's. That man is a stumbling block. There'll be no peace here while he's on the throne, robbing the people and torturing our children.

As usual, the neighborhood folks started milling in the street in order to listen to Jesus.

John: Jesus, let's go inside first.

Jesus: No, John. The people must know what's happening in our country. They had the right hand of this man's son cut off, do you understand? If it were your own hand, would you just keep quiet?

John: Okay, okay, but there are lots of squealers around. You can never tell.

Jesus: Hey, all of you, listen to me! If anyone here is a friend of this fox, disguised as the king, tell this to him on my part: he who lives by the sword shall perish by the sword. You cut off the right hand of Abiathar's son, and God will throw you into the fire with your two hands. You cut off a foot of Manasses's son, and the Lord will throw you into the fire with your two feet. You gouged somebody else's eyes with a nail, pulled out fingernails with a pair of pliers, castrated men and raped women in jail, and mutilated the sons of Israel. God will throw you and your whole body into hell, where the worms will feast on it. You had the prophet John beheaded. God will have a large millstone tied around your neck and have you thrown into the depths of the sea. You and the rest of the criminals do not deserve to breathe the air nor step on this ground. Tell Herod all this on my behalf.

Jesus turned and went inside the house. He was enraged. He sat on the floor, buried his face in his hands, and remained quiet for a long time.

•

About twenty years before Jesus was born, King Herod established the city of Tiberias, on the west bank of the Sea of Galilee. It was named in honor of Tiberius, the Roman emperor. Herod made it the capital of Galilee, instead of Sepphoris. Tiberias was the regular residing place of Herod Antipas, where he had his palace built. For many reasons it was a hated city, not only because of the king's presence but because it was built on a cemetery — and, therefore, for the Pharisees, was "impure" — and was dedicated to the emperor of Rome. For this reason, the nationalists found it a despicable place. Today, Tiberias is one of the most populated and modern cities of Galilee, with several hotels, good restaurants, and sports centers to boast of.

In the basement of the palace — as was common during the period — were the dungeons that served as a prison for Herod's foes. Although in Israel torture did not exist as a form of punishment for prisoners, Herod the Great employed excessive torture during his reign, in violation of the Jewish law. His son, Herod, the contemporary of Jesus, brutal as he was, followed in the footsteps of his father. His greed for power and the diminishing popularity of his reign, dependent on Rome, as well as the people's discontent, made him a ruler capable of committing any crime in order to save his throne.

Torture has existed throughout history. Human beings, degrading their condition, make others suffer in order to dominate, to subjugate, and to obtain information. Torture is almost always linked to the unjust exercise of power. We must confess that even the official church has engaged in torture. Only five hundred years ago, heretics were burned, nonconformists and nonbelievers were horribly tortured, and all types of pressure was employed over the "enemies" of the church. The theme of torture is "basic" to a Christian reflection. Its eradication, its rejection by any means, is a Christian task, a matter of urgency and priority.

This text in the gospel that deals with the "scandal of the small people" has been often used to illustrate the theme of corruption of minors, child pornography, and the like. In biblical language the phrase "the small people" does not refer only to children. The small people are the poor, the disabled, the oppressed, the powerless who are crushed by people in power. For these little people, humans like the blood-thirsty king are a scandal (the word originally meant "stumbling block"). That is to say, people like Herod are deterrents to poor people's growth, development and life. That is why Jesus says Herod will be hurled into the sea with a millstone tied around his neck. In Jesus' day, wheat flour and flour from other cereals were obtained by running the grain through a mill. The mill was an instrument composed of two pieces of stone, one turning over the other. Mills were basic in a home. They evolved into different shapes through the centuries. In Jesus' time, the so-called ass-mills were utilized. The stones were so huge, only an ass (or a donkey) could turn the stone that was on top of one fixed on the ground. This was the kind of mill used by various families. Several of these very heavy stones were found among the archaeological ruins of Capernaum. Seeing the size of this piece, one can imagine the tremendous impact of the phrase used by Jesus, one that is "exaggerated," according to the typical, Middle Eastern manner of speaking, reflecting Jesus' grave criticism of the exploiter of the poor.

(Matt. 14:1–2; 18:6–9; Mark 6:14–16; 9:42–48;
Luke 9:7–9; 13:31–33; 17:1–3)

64

Trees That Move Around

Bethsaida Square was lined with almond trees. Every morning Barnabas would sit under the shade of one, the shadiest of all. He was a poor old man who always wore a black thick mantle, stained and tattered, on his shoulders.

Barnabas: I think there's ice trapped in my body, woman. I'm always cold. Were it not for this blanket you have sewn for me...
A Man: Hey, crazy old man, are you talking to someone?
Barnabas: Oh, I don't know. The truth is, I don't know what to do. If it was just me, I'd go away to a far place. But what would these trees do if I left? Poor creatures, they'd have no company. I believe, though, that I must go. Yes, I'll have to do it.

Barnabas had been talking to himself for many years. For many years too, his eyes could not see the light of day. He became blind when a few pieces of ember landed in his eyes while his wife was cooking food on the kitchen stove. A year later, his wife passed away without having left him a child. Barnabas remained alone, with the memory of his dead wife, and living on alms as he sat beside the trees in the square.

Barnabas: Just a few alms, please, and God will reward you with good health! For the love of God, give me some alms!
A Boy: Here comes, Barnabas, the blind! Come, let's give him some "alms," ha, ha, ha!
Another Boy: Don't laugh too much, you fool, he might find out! C'mon, let's go...
Barnabas: The trouble is, I can't go that far, woman. There are many stones in the road, and my cane is not of much help. If you were here with me, then it'd be different....
Boy: See how he talks to himself? He's crazy! Look at his face!
Barnabas: Just a few alms, for heaven's sake!

Boy: Here, old man, take it — these are my little savings; this will tide you over the whole week.

The boys, changing their voices, put a small sack of cloth in Barnabas's hands. It was quite heavy.

Barnabas: But, lady, why do you have to give me so many alms?
Boy: It's all right, old man. We've got our eyes and you don't. All this is for you, so you need not come here everyday to beg. You've suffered enough.
Barnabas: Thank you, lady, thank you. I told you, dear wife, there are still good people in this world.
Boy: Goodbye, old man, and God bless you!

The boys, who were controlling their laughter, left the almond tree where Barnabas was, as he joyfully opened the small bag given to him.

Barnabas: But but, what's this? Oh, what wicked creatures!

From the bag full of small and fine pebbles from the river came a handful of cockroaches that started to run up his arms inside the folds of his mantle. The blind man slapped them away, while the boys doubled up with laughter, seeing him leaping and hurling invectives.

A Boy: Ha, ha, ha! Old Barnabas has got eyes but can't see! Old Barnabas has got eyes but can't see!
A Woman: Has anything happened to that crazy old man?
Boy: No, nothing, except that he's teaching the cockroaches how to dance!
Woman: Well that beats everything! What else is left for him to do? Well at least he gives us reason to laugh. Otherwise, of what use is this poor fellow?

Almost everyday something similar happened in the shady square of Bethsaida. Blind Barnabas was the laughing stock of the town. Everyone made fun of him.

A Boy: Hey, old man, guess who it is this time! Puah!
Another Boy: It's your turn now. Now! Puah!
Boy: Guess who it was, guess, Barnabas!
Barnabas: Wicked creatures! Rascals!

That morning, when we arrived in Bethsaida Square, a group of boys had the blind man tied around an almond tree with a rope. They took turns spitting at him, trying to hit him in the eyes with their saliva and asking him to guess who had done it. Some people gathered around and joined them.

Jesus: What's going on here?
Woman: I don't know, stranger. This blind old man's gone a little crazy.
John: But why are they spitting at him?
Woman: Leave him alone, damn it! Poor man! Well, it's a children's game, you know. They must amuse themselves with something, no?
Jesus: Of course, and the grown-ups are enjoying it too, aren't they?
Man: Look, stranger, you meddler, what've you got to say, huh? As far as I know, everyone can have fun with anything he pleases. Am I right or wrong?
A Boy: Let me go! Let me go! It's my turn now!
All: Old Barnabas has got eyes but can't see! Old Barnabas has got eyes but can't see!
Jesus: Listen, friend, if you were blind, would you like people to do the same to you?
Man: I'm not blind, so what the hell do I care! If you're not enjoying the game, beat it man!

The game was over when we returned to the square at noontime. But old Barnabas still had his hands tied around the tree. He was panting and talking to himself, his face full of the boys' saliva.

Barnabas: And I'll take a ship, woman, you know, one of those that cross the lake, and I'll go away. There, on the other side of the lake, they say that people are different, that the boys respect you and people give you a hand.
Jesus: We're from the other side of the lake, old man.
Barnabas: Huh? Who who are you?
John: We got here this morning and we saw you in the square.
Barnabas: You demons! What, what will you do this time? Go away! Go away and leave me in peace!
Jesus: We're here to untie you, old man. Don't be afraid. We never liked the game they played on you, old man.
Barnabas: Where are you from?
Jesus: We came from Capernaum.

Barnabas: From the other side of the lake?

John: Right. Have you ever been there?

Barnabas: When I could still see, yes. But that was a long time ago. I can't even remember anymore.

Jesus: C'mon, John, let's untie him.

Barnabas: What will you do to me? Please, have pity on me!

Jesus: Don't be afraid. We won't hurt you. Don't be afraid.

Barnabas: They're all a bunch of rascals! They all laugh at me the whole day and I, I'm helpless.

John: Cheer up, old man, you're free.

Barnabas: Free? Tomorrow and the day after tomorrow, they will tie me up and do the same thing again. It's always the same.

Jesus: Have they done this to you before?

Barnabas: This and more. If they don't spit on me, they beat me, or they hurl cockroaches at me, making me flee, and this hurts me. Well, I've become used to it and I don't care anymore.

Jesus: You don't care anymore? So, why are you weeping?

Barnabas: Because it hurts every time. No, I'm not used to it. I'm always hurt.

Jesus: Come old man. Let's get away from here.

Barnabas: You want me to go?

John: Sure, come with us.

Barnabas: But, are you out of your mind? Where will you bring me?

Jesus: To a place far from here, old man, where no one will harm you.

Barnabas: But, but, I can't simply do that. How can I go and leave the trees alone? See what I told you, woman? I really don't know what to do now. These strangers want me to go with them, and if I do, who'll keep these trees company? Well, if you want me to go with them, woman, then I go, but don't blame me later on.

Jesus: Let's go, old man. Here take my hand. Hold on tight so you don't stumble. Let's go.

So we left the square, passing through a narrow street that was lined with palm trees, and proceeded outside the city. Barnabas was supported by his cane and the brawny and callused hand of Jesus. He was limping a little.

John: What's wrong with your foot, old man?

Barnabas: What else? A few days ago, they burned it with a lighted stick. "Guess who did it to you." If I only knew! Rascals!

Jesus: That's all over. They won't harm you anymore.

Barnabas: Yes, because if they come back, they'll tie me up again, even if I don't do anything to them. So why do they always pick on me and beat me? Tell me.

John: Forget about these people, old man.

Barnabas: You can say that again, young man. Even my wife tells me to ignore them. But I can't, because, because I hate them, you know? Before, when I could still see, I didn't know the meaning of this word, hatred, but now, I do. It's something that you keep inside your heart, and it stays there. Yes, woman, this is an ugly word to utter, but I can't help it, because I feel it! Of course, you haven't experienced what I have!

We continued walking, staying away from the city. The noonday sun scorched the road and made the leaves of the trees glitter. Blind Barnabas could not see the light that was blinding all of us.

Barnabas: You know what, I think people are worse than the beasts. Beasts kill so they will have something to eat, but people cause you harm for the fun of it, and they make fun of you! Do you know what these people do to me? They spit on me, on my face, in my eyes. Do you understand?

Jesus: Hey, old man, wait a minute. Puah!

Barnabas: What are you doing? No, no, don't do that young man. No, no, you don't...

Jesus spat on his hands, wet his fingers with the saliva, and touched the blind man's eyes.

Jesus: Hold it, old man, keep still. You know something? People are bad at times but God is always good.

Barnabas: Hey, hey, what're you rubbing in my eyes?

Jesus: Nothing, don't worry. C'mon, open your eyes.

Jesus removed his fingers from Barnabas's eyes.

Jesus: Can you see anything, old man?

Barnabas: I, I, yes, yes! I see a lot of trees. I can see you and your friends. They look like trees moving around.

Jesus went near the blind man and put his hand on his eyes again. Barnabas was weeping.

Jesus: What's wrong, old man? Why are you crying?

Barnabas: I can see the trees again, young man. There in the town square, the almond trees were my only friends, you know. They have given me shade, and when it was time, their fruits. Now, I'll see them again. The people, no I don't want to see them.

John: But you're seeing us.

Barnabas: You have been my friends like the trees.

Amid his tears, Barnabas started to distinguish the road, the stones, and the flowers. And there, from afar, the silhouettes of the houses of Bethsaida.

Barnabas: I don't wish to go back there.

Jesus: No, don't go back to that town. Better take this road. By afternoon, you will arrive in Chorazin. Stay there. Don't tell anyone what happened. Neither should you do to anyone what you didn't want others to do to you.

Barnabas looked at us with his small and wrinkled yet sparkling eyes. Limping, and with his long cane, he began to walk. As always, he was talking to himself.

Barnabas: You should have seen him, woman. He was a man, but he seemed like a tree. He could give you shade and support. You should have seen him, woman.

Old Barnabas moved away until he was lost in the horizon, illuminated by the huge red sun of Galilee.

•

Bethsaida, meaning "house of fish," was a small city on the northern edge of the Sea of Galilee. Here were born Philip, Peter, and his brother Andrew. Philip the tetrarch called it Julia in honor of the imperial Roman family bearing this family name. No remains of this city can be found at present. It is believed that the floods coming from the River Jordan and leading into the lake buried the ancient fishing village.

Blindness was a common sickness in Israel in Jesus' time. The dry climate and the intense heat of the sun contributed to the disease. In general, blindness was prevalent all over the ancient world; it was often due to poor hygienic conditions and ignorance of disease. It was thought to be incurable and was believed to be a special kind of God's punishment. As a consequence of their ailment, the blind were outcasts.

Sick persons do not always evoke in others a feeling of compassion and mercy. On occasion, they become the object of ridicule and maltreatment. A person who is useless, different, abnormal, sometimes becomes the laughing stock of everyone. It happens in school, where one always finds a weakling, a stout one, an ugly one who is made fun of by others. It often happens in the towns, in the neighborhoods, and at work. When Jesus approaches Barnabas and gives him back his eyesight, it is a sign of Jesus' special closeness to the dejected and the ridiculed. God feels a special affection for them.

Although one may apply various critical norms in reading the miracle stories in the gospels, and one may come to different conclusions about them, there always remains a nucleus which is absolutely historical. Jesus performed miracles that astounded his contemporaries. Basically these were healings of real diseases, though related with special psychological situations. Among these cures were the so-called expulsion of demons, madness, hysteria, epilepsy, and the healing of lepers (within the wide gamut of diseases that this word encompassed), paralytics, and the blind. In modern language today, such healings would fall within that branch of medicine called "the therapy of transcendence."

Do unto others what you would want others to do unto you: this is the so-called golden rule of the gospel (Matt. 6:12). With this, Matthew summarizes the beatitudes pronounced by Jesus on the mount. Certainly, it is a very practical conclusion, since the entire Mosaic law can be capsulized in love — in deed, not in words — that we should have for others.

(Mark 8:22–26)

65

Foreign Dogs

In those days, we went up into the country of Tyre. We crossed the border of Israel in the north, near the Waters of Merom, and went through land full of forests.

Peter: This is my first time to set foot on foreign land!

John: You're not the only one, stone thrower. It's the first time for everyone. How about you, Jesus. Have you ever been beyond the border?

Jesus: No, never. We from inland travel very little.

John: Well, since all of us are traveling outside Israel for the first time, we must all be careful. They say half of the people here are thieves and the other half are usurers. So we've got to be alert!

Jesus: What I've heard, John, is that in business, there's no one who can beat these Canaanites.

Philip: Yeah, that's true. When it comes to those things, I'm in the know. If you want good textiles, get them from here. If you want quality glass, you'll find it here.

Peter: And if you want first-class cheaters, they also come from here.

Philip: What these people sell you with one hand, they also get it back with the other. All our townmates who have been in this place know their tricks.

Jesus: We must be coming close to Tyre. Isn't that what we can see from afar?

Tyre, one of the principal ports of the country of the Canaanites, was a white city built on rocks, by the sea. Here lived Salathiel, an Israelite friend of old Zebedee, who had invited us to come there.

Jesus: Where could the house of Salathiel be?

John: The Israelites' district is here, on the outskirts. We shouldn't be far from it.

Jesus: Let's ask someone.

Peter: Better if we can find it by ourselves.

Jesus: Why, Peter?

Peter: Because I don't trust these foreigners. To each his own. We go our own way and they go their own.

A minute later, the accent of people conversing in the streets told us that we were in the neighborhood of our Israelite countrymen. We asked an old man with a long gray beard for Salathiel's house, and he himself, limping and supported by a thick cedar cane, brought us to his house.

Salathiel: Welcome, countrymen! I was expecting you tomorrow, but old Joachim informed me of your arrival. This is really a nice surprise!

Peter: We left one day earlier. Things are not so good in Galilee.

Salathiel: What? It's Herod again and his usual thing, isn't it? Everyone here knows what's going on there. But, well, please sit down. The wine will be brought any minute now, and that's what matters. Methelia, Methelia! Bring in two jugs of wine, right away! Oh, please pardon our wine. Our wine here is no good. It's dirty water tinged with purple! And well, Jesus, Peter, John, I have long wanted to meet you. The news that you are agitating the whole of Galilee has reached us here. I want you to speak with my countrymen later. Even in this country, a lot of things ought to change, yes sir!

Philip: This place is quite big, isn't it? When we got here and went into the square, we couldn't even get through.

Salathiel: You came on a market day. Those foreigners are the finest hawkers in the world! Today they're all out in the streets, while we stay here at home, he, he, he! Yeah, we're together and not bothered!

Jesus: About how many Israelites live here, Salathiel?

Salathiel: Well, that's not difficult to know. Everyone lives in this area. I think we're about three hundred, excluding the women and children. We manage very well. These foreigners need us. Work is never scarce. The Canaanites may be astute businessmen, but without us, they would do very little! Wherever one of us is, business prospers, and even stones are converted into silver, yes sir!

Salathiel explained to us how life was for our compatriots in that foreign land. He had lived there for many years. He was a sort of patriarch for his countrymen.

Salathiel: It's difficult to live among pagans, young men. These foreign dogs may be very knowledgeable about purple, but that's all they know. They're ignorant of other things. They have a god in every neighborhood. Just imagine. Ah, only when you live far from your country do you realize to thank the Lord for having been born in a town like ours. God did the right thing in choosing our country as his own! Well, damn, the tongue also deserves a rest. Aren't you hungry?

Peter: Yeah, Salathiel. The last time we got a glimpse of bread was when we passed through the border.

Salathiel: Well, in that case, let's all go and eat! In a short while, a group of our countrymen will be here to tell you what they're doing here in Galilee. Hey, Methelia, Methelia!

Methelia: Sir?

Salathiel: Have the food ready. And hurry up, because we're starved!

Methelia: Right away, sir.

Salathiel: Ah, every time I think that one of these Canaanites sleeps under my roof, it makes me sick to my stomach, but at least I'm consoled by the fact that she is under my orders.

Jesus: Has she been with you for a long time, Salathiel?

Salathiel: Her husband abandoned her when they were newly married and left her with a daughter about four or five years old. So I bought her as a maid. That was a good deal, you know. And she was cheap. Ah, a bitch like that is not worth the dust from the sandals of one of our women. Have you noticed how ugly they are? No amount of ornaments can hide it!

Soon, Methelia returned with a big pot of lentils and a tray of eggplant and put them on the table. In her young face the color of olives, like the rest of the Syrophoenician men and women, could be seen wrinkles, telltale signs of her tears and suffering.

Salathiel: Okay, let's pray to God that he may bless the food! "We praise you and bless you, God of Israel, who has placed our country above all nations! Remember, Lord, all of us who live outside the country, in the midst of pagans who know not your love and the foreigners who have no respect for your laws. Grant that we may again partake of the bread in our own land!"

All: Amen, amen.

Salathiel: Come and get it, fellows. Eat all you can and nothing should remain on the table.

When we were almost through eating...

Salathiel: With you gathered at my table, I feel near my beloved Sea of Galilee. But I'm not losing hope, no sir: one day I'll shake the dust off my sandals right in the noses of these pagans and I'll return to my land. "Larara Galilee, my beloved land"...

All: Fine, fine!

Salathiel: Hell, how nostalgic!

Methelia: Sir, you wish nothing?

Philip: How's that?

Methelia: You wish nothing?

Philip: Hey, Salathiel, what the hell is this woman asking me? I don't understand a thing!

Salathiel: What is it, Methelia?

Methelia: You wish nothing, sir?

Salathiel: We want you to go and leave us in peace. Go to the kitchen, where you belong.

Methelia: And the wine, sir, I put here?

Salathiel: Ha, ha, yes, "put it there." Ha, ha. Did you hear? She doesn't even know how to speak! Ha, ha. You'll see. You'll see. Hey, Methelia, tell my friend what you put in the soup for its nice taste.

Methelia: Sir, I put parle...

Salathiel: Parle! Parle! It's been five years and you haven't learned the word "parsley!" Ha, ha, ha! C'mon, why don't you tell them the name of the flowers I asked you to pick from the garden.

Methelia: Sir, they are lilies and dissies.

Salathiel: Ha, ha! Oh, I'll die laughing! I taught the word, but nothing! Ha, ha, ha! Heck. Look, Methelia, do you see that bearded man in front of you? He's a famous doctor, a healer. Ask him to do something for your "daufter." Ha, ha, ha! C'mon, tell him, tell him...

Methelia, the servant from Canaan, looked at Jesus with a ray of hope in her deep, dark eyes.

Salathiel: This poor creature does nothing but weep for her daughter, for her "daufter," as she says. Ha, ha, ha! She cries the whole day. Your daughter was born sick and not even the doctors nor your tears can cure her. Put this into your head and try to understand, Methelia!

Methelia: Are you a doctor, strrangerr?

Salathiel: Ha, ha, ha! Yes, he is a heallerr! It gives me a good laugh when I hear these Canaanites speak!

Methelia: Strrangerr, help my daufter!

Salathiel: Here we go again. C'mon, Methelia, beat it, I'll call for you if we need something.

Methelia: Help her, strrangerr!

Salathiel: What a big bore you are! Now, leave. Mind the kitchen fire while we enjoy our lentils here.

But Methelia did not leave. Rubbing her hands on the dirty apron, and teary-eyed, she even went closer to Jesus.

Methelia: My sick daufter, help my daufter! Cure her, great prophet!

Salathiel: What do you know about this man? Of course, eavesdropping behind the door. As always! Listening to gossip and poking your nose in everything is all that you know!

Jesus: Wait a minute, Salathiel, let her . . .

Salathiel: No, Jesus, I've lost all my patience. Pff, this is what I get for being too familiar. You give a finger and they take your hand. Peter, John, Philip, I'm sorry. C'mon, go away from here, and weep all you can in the kitchen.

Then Methelia threw herself at Jesus' feet, sobbing.

Salathiel: Hey, what's this? Have you ever seen such a brazen act? Jesus, why don't you scare this bitch away! Don't waste your time on her c'mon, c'mon.

Methelia: Please help my daufter, help her!

Jesus stared at Salathiel, the Israelite, and smiled with sarcasm.

Jesus: Woman, how am I going to help you? It is not fair to take the children's bread and throw it to the dogs.

Methelia: That's right, stranger, but even the dogs eat the crumbs which fall from their master's table.

Methelia, her head bent, like a beaten dog, remained on the floor.

Jesus: Get up, woman. Nobody should be at the feet of anyone. Get up and go peacefully. Your daughter will be well, I assure you.

When Methelia left to look for her daughter, Jesus turned to Salathiel, the old patriarch of the Jewish neighborhood of Tyre.

Jesus: You were born in Israel, and nurtured by the history of love of our God, but you understood nothing. For God, there are no barriers. He removes them from among all nations like dry grass. For the Lord, this is not a land of dogs but of people, like all the rest. No one is a stranger in the house of God.

Two days later, we returned to Israel, our country, passing over the road of the Phoenicians. We hardly felt that we were crossing the frontier because the land had the same color, the trees bore the same leaves, and the birds sang the same tune everywhere.

•

The Roman province of Syria was a foreign territory where a great number of Israelites used to live, and, therefore, there was much contact between Syria and Palestine. This contact was even more intense with the northern province of Palestine, Galilee, which shared a border with Syria. The territory of Syria contained two important cities of the Phoenicians, Tyre and Sidon. The Phoenicians were great navigators and merchants of the ancient world. The ruins of Tyre and Sidon currently lie within the territory of Lebanon.

Tyre was an important center during the time of the gospels and lasted for centuries. Its two ports were actively engaged in commercial activities with other Mediterranean cities, as well as industries such as metals, textiles, dyes (specially purple), and glass. A flourishing Israelite colony was established there. Since the Jews were well known for their business acumen, they succeeded rapidly in this undertaking. But since they were a nationalistic people, they never mingled with the inhabitants of Tyre, who, in the gospels, are called Syrophoenicians or Canaanites.

The gospels tell us that only on this one occasion did Jesus leave for a foreign country. Only with this Canaanite woman and with the Roman centurion who had an ailing servant did Jesus show a sign of the Kingdom of God by healing non-Israelites. But by those healings he demonstrated that he absolutely rejected the kind of nationalism embraced by his compatriots. This was a novelty and a scandal for them at the same time. The Pharisees, the Essene monks, and the people in general believed that foreigners would have no claim on the much-awaited Kingdom of God. It was their belief that God would discriminate against non-Israelites. Jesus completely destroyed this deeply rooted nationalistic tradition.

Even in our time, there are nations which feel a certain superiority over others and therefore feel they have a right to rule over them. There are also races who think they are more intelligent and more capable than the rest. In the name of this supposed superiority, they colonize, dictate laws, discriminate, persecute, and kill. These ill-fated ideologies led, in Latin America, to massacres of indigenous inhabitants with extremely varied cultures, to the creation of encomiendas, as well as to the imposition of tribute. Eventually, it led to the enslavement of men and women of African origin, violently uprooted from their countries. The indigenous part of Latin America (more than 15 percent of the population) is composed of survivors of that historical crime. The thirty million blacks presently living in these countries are children and grandchildren of slaves brought to the continent like beasts, by white men who thought it was their right and even obligation to enslave them. In doing so, they invoked the name of God, as they continue to do today, in order to justify racism and discrimination of any type.

Science has proven the absolute fallacy of the racist's mind affirmation that some races are superior to others. Biologically speaking, each human group has distinctive physical and psychic characteristics, not necessarily better or worse than those of the rest, nor more valuable than others. Above all, historically speaking, races and countries have had unequal opportunities in developing their own set of values and expressing them. On the level of racism, it is easy to discover the plan followed by the oppressors and the oppressed. What makes it more horrible is the fact that these oppressors are mostly nations with a long history of Christianity. The whole gospel rejects nationalism and racism. Christianity in its original form combats any form of discrimination: there is neither Jew nor pagan, slave nor free man, male nor female (Gal. 3:28). Neither will there be a black or a white, an Indian or a Latin, a Mulatto or a Mestizo. We are all the same in the eyes of God. We are all God's children. Jesus makes use of irony with the Canaanite woman. He speaks to her, "It is not fair to take the children's bread and throw it to the dogs." His words highlight Salathiel's lack of compassion and his glaring nationalistic arrogance. "Dog" is a word of insult in Aramaic as well as in Arabic. The dog is considered a despicable and impure animal, for being a stray and for eating rotten and unclean meat.

As a Christian, one cannot talk about borders separating all peoples. A wrong concept of nationalism is no less than a collective expression of egoism or false pride. While respecting the culture of each nation, its history and peculiarities, the Christian must be (as has always been said) a "citizen of the world," an "internationalist," sensitive to the pains and joys of people of every country. The Christian must be in solidarity with the struggles and just gains of all nations. In the world we live in, where the fate of a nation can no longer be detached from that of its neighbors, for better or for worse, this is not only an ideal theology but a historical reality. In this episode, the miracle of Jesus directed toward the daughter of a foreign woman is a sign that before God there are no borders or races. God gathers people from the four corners of the earth, and the only sign that will distinguish the citizens of that nation are freedom, life, and justice chosen by those who comprise it.

(Matt. 15:21–28; Mark 7:24–30)

66

Possessed by Beelzebul

After passing through the Phoenician cities of Tyre and Sidon, we made a round through the various towns of Decapolis and proceeded once again to the Sea of Galilee. I remember we were almost at Chorazin when we came across a crowd of farmers running and screaming like crazy.

In front of the crowd was a man who was panting and stumbling every now and then. He was short and untidy, his tunic in tatters. Behind him was a group of men with boards and stones in their hands, running and cornering him like a beast.

Neighbor: Go away from here, Satan! Go away, go away!
Woman Neighbor: Off you go to the desert! Demon! Outta here!
Another Neighbor: You're Beelzebul! You're Beelzebul! You're Beelzebul!

A stone flew over our heads and landed right on the neck of the poor creature. Whirling, the man fell to the street. He was motionless.

Neighbor: Seraphio is cursed! Seraphio is cursed!
Woman Neighbor: Don't get too close. This man is possessed by the devil.
Neighbor: Seraphio is cursed!

Jesus and I forced our way through the enraged multitude and finally saw Seraphio, who was whimpering on the ground, his head supported by his two hands. He was trembling with fear.

Another Neighbor: Send for the Pharisee. Send for the Pharisee.
Pharisee: Here I am, damn it! Let me pass, you bunch of troublemakers.

An old man with his prayer cloak hanging from his shoulders appeared in front of everyone.

Woman Neighbor: This damned fellow needs special incantation.
Jesus: Hey, what's all this hassle? Who's this fellow?
Neighbor: He's possessed by the devil. Can't you see?

Jesus: Why, what happened to him?

Woman Neighbor: What else could happen to him? The devil slipped into his body, like he swallowed a fly.

Neighbor: The poor creature has been hiding for a week. If it hadn't been for old man Clete who found him this morning, we wouldn't have known what happened to him. Do you know where he found him? There, right inside the well, like a mouse trapped in his hole, dropping all his shit in the water that everyone drinks.

Neighbor: Damn! If not for Clete . . . He took him out with a rope!

Another Neighbor: Say the prayer fast, Pharisee, and hurry! This man is dangerous! He's possessed by the devil!

Jesus: Are you sure he's possessed?

Woman Neighbor: Of course. Look, this devil's gotta be really strong. The possessed one can't even hear or speak. He's tongue tied and his ears are covered.

The Pharisee was already preparing to pray, so he signaled us to keep quiet.

Pharisee: I want complete silence, so the Lord will hear our prayer. If anyone sees the devil leave this man, throw him at once to the ground to prevent him from entering another person's body.

We were all on tiptoes in order to get a view of poor Seraphio, who was curled up on the ground. Then the Pharisee raised his hands and began to exorcise the demon from the deaf and mute man.

Pharisee: Stay away from this man, Satan! Go away, get away from here, and leave the body of Seraphio. I command you, in the name of the Lord! Satan, filthy serpent, monster of broken hooves, beast with seven horns, get out! Go away, stinking devil, leave this man, unclean devil, deaf devil, mute devil! Beelzebul, conqueror of man, temptation of woman, go away from here, drown yourself into the sea, burn yourself in fire, go back to hell! This man is not moving. He does not even hear or speak. He's got the devil all over him! But I'll get him, yes sir, I'll get the devil out of his body at any cost!

Woman Neighbor: Hey, Pharisee, why don't you try it with a candle? They say that the demon is like a scorpion that emits its own poison when threatened by fire.

Pharisee: Yes, let's try it with fire. You four, tie his hands and feet. Make it tight so he won't kick. Then bring me a torch. We'll put the candle on his feet, to make him talk. The mute devil hates the candle.

The Pharisee took a burning torch and placed it near the sole of Seraphio's feet. He looked at us terrified.

Seraphio: Aaaaagghh! Aaaaaagghhh!

The air was filled with the smell of burned meat. The deaf-mute twisted but could not escape from the four strong men who held him on the ground.

Seraphio: Aaaagghh! Aaaagghh!

Pharisee: He's a very powerful demon, more powerful than the candle. He has his tongue tied in four knots. But don't worry, now we'll remove the cover from his ears. The deaf demon flees from boiling water. Hey, bring me the pot so I can remove the stuff from his ears. Hold him tight and turn his face!

The Pharisee poured the boiling water into Seraphio's ears. He was kicking like mad.

Seraphio: Aaaagghh! Aaaagghh!

Pharisee: Do you hear me? Do you hear me? Can't you hear anything, damn!

Woman Neighbor: Maybe there are seven of them, Pharisee, that's why the ears don't melt.

Pharisee: Please wait. Let's try the needles. My father exorcised not seven but seventy demons from a witch's body! No demon can ever stand the prickings he'll get in the groin! Hold him tight!

Jesus, who was beside me, lost his cool and pounced on the Pharisee.

Jesus: For God's sake, stop it! Do you wanna kill him? Is that what you want?

Pharisee: This man is possessed by the devil. We must get the devil out of his body.

Jesus: At the rate you're going, you'll soon be pulling out his soul. Leave him alone, damn it! Don't you see he's already suffering?

Pharisee: Ha! This only proves you don't know him. He's got the deaf and mute demons inside him. Isn't that enough? I couldn't get them out with candle or boiling water.

Jesus: I'm not surprised.

Pharisee: Why do you say that?

Jesus: Have you forgotten what the prophet Elijah found out in the cave of Sinai? That God was not in the fire nor in the hurricane, but in the soft breeze.

Pharisee: What do you mean?

Jesus: This man doesn't need a burning torch but the warmth of a helping hand. He doesn't need boiling water. Just a small amount of saliva will do.

Pharisee: Hey, stranger, wait a minute, what will you do?

But Jesus was already leaning over the deaf-mute lying on his back on the ground, breathing irregularly and with a terrified look on his face.

Seraphio: Ahh, ahh, ay.

Jesus: Don't be afraid, brother, I won't harm you.

Jesus wet his fingers with saliva. Then he touched Seraphio's tongue and ears and gently blew over his forehead.

Jesus: Look, I told you, Pharisee. The Spirit of God is like a soft breeze. This man's already cured.

Pharisee: This is all a hoax! How can he be cured? I'm the only one here who knows about exorcism, do you hear? This poor creature's possessed by at least seven demons that make him deaf and mute.

Seraphio: You, you are the seven demons!

When Seraphio spoke those words from the ground, we milled around him all the more. Some of us even shoved one another just to get a glimpse of what happened to the deaf-mute. The stronger men threatened with their boards to maintain some order. Then the Pharisee spoke.

Pharisee: My dear neighbors from Chorazin, as you can see, Satan takes to his kind. We wanted to get rid of this deaf-mute, but a greater evil is in his stead. This stranger who has anointed him with saliva is more evil-possessed than Seraphio.

Woman Neighbor: Why do you say that, Pharisee?

Pharisee: Why? Because only a nail can pull out another nail. If he was able to exorcise the devil out of this wretch, then he could've done it only through the power of Beelzebul.

Another Neighbor: How's that possible, Pharisee? If Beelzebul had driven away the same spirit, then he would have been crazy fighting his own self.

Pharisee: Shut up woman, or you might end up being possessed by the devil too. Neighbors, this stranger drove away the devil with the power of the same devil. So why don't you all stone him? Did you hear me? This man is possessed by the devil!

But the farmers of Chorazin did not move to stone Jesus nor to hit him with their boards.

Pharisee: I repeat, the same Beelzebul has come in to our midst. He's right here before you!

Woman Neighbor: Well, I didn't know that the devil was a fine, young man!

Pharisee: Oh yeah? So you're disobeying my command? Right now, I'll inform the great rabbi, Josaphat, that all of you have been influenced by this devil of rebellion! Everyone's under the power of Satan! You are all possessed by evil!

The indignant Pharisee shook off the dust from his tunic and left. The people were waiting for Jesus to speak.

Jesus: No, my friends, Beelzebul is not here. It's the Kingdom of God that has come. The devil is conquered, and he can't do anything. There's no more demon to fear.

An Old Woman: You can't say that, young man. No one can ever surpass the demon, whose tail is so long, it measures forty feet. They say that when the Lord puts him in jail, he opens the door lock by using his tail. That's why the demon's always free!

Jesus: No grandma, that's not so. The demon is well tied up, because God's already cut off his tail. It's only God who's powerful. Truly, the devil can no longer slip into someone else's body. Don't be afraid. Only the Spirit of God can enter our soul, because he has the key to our being. The devil can't do anything before God, who is most powerful.

Neighbor: Look, stranger, Isaac, the Pharisee, has spent all his life pursuing witches and demons. When this thing happened to Seraphio, I told him: "You have more faith in the devil than in God. You never speak about God, but Satan and his hell."

Old Woman: Well, he's done a good job for him. Ha! This is what the devil wants, my son, that you don't mention the Lord, but him. This I know for sure!

Jesus: Don't tell me, grandma, that you have seen the devil and his tail. Or have you?

Old Woman: Well, not really, but...

A Woman Neighbor: What about you, stranger, you who come from afar? Have you seen the devil?

For a moment Jesus became pensive as he rubbed his beard...

Jesus: As a matter of fact, no. I haven't seen the devil yet. But I've seen a lot of evil deeds. Yes, here in Chorazin and all over these towns. That's why, I tell you, the devil doesn't really have to exert too much effort here. He goes around with arms akimbo as we do everything for him with our evil deeds. Isn't that right, Seraphio?

Seraphio: Yes, yes! You burned me. You threw stones at me. You're the devil all of you!

Seraphio pointed an accusing finger at all his neighbors who had maltreated him, and with his brand new tongue he repeated his accusation.

Seraphio: You, all of you are demons!

•

There may have been a lot of deaf-mutes in Israel, since in the Book of Leviticus, there is a special law applying to this group. It is prohibited to throw a curse against these people, who, because of their handicap, are too helpless to defend themselves (Lev. 19:14). As in the case of other ailments, this disorder was attributed to the devil and the evil spirits. It was likewise believed that in Messianic times, the deaf would hear and the mute would speak (Isa. 32:1–4).

In this period in history, all diseases against which people felt specially defenseless intensified beliefs in the power of the devil, and exorcisms — prayers, gestures, invocations — were practiced to confront these spirits and drive them away from the sick person's body. Oftentimes these practices turned out to be cruel and violent because the ones performing the exorcisms thought they were struggling against the devil. At present, some people still blame the devil for the strange behavior of other people. Today, spectacular exorcisms are performed with the purpose of winning the battle over the devil. Such a mentality needs to be overcome, and the gospel of Jesus is a help to rid one's self of such beliefs.

The gospels speak of Satan (i.e., the adversary), one of the names of the devil, who is also called Lucifer or Beelzebul. The gospel writers do this precisely to point out negative deeds which they know are not pleasing to God, yet which they cannot explain very well. In writing about the power of the devil, they appear as people of their time – with all the limitations in various fields of knowledge – manifesting their own bewilderment, their disorientation. In their texts, however, they try to express, over and over again by means of symbolic language, what for them is decisive: that Jesus has all power over the devil, and his complete trust in the Lord makes it easy for him to defeat the devil. The gospels aim to free us from fear of the demon, from this false idea, rooted in various people, of two gods: the good one, God; and the bad one, the devil, who has similar powers, yet opposite intentions. The whole life of Jesus is the joyful proclamation that the only God is the Father who loves us.

The traditional "faith" in the devil has been catastrophic. It has sown terror in people's heart; it has made us believe that we are a plaything fought over by good and bad angels, with the stronger coming out as the winner. It is easy to blame the devil for an evil event of our own doing and for all injustice. In this sense, faith in the devil is absolutely contrary to Jesus' message, which is the word of liberation, a reaffirmation of God's kindness. God embraces people and history and demands that each of us take to heart the responsibility for our actions. Other horrible consequences of professing "faith" in the devil were the persecutions which occurred against witches and those thought to be possessed by the devil. Witch-hunting and burning are among the dark chapters in the history of the church in Europe. From the eleventh to the sixteenth centuries, persecutions spread like famine through all regions of Europe, with victims estimated to reach millions. The majority were poor women farmers who were accused of being possessed by the devil, either because they were ugly or pretty, or were extremely happy or silent. They were tortured and burned. Yes – as Jesus said: "The tree is known by its fruits" – the tree of faith in the devil has given rotten and bitter fruits throughout history; and if only for this, it should be uprooted.

Jesus was accused of being possessed by the devil, precisely because of the enormous freedom he manifested before these and other false beliefs, and for his opposition to priests and other authorities enslaving the people by way of their beliefs. The powerful of this world always make real demons of their enemies, of those who denounce them. Calumnies and suspicions haunt those who struggle for a better world, as they are depicted as agents of the very same forces of evil. The mechanism used in the systematic defamation is the same as that used against Jesus, a mechanism that aims at nothing else but to hide the truth. The "devil" is on the other side. The cruel person, the blood-thirsty and the unjust one — these are the devil, or, at least, his best accomplices. There is no need to resort to the devil to explain the evil in this world as long as there are still many unjust people, criminals, and enemies of life.

(Matt. 13:22–29; Mark 3:20–26; Luke 11:14–23)

67

The Messiah's Staff

In those days we traveled to the north, to the mountainous region of Caesarea Philippi, near the springs of the Jordan. The farmers living there wanted to hear about the Kingdom of God that would bring justice and peace on earth.

Jesus: ... And if your son asks you for bread, will you give him a stone? Of course not. If he asks you for fish, will you give him a snake? Of course not, because he's your son. Well, this is what we are proclaiming here, that God is our Father who loves us. We, his children, ask him to give us a hand. God will not fail us!

As usual, Jesus easily won the attention of the people. He joined one story with another and the residents of Caesarea never grew tired of listening to him.

Jesus: Friends, the Kingdom of God is at hand! Our liberation is here! The Messiah is at our door. When he comes, he'll bring in one hand a balance for meting out justice and in the other, a staff to rule without privileges.
A Man: Very good! Long live the Kingdom of God!
A Woman: May we see the Kingdom of God soon!

Then, amid applause and shouts of the people, appeared a huge man with sun-burned skin and a very long beard, like that of the ancient patriarchs. He was making his way through everybody until he reached Jesus. He was an old Bedouin from the plains of Gilead.

Melchiades: Speak no more, brother. That's enough. I am Melchiades, a shepherd, grandson of Yonadab, of the tribe of the Rechabites, shepherds all, as God has commanded us. Crossing the desert, we have learned to read the sky and the eyes of people. Your eyes are dark like the night and brilliant like the stars. I can read through them.

The old Bedouin drew closer to Jesus and put a hand on his shoulder.

Melchiades: Listen, brother. Our tribes have been scattered for a long time, for many generations, for many years. We're like sheep without a shepherd. Thank you for having come. Here, take this: this is for you.

Melchiades, the Rechabite, held up in his right hand a long and knotted old staff.

Melchiades: With this staff I've pastured my flock since I was young. With it I drove the wolves away and led my sheep through the plains. It belonged to my grandfather. Look: it's a shepherd's staff like David had in his hands when old Samuel found him and presented him before his people.

Jesus: What do you want me to do with it?

Melchiades: It's yours. Shepherd your people. You're the man we need so that things may change.

Jesus: But, what're you saying, grandfather? I . . .

Melchiades: Take the staff. Hold it tight with your hands so that the warmth of your blood will give life to the dead nerves of its wood.

And the old Bedouin handed the staff to Jesus.

Jesus: But grandfather, I . . .

A Man: Very good, Melchiades! That was very well said and done!

A Woman: We're behind you, Jesus! You can count on us!

Man: Us too!

The thirteen of us remained talking late into that night. Soon the sky became flooded with stars. Up there at the far end was Mount Hermon, bathed by the soft moonlight. The snow covering the slopes was just beginning to melt, as a welcome gesture to the forthcoming spring.

Jesus: This Rechabite shepherd must be crazy.

Peter: You're the crazy one, Jesus, if you don't take this chance. The people are excited about you.

Jesus: They are excited over the Kingdom of God.

James: And about you, too.

Jesus: James, listen to me.

James: No, Jesus. You can't deny it. You've got the people in your hands, just like that staff. Just a word from you is enough to mobilize them.

Jesus drew some lines on the ground, with the long and knotted staff given to him by old Melchiades that afternoon.

Andrew: The people expect much from you, Jesus. Don't disappoint them.

Jesus: And what can they expect from me, Andrew?

Andrew: A lot. They expect you to continue awakening them, to lead them so this country will mend her ways, which will end once and for all the abuses and they can live in peace. This is what they expect.

Jesus: But are they out of their mind? Who do they think I am?

Judas: A prophet, Jesus.

Philip: Do you know what a woman told me today? That when she looked at you sideways, you reminded her a lot of John the Baptist. She even bet five against one that the prophet John had resurrected and his soul had slipped into your body.

Thomas: Wh...wh...what a joke! Th...th...they might have his head cut off again.

Andrew: No way. I heard something else. They say that the prophet Elijah got down from his chariot and lent you the whip he used for his horses. You speak in the same way as the prophet from Carmel!

Jesus: Bah, this is plain stupidity.

Judas: The other day, they asked me if you have a wife. I said none.

Jesus: Why did they want to know that?

Judas: Well, because the prophet Jeremiah also didn't get married. They say you look very much like him.

Jesus: Of course. I also look like the prophet Amos, who was also a farmer. And the prophet Hosea, since I also come from the north. Very soon they'll say I was swallowed by a whale which threw me out of his belly like Jonas. I don't know how people can make up these stories.

James: It's not the people, Jesus, it's not them.

Jesus: And who else?

Peter: Look, dark one, we've been together for quite some time, for several months, and we've formed ourselves into a group, so we can speak out what we think, right?

Jesus: Why of course, Peter, that's what friends are for. What's the problem?

Andrew: Jesus, you've performed things right before our eyes which... The case of the deaf-mute of Chorazin...

James: And that girl, Jairus's daughter, who was dead. I even saw her.

Philip: And the Roman captain's servant.

Andrew: How about Flor, the paralytic, and Caleb, the leper, and the madman, Triphon. And the...

Jesus: Okay, okay, that's enough. So what? God's the only one who has the power to cure. He takes my hands, or yours or somebody else's, and does what he wants. A lot of people do even greater things.

Judas: But that's not all, Jesus. It's the way you speak. Admit it: your words hit like David's when he hurled stones from his sling.

Peter: You smell like a prophet, Jesus, and not even alum can remove it.

Andrew: You have a way with people. You talk to them and they listen.

Jesus: The people, the people! Today they say this but tomorrow they say that. What do you say? Let's lay our cards on the table, now that all thirteen of us are here. What do you really expect from me?

Peter: What every one else expects from you, Jesus. That you lift the staff and lead the people.

Jesus: You don't know what you're talking about, Peter. Who am I to do that? Who am I?

Peter: You? You're the Liberator that Israel has been waiting for!

Jesus: But, Peter, have you gone out of your mind? How can you say that?

Peter: I say it because I believe, damn it! And I'm just dying to say it. I already told Rufina and my mother-in-law. Even the two women think the same.

Jesus: Peter, please...

Peter: Yes, Jesus. Remember the other night? I saw it with my own eyes. We were on the boat, on my boat. Suddenly, there was lightning and the wind from the Great Sea blew. It was a horrible storm. And I saw you walking on the waves. The wind stopped. You gave me your hand and I took it and I walked over the lake, don't you understand?

Jesus: Yeah, yeah, I understand. If you don't stop dreaming, then one day you'll wake up drowning.

Peter: You're the Messiah, Jesus! You've come to free our people!

When Peter said those words everyone became silent. We were waiting for Jesus to reply. All eyes were glued on him, who was nervously clasping the staff of the old Bedouin.

Thomas: Don't w...w...worry, Jesus. We're b...b...behind you.

Judas: You can count on us. That's what this group is for.

Andrew: You gotta make up your mind, Jesus. If this comes from the Lord, then you have no way out.

Peter: It's not the people, nor us. It's God who has given you the staff of leadership.

Jesus looked at us, slowly, one by one, as if asking permission to utter the words blocking his throat.

Jesus: Yeah, you're right. You can deceive the people, but not the Lord. For many days and nights, I've been thinking about this. Ever since the prophet John died, I felt that something's changed, as if God were telling me: your time has come, the way's been prepared.

Peter: God doesn't give you a load that you can't carry! So cheer up, Jesus! God will not fail you!

Judas: And neither shall we!

James: Remember what the old man Melchiades said? Lift the staff and hold it tight! With you, we'll all move on.

Then Jesus raised the long and knotted staff of the Rechabite, held it tight with his two hands, and in one stroke split it in the middle.

Philip: Hey, dark one, what's the matter? Why did you do that?

Jesus: Because Elijah was persecuted, Jeremiah was thrown into a pit, and John's head was cut off. Look at this, everyone: this staff is broken, and that is the fate of all prophets; this is how the Messiah's life will end too.

Peter: Don't talk that way, Jesus. We'll defend you, damn it! Isn't that right, fellows? By the good star of Jacob, nothing bad will happen to you.

Jesus: First, you're pushing me forward, and now you're throwing me the bait. No way, Peter. Let's settle this once and for all. They're gonna break my bones like this cane, but you're gonna have to fight to the end too. From now on, each one should carry his cross too, so that later, each one is ready for anything.

Peter: C'mon Jesus, stop talking that way. Be ready and have courage!

Jesus: You too, Peter. You'll be behind me.

Peter: What did you say, dark one?

Jesus: Peter, Peter, the stone thrower. Now they'll throw stones at you, but don't worry. You're a good piece of rock for foundation. They won't crush you, not even with hammer blows.

Judas: Well, well, let's not get sentimental. Now we're one and united, and that's what really matters.

James: And we're gonna move on, whatever the cost.

Andrew: Whatever happens, this group won't disband.

Philip: Well said, Andrew. Not even the devil with his pitchfork can go against us, isn't that right?

Jesus: Of course, Philip. The friendship that we've formed here on earth, not even heaven can destroy. Do you agree?

Thomas: Of course! Just like a good lock with thirteen keys, every key meant to work with the lock!

Jesus: Peter, you keep the keys so they don't get lost!

Peter: So, we'll work hand in hand, forever!

James: Hand in hand, fellows!

Dawn came at Caesarea Philippi. The night slipped from us as we continued our conversation, and now we still had a couple of miles ahead of us. After stretching our legs we resumed our journey toward the south, to Capernaum. Mount Hermon was sparkling white behind us.

●

The city of Caesarea Philippi was founded by Philip, the brother of King Herod, about three years before Jesus was born. It was named Caesarea in honor of Augustus Caesar, who was then the emperor governing in Rome. The city was situated to the north, sharing the border with Syria. The River Jordan originates from Caesarea, and from there descends and passes through the land of Israel. The river is formed by three springs, one of which is the fount of Dan, thus giving it the name: Jor-Dan (that which descends from Dan). In biblical language, it is common to hear the expression "From Dan to Beer-sheba" to define the geographical boundaries of the land promised by God to Israel: from the north where the fount of Dan was, to the farthest end to the south, the Bedouin city of Beer-sheba. Caesarea Philippi is presently called Banias.

The Rechabites were a group of Israelites who, for many centuries, and out of loyalty to their religious principles, lived as shepherds, rejecting the life of sedentary farmers. They never drank wine, were zealous for their traditions, and only entered the cities by chance and on special occasions. They represented opposition to urban civilization and respect for the memory of the ancient tradition of the desert, when Israel was a country of wandering people (Jer. 35:1–19).

Just as the time of his baptism and the proclamation of the good news in the synagogue of Nazareth were decisive moments in Jesus' conscience in relation to his prophetic mission, this episode of Caesarea Philippi marks a milestone in his life. Up to this moment, Jesus, driven by the Baptist's example and supported by his disciples, plus a continuous fluctuation between pain and hope from his people, has manifested himself before his compatriots as a prophet. As such, he has spoken and acted. He feels heir to the prophetic tradition of Israel and acts with such a conviction. In Caesarea, he takes one step further. In fact, the freedom with which he speaks about the law and interprets it, and the certainty with which he presents himself as emissary of the Kingdom of God who would change the course of history, brings him closer to that awareness of being the Messiah. This "leap" in the conscience of Jesus takes place in Caesarea — inasmuch as it's possible to determine a concrete place and time.

Jesus accepts his messianic mission to the community. God chose Jesus as the Messiah of Israel, but the choice did not mean Jesus was to remain on the sideline with the people he was to serve. Similarly in the church and the Christian community, no vocation should come "from above," nor should it be decided "singly." All vocations, charisma, and service, if understood to be intended for the community, must be guaranteed by those who make up the community. Thus, we shall see the fulfillment in history of what was Jesus' ministry.

When, in the gospels, Jesus speaks of his passion that is to come, of his death, this ought not to be understood as a "prophecy" in the limited sense of this word, as if he were a reader of his own future. If understood this way, then the dramatic consequence of his life would not have been a historical fact. Everything would have been predetermined from the outside and anticipated from the beginning. What these words mean is that, at this level of his activities, Jesus was already anticipating a violent death. He had violated the law of the Sabbath — the core of the system — and this was reason enough to be sentenced to death; he had been accused by the powerful priests of being possessed by the devil, which was also punishable by death according to the law; he had had encounters with the authorities and with the landlords; he associated himself with people despised by the powerful, awakening them to their real condition as exploited people, and with the others who were feared as subversives, the Zealots. He was actually instigating a real people's movement. The religious leaders as well as the political authorities considered him to be a dangerous element every time, a rebel. And he was all too aware of this. For this reason, Jesus never ruled out the possibility — it was almost a certainty — of his violent death, like the fate of all the prophets. His faithfulness to the mission entrusted to him by God and the people made him move on, whatever the risk. This growing awareness of his important mission did not alienate him from his friends. On the contrary, Jesus was a leader who inspired trust among his followers. He had a sense of humor and never considered himself important, nor set "a distance" from them. By being "one of them" he likewise revealed God's nearness to us.

(Matt. 16:13–24; Mark 8:27–33; Luke 9:18–22)

68

At the Summit
of Mount Tabor

In those days, Peter, James, Jesus, and I were on our way to Nazareth. We took the route of the caravans, bordering the Sea of Galilee and crossing through the Valley of Esdraelon. The summer sun was a golden globe, shining on the wheat fields which were then ripe for the harvest.

Jesus: You haven't scaled the mountain, have you, Peter?
Peter: Where, Jesus?
Jesus: The mountain. When I was a little boy, I used to slip out of the synagogue. There were three or four of us from the village who'd get together and hike to the mountain. We'd reach the top with our tongues hanging out, yeah, and our sandals half worn-out, but it was worth the effort.

To our left stood Mount Tabor, round as a dome, separating the old territories from the tribes of Issachar, Zebulun, and Naphtali, the lone guardian of the fertile plains of Galilee.

John: Peter, James, tie your sandals well!
James: What's that, John?
John: I know this dark one damn well. Can't you see he's about to go up?

Suddenly we were going up the mountain slope toward its summit, inching our way among pine trees and turpentine trees abounding on the slopes.

Peter: For God's sake, I'm breathless. Pfff! I'm out of breath. Wait, Jesus.
Jesus: You gotta be getting old, Peter. Pff! I used to run up this mountain when I was a little boy.
Peter: Hey, John, James, come over here!
John: Those sheep, where did they come from?

125

James: Where there's a flock, there must be a shepherd too. But where is he?

Peter: C'mon, let's go on climbing!

There on top of the mountain was old man, Joel, above a rock with his bamboo flute. His eyes were lost on the horizon.

Jesus: The shepherd! The shepherd!

Joel: Here I am! What do you want from me, or what do you have for me?

Peter: All we can do is greet you, old man! What about you?

Joel: I can spare you some cheese and all the milk you want! Come, come, my countrymen, the milk from my sheep is purer than Susanna!

Jesus: Hey, are you the old man Joel?

Joel: Yes, that's my name. How did you know my name? Did a little bird on the road tell you?

Jesus: No, I used to scale this mountain when I was just a kid, and I used to see you around this place.

Joel: Of course, this is my home. Others build their houses, but not me. I have no hut of my own. I prefer the open air. The sky's my only roof. C'mon, try this goat's milk, it's gonna refresh your throat!

John: Thanks, Joel.

James: Doesn't this solitary life bore you, old man?

Joel: Music is man's best friend, don't you forget that. Look over the valley. Not even Methuselah with all his years had time to contemplate all this beauty. You who're from the lowland, who live in the cities and villages, learn how to read and go to the synagogue to listen to the Holy Scriptures. I know nothing about the written word, but that's not necessary, do you hear? This is my book and this is enough for me.

Old Joel showed, with his callused hand, the Valley of Esdraelon which opened before our eyes into a green vast expanse of land.

Joel: Look well, young men. This is the land promised by God to our fathers, the land where milk and honey flow, the most beautiful land of all!

Peter: Hey, old man, what's at the end of this. Is it the lake?

Joel: Yes, the Sea of Galilee, round as a bride's wedding ring. They say God slipped it onto Eve's finger when she became his wife. But look over there, countrymen: do you see?

John: Where, old man?

Joel: Over there, right behind all this. It's Mount Hermon, where snow continues to fall, white as the beard of our Lord! God blesses our land from there. Now, look at the other end where the lands of Samaria are found, where Mount Ebal and Mount Gerizim seem to join the clouds, and right between the two was the city of Shechem, nestled like a locket in a woman's bosom. This is where our father Joshua reunited with all the tribes of Israel and made an alliance with God, a blessing for those who complied and a curse for those who did not.

John: Old man, what are these mountains nearby?

Joel: Ah, those are the mountain heights of Gilboa where the Philistines murdered Saul, the first king of our country, and Jonathan, his son and friend of David who was also a music lover, played the flute for his dead friend. Look over there, to the west. Do you see something like a green spur coming out of the land and sinking into the Great Sea? That is Mount Carmel, Elijah's country, the first prophet who took the cause of the poor of Israel and defended their rights. Ah, Elijah! His tongue was like a whip in the hands of God. He made the kings tremble and all those who oppressed the poor. And when God took him in the chariot of fire, his spirit was scattered like sparks among the new prophets. Do you understand what I'm telling you, countrymen? Each of these mountains you see from here is like a page of a book, where the history of our people is written.

Jesus: But that history traces its beginning to another mountain, old man, the greatest of them all, that which cannot be seen from here.

Joel: You're right, young man. Mount Sinai is very far from here, some-where in the south, which only the eye of an eagle can reach. It was in that wilderness that God felt he should call on Moses through a burning bush. From here, he was sent to Egypt to liberate his brothers and sisters. Moses faced the Pharaoh, took all the slaves with him, and crossed the Red Sea and the desert, bringing them to Sinai, the holy mountain, the one with two peaks on the summit, like the open knees of a woman about to give birth: and it was there a free nation was born, our country, Israel.

John: Gee, old man, I get emotional, just listening to you.

Joel: My children, you're so young and you don't know. So many things have happened and what is yet to happen . . . God never keeps still. I'm sure he's in for something this time. Know something countrymen? God is like a goat: he loves the mountain. Sometimes he's with Elijah on Mount

Carmel, other times with Moses on Sinai. But he always fights for justice and defends the humble. Remember what our ancestors used to call the Lord? *El Shaddai*, the mountain God, because every time he's not pleased with the way things are down there in the great city he goes up to the mountains. And from there, he laughs. That's right, God laughs at the kings and the Pharaohs. Great nations make wars and the powerful oppress the poor. They'll not sing victories, though. God'll send a liberator on Mount Zion. He'll be my beloved son, with whom I'll be well pleased.

Up to this day, my eyes can still picture that moment: the blue horizon, the immense valley cut into cultivated lands like pieces of cloth of a hundred colors, the sun half-hidden behind the clouds, and the breeze coming from Mount Hermon seeming to augur rain.

Jesus: You're right, old man. It's in the mountains that the eyes are cleansed and the ears are opened to listen to the voice of God. It is there that the God of Israel spoke in whispers to Elijah and where he spoke with Moses face to face. Yes, God is alive and lets his presence be felt. From each of these mountains he continues to pave the roads of people on earth, interweaving them assiduously with the hands of a zealous woman. The work is done in God's time. He comes to build his house on a high mountain, on the summit of the mountains, so that we, the children of Israel and all the other nations, can climb up to it. Because God is the God of all, whether near or far. He's not content in gathering only the dispersed tribes of Jacob. No, because liberation abounds. There is much forgiveness and mercy for all children. And God's Anointed One, the Messiah, awaited for so long by our people, shall remain on top of the mountain to be the guiding light of the people, so that there will be salvation in all the confines of the earth.

Peter: That was great, Jesus! I told you, you inherited Moses' beard and Elijah's tongue. Keep on talking, don't be silent, the world's liberation is at hand, and there's no stopping it.

James: It's the storm that's coming soon. C'mon fellows, let's stop being poetic for this one minute and let's all go down, if we don't want to get drenched.

Peter: Hey, what's that nonsense you're saying, James? No, no way! Didn't you hear what Jesus said? Everything's going fine.

John: Are you outta your mind, Peter? Don't you see the storm coming, and there's not even a hut here to shelter us.

Peter: Then let's go make one, damn it! Let's build three, if need be! But no one is to move from here, no one!

Peter, in his excitement, looked up to the sky. The dark clouds were already touching our heads. In a few seconds, the first drops of rain fell.

Peter: Does the rain really matter, guys? Wasn't there lightning and thunder when God appeared on Sinai? The same thing happened on Carmel. This is because God roams freely in the mountains. Yes, yes, and now, Elijah will descend in his chariot of fire, and Moses likewise, with a burning bush in his hand.

The clouds fell furiously over Mount Tabor, and we were drenched to the bones. The lightning rays crossed the sky like lances, illuminating with splendor the faces of the shepherd, Joel, my brother James, Peter, and Jesus.

Peter: Well, and now what? Is everything over?

Jesus: No, on the contrary. This is just the beginning.

Peter: What's gonna happen now, dark one?

Jesus: Nothing, Peter. If you don't wanna catch cold, start moving and let's go. Or would you rather stay here above and watch the lightning?

Peter: I don't know. I was expecting more to see the Lord even halfway, but . . .

Jesus: Listen, Peter: God's in the mountains, that's right. But the people are down there. Look . . .

Jesus looked over the Valley of Esdraelon, interspersed with small villages where the poor of Israel earned their daily bread with their sweat and their tears.

Jesus: That's where we gotta go, Peter. That's where we gotta kindle the flames in the people's hearts. Leave the burning bush and the chariot of fire alone, and let's all go down. This was what Moses and Elijah did: to show concern for their brothers and sisters, to work unceasingly in helping them to fend for themselves. So, move on! And hurry! Let's light a fire all over the earth and keep it burning!

Peter, my brother James, Jesus, and I descended the slopes of Mt. Tabor, which became slippery after the downpour. The old man, Joel, was left on top of the

mountain, with his flock and his bamboo flute. Below were the fields and cities
of Galilee, lying in wait for a change, a renewal, a transfiguration.

•

Mount Tabor is an isolated mountain to the northeast of the beautiful
and fertile Valley of Esdraelon. It has a round shape and is 580 meters in
height. From the early days it was considered a holy mountain on account
of its beauty and location within the territorial borders of the tribes of
Issachar, Zebulun, and Naphtali. Although the gospels do not mention
the name of the mountain where Jesus ascended with his disciples in this
episode, tradition has always situated his transfiguration on the summit
of Mount Tabor. The mountain is about thirty kilometers from Nazareth
and boasts an abundant vegetation. In 1921, the grandiose Church of the
Transfiguration was built on top of the mountain. The exterior part of the
church reminds us of the silhouette of the three tents referred to by Peter
in the evangelical text.

From the top of the mount can be viewed one of the most fascinating
scenes in Israel. At the foot of the mount extends the plains of Esdraelon
or of Jezreel (which means "God has sown it"), as if wanting to bring out
the exuberant fertility of this land (Hos. 2:23–25). Jezreel (Esdraelon) is an
immense valley in the form of a triangle, surrounded by Mount Carmel, the
mountains of Gilboa, and Galilee. It served as a connecting link between
eastern and western Palestine, and therefore was a frequent setting for
important wars in the history of the nation. The old shepherd, Joel, viewing
all the mountains from the heights of Mount Tabor, traces the important
moments in the history of Israel. He refers to Mount Hebron, the northern
border of the land promised by God to his people, as the guardian of the
country. It is always covered with snow (Psalm 133). Mounts Ebal and
Gerizim, located on Samaritan lands, were the setting of one of the most
solemn moments in the history of the people (Josh. 8:30–35). The Israelites
were defeated by the Philistines in the mountain range of Gilboa, where
Saul, the first king of Israel, was killed, as well as his son, Jonathan (1 Sam.
31:1–13; 2 Sam. 1:17–27).

Joel makes special reference to Mount Carmel, the mountain of the
prophet Elijah. Carmel (the name means "garden of God") is a very fertile
mountain about twenty kilometers long, situated between the Mediterranean and the plains of Jezreel. Elijah performed some of the most
spectacular signs here (Rev. 18:16–40). At present, Carmel is called Yebel-

Elyas, the "mountain of Elijah," and thousands of pilgrims come to venerate the first great prophet of Israel in a cave that was excavated at the base of the mountain, the cave of Elijah. Here they pray and come together in pilgrimage, sing and eat symbolic food.

Elijah (his name means "Yahweh is God") lived about nine hundred years before the birth of Jesus. He was the great prophet of the kingdom of the north of Israel, when the nation was divided into two monarchies. His popularity was so immense that people wove all kind of legends about his person, converting him into an unforgettable myth. He performed great miracles and confronted the kings. He did not die, but instead, went up to heaven in a chariot of fire, and most important of all, would return to pave the way for the Messiah. All these were very vivid ideas in Jesus' time. Elijah was always the prophet par excellence, and the proclaimer of the coming of Messianic times. Because of all this, it was but natural that in this episode of the transfiguration, which is replete with symbols, Elijah should appear with Jesus, as a guarantee that his prophetic spirit was in Jesus; and more so, to become witness to the much-awaited Messiah. (The story of Elijah appears in the First Book of Kings, chapters 17, 18, 19, and 21, and in chapter 2 of the Second Book of Kings. References to Elijah are innumerable in the entire Scripture. Elijah appears as a prophet of justice in a special way in the episode of the vineyard of Naboth [1 Kings 21].)

The shepherd, Joel, also makes special reference to Sinai, Moses' mountain. Mount Sinai, also called Horeb in the Bible, is the most sacred mountain of Israel. Here, God appeared to Moses in a burning bush and revealed his name — Yahweh. Here, he handed over the commandments and made an alliance with the people when they marched in the desert. Sinai is situated in a territory which now belongs to Egypt, on the Sinai Peninsula, on a desert plain, in an area inhabited solely by Bedouins. Sinai is endowed with savage beauty which cannot easily be compared with that of other areas. Moses, who lived eighteen hundred years before Jesus, was an exceptional figure for Israel. A father and liberator of his people who formed them and led them to the Promised Land, he spoke face to face with God. He was, above all, a legislator who gave the Holy Law to Israel. No biblical figure had as much worth and authority as Moses. That's why he must likewise appear with Jesus in the scene of the transfiguration. When God started a new law with the peasant from Nazareth — the law of freedom, and a new alliance, that of justice and love — Moses was there as witness to Jesus' being heir to the best traditions of his country. (The entire book of Exodus is important in knowing the story of Moses, especially chapters 1 to 24.)

In Israelite thinking, the mountain, because of its proximity to the sky, was the place where God manifested himself. Other neighbors — the Assyrians, the Babylonians, the Phoenicians — thought the same way. The mountain, therefore, is a holy place par excellence. Later on, another complementary idea emerges: God elects some mountains as his special abode. Thus, Mount Zion (in Jerusalem) is spoken of several times in the Old Testament as his dwelling place, as a place for banquets during messianic times. Besides, there is an ancient tradition in Israel referring to God as El-Shaddai. God himself must have revealed this name to the old patriarchs (Gen. 17:1–2). El-Shaddai means "God of the mountains." The Book of Job mentions, on many occasions, this beautiful name of God.

Taking into consideration all these elements — sacred mountain, Moses (the law), Elijah (the prophets), the clouds (likewise a feature in the Exodus), resplendent light — the evangelists created a symbolic frame indicating to what extent the prophecies of the ancient writings of Israel were realized in the person of Jesus. What is thus presented to us is the so-called theophany (God's appearance or manifestation). This style is used in a number of the theophanies of the Old Testament: Exod. 24:9–11 (God appears to Moses and the ancients); 1 Kings 19:9–14 (God appears to Elijah through the wind); Ezek. 1:1–28 (God appears to the prophet Ezekiel in a chariot). In all these descriptions, there is always a series of symbolic elements whose culminating point is that moment when the voice of God is heard. In the transfiguration, God utters the words of Psalm 2: "You are my Son." The ideas in this psalm provide the backdrop for the theophany of the transfiguration, as it appears in this episode.

Here, Jesus expresses himself in prophetic and poetic language, born out of the atmosphere of warmth that the shepherd has elicited through his biblical evocations. In his words, Jesus puts together all prophecies making reference to the holy mountain, the Messiah, the day of salvation, and God's plan of liberation (Isa. 60:1–4; 61:1; Mic. 4:1–8). What Jesus announced was never "his" glory, "his" power, "his" transfiguration.

The good news he brought us is not a cheap vindication of his greatness, like a superstar who, with marvelous gestures, seeks to dazzle an astounded public. The good news Jesus proclaimed and for which he gave his life was the transfiguration of the world: a new world where the message of justice of the prophets could be a reality. What he has announced is the transfiguration of history. This history, which at times seems wanting in meaning, absurd, bathed in too much blood, is one led by God toward the final consummation of the world — a history which the hands of the God of the mountains will one day rescue. Then it shall be transfigured history.

(Matt. 17:1–13; Mark 9:2–13; Luke 9:28–36)

69

Ishmael's Questions

At the foot of Mount Tabor is a small village surrounded by palm trees called Deboriah (in memory of Deborah, that courageous woman who fought for the freedom of her people). Ishmael lived in Deboriah. He had a leather shop and an only son, Alexander. One day there was a celebration in Ishmael's house. His son was engaged to Ruth, a young and beautiful neighbor. They were already planning the date of their wedding.

A Woman: This young lady is very fortunate, of course. Alexander is just the right guy for her.
Woman Neighbor: You bet! He's a fine young man, hard-working, whose father is very religious.
Woman: May God bless them and may they stay happy forever.

Alexander danced in the circle of men. His friends pushed him to the center, and started clapping, goading him to recite a few lines for his sweetheart. He was tall and strong, and full of vigor.

Alexander: "The stars in the sky / do not have as much joy / as I do, when I sing to you / beloved...

Then it happened. Alexander, as if struck by lightning, fell on the floor. His mouth was foaming, and he was kicking. His friends rushed to him without knowing what to do to help him.

A Friend: Hey, go and tell his old man, Ishmael. His son is having an attack!
A Woman: He looks terrible!
Friend: For God's sake, let him breathe! Don't push!
A Woman Neighbor: He's relaxed now. Come, Ishmael, help me to bring him inside. Poor guy!

Ishmael: He had it when he was a little boy. I thought he was already cured. Imagine, it happens again today, when he was about to announce his wedding.

Woman Neighbor: Don't worry, Ishmael. God willing, it won't happen to him again. Have faith in God.

Ishmael: Yes, I hope so. May God listen to you, Sarah, may God hear you.

After that, however, his sickness became worse. The attacks kept recurring. Any moment, during mealtime, in the leather shop where he was working with his father, or when walking around town, when he least expected it, Alexander's eyes would remain wide open, he would leap like he was struck by a whip, then fall to the ground, gnashing his teeth. His body would twist forcefully, so that four men had difficulty subduing him. Then, he would get up, very exhausted, with no knowledge of what had happened to him.

Ishmael: Oh my God, please help me! He is my only son, my only joy. Heal him, Lord, I beg of you, I implore you with all my strength. Is it true that he will never have these attacks anymore?

Every night, he prayed the same prayer, and was disappointed every time. Alexander's illness was getting worse.

Doctor: I'm sorry, Ishmael, but how can we tell you?

Ishmael: You who have studied should know of a cure, some herbs, perhaps.

Doctor: It's so terrible a disease, we don't even know its name. It's so bad, the devil himself must have invented it.

Ishmael: But, damn, you're a doctor.

Doctor: Ishmael, the disease was born way ahead of medicine. It always has an edge.

A Woman Neighbor: That's life. Be resigned to your fate, Ishmael.

Ishmael: Yeah, right. I must be resigned to my fate. It's so easy to say that, isn't it? Because he's not your son.

Woman Neighbor: You're not alone in your suffering, Ishmael. Remember my friend Leah, whose son was born dumb. She's worse than you. What about little Reuben, who became blind after a stone hit him. And remember Rebecca, poor girl, who's got more humps on her back than a camel?

Ishmael: Yeah, yeah, stop mentioning all the sick people in town. I know: Rebecca the cripple; my friend's grandson, whose face is burned; Annette's son, the lame one; the other, armless one. Am I to be consoled by this?

Woman Neighbor: Well, they say that the illness of many gives solace.

Ishmael: To fools, yeah, to fools! That there are people worse than my son, Alexander, that others suffer more than I do, doesn't solve anything. Their suffering in no way relieves me; neither is my sorrow any consolation to them.

Woman Neighbor: You ought to be resigned to your fate, Ishmael.

Ishmael: No, no, there's no way I'll be resigned to my fate! I can't bear to see my eighteen-year-old son limp as a rag. His friends have stayed away from him. They feel pity for him. His girlfriend has abandoned him. She's scared of him. Now you say I must accept my fate, seeing my son abandoned on the ground like a mad dog?

Woman Neighbor: You must accept the will of God.

Ishmael: The will of God! Was it God, therefore, who sent this disease to my son? And may I know why?

A Friend: Because you're a sinner, Ishmael. God has punished you by hurting you where it hurts most. This is what happens.

Ishmael: Oh yeah? So this is God's justice? The parents eat the green grapes, while the children bite their teeth. Let the Lord impose a penalty on me, but not on my son, who's done nothing wrong!

Friend: You can't say that. No one's innocent in the eyes of God.

Ishmael: Then why does God pick on my son and not yours? Tell me, why?

Friend: Because the Lord does what he wants. And what he does is okay. Who're you to exact an accounting from God?

Ishmael: Who should I ask? Whose fault is it that my son should get sick? C'mon, tell me.

Rabbi: God isn't the culprit, my son. How can you talk like this about God? God is kind. He's our father, and seeks our happiness.

Ishmael: If that's so, then why doesn't he cure my Alexander? I have prayed to him and asked him, day and night. He doesn't hear my prayer.

Rabbi: Yes, God hears you, Ishmael, but . . .

Ishmael: But what? Can't God do anything? Then why not cure my son?

Rabbi: Sometimes God makes something good from bad.

Ishmael: Wouldn't it be easier for him to take out the bad? That way he'd get done sooner.

Rabbi: We ourselves cause many of our ills and sufferings. Look at that crazy man, Saul, his intestines became rotten because he drank a lot. And now his widow is blaming God for everything!

Ishmael: My son's name is Alexander and not Saul! And my son did nothing bad to make him sick!

Rabbi: Who knows what God is planning. The ways of the Lord are mysterious.

Ishmael: Of course, and because of this, you want to silence me. Well, I'm not keeping quiet, do you hear? God has no right to do this to my son. You say that God is our Father. Doesn't it hurt him to see many of his children suffering? What kind of father, then, is one who doesn't mind seeing my son suffer on the ground?

Rabbi: God doesn't suffer, Ishmael, because God is God.

Ishmael: Then he is nothing! To hell with him!

Rabbi: You don't know what you're saying, Ishmael. Take it easy

Ishmael: No, and I know what I'm saying. I have prayed day and night, but God doesn't answer me. I lifted my face to heaven and said to him: Why, why do you treat my son this way? What's he done to you? If you're bad God, then make me suffer, not him. But if you're a good God, why don't you cure him? What would it cost you if, indeed, everything is possible for you? But God never answers me. He's deaf.

Rabbi: Come, Ishmael. Go home. Rest a little. I know this will pass.

Ishmael: Yeah, for me, this'll pass, but my son Alexander will continue to be sick. You'll go back to your work and to your own life. But Alexander will still be sick. God will continue to hear the angels sing above, while my son continues to be sick and embittered! Why, why, why?

Rabbi: Be patient, Ishmael. This is all I can say: Have patience and more patience.

Ishmael: No. keep it all for yourself, because I don't need it. Don't worry, I won't be asking anymore, I got the answer already. Do you know why God doesn't cure my son? Do you know why? Because he doesn't exist! Yes, and don't look at me that way. That's the only excuse that he can give us, that he doesn't exist. That's the truth. There's no one in heaven. And when we pray, our prayer comes back and falls flat on our face.

That day was market day in the village of Deboriah. Peter, James, Jesus, and I passed by, after our descent from the mountain. In a stall, a man, quite

old, with large bags under his eyes, as if he had wept a lot, showed us some leather shoes.

Ishmael: This is good leather, strangers, look.

Beside him was a tall young man with stunned eyes, who was showing us, through gestures, other items.

Ishmael: For two denarii, and you can wear them right away. C'mon.
Alexander: Ayyy!
Ishmael: Alexander, my son, my son!
Alexander: Aggg! Aggg!

In no time the boy at the fruit stall fell down. He was twisting amid spasms. Ishmael, his father, tried to open his mouth to insert a piece of cloth so that the boy wouldn't bite his tongue.

A Friend: Why do you have to bring him here, damn it? Why don't you leave him in the house, or lock him up! He's dangerous, damn it!
Ishmael: Don't you curse my son, for he's done nothing wrong. Curse God who is responsible for this!

Then Jesus went near the boy's father.

Jesus: For how long has he been suffering from this illness?
Ishmael: Since he was a little boy. For many years, he was okay, but now . . .
A Woman: Ishmael, this man who just asked you is the Nazarene who many are talking about. They say he's God's prophet and has cured a lot of people.
Ishmael: Prophet? You're a prophet? You speak with God? Please ask him on my behalf: Why is my son suffering, why, why? Pardon me, stranger, it's just that, it's just that I can't stand it anymore. I'm tired, tired of praying, because God doesn't listen to me. If you're a prophet, if you can do something for my son . . .
Jesus: Do you have faith? Do you believe in God?
Ishmael: Now I don't know what to believe in.

Jesus sat beside the young man who was breathing laboriously and wiped his face, which was wet with sweat.

Jesus: There's hope after all.
Ishmael: Is that all?

Jesus looked at the young man's father for a long time. Like him, he was teary-eyed.

Jesus: If I told you that God is also suffering for your son, would you believe it? That God also weeps seeing so many sick suffering. No, you're not alone, brother. God is with you, staying by your side and sustaining you. What more can I tell you? Come, let's bring him home, lie him down, so he can rest. Let's go, he's more relaxed now.

Ishmael: Will he have another attack?

Jesus: Even if he will, there's still hope.

Jesus helped the old man, Ishmael, lift his son from the ground. Then he supported Alexander by the shoulders and silently walked with him and his father through the dusty road crossing the small town of Deboriah, to their home, in the shadow of Mount Tabor.

•

Deboriah was located at the foot of Mount Tabor. It was a town that belonged to the Israelites of the tribe of Zebulun. It was named in memory of Deborah, a prophetess and "mother of Israel," who served as judge in the first periods of the history of the people when they were winning battles for the country. Their victory hymn (Judges 5:1–31) is one of the masterpieces in Hebrew Literature. At present, Deboriah is still a small village, inhabited now only by Arabs.

Through the description in the gospel of the symptoms of this sick young man, we can deduce that he was suffering from epilepsy. Today we are aware that the cause of these attacks and sudden convulsions is generally a lesion in one part of the brain. While it cannot be entirely cured, epilepsy can be controlled. In Jesus' times, nothing was known about this, and those afflicted with it were specially feared. Ignorance of the disease and what to do about it made the situation deplorable. Very often, its cause was attributed to the devil. It was also believed that it was a form of God's punishment for some hidden sin of the victim and his family.

In the face of his son's suffering, Ishmael, the father, prays, seeks, and asks questions. He does not resign himself and ends up rebelling, shouting to God for an answer, believing that God is the only one who can grant it to him. His attitude and his questions are parallel to those of Job. About five hundred years before Jesus' birth, an anonymous author wrote one of the most important and beautiful books of the Bible, the Book of Job, which is about a good man who experienced all kinds of calamity. The pages of the book contain his reflections on sorrow, which he considers absurd, unjust, and undeserved. He meets three friends, who seek the reasons for his misfortune. Above all, he faces God, who is ultimately the one responsible for his ills.

This Job, who becomes rebellious in the face of suffering, and who implores God himself, signified an authentic revolution in the religious thinking of Israel. Until then, it was believed that while on earth, people already received the reward or the punishment for their deeds. A good person became happy and prosperous. A bad one experienced failures and sufferings sooner or later. The Book of Job radically contradicted these ideas. Its theme can be summarized in one important question: Why do the good suffer? What is the significance of the sorrow of the innocent? Throughout its thirty-eight chapters, and in all possible ways, Job asks the same question again and again. After this book, the reflection of the people of Israel on sorrow, individual responsibility, and God's plans would vary substantially. Job's case paved the theoretical way to begin to understand the possibility of immortality, the transcendence of human life beyond earth.

Job — like Ishmael — is not convinced of the reasons offered by his friends. There were no valid "reasons" then, nor today, for the suffering of the innocent. It is an oversimplification to say that in suffering, God always consoles the one who suffers, since there are some who do not feel such consolation, who are desperate and embittered, unable to overcome the pain they experience in themselves or in the people they love. The suffering of the innocent is a mystery. That is why Jesus does not offer Ishmael any "reason"; he does not look for motives, nor blame anyone. He just makes his presence felt. He is there, beside the suffering father and the sick son. That's all. Christian faith does not give "convincing" answers to everything, much less to "absurd" pain. This is not to propose a resigned acceptance, because pain always ends up in mystery, where perhaps the only thing that we can do for others is to share with them their suffering (Rom. 12:15). Obviously, there are pains and sufferings about which we can "do" something. Death by starvation, the suffering of people who are unemployed, the pain of women exploited by their husbands, the lack of education of numerous children, the lack of shelter and medical attention, and so on, are sources of pain. Neither one's presence nor sharing is enough for this type of suffering. Christian faith compels us to do more in trying to get rid of this suffering, to combat and to fight against it.

It is another kind of pain that renders us impotent and demands of us Christians a faith and a hope that do not come easy. There are diseases that cannot be fought no matter what the means at hand. There are accidents that claim the lives of good persons, whose foresight escapes human control. There are children and young people who die before they have barely lived, and the cause of their death simply perplexes us because it is unexpected. There is likewise the pain experienced by the human heart (unrequited love, betrayal of friends, misunderstandings, failures, loneliness). At the end of it all is death, which is always painful even if it comes "in due time." These are the pains that confront us in our limitations and helplessness. Faith is, therefore, not a consolation, like aspirin. Perhaps it only serves as a fragile support, knowing that God suffers when he sees us in pain, that the heart of a Father is touched with the pain of his children, that he will also take away our sufferings and that one day, God will wipe away all the tears from our eyes (Rev. 21:1–5).

(Matt. 17:14–21; Mark 9:14–29; Luke 9:37–43)

70

With Lighted Lamps

Rabbi: The same Lord had said: "It is not good for man to be alone." So he gave him a woman for companion. Raphael, take Lullina as your wife in accordance with the law and the written commandment in the Book of Moses. Receive her and bring her as a family member to the house of your father. May the Almighty God always guide you and bring you peace!

That night, the fishermen's village of Capernaum was having a feast. Raphael, one of the twins of the big house, was getting married to Lullina, the daughter of an old boatman. The sounds of drums and zithers echoed through the village, inviting everyone to the dance in honor of the bride and groom.

Women: "The bride is like a lily / the groom, a carnation / who blushes like the flower / when his bride looks at him."

The women danced around Lullina and the men formed a circle around Raphael. After a while, we were served the food prepared by the groom's father. We sat on the floor, beside the trays of pastries and jugs of wine. The music played continuously, our faces drenched with sweat, dazzled with great joy.

James: It's good to die at a wedding, fellas! If I have to go, then let it be when I'm dancing and feasting!

John: And drinking! Here's a toast to Raphael and Lullina, the newlyweds!

Peter: And I drink a toast to those who have stuck to their wives for forty years!

A Man: And to those who are due to tie the knot but haven't made up their minds!

Peter: Hey, Jesus, that last toast is intended for you! Damn it, how many weddings have you been to? Hasn't the fever gotten you yet?

Jesus: As you can see, Peter, I haven't swallowed the bait.

John: I bet this wedding is a lot better than that of my friend Reuben . . .

142

James: Certainly! Wasn't it there that your tunic got burned, John?

John: Right. There was some delay among the participants to the wedding, and later, the hassle with the oil lamps. Remember that, Jesus?

Jesus: Of course I do. I was with the groom and his friends in his house. We left together for a place nearby, and there we waited for the coming of the bride. It went like this:

A Friend: Are you nervous, young man? This is the greatest night in your life!

Reuben: No, I'm not. Brrr ... I just, I just feel cold and ...

Another Friend: Gee, you don't talk of anything here but love, man! And love is at its best with a shot of wine! Here's to your health, rascal!

Friend: Long live the groom!

Friend: Long live the bride!

Jesus: Right from where we were gathered, we saw a group of young ladies pass by, illuminating the dark night with their oil lamps.

Ladies: You stole my heart, my beloved husband, you stole my heart, with your look and your words of love

Jesus: The young ladies accompanied the bride to the groom's house. Then they went out and stayed by the door, awaiting our coming.

Reuben: When all the stars shine in the sky, then it's time for us to go!

A Friend: Oh, we've got enough time! There's just a lone star up there.

Another Friend: There's no hurry, fellas. Let the ladies wait! We gotta finish this barrel yet!

Jesus: At the door of the house were ten friends of the bride, who were waiting with their lighted lamps.

Young Lady: You're gonna get your dress soiled if you sit on the floor, Annie. Don't forget you just borrowed it.

Annie: Don't tell me we're gonna be standing here all night. I'm tired because of dancing, and my feet are hurting.

Another Young Lady: I'm sleepy. That's all. Hmmm, I guess we've had too much wine.

Young Lady: Hey, how foolish you are! Look what we've got here, one sleepy-head, and a sloppy one. Lousy, huh? Listen, why don't we sing, to keep us all awake! C'mon!

Annie: Yeah, let's sing some ballads. Hey, this lamp is running out of oil. I didn't bring extra oil.

Young Lady: Neither did I, but I think this will get us through.

Young Lady: Stop arguing and let's go on with the songs!

Jesus: The bridesmaids began to sing to pass the time. We could hear their singing and their happy voices from where we were.

Young Lady: Here comes my love, through the field he comes / through the field he comes, I can hear his voice ...

Jesus: And when the sky became studded with stars, the young ladies' songs became softer. The girls grew tired of waiting. From afar, we saw that some of the lamps had stopped burning.

Young Lady: Hey, Annie, look at these girls, they have fallen asleep, and their light is extinguished.

Another Young lady: I think they ran out of oil.

Young Lady: Well, sleep tight, ladies!

Annie: Hmmm! Oh, Miriam, I'm sleepy too; my eyes are getting heavy! Hmmm!

Jesus: The groom and his friends were finally ready.

Reuben: Well, fellas, the barrel is empty, and I guess this is the end of it. I gotta say bye-bye to my bachelorhood!

A Friend: Your time has come, Reuben! Be ready, for tonight you're the king of the party!

Another Friend: Hic! Let's drink the final toast to this man who will join his better half, at last!

Jesus: Then, when it was midnight, we headed for the house where the grand celebration was to take place: the meeting of the bride and groom. The bridesmaids were still sleeping by the door, one slumped over the other.

Friend: Hey, the groom is coming! Ain't you gonna welcome him?

Young Lady: Oh, oh, the groom is here! Wake up, Annie. You too, Miriam!

Annie: Oh, the light from my lamp is gone!

Young Lady: And so's mine!

Another Young Lady: And mine too! What are we gonna do? Oh my God!

Young Lady: Try to fix them! I haven't got even a drop of oil!

Another Lady: This is what you get for being careless! Go and buy some oil at the store. Hurry!

Young Lady: And don't be late for the party!

Another Young Lady: Run, Annie, run. Oh God!

Jesus: So the five bridesmaids who did not bring enough oil hurriedly left to buy oil in the square. While they were away, we arrived at the house, singing and clapping with the groom.

Young Ladies: Open the door, my dear, for the groom wishes to enter!

Young Men: Open the door, my love, for your master is here!

Young Ladies: Open the door, lady, most beautiful one!

Young Men: Open the door, beloved, for outside, it is terribly cold!

Jesus: The other five ladies with their lighted lamps opened the door for us and led us inside the house, where the bride was anxiously waiting. She was dressed in blue, with a crown of orange blossoms around her forehead.

A Man: Let's begin the great celebration!

Jesus: Then the door was closed. The dance began. There was much food, and every guest was happy. A few minutes later, the careless bridesmaids came back from the store, running...

Annie: Please open the door! We're back!

Young Lady: Open the door, please, and let us in!

Servant: Who's banging the door, huh?

Young Lady: Our other companions. They forgot to bring enough oil, so they came late.

Annie: Please open the door and let us in!

Servant: Stop disturbing us, damn it! Get away from here! It's your fault. You were not vigilant. Who told you to sleep and be late?

Peter: Then what happened, Jesus? After having waited, were they left outside the house?

Jesus: Well, Peter, the truth is these girls were not alert.

James: Serves them right, for being foolish and nonvigilant.

Peter: Okay, okay. The girls failed to do their part. But the groom, what did he do, Jesus? Didn't he open the door for them?

Jesus: The groom did what every groom is expected to do, Peter. When he learned what was happening outside...

Raphael: Hey guys, are you having fun, tonight? Did you like the pastries? What about the wine?

John: Everything is wonderful, Raphael. Here's a toast to you and to Lullina!

Raphael: And to all of you, my friends! A toast to all of you!

Raphael, the groom, came to where we were. He was radiant with joy.

Raphael: And who's up next, huh? Is anyone preparing to get married soon?

Jesus: No, not yet. It's a lot easier to tell stories about weddings! Say, Raphael, what would you do if tonight, five of your wife's bridesmaids came late for the party because they had run out of oil, if when they came back from buying oil, they found the door of the house locked? Would you let them in or not?

Raphael: But of course, Jesus! How could I leave them out in the cold? My house is always open; it never closes at night. Today is the happiest day of my life, and I wouldn't want anyone to be left out in the cold of night. Well, guys, enjoy yourselves!

James: See you later, Raphael!

Jesus: You see, Peter? This was what the other groom did. All grooms do the same:

> *Annie:* Please, let us in, please!
>
> *Servant:* Don't bother us, damn it! Get away from here! It's all your fault. Who told you to sleep and be late?
>
> *Reuben:* But what's going on here, Theodora? Who are you quarreling with, ghosts?
>
> *Servant:* No, master. With five negligent young ladies who didn't come on time. Too bad for them. Let them wait outside. This is what is commanded of us: to close the door.
>
> *Reuben:* Well, go ahead and open it, c'mon.
>
> *Servant:* What was that again, master?

Reuben: Open wide the doors! Let the five young ladies in. They must be very tired! They've waited for a long time! C'mon, hurry, open the door and let anyone in who wants to enter! Today is a joyful day and I want everybody to join me in the celebration! This is a wedding, yes sir, and the party is for all!

Jesus: That's right. All grooms do the same thing. The joy of a wedding fills the heart. I believe God will also do the same at the end, at midnight, when we all get back to our homes with but little oil left in our lamps.

The sounds of drums and zithers echoed until dawn. Until then, we continued dancing and celebrating the great joy of that wedding feast, with doors open wide.

•

Weddings were celebrated with great joy in Israel. They usually lasted seven days and were spent eating, singing, and dancing. Although the customs differed in several details from region to region, there was always a culminating moment: the meeting of the bride and groom. In the afternoon of the first day of the feast, they brought the bride to the house of the groom's father, where the banquet usually took place, and a room was specially prepared for the new couple. The groom would go out to meet his wife with special headgear sewn by his mother: the "crown." His friends accompanied him. Usually, a group of young men singing songs and carrying torches would leave the groom during the encounter, to get together later in the house where the feast was celebrated. The bride, who was beautifully adorned, appeared before her future husband, covered with veils. During the celebration, it was the practice among men and women to dance and eat separately.

The so-called parable of the ten virgins is narrated only in the gospel of Matthew. Here, the evangelist wants to make a catechesis to the community on the subject of vigilance. Those were difficult times, and when the hour of God's final judgment came, no one was to feel too secure. One must be ready with oil for replacement; one must be prepared; no one should rest on their laurels. On the contrary, one should be ever watchful. This is what Matthew wanted to tell us in this parable that dramatically ends with a closed door to indicate the seriousness of the topic he was talking about.

In this episode, without contradicting the catechetical meaning of the parable, the door remains open at the end. Of the many symbolic elements interplaying in this story, rather than highlighting those of the oil, or those of the night of vigilance, emphasis is placed on the others: the groom, the wedding. From the point of view of catechesis vis-à-vis Christians, one must insist on the importance of vigilance. From the missionary point of view, though, in order to show how God is, how mysterious his ways always are with people, it is valid to focus on the more joyous aspects of the parable. People must be watchful and must take this to heart, but God, in his love and mercy, will always surpass the heart (1 John 3:2).

Certainly, this parable speaks of the end of time, the judgment day and the reckoning. It is an eschatological parable. A unilateral kind of preaching has, for a long time, terrorized the people with regard to the end of the world. The fear of hell, fire, and punishment has been a perennial topic of preachers in order to make people mend their ways, "to convert them." To this day, it is a burden borne on the shoulders of Christians. Consequently, those bleak ideas have given us a lousy image of God: a policeman who takes account of our good and bad deeds and, much to our dismay and to his joy, brings us death at the most inopportune time, hurling us into the cauldron of boiling oil. Christian vigilance is thus reduced to fear and the need to store up merits in preparation for the day (dying with the scapular on, having complied with the nine first Friday devotions, having earned indulgences, may save us at the last hour from the whims of a vengeful God). In the light of all these, we have to open ourselves to the reality of the God of Jesus: a cheerful God, who is preparing a wedding banquet to receive us in the other life, who understands our foibles, wishing only our happiness, with a heart "always greater than ours."

(Matt. 25:1–13)

71

What God Has Joined

James: C'mon, I dare you deny it, now!

Esther: But, where did you get this silly talk, James? Tell me, whoever filled your head with all this gossip?

James: Oh yeah? So you call it gossip? My good friend Zebulun told me! And he doesn't lie.

Esther: And may I know what this good friend of yours told you?

James: You've been in the market, haven't you?

Esther: Of course, I go everyday.

James: You bought some fruit, didn't you?

Esther: Yeah, what's wrong with that?

James: Nothing! But winking at the fruit vendor is something else!

Esther: That's it! You're jealous again! Oh God, what kind of husband have I got?

James: You were flirting with Ruffo, the fruit vendor. Don't deny it.

Esther: Ruffo, the fruit vendor is more than sixty years old. He's got no teeth left in his mouth!

James: You know that's not necessary!

Esther: Oh yeah? So you think this old man and I ...?

James: I'm not thinking anything. I'm positive! My friend Zebulun told me. You listen here: Don't you ever set foot in that market again, ever!

Esther: Really? That suits me fine. From now on, you'll have to do all the shopping for the family.

James: And don't you ever leave this house!

Esther: Why don't you get a watchdog to be sure?

James: I don't wanna be the laughing stock of all Capernaum, do you understand? I, the son of Zebedee, will never tolerate this!

Esther: Of course, but my mother's daughter has to put up with all her husband's idiocy.

James: Hell, I'm the man of this house!

Esther: And I'm a nobody here, is that it?

James: Shut up, insolent woman! And don't you ever shout at me!

Esther: Oh, my God!

James: It's all over, do you hear? Gather all your trash and go back to your mother's house! I don't need you here, understand? I don't wanna have anything to do with you!

Esther: Now you've awakened the girl with your screams! Why don't you nurse her with your milk? Let's see how you do it!

My brother James had been married to Esther, a woman from Bethsaida, for five years. During that time, they had three daughters, and more bickering...

Salome: James, son, I don't understand this. Esther is such a fine woman.

James: Esther is a whore, that's what she is.

Salome: Don't talk that way about your children's mother. Esther is your wife.

James: That's the end of it. I have no wife any more. I told her to pack all her things and get out!

Zebedee: Wait a minute, James. Let's not rush into this. Tell me what happened. Was she unfaithful to you?

James: If she was, I would've given her a good beating she'd never forget!

Zebedee: So what has she done to you?

James: She's nuts, that's it. She winks at every man that comes her way.

Salome: That means there could only be very few, since you lock her up in your house like she's a leper. Poor creature! You don't even bring her over!

James: C'mon, mama, stop defending her.

Zebedee: Okay, tell me: What really happened?

James: My good friend Zebulun saw her smiling at Ruffo, the fruit vendor. That's it.

Salome: For God's sake, James, what do you expect her to do? Spit in his face?

James: Don't be naive, mama. Everything starts with a "simple smile." You turn your back and she plays around.

Just then, Jesus entered the house, in the middle of the conversation.

Jesus: Hey, who's playing around, huh? How're you, Zebedee?

Zebedee: Still alive, Jesus, which is still a big deal in this country.

Jesus: You can say that again! What's up, Salome? Hey, red head, you look so serious, is anything wrong?

James: Right, Jesus.

Jesus: What's happened?

James: I'm divorcing my wife. We're going separate ways.

Jesus: But why?

Salome: It's really nothing, Jesus. It's just that someone has whispered to this son of ours that his wife winked at the fruit vendor.

James: It's no gossip, mama. It was my good friend Zebulun who told me.

Zebedee: And there is no one in all of Capernaum who can beat him as a rumor monger.

James: Not only that. Zebulun has also seen her in the square, and in the street of the tanners. The other day he saw her at the wharf.

Jesus: Say, couldn't it be Zebulun who is "after" your wife? Why, he follows her wherever she goes.

James: Stop kidding me, Jesus.

Jesus: After all, it's only a marriage of five years that's going to waste, all in the wink of an eye.

James: Yeah, that's right. It's better to be alone than to have a bad companion. And I've lost my patience!

Esther: Of course!

James: And look who's here ...

Salome: Esther, my child, James told us about ...

Esther: Oh yes, yes, what our friend Zebulun said. Why don't you sleep with him tonight? After all, you like him so much!

James: There you go again, devil woman. I told you to pack your things and go!

Esther: That's why I came to say goodbye to everyone ...

Zebedee: Esther, child, take it easy. Come, sit down here. Let's have a little talk.

Esther: Talk? What for? All that this son of yours does is yell and give orders like a captain. No, no, I can't stand this lunatic anymore. I'm tired and I'm leaving.

James: What did you say? You're tired? You're tired of what? Of sitting calmly all day long in the house, while I break my back out there on the sea? And now, you're saying you're tired!

Esther: So I do nothing but sit in the house, huh? Who takes care of the children? Who cooks and goes to market, does the laundry, and looks

after little Mila? Who cleans the house and does endless things at home?
You don't think I'm working at all, do you?

James: Yeah, and it doesn't include your gossiping in front of the house!

Esther: Then the master comes home, sits down with his arms folded,
while I have to serve him his food like a great king, since he never bothers
to touch any plates!

James: So this is what I deserve to hear, after spending all day working
like a horse for you and the children. Don't I deserve a plate of lentils
for this?

Esther: Sure, a plate of lentils plus four jugs of wine in that damn pub
where all your money goes!

James: You've got no right to question what I do with my money!

Esther: Yes, of course, while this slave does nothing but serve you, "gratis
et amore." For five years we've been married, and yet you never spared me
a single cent to buy myself a hanky!

James: I'll squeeze your neck if you don't show me more respect!

Esther: The trouble is . . .

James: The trouble is that's enough! You women are chatterers. You've
heard her talk, Jesus. Tell me, am I right or not, in divorcing this witch?
Answer me.

Jesus: Well, James, I think it's she who has the right to junk you.

James: What?

Jesus: You heard me. What I don't understand is how Esther has
managed to put up with you for so long.

James: Oh, yeah? So you're against me? It's okay. You can all go to hell!
You ought to be the first, Esther. C'mon, get out of here, so you can wink
at that fruit vendor once more!

Jesus: It's funny the way we are. We men are very strict with women,
and yet we don't realize how much they have to put up with with us men;
we make it difficult for them, as if we're making them swallow camels as
big as this . . .

James: Why do you say that now?

Jesus: Why do I say that? Look, James, we know ourselves very well. It's
better to talk, isn't it?

James: Fine. We'll talk. But I know this, and you can't talk around it:
I'm a man.

Jesus: Yeah, of course, of course. And God gave the commandments to
Moses, not to his wife.

James: It was Moses who gave men the right to abandon their wives and be divorced if they had good reason. Right?

Jesus: Yeah, because maybe he was thinking of the brutality and callousness of men. So Moses thought: "It is better for the wife to kick him out of the house; that way, at least he won't beat her to a pulp." But it wasn't so at the beginning, do you hear? God wanted the man and the woman to live together with the same rights and obligations for both. What God has joined, let no one put asunder anytime he pleases.

Salome: Well, I'd rather we talk than see you quarreling with one another. This is how people get to understand each other. What do you say, Esther?

Esther: We talk? Your son isn't capable of talking. All he can do is shout while I bow down my head: that's his idea of talking.

James: Well, the husband is supposed to have the last say, don't you think so?

Esther: Sure, you have the last say, and the first and the middle too.

Jesus: God had the first say when he took out the woman from Adam's rib. He didn't take her out of the sole of his foot, nor did he mold her from another clay. He took her from here, beside the heart. God didn't want to give him a slave, but a companion.

A Girl: Your blessing, grandma!

Another Girl: Grandma, grandma!

At that moment, Esther and James's three daughters entered the house. Mila, the eldest, was four years old, and had very long braids. Terina, the second, was holding Naomi by the hand. The latter, who was the youngest, could hardly walk.

James: Why did you bring the girls, Esther?

Esther: Why did I bring them? I'm taking them with me.

James: What?

Esther: I'm taking them to Bethsaida. They're my daughters, aren't they? I brought them into this world.

James: Oh, of course, and I didn't do anything? Is that it? A little angel who passed through the window did it. Look at their hair: it's as red as mine. The girls will stay with me. My mother, Salome, will look after them. The girls stay here, do you understand? They stay here!

Jesus: That's enough, James, stop screaming! You say their hair is as red as yours. Don't look at their hair, but their eyes: look at them. Come, Mila, come. Look at her eyes, James. They look at you with fear, because, ever since your children were born, they've heard nothing but your screams and received nothing but beatings. You yourself have said before: it's better to be alone than to have a bad companion. That's true. It's better for your children to be orphaned than to have a father who's like a centurion. Go ahead, Esther, take your daughters with you. May God help you to be a mother and father to them at the same time.

James: Hey, what're you saying, Jesus? That, that can't be. Wait a minute, Esther, wait.

Esther: Now what?

James: I well, I...

Esther: You, yes, you, who always protest against the abuses of the rulers and of King Herod, are a tyrant, worse than they are to your family. James, the son of Zebedee, who talks about justice and sharing the world's wealth with others! Yeah, yeah, but with your wife, you're incapable of sharing even your wages! Is this the kind of justice you're talking about?

Jesus: Your wife is right, red head. We keep on saying that things ought to change in our country. I guess we have to clean our own backyard first, don't you think?

James: But, I, I... What must I do in order to...? The truth is, I, I...

Jesus: Forget about yourself! That's what you've got to do, James! Forget about yourself and think of your wife a little, of making her happy.

James: Well, Esther. So I say you... Pff... If you want, we can... Hell, how difficult it is to ask for forgiveness. You know what I mean, what I ask of you... King David also made a mistake, and look, he ended up singing psalms.

Salome: Well, whatever it is that you want to say, say it at home. These little creatures are already hungry, and it's time I serve the soup!

Esther's face was brightening up. The girls immediately left running toward home and, as always, made a lot of noise. The truth is my brother James was a difficult and stubborn man. But he was different that day. And little by little, he and all of us learned how to treat others the way we would want others to treat us.

•

The gospels hardly tell us anything about the daily lives of Jesus' disciples. But as in any other life, they also experienced joys and sufferings and passed through difficult moments, whether great or small. Like any-one, they also had their bad moods, quarrels, and silly moments. And like all people, they also had internal struggles to become better individuals. James's argument with his wife — a spat common among married cou-ples — gives an occasion for Jesus to share with him and with the rest of the family his ideas about marriage: ideas that were enormously novel in his time.

Jewish laws and customs regarding women were without any doubt pro-masculine. A daughter was under her father's care until she became twelve years old. After this, she could get married — very often, the father chose the groom for her. Thus marriage served as a kind of transition of the woman from her father's custody to that of the husband. Once married, the woman had the right to be supported by her spouse, although her husband's rights were superior by far. The wife was obliged to perform household chores and to obey her spouse with an obedience that was understood to be more of a religious duty. She was virtually his servant. Above all, the husband enjoyed two rights which totally tilted the balance with respect to the nonexisting conjugal equality: the right to have as many lovers as he pleased, if he could maintain them, and the right to divorce, which depended exclusively on him.

Divorce was practiced in Israel. And the "evil" that sprang from this practice was the fact that such unilateral dependence on the man gave rise to a situation that was truly unjust for women. The law of Moses al-lowed for the repudiation of the woman (Deut. 24:1). But in his time, Jesus questioned the reasons for her rejection, and the legal motives for divorce. There were two ways of interpreting this old law. For some people, the granting of divorce could be justified only by grievous reasons (principally adultery). For others, flimsy reasons were sufficient: for example, the wife had burned the food, spent too much time idling and gossiping with neigh-bors, and so on. In practice, and since society was intensely "macho," the latter was imposed. Thus, there were divorces motivated by whatever rea-son. Because of the stigma she was carrying, the rejected wife was left in a situation of serious abandonment. Right from the start, she hardly had an opportunity to live without being dependent on a man.

What Jesus basically teaches us regarding matrimony has a lot to do with the customs of his country. The famous phrase "What God has joined let no man put asunder" does not state an abstract principle on matrimony. "Man" must be read as "the male." Jesus concretely rejects masculine arbitrariness. Let no "male" separate what God has joined. This means that the family should not be left to the whims of the man, and that the wife should not be rendered helpless because of the intransigence of the husband. In the face of confusing legal interpretations about divorce, which were always favorable to the husband, Jesus goes back to the beginning. The history of creation as told in Genesis points out the fact that God created man and woman in God's image. Therefore, they are equal in dignity and have the same rights and opportunities. This is not to say that if the woman is to decide the divorce, then separation becomes valid. No, the Christian ideal is, obviously, matrimony "forever," since it entails responsibility and love between the couple, which is really what is desirable. This is viewed not only from the Christian angle, but also from the point of view of human maturity. The separation of spouses will never be a solution, a panacea for the disease. As in all medicine, this "remedy" must be dispensed with precaution, only when it is really necessary, and when there is no other way out. It is a painful decision, with many social consequences — especially for children. Therefore it should not be taken lightly. The same applies as in medicine: an overdose can kill the patient.

(Matt. 19:1–9; Mark 10:1–12)

72

Along Different Roads

Beside the big square in Capernaum, in the fishermen's barrio, there is a well they call "the whispering well." Every morning when the sun rises above the horizon, the women gather by the well to fetch water.

A Neighbor: Have you seen the face of that girl? How deep are the bags around her eyes! She was so quiet. She didn't even utter a word while she was here. And to think what a blabber-mouth she usually is!

Old Woman: She's too young to be sick. She's in love "She's love struck." Didn't you hear how she sighed while she was leaving?

Salome: Good morning everyone! How's everything this morning, neighbors?

Another Neighbor: We've got energy to work, Salome, while we're still strong and healthy.

Neighbor: You can say that again. Well, we've been talking about young Rachel.

Salome: What's happened to her?

Old Woman: Haven't you seen here lately? She looks very pale and stares with a blank look on her face.

Neighbor: You talk to her but she doesn't respond.

Salome: She must be sick.

Neighbor: Nothing of the sort. She's just in love. The girl's in love. And you ought to know this, because in a way it also concerns you.

Salome: What are you talking about? What have I got to do with the girl's being in love?

Neighbor: Salome, how come you haven't discovered it yet? Rachel is interested in Jesus of Nazareth. Don't tell me you haven't noticed how she looks at him every time he speaks.

Another Neighbor: And don't deny that she's been going to your house everyday this week.

Salome: Well, the girl needed some salt and she came to ask me for some.

Old Woman: And the following day, she wanted a tomato.

Neighbor: And some flour the day after.

Salome: Well, yes.

Neighbor: Can't you see, Salome? She goes to your house hoping to see Jesus.

Neighbor: She also goes to the wharf like a crazy girl, goes up and down the street, and thinks she might see him with your sons. She's fallen for him. She can't deny that.

Salome: I wonder if what you're saying is possible.

Neighbor: Of course it is. Why don't you find out yourself and then tell us, huh?

Salome went back to her house and found Rachel milling around outside the door.

Rachel: Good morning, Salome!

Salome: Good morning. Ah, it's you. Come in, come in. What's up? Do you need anything, Rachel, my child?

Rachel: Salome, I need a little oil.

Salome: Why? Did you run out of oil?

Rachel: Well, I've got very little left, and I'm not sure if I'll have enough for tomorrow. I'd better be sure.

Salome: Of course, of course. But why don't you come in? Don't stay there at the door.

Rachel: Are you, are you alone?

Salome: Yes, my child, old Zebedee and the boys are out fishing, as always.

Rachel: Yeah, of course, they're working.

Salome: One must work in order to eat, child. God said that since the beginning; you must earn your bread by working hard.

Rachel: And, and no one else is here, is that right? Then, I'm going now.

Salome: What about the oil you needed?

Rachel: Gosh, I forgot. With so much work I have at home, I forget everything, and what with ten brothers to attend to...

Salome: Don't leave yet, child. Why don't you sit for a while so we can chat? That way, you can relax a little.

Rachel: Well, but...

Salome: Nothing. C'mon, sit here. That's right. How I wish I had a daughter like you that I could chat with. But you've seen what I have, two boys. When you have your own children, ask the Lord to give you sons and daughters. Men are the bread-winners, while we are the molders.

Rachel: Oh, Salome, how can I have children? I've got a long way to go yet.

Salome: No, my child, you're of marrying age now. And I bet you often think of it too. Am I right?

Rachel's face became redder than the scarf she was wearing on her head. She was quiet. But her heart was about to burst.

Salome: Look, child, I, I want to help you. Tell me everything. You have no mother, and somehow you've got to tell someone what's inside your heart.

Rachel: Ma'm Salome, oh, Ma'm Salome, it's been a month that I can't sleep and ...

Salome: And at night, you think of him. You think of Jesus, don't you?

Rachel: How, how did you know?

Salome: Oh my child, love is like a bell. It creates a loud noise for everyone to hear.

Rachel: Do you think it's something wrong?

Salome: No, my dear, why would it be wrong? You're just in love. I'd be very happy if that guy found a girl and married her once and for all. With the kind of life he has, it would be good for him to get married, so he could settle down.

Rachel: Do you think he'd fall for me?

Salome: Well, child, this Jesus is a little weird, and I wouldn't know how to explain that to you, but don't worry, I'll help you. He's been living with us for quite a while now, and I'm beginning to know him. Yeah, let me handle this.

That night, when the men came back from fishing, Salome talked to Zebedee about her chat with Rachel.

Salome: Old man, you've got to talk to Jesus. And talk to him clearly.

Zebedee: Sure, I'll talk to him. If you insist that this girl is deserving.

Salome: Rachel is a nice, hardworking, and loving girl. Besides, she's pretty. I think she loves him very much. What else would he want?

Zebedee: Ah, old woman, no one will ever know. Jesus is Jesus. Okay, I'll talk to him. Man to man. I wonder why this rascal doesn't get married. Every time I see him leave for the square to work, I've always asked myself that question, and when he gets back at night nothing! I think he's a little weirdo!

The next time Zebedee saw Jesus alone, he decided to bring up the subject.

Zebedee: I'll get to the point, Jesus.

Jesus: Sure, Zebedee, to the point.

Zebedee: For several days, I've been trying to talk to you, seriously and candidly.

Jesus: Why, is something wrong?

Zebedee: Jesus, I'm talking to you as a father and as a friend. I'm very fond of you, young man. The truth is, and I'm talking to you as a man, I don't understand why you haven't gotten yourself a wife and have continued to be a bachelor.

Jesus: Oh, is that it?

Zebedee: Yeah, that's it. Now answer me.

Jesus: Well, I don't know. I thought you were going to ask me to forget all about this mess I'm into, and I wasn't expecting your question.

Zebedee: Listen to me, young man. Life goes by fast. A man's strength wears off sooner than you'd expect. You always talk about God, what he wants. Well then, if God had put in man the seed of life, it was for him to sow it in the woman, so that she wouldn't remain sterile. Is that right or wrong?

Jesus: Sure, it's right. The Lord wants to see all trees bear fruit.

Zebedee: So why the hell do you remain alone?

Jesus: But I'm never alone, Zebedee. Ever since we formed our group and started to work for the Kingdom of God, I've always been surrounded by people.

Zebedee: No, no, you can't get away from me the way the flying fish do, rascal. I mean "alone" at night, without a wife, without children. You will always be surrounded with people, but one thing doesn't cancel the other. Don't you try to confuse me. Look, Jesus, when a man has no wife, all his energy goes up to his brains, and he ends up a crazy man! I wouldn't want the same thing to happen to you.

Jesus: Do I look like a mad man?

Zebedee: No, that's not what I mean, but . . .

Jesus: Look, Zebedee, now I remember something I heard once in the synagogue: that the solitary man is not a dead tree, because even single people have a place in the house of God.

Zebedee: There you go again. Say, Jesus, let's forget about those beautiful words and let's get to the point. Don't you like women? Or are you gay? Is that it? No, no, don't tell me anything! I've never thought of that as a reason for your not wanting to get married.

Jesus: Don't talk that way, Zebedee. Gays are not filthy slobs.

Zebedee: Ah, no? So what are they?

Jesus: They are also people whom God loves. Neither are they dead trees.

Zebedee: C'mon, Jesus, don't defend them!

Jesus: Neither should you criticize them, Zebedee. What do you know about them and their problems?

Zebedee: Okay, okay. You're not one of them. Why don't you get married then? Don't tell me you haven't found a woman of your choice.

Jesus: Well, I met a girl once a couple of years ago. But I wasn't sure.

Zebedee: You'll be an old bachelor all your life! Is that what you want?

Jesus: Wait a minute, Zebedee. To be single is one thing and to be an old bachelor is another.

Zebedee: Bah, a single man is half a man, and the daughter who remains a virgin is a shame to her parents.

Jesus: Those who are self-centered are the ones who are only half a man or half a woman, and you can be married and be self-centered. Whether you're married or not isn't the issue.

Zebedee: Jesus, listen to me, there's a girl in town who is in love with you.

Jesus: So, that's where we have been heading.

Zebedee: If you can't see that someone is in love with you, then somehow you must be told about it, damn it!

Jesus: And who is she?

Zebedee: She's Rachel, the late Hagar's daughter, who has several little brothers.

Jesus: Oh, yeah, now I know. She seems to be a nice girl.

Zebedee: She's a very nice girl! She'd make a good wife for you!

Jesus: Yeah, that's possible, Zebedee, but . . .

Zebedee: No more buts. Today you're going to see her, talk to her, and then you can start planning things.

Jesus: Wait a minute, Zebedee. Don't rush.

Zebedee: What's the matter? Don't you like her? You prefer another one? Is that it? That's okay. Trust me, young man, this will be between the two of us only.

Jesus: I love all of them, Zebedee.

Zebedee: Lies! If you say you love them all, then you don't love anyone at all!

Jesus: Really, I love all of them! That's why I wanna be free to be able to help them.

Zebedee: Who do you think you are, the protector of abandoned women?

Jesus: That's not it, Zebedee. The truth is I want to work for my people. You know how difficult things are now. Look what happened to the prophet John. He was beheaded. How can one have a wife and support her in this anguished state? What will happen to the children? If they lose their father, who'll earn a living for them? Really, Zebedee, I need to have free hands, more so at this time. God is so much in a hurry that even in my sleep, I have my sandals on.

Zebedee: You make things look horrible, Jesus. I didn't say you should put your arms up and do nothing. But, hell, can't you go on with the struggle and be married?

Jesus: Well, of course you can. Look at Peter, who has his wife, Rufina, his four sons, and another one who was just born. There's James, who is also married. John is single, but Andrew has a girlfriend, and he's getting married soon. There's a place for everyone in God's Kingdom, where everyone counts, whether married, widows, or single.

Zebedee: But you . . . you . . .

Jesus: What about me, Zebedee?

Zebedee: You haven't done anything in order to get married!

Jesus: Nor have I done anything so as not to get married!

Zebedee: So, what now?

Jesus: Nothing, Zebedee. Let each one take his or her own road and see what God asks. Look, God called Abraham from the north and Moses from the south. Along different roads, the two men arrived at the Promised Land.

•

Only the gospel of Matthew mentions what Jesus said about "the eunuchs, the castrated, the celibates for the kingdom," which provides support for this episode. The text is one of the "enigmatic" sayings of Jesus, in the sense that it is difficult for us to comprehend the exact meaning today as well as the exact historical occasion. The saying is likewise enigmatic considering how strange it must have seemed to his contemporaries. Everything seems to indicate that Jesus tried to explain with these phrases his personal situation to those who questioned him about it.

In Israel, neither virginity, nor the state of being single, nor celibacy was understood to be a stable situation or was viewed as being of any value whatsoever. Rather, these states were antivalue, a disgrace, and something negative. The virginity of a woman was most appreciated only before matrimony. Such virginity before marriage had to be protected. It was an honor not only for her but also for the family to bring it to matrimony. But a woman who did not marry and have children was a disgrace, a family stigma. This was also true for the man. An unmarried man, for whatever reason, was viewed as somewhat weird, as incomprehensible, unless he had made a special vow (some of the Essene monks, for example). The principal value was sexual relations and fertility. The rest did not figure in the set of values of the people. Therefore, they were understood to be contrary to the will of the God of life. All Scriptures highlight the importance of matrimony, the sexual union between the man and the woman, as something positive, beautiful, and an ultimate expression of human relation as the most appropriate image of the love that God feels for his people. Whatever contempt, disdain, or rejection there is of human sexuality has nothing to do with the biblical message; it is in contradiction to the biblical message.

Jesus did not marry. Although this is not explicitly said in any text in the New Testament, we consider it as something historical. Given the same data, the same can be said of John the Baptist. Nevertheless, that Jesus did not marry does not mean that he was asexual, that sex meant nothing to him. Jesus was a man, not a woman. As such, he had a male sexual dimension. In this sense, it would not be out of place to think that there were women attracted to him. Nothing of this sort appears in the gospels, not because it did not exist in his life, but precisely because in the thinking of his contemporaries, it was somewhat natural not to write about the topic. Neither do the gospels say that Jesus sneezed or suffered from stomach pains or hummed a song. It is practically certain all these occurred. Textually speaking, Jesus refers to three types of eunuchs (the unmarried, the impotent, the men without wives). The first are "those who were born that way from their mothers' womb." There have always been males who, due to some physical defects — generally congenital — cannot have sexual relations with women. Within this group is included the homosexual. The other group referred to by Jesus was composed of those "who were made eunuchs by others." These are the castrated boys and men. Throughout history — and even today — male castration has been institutionalized. In Oriental courts, the kings castrated their men who served as guardians of their harems, in order to make sure that they did not have any relations with their women. In other countries, castration was done in order to obtain greater intelligence, for example, among the teachers. War, pleasure, and power were considered to correspond to man, while delicate work, a certain knowledge, and so on, were considered to be the province of the woman — or "effeminate," when done by a male.

In Israel, religious law did not allow the castration of men or livestock. The castrated man could not enter the temple or the synagogue, nor could a castrated animal be offered as sacrifice. However, there were several castrated men in the courts of the kings of Israel, influenced by other Oriental countries or because they were brought in as slaves. Finally, Jesus speaks textually of a third group of men: "Those who have been made eunuchs for the Kingdom of God."

This type of singleness or virginity — the celibate "for the kingdom" — is a new category that Jesus brings. After him, Christianity presented an alternative to the panorama of sexuality, as it had been understood until then in the Old Testament. This alternative was "relational celibacy." That is, celibacy is not a value in itself, but in relation to the kingdom: for the kingdom. That was Jesus' option. He did not marry not because he was sexually abnormal or was castrated, not because he was impotent or was a type of "old bachelor" who was scared of women and shied away from them. Neither was he the type who sought a solitary life as a rejection of communal life or a life of coexistence.

Rather, he remained single and rejected matrimony for the "sake of the kingdom." Jesus profoundly lived the "urgency" of the Kingdom of God. He conceived of his mission as something tremendously important, which needed to be carried out in a short time. The time was short. And God's time was passing, and there was no time to waste.

The way he understood his vocation is at the bottom of Jesus' option not to marry. To serve the kingdom is, in essence, the justification of Christian celibacy. When commitment to the kingdom is radically lived, one can be in a situation that is truly compatible with a normal family life. But celibacy allows for a certain mobility, poverty, and freedom which, in principle, marriage cannot offer.

Any stand on sexuality is valid before God. There is no need from the biblical or Christian point of view to categorize virgins and married ones as "better" and "worse," as first- or second-class Christians, as perfect or imperfect. Much less are condemnations necessary. As regards homosexuality, the gospels — which do not mention anything explicitly — say it all in the context of proclaiming very strongly human freedom and the respect for people. In any case, society's rejects — the ridiculed, the outcasts — are the privileged ones in God's love. It is important to recall the beautiful phrase about them from the prophet Isaiah, a phrase that Jesus remembers in this episode (Isa. 56:3–5). God so loves them that he makes them heirs to his promise (Wisd. 3:14).

Everything mentioned by Jesus in Matthew's text makes explicit reference to the male. Female sexuality, its characteristics, and its problems were avoided as subjects of serious consideration until relatively recently. Until very recently, it was thought that the only value in female sexuality was fertility. Woman's pleasure in sexual relations was viewed as something suspicious, if not bad. On the other hand, since it was not a woman's "decision" to marry or not, but her parents', neither could the question of female celibacy be presented. Nevertheless, in other societies at present, and with the evolution of ideas, we can say that what is basic in Christian celibacy — greater freedom to live and die for the kingdom — is equally applied to man and woman alike. They are equally capable of this option which they can fully carry out as members of society.

(Matt. 19:10–12)

73

The Death of a Greedy Old Man

Woman Neighbor: Holy God, have you seen how Manasses is suffering?
Another Neighbor: Poor man, he's always been so good!
Neighbor: That's life, woman, he'll end up in the grave. But what a misfortune!

For two days, old Manasses, one of the richest men in Capernaum, had been agonizing on his soft, wooden bed. And for two days, his neighbors flocked to his house awaiting the end.

Manasses: Oh, damn!
Neighbor: What's hurting you, old man?
Manasses: Everything! My whole body aches! Oh, oh!
Neighbor: Do you want anything, Manasses? Some water, perhaps? or hot soup?
Manasses: I want nothing, damn it! All I want is to get up from this damned bed and drive you all away from my house.
Neighbor: What's keeping this old man from dying?
Another Neighbor: Only the good die young, don't forget.
Neighbor: Poor Manasses, he's been good, very good! Death is like a thief in the night. It comes any moment, and it's coming for him.
Manasses: Oooh! Damn . . . Daaaamnnn . . .
Neighbor: Is he dying?
Another Neighbor: Wait a moment. Let's see. Yeah, I think so.
Male Neighbor: I guess he's passed away already! He's very pale!
Neighbor: Yeah, he's dead!
Another Neighbor: May he rest in the peace of the Lord!
Another Neighbor: May the angels take him to Abraham!
Neighbor: And let's see what we can take along with us!
Neighbor: I'll take the chickens!
Another Neighbor: But didn't I tell you that the chickens were mine?

Male Neighbor: Hey, don't quarrel! There's enough for everyone! The poultry yard is full!

Another Neighbor: Hey, Clete, take a look at that chest and see what's inside!

Neighbor: Hey, madame, this sack of flour belongs to someone already.

Woman Neighbor: Oh dear! After having waited since yesterday, do you mean to say that I'll be left with nothing? To hell with you! That sack is mine!

Male Neighbor: It's mine! And the flour too!

Woman Neighbor: Where do you think this old man hid his money, huh? That's more important!

Manasses's neighbors ransacked the whole house for any loot, while the mourners intoned their mourning songs. The children, each one carrying three or four chickens, leaped over the garden wall. Meanwhile, their mothers searched thoroughly through the chests.

Manasses: Ooooh! I am not dead. I am not dead, and I don't intend to die yet!

Everybody, with hands full of the loot, stopped, scared stiff. Manasses, who was seated painfully on his bed, looked at them defiantly.

Neighbor: Who the hell said he's dead?

Woman Neighbor: Old Manasses has a long way to go. Be patient!

Manasses: No, no, I don't want to die. Go away, vultures! Go to hell, all of you! All you want is to rob me of my wealth. Everything is mine! And it remains here, in my house oh, oh . . .

Woman Neighbor: C'mon, Manasses, take it easy; that's it, that's it.

Woman Neighbor: Don't exhaust yourself. Rest. Just rest.

Manasses lay down again, his eyes closed, and he was nearly out of breath. Things went back to normal, while the old mourners pulled their hair but stopped weeping. At this moment, when even the chickens were running loose in the garden and the entire house was in disarray, the two sons of Manasses appeared at the door. They lived in Perea, which was a long way from Capernaum, and they had received the news about their dying father.

Joel: What the hell is all this mess?

Woman Neighbor: Look who're here, Joel and Jason!

Jason: What's happening here? What're you all doing here?

Woman Neighbor: We're here to help your dying father.

Woman Neighbor: He's been in a lot of agony, poor man.

Joel: And you've been helping yourselves as well, to everything that you see in all corners of this house!

Manasses: They wanted to strip me naked of my wealth. Damned vultures! Get out of my house, I'm commanding you! Oh, oh, oh!

Joel: Out, out, all of you! Get out of here!

Jason: Papa, poor Papa.

Joel: Out, out you go, everybody, damn it! And the mourners too! And don't take anything from here, do you hear? Not even a needle should be taken away from here.

One by one, with bowed heads, the neighbors left Manasses's place. The long hours of vigil had been in vain: the sons of the rich farmer, heirs to his fortune, had arrived in time.

Manasses: Are they gone?

Jason: Yes, Papa.

Manasses: They wanted to strip me naked of my wealth.

Joel: But they have not succeeded. Oh, Papa, see how people can be so cruel. All they could think of is taking possession of the wealth that you painstakingly accumulated!

Jason: We learned about your condition only yesterday. That's why we didn't come before.

Manasses: I . . . I'm dying, damn it! I'm ill. It's just that . . . It's just that . . . Oh, oh, I feel so bad, oh . . .

Joel: You had better rest, Papa. Let's make you comfortable. That's it, that's it.

Manasses: Oh, oh, oh.

Jason: Where do you think he's put his money?

Joel: How would I know?

Jason: Yeah, you know it, Joel! You know where he put it, don't deny it!

Manasses: Oh, oh, oh!

Joel: Sshh, don't shout, Jason; he might hear us!

Jason: He might hear us, he might hear us! Well, let him hear us. What do I care? Half of that money is mine. You know that as much as I do.

Joel: You know fully well that all the old man's wealth belongs to me, and only to me. I'm the eldest son and according to the law, it belongs to me. The law is the law.

Jason: The law says that the younger son has a right to the inheritance.

Joel: Not if the inheritance is little, so the money can't be divided. Then it all goes to the oldest son, to me.

Jason: Do you know how much Papa earned? You say it can't be touched, because you want to have it all. Damn you, greedy man! You're already rich, yet you want to have more!

Manasses: Oh, oh, oooh!

Joel: Yes, Papa, we're here beside you. Take it easy, Papa. We know you're suffering! Now let's see who's the avaricious one. Your wool business is going fine, isn't it? What do you need the money for, huh? To give alms to the poor? You can't deceive me, Jason. You're more ambitious than an Assyrian king!

Manasses: Oh, oh, these pricking pains!

Jason: What's wrong, Papa?

Joel: Do you need anything?

Manasses: I, I don't want to die.

Jason: Don't think of dying now, Papa. You're as strong as cedar from Lebanon. You'll be all right. Tomorrow or the day after tomorrow, you'll get up from your bed, I'm sure. And you'll continue working on the farm.

Manasses: This year harvest has been so good, did you know? There's no more room for wheat in the barns. Ha, ha. I'm goin' to tear down the old barns and build bigger ones beside the house, and money will flow like honey. Yes, it'll flow like honey! Oh, oh, oh, it's painful!

Joel: What does he need the money for? To hide it in a pit underground? What a miserly old man.

Jason: And you, what do you need it for? So that you can spend it all as you please?

Joel: How selfish you are, Jason. Papa is panting like a wounded dog, while here you are thinking only of the money.

Jason: And what's on your mind, you wretch? Your eyes have been sparkling like gold ever since you got here!

At Zebedee's house Jesus stood up suddenly and moved toward the door.

John: Where are you going, Jesus?

Jesus: To old Manasses's house, John. Do you know that he's dying?

John: Yeah, but my friend Clete says he's got a long way to go. That old man is holding on to his life like a leech. Nothing can banish him from this world

Manasses's house was almost dark when Jesus and I reached it. In one corner of the room the two brothers were whispering to each other.

Jesus: May we come in?

Joel: Who are you?

Jesus: We know your father.

John: They told us he was very ill, and so we have come to visit him.

Jason: To visit him and to find out what you can get from him. Am I right?

John: Why do you say that?

Jason: Because all those who visit him have sharp fangs ready to take advantage of our poor Papa!

Jesus: You must be his sons who live in far away Perea?

Joel: That's right. We arrived a few hours ago.

Jason: So, you're our father's friends.

Jesus: Well, not really friends. Manasses never had friends, and that's the truth. He lived all by himself, ate and slept all by himself, and, in the end, he even talked to himself.

Jason: And he never bothered to tell anyone where the hell he hid his money. He's dying and we'll have to demolish the house and dig into the entire farm just to find it!

Joel: Why do you say "we"? You won't be doing anything because this inheritance is mine. Do you understand, Jason?

Jason: Damn you, Joel, there you go again! I've told you a thousand times that half of that money belongs to me, to me! Let's see, please tell us if I'm right or wrong: our father saved . . . Tell him, stranger, tell him that the law provides that he has to divide the inheritance with me!

Joel: Don't involve anyone in this! This is just between you and me!

Jesus: Listen, friend, who am I to meddle in your mess? I'm not a lawyer or a judge.

Jason: Papa's money is mine, Joel!

Joel: It's mine, Jason!

Manasses: Papa's money belongs to Papa! It's mine, mine, and not even you or anyone else can take that away from me! Scoundrels! You, my sons, are also thieves who want to rob me of my fortune and leave me with nothing!

Jesus: C'mon, old man, take it easy. I'm Jesus, staying in Zebedee's place. And this is John. We came to visit you.

Manasses: You have come to see what you can steal from my house. But you'll leave with your hands empty. I don't intend to die. I'll have new barns constructed for my wheat this year and for many years. Oh, oh . . .

Jesus went near Manasses and gently closed his eyes.

John: He's dead.

Jesus: This is sad, isn't it, John? Old Manasses thought of nothing his whole life but to amass wealth. He had no time for anyone. He never wept for anyone, neither did he know how to be happy. Of what use were all these things of his? Nothing. They were there for the moths to feed on. He came into this world naked and left this world naked. What's the use of piling up things if he has lost his life? Let's go, John.

Jason: Where the devil could he have hidden the money, Joel?

Joel: The old man's money is mine, Jason, and don't you insist anymore!

Jason: Go to hell, Joel, I tell you.

While the neighbors and mourners kept on coming to the house, old Manasses's sons started to search the whole house, hoping to find in some nook their dead father's savings. They were like two vultures tearing at a carcass.

•

The Roman conquest brought to Israel, among other things, a radical transformation in land ownership. Before then, it existed in two forms: the *latifundium* (or large landed estate), which came about by expansion, and communal property, which was divided into lots and tilled by cooperatives or by families. The collection of taxes imposed by the Romans led to the gradual impoverishment and indebtedness of farmers. Many were forced to sell their lands. This hastened even more the process of concentration into big landed estates. This system of landed estates was eventually imposed because it turned out to be more profitable. The figure of the big landowner, the proprietor who continuously accumulated wealth, had huge granaries, and enjoyed profits "without having to work," was very common in Jesus' time, especially in the Galilean region. In the upper reaches of the Jordan, along the banks of the river and in the mountains of Galilee, the arable lands were already large estates. Some parables, like that of the "rich fool," are told in the gospels in such a vivid manner that it is believed that Jesus didn't make up the story, but simply referred to a fact well known to his listeners. In our episode, Jesus appeared among those who were awaiting the death of the landowner Manasses, people eager to hear what Jesus had to say about avarice, life's meaning (Matt. 16:26), and real wealth. Jesus was not alien to the history of his time. He came with messages and lessons about compassion for those who came to listen to him. His words, his good news, reflected his thoughts on everything he saw and experienced. They were the consequence of his observations and his having lived with the people. This is also true for us, as we form our own conclusions about life in this world, when we live and share our experiences with others. Jesus strongly criticized the rich and showed how he distanced himself from money. Wealth hardens the heart and alienates people. Jesus saw a serious danger in riches, since they become a supreme value in life and a substitute for God (Matt. 6:24). Much as one may claim to be maintaining faith, one becomes an enemy of God through avarice, ambition, and covetousness. This is because the values of the Kingdom of God — the full surrender of life, unity among brothers and sisters, loyalty, respect for others, the desire to share what one possesses, the drive to serve and construct a just world — are diametrically opposed to ownership and accumulation of wealth, which should be an important consideration for those who idolize the god of money.

(Luke 12:13–21)

74

The Judge and the Widows

Peter: Look, Jesus, this is ridiculous. We've already used twelve pairs of sandals in announcing that things are heading for a change and that justice and liberation are at hand. But what have we accomplished up to now?

Jesus: Be patient.

Peter: Yeah, be patient. You've gotta open your eyes, dark one! This is getting us nowhere. It's like moving a mountain.

Jesus: And it will move, Peter. The moment we really have faith in the Lord and in ourselves, we shall indeed move mountains and cast them into the sea. I learned this lesson from my mother. When I was a little boy in Nazareth, my mother, who was already a widow, worked on the farm of the landlord Ananias. We heard conversations like this:

Susana: What a rascal this Ananias is! How I wish this millstone would crush his kidneys!

Rebecca: For three weeks we have been gathering olives for him, and yet he doesn't want to pay us. No, this can't be. I swear, by the trumpets of Jericho, that the whole world will know of his brazenness, and this old man will have to pay us to the last denarii, or else!

Michal: Or else what, Rebecca? No, woman, save your strength. What can we do if he doesn't pay us? Nothing. If our husbands were alive, they would defend us. But what can we do? We're widows. Take the yoke upon us and work like beasts.

Jesus: My mother, Mary, and her neighbor, Susana, together with the other widows of Nazareth, had not been paid their wages after harvesting olives from Ananias's farm. They were furious, for this happened many times: the landowners took advantage of the single women, who were hired to gather olives or tomatoes or figs. They got paid very little or nothing at all for the work.

Mary: We've gotta do something about this, neighbors. We can't go on like this, doing nothing, while our children go hungry.

Michal: Is there anything we can do, *comadre?** This is the fate of poor people like us, so let's just accept it.

Mary: What fate are you talking about? No Michal. I don't buy that. Do you know what Joseph, my late husband, used to say? May he rest in peace. He said that our destiny is in our own hands.

Susana: That's right, Mary, but we women are weak, don't forget that.

Mary: How can you say that, Susanna? Wasn't it Judith's hand that cut off the head of that giant whose name I don't even remember? When the men of Israel lost courage, who led the people against the attacks of the Canaanites? It was Deborah, a woman like you and me, in whose veins flowed blood and not water. And wasn't Queen Esther a fighter too?

Rebecca: Mary's right. The trouble is, the woman, for being alone, loses heart and ends up hiding in a cave like mice do.

Mary: Well, then, let's get out of this cave and punish the cat.

Susana: Yes, we've gotta do something for our sake, and for our children!

Mary: C'mon, let's all go to Cana and file a complaint against that old swindler. What are judges for, but to give justice, right? Let's see the judge right away, so he can take up our case in court.

Jesus: My mother and the other widows left Nazareth and headed north toward Cana where old Jacinth, the bald and fat judge, lived.

Rebecca: Judge Jacinth! Judge Jacinth! Judge Jacinth!

Jacinth: What's going on here? Damn it! Who are you?

Susana: We are the poor widows from Nazareth! We're here to tell you something! Please open the door!

Jacinth: Some poor widows. What do you want? Why do you bang my door?

Mary: Because we were deprived of our three-week wages after having worked under the sun.

Jacinth: So what?

---

*The *comadre* is a co-godparent or neighbor. There is no exact equivalent for the word in English. Trans.

Rebecca: You're a judge, aren't you? Aren't judges supposed to give justice?

Jacinth: We put troublemakers like you in jail. I'm very busy now, so please stop bothering me.

Mary: Sir, please wait, don't go away. You see, this old leech Ananias, whom you know better than we do, hired us to gather olives for him. A week passed, but he didn't pay us. The second week and the third week came, but nothing. Do you think this is fair?

Jacinth: So what do you want now?

Susana: We want to sue him in court, and we'd like you to give us justice.

Jacinth: Well, let's start from the beginning: If I defend you in court, how much are you going to pay me?

Michal: How's that again, judge? Please speak more clearly. We come from the poor district.

Jacinth: I say, if I take up your case, how much money are you going to pay me, damn it?

Mary: Well, sir, as you can see, we're all widows, poor widows at that. Besides, how can we pay you if Ananias doesn't pay us yet?

Jacinth: I understand. In that case come back next time. I'm very busy today. That's right, come back next week I'll see what I can do for you.

Jesus: So, from Cana, my mother and her neighbors walked seven miles back to Nazareth. After a week...

Susana: Please give us justice, sir! Judge Jacinth, please!

Rebecca: We'll pay you something from what Ananias will have to give us, if you defend our cause.

Jacinth: Something, something. How much? Tell me, how much are you paying me?

Michal: Well, we can collect ten denarii or even fifteen from all of us.

Jacinth: Damn it, fifteen denarii! I'll be damned. You're paying me fifteen denarii! You've come to ask me to confront the most powerful man around, who, by the snap of his finger, can have me hanged, and, in return, you're paying me fifteen filthy denarii! Puah!

Susana: Please understand, sir, that we're only poor.

Jacinth: Of course I understand, and you too must understand that I've got much work to do, and I can't attend to you. Ehem. That's it, come back next week and we'll see.

Jesus: Seven miles of journey back to Nazareth. After a week, they again traveled seven miles to Cana.

Susana: But sir, how long do we have to keep coming back?

Rebecca: Our children are skin and bones already!

Michal: See these breasts of mine, judge! They've dried up! We're all desperate. We can't stand this anymore. Our children are dying of hunger, and they're getting sick.

Jacinth: What have I gotta do with that, huh? I didn't give birth to those kids. So why bother me? Why don't you settle this among yourselves? Go away and stop pestering me.

Mary: Fine, don't do it for our sake, if you don't want to.

Jacinth: And for whose sake, may I ask?

Mary: Do it for the love of God, judge!

Jacinth: Ha, ha, ha! For God? What do I care about God? He's up there in heaven, while I'm down here on earth. Didn't you say that God gives justice to the poor? Why don't you go get yourselves a long ladder so you can reach him and ask his help? And stop bothering me!

Susana: Pff. What a sour character he is.

Mary: No, Susana, it's just that the fox in Ananias has gotten to him, do you understand?

Michal: What'll we do now, Mary? We're doomed.

Mary: No, we'll keep fighting!

Rebecca: But Mary, are you out of your mind? How can we fight without even a stick as a weapon!

Mary: We don't need sticks or swords for this, Rebecca.

Rebecca: So what do we do, Mary?

Mary: All we need is patience.

Susana: What for?

Mary: To put an end to his patience. Remember what Moses did in Egypt? The Pharaoh had everything, including war chariots! Moses had nothing. Well, the only thing he had was a stubborn head. Moses gathered all the Israelites and tested the Pharaoh's patience: by turning the water red, infesting the houses with toads and frogs, and turning the city into total darkness.

Susana: But Mary, we're just a handful of widows. Moses did it because he was a man and many people rallied behind him.

Michal: We're just like mosquitoes, while they're like elephants.

Mary: That's precisely the point, Michal. That was one of the ten plagues of Egypt, that of the mosquitoes. This I can assure you: a band of attacking mosquitoes can render sleepless all of King Solomon's elephants in the palace. Come with me; we're all going back to Jacinth's house!

Jesus: And so the obstinate peasants, together with Mary, my mother, who was their leader, went back to the front door of the fat judge.

Jacinth: You're here again! Damn it, I told you to go away and leave me in peace. Are you all deaf? What are you waiting for?

Mary: We're waiting for the judges of Israel to give justice to the poor.

Jacinth: Well, you've got to do it sitting down, because it will take a long time.

Mary: That's exactly what we're going to do. Neighbors, let's all sit down.

Jesus: When my mother said that, all the widows sat at the front door of the judge's house.

Jacinth: To hell with all of you! Okay, you may stay there, until your asses get numb. Damn you, peasants; your heads are as hard as stones.

Jesus: The judge slammed the door. After a while...

Jacinth: You're still seated there? By Jove, have you all lost your minds?

Susana: No, it's you who's losing your patience, judge!

Mary: We won't move from here until we get some justice.

Jesus: Then the judge slammed the door again.

Rebecca: You'll bring your house down if you keep slamming your door like that, judge.

Susana: What do you think, Mary? Will we achieve anything?

Mary: Our ancestors suffered for four hundred years in Egypt, until finally they obtained their freedom. We won't budge from here.

A Man: Hey, who're you? Are you begging alms from the judge?

Rebecca: We want justice, not alms.

Susana: We labored for three weeks gathering olives at Ananias's farm, and now he doesn't want to pay us.

Man: What a thief! What about the judge? Has he done anything yet?

Mary: That's what we've been waiting for. But you see, Ananias has slipped the judge money, and he in turn has slipped something to the captain, and so on and so forth.

Man: Yeah, you're right. The powerful protect one another, while we keep on pushing each other. Hey, fellas, come on over here, all of you!

Jesus: That man started to call his friends who were idle in the square and inside the tavern. Soon, a great number of people from Cana joined the widows from Nazareth.

Jacinth: Well I'll be damned! What do you want? I'm not the governor of Galilee, neither am I here to give you candies or sweets. So all of you: get lost and leave me in peace, you fools.

Jesus: More and more people joined them at the front door. They were like a plague of mosquitoes.

Jacinth: That's enough. To hell with all of you! Come inside and let's settle this matter once and for all.

Susana: So the judge has finally relented. He's tired of the mosquito bites.

Jacinth: I couldn't stand the scandal anymore. However, I want you to bear this in mind: I'm doing this not for God's sake, not for you, nor for your "starving children," but because I want to get rid of you and get you out of my sight.

Jesus: Judge Jacinth took the case to court, and the landlord Ananias had to pay the widows' wages. Yes sir, they won the fight! That's how all wars are won: you fight until the end. It's the same thing with the Lord. We pray day and night, without ceasing. If we do, he'll never let us down. He'll give us justice.

Rufa: God bless your lips, Jesus, and God bless the woman who brought you into this world.

Peter: Very well said, Grandma Rufa!

Jesus: Yeah, even more, God bless all those who fight to the end, whatever the cost.

•

In many ways, the women peasants of Israel had more freedom than those in the city. The need to feed a family caused them to work side by side with the men on the farms. The women and men harvested the grapes together; sometimes the women were hired to work alone.

When the Bible refers to a widow, we should never assume that she was old. Many girls got married at the ages of twelve or thirteen, and a lot of women became widowed at a very young age. Considering that when Jesus initiated his activities in Galilee his father had already passed away, Mary was widowed at thirty or forty. Her social condition made her dependent on her son, whose duty it was to support her. Likewise, she certainly had to work. The parable of the "evil judge" or that of the "persevering widows" in this episode is told by Jesus to his friends as a real experience of his mother and some widows like her.

The administration of justice in Israel traces its origin from the people's history, beginning with the ancestors designated by Moses. However, there is no remaining exact data from Jesus' time that show how justice was meted out and how cases were presented in court. The institutionalization of justice varied according to regions. Mary and her friends went to look for a local judge, who was residing in Cana, since Nazareth was too small a locality to have one. These judges decided less important cases in small localities. Sometimes, the rich would "buy" them off with gifts, and so no real justice was delivered in their decisions.

The prophets of Israel always fought for justice for the poor. They identified God's law with the rights of the poor. Among the poor were the foreigners, the orphans, and the widows, who were defenseless and, therefore, deserved justice more than anyone else. The prophets denounced the corruption in the courts, the bribes received by the judges, and the injustice they committed against these unfortunate souls (Amos 5:7–13).

In the history of Israel, a lot of women became known for their active part in the people's struggle. Deborah, the judge of Israel, won several battles (Judges 4 and 5); Esther, a very popular heroine, and Judith, who defeated the tyrant Holofernes, were significant female figures in the history of Israel for their courage and cunning. Mary, Jesus' mother, likewise left a mark in the history of Israel by helping establish the Kingdom of God through her work, her constant fidelity, and her courage in the face of adversity.

Mary, the mother of the people, a peasant and a laborer, ought to serve as inspiration to women. There is so much in common between her and the women in various societies today. Mary lived in a male chauvinistic society. She engaged in manual work and experienced the suffering of the poor: scarcity, insecurity, and discrimination. She had a son whose commitment to the cause of justice put her own life in jeopardy. Without fully comprehending Jesus' mission, she collaborated with him.

Mary is not only venerated but "adored." In the Magnificat, a hymn of faith in the Lord and a source of inspiration and hope for the poor, can be found all the elements necessary for a genuine veneration of Mary.

Like any child learning from his parents, Jesus learned the fundamental values in life from Joseph and Mary. He acquired Mary's tenacity, her constancy, that typical peasant obstinacy that can "move mountains." If the parable of the "evil judge" has been commonly regarded as an exhortation to the constancy of prayer, Jesus, in this episode, broadens its meaning: in prayer, we must also be as consistent, patient, and insistent as Mary. Prayer and action go hand in hand; they are nurtured by the same spirit and inspired by the same attitudes. Thus, Jesus presents Mary as a model of constancy of action.

There will be no freedom for women until men and women alike take part, hand in hand, in the construction of a world that is different from the present: a world that is free from discrimination of any type.

In this account, the widows' strategy to win the sentiment of the unjust judge was tenacity, in the form of nonviolence. They insisted, journeyed several times, pressured the judge with their words and screams, and staged a sit-down strike until they overcame the judge's resistance. Their unity gave them strength and victory.

(Luke 18:1–8)

75

The Feast of the Tents

Every autumn, when the barns are filled with wheat and the vineyards are teeming with grapes, all Israel travels south to celebrate the feast of the tents. For seven days, Jerusalem is dressed in green and adorned with leaves. Hundreds of huts made from palm trunks and branches surround the walls of the holy city in remembrance of the tents where our fathers lived during their long journey in the desert. The wine from the new harvest is drunk in abundance; euphoria spreads through the narrow streets of King David's city.

A Man: I bet my five donkeys he's coming to the feast.

Another Man: I won't call your bet. He's a marked man. He knows that if he comes, the Romans can grab him anytime.

Man: I wish I could see him at close range and listen to him. He's a prophet. Israel is never wanting in wine and in prophets. I drink to our country: the greatest in the whole world.

Another Man: Watch your tongue, big ear. Much more is said of Jesus of Galilee. John was a prophet, so they cut his head off. With Jesus, it's more. They say he's the Messiah.

Man: So they'll have him beheaded too?

Another Man: On the contrary, he'll have the Romans beheaded, damn it! If he's the Messiah, he'll come with his sword this long and — zas! Down with the imperial eagle! Ah, that'll be the day of grand feasting in Jerusalem. I give a toast to the Messiah of Galilee!

On the first day of the festival, when the first star began to shine in the sky, the big torches in the temple of Jerusalem were lighted. All night, the streets were crammed with singing and laughing pilgrims. Jerusalem jubilantly stood watch for a week-long festivity in thanksgiving to God for the fruits of the new harvest. Meanwhile, in Nazareth . . .

Mary: So my son, aren't you going to Jerusalem?

Jesus: I don't know, mother, I still don't know.

Mary: Your cousins wanted to go along with you.
Jesus: I see. The problem is I don't wish to go with them.

When that year's harvest was over, Jesus went to Nazareth to see his mother. Some of his friends went with him. The wheat fields lay idle after a long harvest time. The grapes had been sent to the winepress.

Jesus: How about you, mama? Aren't you going to the festival?
Mary: No, son. There's a lot to do around here. My comadre Susana is sick, and so is Nepthali's wife. Someone's got to look after the children.

Jesus' cousins, Simon and Jacob, entered Mary's house with their walking canes in hand.

Simon: You work so hard, Mary. Maybe that's your secret in staying young. So, what now, Jesus? Have you decided yet? Are you going with us to Jerusalem?
Jesus: No, I'm not going. I'm staying in Galilee.
Simon: What? But people keep on talking of the marvelous things you're doing. That you have the makings of a prophet. And now, what? Don't tell me that the prophets of today are hiding under the ground like moles. Since you can do such great things, come with us and perform these deeds in the capital, for people to see you. Jacob and I shall be your barkers. "Hey, the prophet is here! He's our cousin!" We'll gather the people. You talk to them and we promise to applaud you, cousin, when you're through.
Jesus: No, I'm not going, Simon. Save the applause and get going. The festival started last night, and you might be late. I'm not going.
Simon: Bah, what a snob you are, Jesus. Go and join your friends in Capernaum. Let's go, Jacob, and hurry up!
Jesus: Mama, tomorrow at dawn, I'm leaving.
Mary: Where to, son, to Capernaum?
Jesus: No, to Jerusalem, to the festival with James, Peter, John, and the rest of the group.
Mary: I knew you were going. Your lips were telling Simon and Jacob that you wouldn't go, but when I looked at you, your eyes said otherwise. Jesus, my son, be careful. Jerusalem is not Galilee. The Romans are all around and they find out everything.
Jesus: Are you still afraid, mama?
Mary: No, son, why should I be? But it's no longer like before. Back then, I could scold you like a little boy. "Jesus, don't do this, obey

your mother." No, now I know I can't be a hindrance to you. Many times I've thought about the things you told me in Capernaum; do you remember, son?

Jesus: Of course I do. And the truth is, I was a little harsh with you that day.

Mary: No, son. It was I who was arguing with God like our grandfather Jacob, who, one night, dared wrestle with the angel who subdued him in the end. The same thing happened to me, you know. I was telling the Lord: "Why don't you look for somebody else? Why take a fancy to my son? He's the only one I've got. Why do you want to take him away from me? Joseph is gone and I'm getting old. At least I'd like to see my son settle down with a decent girl, have a secure job, and maybe I can even take care of my first grandchild." This was all I asked. It wasn't much, was it? But you see, God's will prevailed, as always. He stretched out his hand to you and said, "You are the one I have been looking for." It's all right, son. He won. He is the stronger one.

Jesus: You're a courageous woman, mama.

Mary: Of course not, I'm scared to death. I just obey without a clear idea of the Lord's plan for you. But don't worry, I won't be in your way. On the contrary, I would like to follow you to help you, though I don't know how.

Jesus: But, mama, you were the one who pushed me into this. You used to tell me: "The Lord wants to humble the great and exalt the humble." You taught me that. And that's what we have been doing all along these months in Capernaum and in the cities by the lake.

Mary: And in Jerusalem?

Jesus: The good news must be proclaimed in Jerusalem too, and now is the time to do it.

Mary: Take a little of this milk before you go. You've become so thin, you might not be able to make it even to Samaria. C'mon son, drink this and see how good it is.

When we arrived at Jerusalem, the festival was almost half over. As we approached the temple, we saw the procession coming out. Men, women, and children, all waving branches of palm and willow, sang along the streets. The priests repeated the same ceremony at the atrium: God's ministers, intoning psalms of the tents, went around the altar.

Priest: Lord, give us salvation! Lord, grant us success!

All: Blessed is he who comes in the name of the Lord

The temple's atrium was filled with drunken men and children chasing sheep. Jerusalem reeked of ripe fruit as it happily bade farewell to the year that was to end.

A Man: Hey, countrywoman, look who's here! The prophet from Galilee.

A Woman: You're drunk, that's why you're seeing prophets everywhere!

Another Man: I'm telling you, woman, look at that cloak with patches. Yeah, it's him. Hey, folks! Run! The prophet has arrived! The prophet has arrived!

People responded to the man's screams by milling around us at the gate of Corinth. A group of men pushed Jesus up onto a bit of rock.

A Man: Hey you, Galilean, what're you doing here?

Jesus: Celebrating this year's harvest; it was good!

Another Man: Speak louder, for we can't hear you over here! Damn it, pig, stop pushing!

The gate of Corinth was like a cockpit in turmoil. Everybody wanted to get close to the newly arrived prophet.

Jesus: We have come to celebrate this year's harvest and to inform you of what is happening in the north. Yes, the farms have yielded wheat and grapes, that's right. But the Lord is announcing a greater harvest, a feast and a banquet to be celebrated by all people on earth. Friends from Jerusalem: we are here to bring you the good news! The Kingdom of God has come!

Man: Oh, great, so this is Kingdom of God.

A Woman: And where the hell is it?

Jesus: You don't have to look up to heaven nor anywhere else, woman. It's right here, where we poor people are gathered.

Another Man: Long live the Galileans! In Jerusalem and all over the country!

Another Woman: Hey, young man, yes, you, who speak so beautifully, will you explain to us one thing: what must we do in order to enter this kingdom? And who'll be left behind?

Jesus: The door to the kingdom is narrow. One must pass through it with empty pockets. Only those who share what they have shall pass through it. Those who deny the poor shall be left behind. Those who think they are first shall be last, and the last shall be first. Those who are at the end of the line shall go in first.

A Man: That's very well said, Galilean!

We had a difficult time leaving the temple. The people were shoving each other. They all wanted to see Jesus. The Roman soldiers watched at a close distance to prevent major trouble. Some Galileans invited us to spend the night in their bamboo tents. At nightfall, we stayed in one of them, while people from the capital continued talking and arguing.

A Neighbor: Did you notice how he spoke? I tell you, this man is the Messiah!

Another Neighbor: But have you ever seen a Messiah in broken sandals? You must be out of your mind!

Another Neighbor: Besides, the Messiah can't be a Galilean. He must come from the family of King David.

Neighbor: So, what family did this guy come from? That's what we don't know.

Neighbor: He's got to be the son of David! Either he comes from David's family or he is not the Messiah.

A Teacher: My friend, how can he be the son of David, when there's a psalm in which David calls the Messiah father instead of son?

Neighbor: What psalm are you talking about? This guy speaks so clearly, he's got the word of God on his tongue!

Pharisee: How can the Messiah be the son of David when David himself calls him father? As another psalm says, no one can be the son of his own son.

Neighbor: Listen, I don't understand a word you're saying or everything the Galilean says, so why don't you just get lost and sing your psalms somewhere else.

Neighbor: This Galilean was born in a poor town called Nazareth. Do you think the Messiah would come from there, huh? Don't be silly! When he comes, no one will ever know where he comes from. But he suddenly will appear. Zas! The heavens will open and we shall see him. He's the tricky type, you know. Let the Messiah go to sleep tonight, while we all go to Aziel's inn! The best wine in Jerusalem is kept in the barrels of that scoundrel!

That night, the prophet from Galilee was the talk of the whole town: from the district of the potmakers, the water carriers, to the street of the prostitutes and the big market. Nobody could come up with a good answer to the main question about him. The autumn's new moon, as it faintly shone over the walls of the holy city that was surrounded by tents, was at its highest point in the sky. Jerusalem, weary after the festival, was just beginning to succumb to deep slumber.

•

At the start of autumn, in September, the people of Israel celebrate the feast of the "sukkoth" (feast of the tents and huts). This brings to a close the fruit harvest and the gathering of grapes. Of the three pilgrimages held by the Israelites in Jerusalem annually — the Passover, the Pentecost, and the Tents — the last was considered to be the most festive and popular. For seven days, the people lived in huts/tents that were put up on terraces or on patios of the houses, along the expanse of the temple, or in public squares around Jerusalem. These huts were constructed in remembrance of the tents where the Hebrews lived for forty years during their journey through the desert and to the Promised Land.

In Jesus' time, and as influenced by the prophetic texts (Zech. 14:16, 19), the people associated the feast of the tents with the triumph of the Kingdom of God and the Messiah. This episode shows the enthusiasm of Jesus' cousins over his becoming more and more popular each day and their excitement, for their own interest, over Jesus' going to Jerusalem for the festival. At this point, Jesus was already a very popular prophet not only in his own Galilee but also in the south, in Judea, and even in the capital. At this point too, Jesus was fully aware of the conflict brought by his words, his actions, and the people around him: the poor, pursued by the law, "the damned," "the leftovers" of that society.

This episode covers the second time that Jesus visits Jerusalem. He does it semiclandestinely, because after the news that Herod was after his head, he did not think it prudent for him to be making noise. In this case, although he does not reject the idea of spreading his prophetic message widely among the pilgrims who converged on the capital, he shuns the spectacle proposed to him by his cousins.

If at this point Jesus was already aware of a violent death, Mary, too, had the intuition that this could be the end of her son. That is why she was afraid. Mary was a courageous woman and a woman of faith, although this faith does not suppress fear or weakness. Mary, constantly fearing the consequences of his actions, suffered because of her son's commitment; she had no clear picture of where this commitment would lead. Nevertheless, she moved on and was guided by her faith, which continued to grow and mature in her.

It was also a fact that the roads to Jerusalem were not safe. In Jesus' time, banditry was rampant all over the country. In order to protect their trade, through the routes of the caravans, the Romans took special interest in ridding the roads of bandits. Farmers told great stories about hijackers and were apprehensive of the risks entailed on their trips. It was a special favor from God to be able to reach Jerusalem safe and sound.

At the capital, after the first public speech shown in this episode and summarized in the constant message of the gospel — share, try to enter through the narrow gate by giving, instead of accumulating (Matt. 7:13 – 14) — the people, gathered in Jerusalem for the festival, were talking about Jesus. They wanted to find out if he was or was not the Messiah: they wanted to know if such a man of low origin, with no academic degree, religious title, or formal authority, could really be the One. In those times, awaiting the Messiah was a constant topic of conversation among people. Some rabbis believed that the Messiah could only come from the family of David (he could be his "son"). Others did not give much importance to this aspect, but to what the Messiah could do. In his second trip to the capital, Jesus is already known. Poor people channel their hopes for justice through him.

(John 7:1–13 and 40–43)

76

The First Stone

Husband: Get out of there, insolent woman! Now you can't escape anymore!

Neighbor: Knock that door down and get them out!

Lady neighbor: Adulteress, adulteress!

A mob of men and women shouted as they gathered around Cirilo's house, in a district in Jerusalem where water carriers lived. Stones were hurled against the door while curses were heard all over the place.

Another Neighbor: You'll pay for this, you bitch!

Another Lady Neighbor: We know that you two rascals are inside!

A half-naked man ran from the house and rushed down the street, like a rat coming out of its hiding place.

Husband: Let him go, I'll come back for him some other time. But now it's Joan I must confront!

Neighbor: Get her out of the house, and hurry!

After shovings from the neighbors, the wooden lock gave way and the door opened. Several men milled inside the house. In one corner, a horrified woman was seen crouching.

Husband: Oh! How I want to strangle you, you filthy woman! You bitch. I swear that this will be your last day on earth!

Neighbor: Death to the adulteress! Kill her!

Lady Neighbor: She must die! She must die!

Neighbor: Get her!

Two men rushed toward the woman, grabbed her by the hair and dragged her out of the house. Then an old man snatched away the sheet with which she intended to cover her body.

Husband: Leave her that way, for everyone to see her sins! If she didn't have any qualms undressing before Cirilo, neither would she mind baring herself before everyone! Neighbors, this woman has betrayed me and went with another man! Help me regain my honor that has been tarnished by this woman's infidelity!

Lady Neighbor: Let her die! Let her die!

Neighbor: Go and live with your good-for-nothing lover, you slut!

The two men who lifted her by the arms dragged her through the small, narrow street, while she resisted by kicking. With raised fists, they shouted at the top of their voices, as they headed south toward the cliff of the Gehenna, a cursed district where the residents of Jerusalem burned their garbage and stoned their adulterous women.

Lady Neighbor: Death to the adulteress! Throw her into the pit!

Neighbor: Now, now, look who's here! The prophet from Galilee!

In the midst of our conversation with Jesus near the temple, we saw the angry crowd approaching.

Neighbor: Come with us prophet, and fulfill the law of Moses! The stain of adultery can only be washed out by stoning the guilty one!

Husband: The more hands there are, the more stones shall be hurled! Come with us. Let all your friends come along too!

Neighbor: We caught this whore in the same bed with Cirilo, the water carrier!

Lady Neighbor: She can't give any excuse. We're all witnesses to her offense!

The men dragging the woman cleared the way, and dropped her in the midst of everyone. Her face almost kissed the ground and her knees were already bleeding. Her whole body was wet with saliva and was full of bruises. One of the men, in a gesture of contempt, stuck out his right foot and rested it on the woman's face, pressed against the stones on the ground.

One Neighbor: Who is the prophet here? So it's you? Well, why don't you condemn her now, so that the devil can swallow her up and lead her directly to hell? Come on, what are you waiting for? If you are indeed a prophet, speak up and condemn her!

Lady Neighbor: Let her die! Let her die!

Jesus approached the group of men who were shouting and threatening with their fists.

Jesus: Where is the husband of this woman?

Husband: Here I am. I used to be the husband of this whore, but not anymore. What do you want?

Jesus: Tell me what happened. Has she ever deceived you before?

Husband: Of course! She would always deny it, but sooner or later, it is easier to spot a liar than a cripple.

Jesus: Tell me: How many times, do you think, has she been unfaithful to you?

Husband: How many times? I don't know anymore. Thrice, four times, or five times. She is worse than a bitch in heat.

Then Jesus bent over and, with his finger, drew three, four, five lines on the ground.

Jesus: What else is your complaint against her?

Husband: What else? Ha! Isn't this imprudence, committed in broad daylight sufficient enough? Do you want more evidence against her? She would say, "I am going to visit a sick friend and cheer her up," and the sick friend was Cirilo, the water carrier and butcher from the next block. Wait till I see him. I'll cut him into pieces with his own butcher's knife!

Lady Neighbor: Have you seen how she flirted with my husband, right before my eyes — making me look so stupid? If you had only seen how she wiggled her way in front of our house, while tongues kept on wagging. What a whore she is!

Another Lady Neighbor: This woman has been screwed by every man in the neighborhood!

Lady Neighbor: Tell the prophet how they caught her fondling Jack's son! Come on, tell him!

Another Lady Neighbor: The rabbi wouldn't turn his head for nothing when she passes by if he didn't know a lot about her!

Lady Neighbor: She's got a foul mouth. Everything she utters is loathsome.

Neighbor: If you only knew what she says and does!

Lady Neighbor: You should see how she dresses herself — baring practically all her breasts! What a brazen woman!

All the while, Jesus, in a squatting position, was drawing a line for every accusation hurled against the woman.

Old Man: This harlot's misdeeds are endless!

Lady Neighbor: We knew all along this was coming. She is her mother's daughter, a whore like her mother. Nobody even knows who her father is.

Husband: Enough of this silly talk! What have you got to say, prophet from Galilee?

Jesus: Will someone get me a stone, please?

All: Very well, and be tough with her!

An old man, with a look of malice in his eyes, leaned over to pick up a stone, and gave it to Jesus.

Lady Neighbor: Hit her on the head — like we all do to adulterous women!

Neighbor: Crush her to death! Crush her to death!

Jesus weighed the stone in his hand, as he looked at the woman who was lying flat, her face on the ground, in the middle of the street.

Jesus: My fellowmen, I am sorry, but I can not cast this stone at this woman. If anyone here thinks that he is without sin, let him come forward and do it.

A pot-bellied old man went up to Jesus.

Old Man: Give me the stone. I'll do it. We have to fulfill the law of Moses, which condemns adultery.

Jesus: Make sure it will not rebound on you, as it did on Goliath.

Old Man: What on earth do you mean?

Jesus: Now you listen, just between the two of us. How much interest do you charge when you lend money? Ten percent, twenty, or perhaps forty? This is also against the law of Moses.

Jesus stared at the old man, who was about to throw the stone at the naked body of the woman. Jesus' look was like a razor's blade penetrating through the old man's eyes.

Jesus: The law prohibits that you choke the poor to death because they are unable to pay their debts on time. Do you agree, my friend?

The stone slid from the old man's hand as he turned around and slipped through the crowd.

Lady Neighbor: What's with him? Why did he back out?

Jesus again faced the people who were getting impatient.

Jesus: Who among you wishes to cast the first stone at the woman?
Neighbor: I do. Give it to me. If there is anything that disgusts me — it's infidelity. What an abominable woman!

A tall man, full of arrogance, approached the woman.

Jesus: Say, my friend, what is your job?
Neighbor: My job? I am a businessman. I run a food store.
Jesus: And probably you keep two weighing scales for your business: one to weigh all your purchases and another to weigh what you sell. Tell me, how many have you got, one or two?

The vendor opened his mouth to reply to Jesus, but he couldn't utter a single word. Then he withdrew and disappeared among the crowd.

Jesus: And you, by your looks, must be a lawyer or a judge, a judge who sits on the Great Council. Tell me, my friend, how much of a bribe do you receive for convicting the widow and exonerating the landowner? Do you wish to cast the first stone? How about you? You must be a doctor. Go ahead. Throw the first stone. After all, this woman lives in the slums. You haven't set foot in the place, have you? All your patients come from the wealthy neighborhoods, naturally, because they can afford to pay you.
Neighbor: Stop all this nonsense! This woman is a sinner. You have noted down her sins through the lines you drew on the ground. See how numerous they are!
Jesus: Why do you see the mote in her eye, while you refuse to see the plank in your own?
Neighbor: The mote in my eye? This woman is guilty of the most grievous sin, adultery!
Jesus: It is more adulterous to see priests in cahoots with the oppressive rulers of the people. Yet no one hurls stones at them. It is more adulterous to see God's servants worshiping Mammon, the god of money, but no one lifts a finger to accuse them. All of you are hypocrites. Go and hide yourselves in the mountain caves, because the God of Israel's coming for

the final reckoning, and just as you have done to this woman, you'll be judged the way you judge others.

Jesus leaned back and spoke no more. Then he reached out to erase the lines that he had drawn on the ground. The crowd began to disperse.

Peter: How you left them breathless!

Jesus: It seems the only sin they're aware of is adultery. They waste their time picking on this type of woman and criticizing her sins. Yet the more obvious things and the grave abuses against the poor are committed right before their own eyes, without their knowledge.

Peter bent over the woman who was lying flat on the ground.

Peter: Hey, you're saved. You're very lucky. What's your name?

Joan: Joan, but I...I...

Jesus: Weep no more, woman. It's all over now. Here, cover yourself with this sheet. Take it easy. No one's going to hurt you anymore. Open your eyes now. Look, they've all left. No one has condemned you. Not even God. Neither has he cast a stone at you.

Peter and Jesus lifted Joan from the ground and brought her home to the district of the water carriers, near the holy temple of Jerusalem.

•

The episode of the adulteress — which can only be found in the gospel of John — is not among the ancient manuscripts which are preserved from the original text of that gospel. Some scholars are of the opinion that this text, which is replete with historical realities, must have been deleted from the gospel of Luke and from the writings of John precisely because Jesus' compassion for this sinful woman might have been scandalous to the first Christian communities. It is therefore this aspect that makes the story relevant.

In Israel, adultery was considered a public crime, punishable by death, in accordance with the ancient laws (Lev. 20:1). Customs and traditions had interpreted a number of laws in favor of the male. Thus, a married man was said to have committed adultery only if he had an affair with a married woman. If a woman, however, was single, a prostitute, or a slave, then such an act on the part of the man was not considered adulterous. On the other hand, a woman having an affair with any man was considered an adulteress. A woman suspected of adultery was subjected to a public trial by making her drink bitter water. If her stomach became swollen after drinking it, then this confirmed her adulterous act. If she did not feel any malaise at all, then it was considered a false accusation (Num. 5:11–31). This test was performed by a priest in the Jerusalem temple. The man was never subjected to a similar process. In any case, once adultery was proven, the guilty ones (man or woman) were to be punished by the people through stoning.

Since adultery was considered a public crime, the stain of the sin was to be cleansed publicly. Death by stoning was carried out by the residents of the place where the sinner had been guilty of the sinful act, and usually the place of torture was beyond the walls of the city. Witnesses to the crime were the ones who cast the first stones at the culprit. Other crimes punishable by stoning were blasphemy, divinations and other forms of idolatry, as well as the violation of the law of the Sabbath.

Adultery is a sin against fidelity. In a number of cases, it is also an expression of weakness. In order to save the adulteress from death as mandated by law, Jesus, in this episode, contrasts this "sin" with other offenses like fraud, exploitation, usury, and judicial corruption. In this light, it is evident that acts of injustice committed against the poor and the less fortunate, by taking advantage of their misery, are far more grievous in the eyes of God than the sins of the flesh.

On the one hand, Jesus was always merciful, full of understanding and tolerant with cheaters, prostitutes, and drunkards — the wide gamut of human weaknesses which are related to the flesh and to the cunning existence of the poor. On the other hand, he frowned upon the hypocrisy and injustice of the rich and the powerful. He never branded the sinners and the condemned as a "race of snakes," as the heads of the official religion claimed. Rather, he used that insult specifically for those very persons of power. The Christian community should be able to identify, as Jesus has shown, the real sin that separates people from God and isolates them from each other.

(John 8:2–11)

77

Like a River of Living Water

The last day of the feast of the tents was the most significant. The week-long jubilation at the end of the year and the new harvest was almost over. The pilgrims who were jam-packed into Jerusalem bade their last farewell to the Holy City by attending the solemn rite of the water in the Pool of Siloam.

Abiah: Everything's all set for the procession, huh, Priest Zirah?

Zirah: Right. In a little while, we'll go to the temple to get the silver jug. Are you coming with us, Magistrate Nicodemus?

Nicodemus: Why, of course.

Abiah: For sure he'll be there too. All these days he's been hovering around the temple with his friends from Galilee.

Nicodemus: Who?

Abiah: Who else, but that Jesus of Nazareth. He's been putting our patience to the limits. He does nothing but bring trouble or join the troublemakers.

Zirah: Thank God the Almighty, this will soon be over. The rotten apple must be removed so as not to spoil the rest.

Nicodemus: What do you mean, Zirah?

Zirah: I mean we've already discussed this with Caiaphas, the high priest, who has given us his authorization . . .

Nicodemus: What for?

Abiah: To get the troublemaker. The holiday ends today and so does his glibness. A stint in jail will knock some sense into him.

Nicodemus: Are you out of your mind? You can't condemn anyone without trying him. That's the law.

Zirah: Nicodemus, don't you think we've had enough of his silly talk? He's filled up the whole of Galilee with all his nonsense, and now he wants to stir up the whole capital. Don't you know what happened the other day to the adulteress? They were going to stone her to death, as the law of Moses demands.

Nicodemus: Of course I know. All Jerusalem has been talking about it.

Abiah: Well, now they'll all be silenced! Everything's over! We'll get rid of the agitator from our midst.

Nicodemus: Take it easy, my friends. People say that Jesus is a prophet.

Zirah: Of course, it's the wine that made him see things. A prophet. Bah! Only thieves and rascals could come from Galilee!

Nicodemus: This man is different, Zirah. I talked to him once, and believe me, I ...

Zirah: So you were also hoodwinked by him? Why don't you open your eyes, Magistrate Nicodemus? Has any one of our chiefs and Pharisees believed in him? Look at his followers: a gang of rogues who neither bathe nor obey the law of Moses!

Nicodemus: Hear him speak first. All I ask is that you listen to him speak.

Abiah: We'll get him first. Then we'll figure out what to do with him. Priest Zirah, tell the guards to come. They ought to be instructed on what to do.

Later in the afternoon, the streets near the Pool of Siloam were teeming with people. With branches of palm trees in our hands, we waited for the procession of the priests who headed for the fountain with a silver jug to be filled with holy water and poured later on the temple's altar. The lighted torches illumined the afternoon in Jerusalem.

Zirah: Let us give thanks to the Lord who is good!

All: His love is forever!

Zirah: Let the whole house of Israel declare it!

All: His love is forever!

Zirah: Let the house of Aaron declare it!

All: His love is forever!

Zirah: Let all the friends of the Lord declare it!

All: His love is forever!

The solemn procession reached the Pool of Siloam. A priest, wearing an embroidered dalmatic, descended the wet stairs toward the spring that supplied drinking water to the people of the city of King David. Then he leaned over to fill the silver jug with water.

Zirah: This, my children, is the holy water that purifies, that quenches our thirst, the life-giving water! Praised be the name of the Lord and lift up your branches in his honor!

Then something unexpected happened. Jesus broke out from one corner of the crowd and shouted so loud that everyone could hear.

Jesus: My friends, listen to me! This water is stagnant; don't drink from it! The living water is something else! The living water is the Spirit of God!

A Man: What the hell is this sot trying to do, yelling at the top of his voice?

Another Man: Get him out of there, he's distracting the people and disrupting the procession!

Jesus: My friends, the Spirit of God hovers around the water, making new things like in the beginning of creation. Those of you who thirst for justice, come and be one with us, and in your heart will spring forth a river of living water, like the torrent seen by the prophet Ezekiel that inundated the earth and purged her of all her sins!

A Man: What's all this mess about? How long do we have to put up with this troublemaker? Why can't you shut him up?

Another Man: Hey, isn't he the same guy who they say is a prophet, the one they wanted killed? How can he go on shouting, yet no one is arresting him?

A Woman: Maybe the chiefs of the Sanhedrin have been converted and now they believe that this troublemaker is the Messiah after all!

A Man: What stupidity! The Messiah will descend from heaven enveloped in a cloud of incense! This guy comes from Galilee, reeking of onions!

Jesus was now between James and me. We were surrounded by an avalanche of people. The priests in the procession, infuriated by the incident, left the jug of water and the branches of palm trees, and called for the guards. But Jesus continued talking.

Jesus: My friends, look above you. Look at those torches that illumine the walls of the city. The New Jerusalem will be as bright. I bring you good news which is the light of the world. The news is that God, our Father, is offering us, those who are down here, his kingdom. God is light, and his Spirit is a torch that will give light to the earth; yes, the light to the four corners of the earth, the light that will burn all that's harmful, giving birth to a world where there are no rich or poor, no masters or slaves, a new heaven and earth where only justice will reign.

A Woman: Let's get out of here, Lenore, I don't like the way things are going to end up here.

Another Woman: Damn, why do they have to mix God's work with politics?

A Woman: C'mon, run, the beating and stoning will start any time now.

A Man: This blabber-mouth must be a Galilean.

Another Man: Such nice words, huh? Such big lies.

A Third Man: Shut up, you beast, and hold your tongue! Can't you see this man is sent by God?

Man: What are you talking about? Look at him! He's nothing but a crazy man who wants us all to be like him. Hey, will someone push him down from that wall?

The Other Man: This man is possessed by the devil. Can't you hear it, Nazarene? The devil of rebellion is inside you!

Jesus: No, my friend, there is no devil inside me. I'm here to tell you the truth. The truth hurts, and that's why some of you refuse to listen.

Man: Ignore this kook! He talks a lot! It's the devil who sent him.

Man: What about those soldiers over there? Who sent them?

Woman: Let's get out of here, neighbor. I think things are getting out of hand.

From the cobbled street descending from Mount Zion to the Pool of Siloam four soldiers of the temple who were sent by the priests were heading toward Jesus to arrest him.

A Soldier: That's it, Galilean! You've caused enough trouble already. Beat it, all of you! C'mon, I told you to disperse! Hey, you, get down from that wall or we'll get you down ourselves!

Jesus: Why, what have I done?

Another Soldier: You're under arrest. Come with us.

Jesus: Me, under arrest? What's my offense?

Soldier: We've got orders from the high priest.

Jesus: But why, what are they accusing me of?

Soldier: Search me, and I don't give a damn. We've got a warrant of arrest signed by the high priest.

Jesus: And who is he?

Soldier: Are you so dumb you don't even know who he is? You must be a peasant!

Jesus: Until lately, soldier, you were also a peasant like me, you and your pals. Don't you remember anymore? Sure, I know the high priest of the temple, Caiaphas, a "great man." And you work for him, don't you?

Soldier: Stop that nonsense, Galilean. I said you're under arrest.

Jesus: Let's all go to jail then! This is amusing! Prisoners taking other prisoners.

Soldier: What madness are you talking about?

Jesus: Oh, nothing, except that you are more a prisoner than I am. You, who are guardians of the temple, have fallen into the snare of the priests and your chiefs, and you can't get away from them. You had the same origin as we did, sucked the same milk, and tilled the same earth. Show me your hands, soldier, can't you see we've got the same callused hands? You used to be one with us and you still are. But the so-called great men make you fight against us. They put the sword and the lance in your hands to kill us, and they filled your hearts with hatred. They don't stand up for you. They use you. You are prisoners in uniform with a handful of coins they had robbed from us. And this is the truth. If you understand, then it will set you free.

The murmurings of the people were gradually disappearing. The four soldiers facing Jesus looked at him intently. They were no longer holding their lances furiously. After looking at each other, they gave a half turn and left.

Zirah: These four imbeciles deserve twenty beatings each and a month's arrest! And a fine of fifty denarii! Go to hell, all of you!

Abiah: What has happened, Priest Zirah?

Zirah: Those stupid soldiers. They've let him go.

Abiah: Why? Why didn't they arrest him?

Zirah: Say something, stupid, or you get twenty lashes more!

Soldier: We couldn't. We had never heard a man speak the way he did.

Zirah: I told you, Abiah. This man is more dangerous than he seems to be. See how he has deceived them. Damn this agitator. Out of my sight, the four of you. You'll go to jail for this. And I want to hear the sound of lashes from here. That will teach them to obey orders.

Meanwhile, water continued to flow in the Pool of Siloam. The torches on the last day of the feast of the tents illumined the walls and the massive towers of King David's city.

•

The last day of the feast of the tents was celebrated with the most pomp. The traditional processions were highlighted with bunches and sprays of palm trees, willow trees, lemon and other trees, while psalms were being sung, specially Psalm 118. Liturgy likewise incorporated in the feast the symbol of water: in a procession, the priests carried water in a silver jug from the Pool of Siloam — which was situated outside the walled city — to be poured on the altar of sacrifice. During this rite, people prayed to God for abundant rain in preparation for the new planting season.

Palestine, a land wanting for water, has the Jordan as its only important river. Rain is a decisive factor in the national economy. The rainy season lasts from October to April. In summer it hardly rains. The early rains (from mid-October to mid-November) prepare the land, hardened by the summer heat, for sowing. The cold rains (from December to January), which are more abundant, give rise to fertile lands that extend through the valleys. Between one rainy season and another comes the period of planting that lasts until February. The late rains (March and April) are indispensable to good harvest. That is why, in this feast, people prayed to God specifically for abundant rain. People prayed for a fertile land and for the fulfillment of the prophecies proclaiming the day of the Messiah when water would flow abundantly from the springs of Jerusalem, until they merged with the sea. The feast of the tents was, therefore, tinged with a messianic theme that annually rekindled the people's hope for liberation.

Israel's ancient traditions compared the Spirit of God with water that fertilizes sterile land, reaping from it the fruits of justice, peace, and faithfulness to the Lord (Isa. 32:15–18 and 44:3–5). It was the Spirit that converted Israel to a country of prophets and transformed hearts of stone to hearts of flesh. In Jesus' time, the tradition of the rabbis and doctors, which was more callous and rigid than that of the prophets, had neglected this vital symbolism and compared water not with the Spirit but with the law. The prophetic gesture of Jesus in the middle of the ceremony, his solemn proclamation, aims to bring back the original symbolism of water: that is, water is like the Spirit. And the Spirit of God always creates new things.

From the first day of the feast of the tents, huge candles in golden candelabras were lighted and placed in the women's patio in the temple. The procession of the water passed through this. Each set of candlesticks held four golden bowls with oil, where wicks made of threads taken from the priests' vestment remained lighted. One had to use a ladder to reach these bowls, as they were placed so high that their lights could be seen throughout the whole city. The prophets, in talking about the day of the Messiah, mentioned a light that would surpass the night (Zech. 14:6–7). Those torches, therefore, had messianic meaning. Prophetic tradition had always associated the Messiah with light, such that he was referred to as "the Light" (Isa. 60:1). Starting from this symbolism, Jesus speaks of the Kingdom of God: a kingdom with no shadow of injustice, but illumined by free people. Butting into the middle of the official liturgy, before the religious leaders of the temple, was such a grave scandal that the priests immediately decided to have Jesus arrested and accused of blasphemy.

The "temple guards" sent by the priests to arrest Jesus were composed of Levites, employees of the temple with a rank lesser than that of the priests. One of their functions was to serve as policemen. These soldiers had the power to arrest, to confiscate weapons, and even to mete out punishments. They were not only in the service of the priests; they were also engaged by the Roman military authorities to control people's rallies in Judea. Jesus confronted these armed men with firmness but with understanding, and in spite of their privileged position, these men felt touched by Jesus' words.

(John 7:37–39 and 43–53; 8:12–38)

78

A Samaritan without Faith

Jesus: My friends, what's the use of saying "I believe in God, and I have faith" if you don't care about other people? If a hungry neighbor knocks at your door and tells you, "God bless you my brother," yet you give him nothing to eat, then what's the use of all this? This is what happens to those who profess their faith yet remain with their arms flailing. This faith is dead, like a tree that bears no fruit.

A Man: Very well said! Long live the prophet from Galilee!

We were in the temple of Jerusalem, in the Court of the Gentiles. And as always, the people from the City of David gathered around us to listen to Jesus and applaud him. These were the common people: the potters, hawkers, prostitutes, water carriers. That's why we were all surprised to see the master of the law, in his linen cloak and wearing a thick golden ring on his finger, approach our group.

Master: May I ask you one question, Galilean?

Jesus: Of course. We are all in conversation here. What is it?

Master: I have been listening to you for a little while. I only heard you speak of sharing what one has, of giving food to the hungry. All this is very good, of course; I don't deny it. But aren't you missing the most important point?

Jesus: The most important point? And what is most important?

Master: God. You are forgetting God. Is it because you are a political agitator and not a preacher of Moses' law?

Jesus: The God I speak of is the same God who gave Moses the commandments of justice.

Master: Of course, Galilean, but the law of Moses contains a lot of commandments. What would you tell me if I asked you which of them is the most important?

Jesus: You know the answer better than I do. What did they teach us in the synagogue since we were children? "Love the Lord your God with all your heart, with all your soul, and with all your strength."

Master: So, then, you say that the first thing is to love God above all things, is that right?

Jesus: Of course, my friend. God, above everything else. But where is God? Sometimes you find him where you least expect him. Let me tell you a story. Once there was a solitary peasant going down the road from Jerusalem to Jericho. Mounted on his old mule, that man was happily riding his way back home. He had sold rye from his harvest for a good price, and he was going home to his wife and children:

> *Peasant:* Ho, ho, wake up mule! We still have a long way to go. Oh, dear wife, wait till you hear my story! Larara, lararara! At last, we'll be able to settle our debts with this little money. God, am I so lucky today! Larara, lararara!

Jesus: But it was not a lucky day for him because at one bend of the road, in the middle of the desert, a band of robbers was awaiting him, and when the man passed by...

> *Robber:* Give me all your money if you want to save your skin!
> *Peasant:* No, please, don't do this to me. I worked for this for six months, it's for the food of my children. I'm nothing but a poor man.
> *Robber:* Here, take this!
> *Peasant:* Oh, please, don't! Ohhhh!

Jesus: The robbers gave him a blow on the back of his neck, scared the mule away, and took away all his money.

> *Robber:* I think he's dead. Strip him of his clothes too.
> *Another Robber:* Bah, just dump him in that ditch and let's get out of here before anyone sees us. Hurry!

Jesus: So they left him half dead by the road, naked and without his money. Soon, when the sun shone brightly over the desert, a caravan of camels was seen heading for the road. A priest from Jericho was traveling to Jerusalem to worship in the temple of God, a solemn cult of the children of Israel.

> *Sophar:* I assure you, Priest Eliphaz, the feasts of this year will be beautiful.

Eliphaz: That's right, Sophar. I was told that the high priest has ordered the purchase of the best incense from Arabia.

Sophar: He also bought new cups for the altar. They are made of pure gold from Ophir. Let's hope we won't run out of wine to fill them up!

Eliphaz: Hey, do you see something in that ditch?

Sophar: Where? Oh yeah, but I can't figure it out. Well, is it a dead animal or a man?

Eliphaz: I bet it's a man, a drunk man. He must have drunk more wine than his body could take. He should be ashamed of himself getting drunk on these sacred days. Ah, Priest Sophar, these are the vices that plague our country nowadays!

Sophar: He should be ashamed. He doesn't even have respect for the Lord and his law. He's not even aware of it. Maybe he's dead. Do you think we should get a little closer to see if we can do something for him?

Eliphaz: Look, Priest Sophar, if he is alive, then he'll know how to fend for himself. If he was able to get here, then he should know his way out too. And if he is dead, what's the point?

Sophar: You're right, Eliphaz. That's a very sensible observation. But what if he is only half dead?

Eliphaz: Do you know what I'm thinking of, Sophar? These types of men are an ungrateful lot, so they don't deserve any help. A priest who was a friend of mine gave a lift to one of this kind. He had barely traveled a couple of miles when the guy threatened him with a knife and robbed him of everything he had. Now, isn't that sad?

Sophar: Yeah, I think you're right. I guess this poor fellow is dead. At least, sir, you can give him his last blessing.

Eliphaz: Amen.

Sophar: Well, let's forget about this. Let's proceed with the journey, for we might be late for the ceremony. Hooo, hooo, camels, let's go!

Jesus: In a short while, another traveler passed along that same dusty road. He was a Levite, one of those entrusted to teach God's commandments to the people. He was accompanied by his wife.

Levite: I'm telling you, Lydia, I'm not ready for anything. It's easy to give a talk in a small village, but to deliver a sermon in the synagogue of the capital is something else!

Lydia: There's no need to worry, Samuel. Talk about God's love, that we have to be good, and that...

Levite: Hey, what's that pile over there? Look.

Lydia: Oh no, don't tell me it's a dead man. I'm scared of the dead!

Levite: No, he's just wounded, the blood is still fresh. Look.

Lydia: Oh, this is horrible! Let's go, Samuel. The sight of blood makes me sick. You know that I can't stand it.

Levite: But who is this poor creature? He's so beaten up.

Lydia: He's probably one of those rebels conspiring against Governor Pilate. Of course, they're always in trouble, meddling in politics, and see how they end up. They can't complain.

Levite: As a matter of fact, this fellow can't complain.

Lydia: Remember Daniel's son? He was such a nice young man until he became a rebel. Poor guy! He ended up like this man. I really don't understand why people can't simply live in peace. What do you say, Samuel?

Levite: People are so violent, that's why, Lydia. And of course, they have no respect for the Lord. They are taught the commandments and the good deeds but that's all. Everything enters through the right ear and passes through the left. If they loved God, these things would not happen. Blessed be God!

Lydia: And his holy name!

Levite: And this beast better hurry, or we won't be in time for judgment day! Ea donkey, hurry up!

Jesus: Then it happened that another peasant was crossing the bend on his old and skinny mule.

Samaritan: What a terribly hot day! Who could have ever invented the desert? If I don't take these figs to the market, no one will buy them; but if I bring them with me, they get rotten along the road. And then they say that God does things very well! I'd say the contrary because oftentimes he gives you something that you're helpless about. Damn it, when I get to Jerusalem, I won't even have a fig to crush in the belly of the high priest, Caiaphas!

Jesus: That peasant was a Samaritan who did not believe in God and had never set foot in the temple. When he saw the badly wounded man...

Samaritan: Hey, what happened to you? Damn, this guy looks terrible. He's almost dead. If I'm bad off, this guy has got it even worse. The vultures must all be preparing for the grand feast!

Jesus: The Samaritan got off his mule and went over to the man who was lying in the ditch. First he washed the blood from his face.

Samaritan: This wine will cure your wounds. Let's see if the oil will remove the pain. That's it.

Jesus: Then he tore off his tunic and wrapped him with bandages. He covered him with his cloak and lifted him from the ground.

Samaritan: And they say that God takes care of the world and his people! Well, see how he took care of this poor creature!

Jesus: The Samaritan who did not believe in God put him on his mount, together with the sack of figs that he was bringing to the market. Though he was on his way to Jericho, he returned to the inn in Anathoth, where he attended to him and spent the night watching over him as the fever went up on account of his wounds. When it was dawn, the Samaritan spoke to the innkeeper.

Samaritan: I have to go. I'll pay you in advance. Buy all the medicines he will need, and if the money is not enough, I'll pay you the rest when I come back.

Innkeeper: Hey, what will I tell him if he asks who brought him here?

Samaritan: Tell him another man brought him here, a man like you and me. Goodbye, and good luck. Take good care of him for me!

Jesus: That Samaritan, who did not believe in God, nor set foot in the temple, proceeded on his journey along the solitary and risky road from Jerusalem to Jericho. Now, you who are a teacher of the law, tell me, who among them loved the Lord?

Teacher: Well, the truth is . . . I don't know . . . Of course, the man who helped the wounded did not believe in God, but . . .

Jesus: He went to a person who needed him. If on your way to the temple to bring your offering before the altar you remember that your brother needs you, leave your offering behind, go back and seek your brother first.

The teacher of the law stayed a little while to listen to Jesus. Then we saw him leave hesitatingly.

•

Many times, when Jesus was in Jerusalem, he would talk to the people in the atrium of the temple, using words that were easily understood by all. The lectures of the scribes and doctors who taught in those places were always vague and mysterious, as if to distinguish the "learned" from the ignorant masses. With their moralizing interpretations, they had divested the Scriptures of all prophetic candor. A layman, with no special education, who spoke the people's language and who gave his own, free interpretation of the Scripture to his countrymen in the presence of the experts was amazing to the people and irritating to the authorities in theology. In this text, one of them raises the question of interpreting the law.

The question asked by the teacher of the law is a theoretical one: Which is the fundamental commandment? Jesus does not respond theoretically, but he does so with a practical example, a concrete experience. The religious attitude not only consists of accepting dogmas more or less, of knowing one's catechism with its list of truths and moral norms. Faith is not only in the mind; it is also in our hands, in what we do. Faith demands work, concrete actions which are not only directed to God, whom we do not see, but also to our brothers and sisters, whom we see. This is the essence of the message of Jesus and of the whole Christian faith (Matt. 5:23 –24; James 1:22–27 and 2:14–26; 1 John 3:11–18 and 4:19–21).

Jerusalem, being the capital, was the center of trade for the whole country. In spite of this, communication with the other cities was far from good. The city was separated from Jericho by twenty-seven kilometers, the road running through the desert of Judea. In the barren mountains of Judea are a number of caves and hideouts which have become havens for highway robbers up to the present. Banditry was then very common, and the authorities tried to control it, but it was not that easy. As a form of retaliation, the Romans would sometimes sack the neighboring villages. Apparently in Jerusalem, there used to be a special court that tried cases of looting and drew up police measures against the bandits. At present, the road from Jerusalem to Jericho is amazing due to its barrenness, just like in those times. It is flanked by gray and barren mountains. There is a small chapel in one of the bends — the Chapel of the Good Samaritan — which is a reminder to the travelers of the parable of Jesus.

In the parable, the priests passed through that road first. Priests had to go to the temple of Jerusalem by turns, in order to offer their sacrifice (blood of animals, incense, prayers). In money and social prestige, they were a powerful and privileged group. The Levites were under them in the service of the temple. They were not priests, so they could not offer sacrifices, and therefore, like laypeople, they could not go near the altar. They were in charge of the music in the temple. They sang in the choir and played the instruments during worship. Others served as acolytes; they assisted the priests in donning their vestments for the ceremony; they carried the sacred books and cleaned the temple. Some of them who were trained in the Scriptures also served as catechists. Still others served as police of the temple. In Jesus' time, there were about ten thousand Levites. For them as well as for the priests, the temple in all its service, its splendor, was the fundamental value, the foremost religious obligation. The laws on purity prohibited them from getting near a corpse. By giving all sorts of excuses — ritual purity, haste, the contempt they felt for "the people" — the Levites did not help the wounded man along the road. By doing so, they thought they were doing something pleasing to the Lord.

Having a Samaritan as the third character in his story, Jesus surprised everyone and irked the theologian who had asked him the question. The Samaritans were highly discriminated against by the Israelites, who felt a great disdain for them, a mixed feeling of nationalism and racism. Furthermore, the Samaritan cited here by Jesus is not in any way a religious man. He is an atheist who believes neither in God nor in the priests, nor in anything. Using this as an extreme example, Jesus responds to the theoretical question expounded by the doctor: he who loves his wounded neighbor loves God. This is enough. And it is not necessary to perform this charitable act "for the Lord," but for one's neighbor. Thus, an outcast, an atheist, a despised person is shown to be one who is authentically religious. This moral is the reason the parable of the Good Samaritan is one of the most subversive of the parables of Jesus.

The original word employed by Jesus in this parable is not that indicating "neighbor" but rather the Greek word *plesion,* which is equivalent to *rea* (in Aramaic) and to our "companion." In Jesus' time, it was understood that in order to please God, it was necessary to do good to others, but the question was raised as to who were one's "companions." The Pharisees excluded from their love those who were not like them; the Essenes excluded "the children of darkness" (= the fishermen) as companions;

many Israelites excluded the foreigners; others, their personal enemies. The "companion" — according to the story — refers to anyone who is in need. The last part of the parable shows us who the real "neighbor" is. The atheist who went to the wounded man becomes his neighbor. A neighbor is not only one whom we meet on the road, but also one in whose road we place ourselves. True love demands an active attitude of solidarity, of reaching out, and of reconciliation.

(Luke 10:25 – 37)

79

Blind since Birth

Ezekias: So you see, brothers, our first parents, Adam and Eve, wanted to discover the secret of God the Most High, and know the good from the bad. And they sinned, because this knowledge belonged only to God. Only God can finally judge what is good and what is bad, but we ministers on earth, who work with God, have received from God power to discern what is the good fruit and what is rotten and infested with worms.

Woman: Master Ezekias, since you are an authority on sins, please tell me: Who do you think sinned more, Adam or Eve?

Ezekias: Look, my child, the sin of Eve was greater because not only did she eat the forbidden fruit, she even led her husband to sin, and this, therefore, made her sin greater.

That Saturday morning, passing through the Water Gate to enter the city, we saw Ezekias, the teacher and authority on the law and on the traditions of Israel, teaching the pilgrims who surrounded him. His eyes moved a lot, like an owl pursuing its prey. The other Pharisees, like him, taught Moses' law in the streets of Jerusalem during the days of the feast.

Ezekias: So, having eaten the forbidden fruit, and the sin of our fore-fathers consummated, the two felt embarrassed for seeing themselves naked. Another sin was born that very instant, the sin of concupiscence, then the sin of greed, of lust and the sin of...

Chispa: Hey, Master-What's-Your-Name. You start mentioning one sin and you end up mentioning the others too. Ha, ha, ha!

Ezekias: What is this wretch saying?

Chispa: I said, if the old man Noah had filled his ark with all the sins you have been naming from the time you opened your mouth, then his boat would have sunk right then.

Ezekias: But who is this insolent fellow?

A Man: He's blind, Master Ezekias.

A Woman: They call him Chispa because he's a blabber-mouth. He never keeps his mouth shut.

Chispa: Go ahead, Master-What's-Your-Name. Your story about naked Eve is getting to be interesting! I may be blind, but not maimed, so I can learn a lot with my hands! Ha, ha, ha!

Ezekias: Hey, you miserable beggar, you better shut up and go away from here, so we may experience the joy of meditating on the law of the Most High!

Chispa: Suit yourselves, I've got my wine, after all, which is better! Ahhh!

Ezekias: Foul mouth! Drunkard! Well, let's go on with our discussion. Are there any more questions?

A Woman: If you know what is good and bad, please tell us why this poor fellow was born blind. Could it be because of the sins of his parents, or his own?

Chispa: Oh, oh, my parents are nice people. Leave them alone, will you? Maybe their grandmother is the sinful one! Look at this woman!

Ezekias: The right answer to the right question. Look, knowing the rebellious spirit of this man and the constant mockery with which he deals with the ministers of God, we can be sure that this man has sinned and because of this, he was born blind.

Chispa: Hey, how could I have sinned before I was born? I was born blind. Did I sin inside my mother's womb?

Ezekias: This man has sinned and will continue to sin. His tongue is his own judge and it is very sinful.

Chispa: And yours too. Master-What's-Your-Name, all your spittle must have dried up by now, so why don't you take a shot or wine? Here, take it. You've been talking the whole morning, you've got to wet your whistle! Ha, ha, ha!

Ezekias: My children, let's get out of here and look for a quieter place. With this rascal around, it's impossible to reflect truly on the word of God.

The group of pilgrims left through the narrow street, with Ezekias the teacher. Smiling, Chispa was left there, with his thick cane in his hands. He was very dark, but the wine gave a radiant look to his face. We moved closer and Jesus sat beside him.

Jesus: So, everyone's gone, my friend. Now you can drink your wine all by yourself.

Chispa: Well, as a matter of fact, I was having a lot of fun with them. He's quite a guy, that teacher! I don't know what you think, pal, but what nerve he's got to judge other people, that this one has sinned, and that one is good or bad. Pff!

Jesus: He wants to have God locked up in a cage, like a bird.

Chispa: Did you hear what he said? That I was born blind because of my sins. How's that possible when I never could see? Hah! If I want to pinch a woman, I end up grabbing her boobs! I'm just a poor wretch. And now he calls me a sinner! And that's the height of it! Look, friend, I believe God will not use up all his spit talking nonsense, like this teacher. Don't you agree?

Jesus spat on the ground and made a little paste with his spittle and clay. Then he rubbed it on Chispa's blind eyes.

Chispa: Hold it, you! What're you doing to me? What's the matter? Are you out of your mind?

Jesus: Listen to me, Chispa, go and wash in the Pool of Siloam. Then go and see that blabber-mouth teacher and tell him what happened.

Chispa: Wait, don't go away. Hey, who are you? Tell me, who are you?

After a while . . .

A Woman: Look, Lyna, isn't that Chispa, the blind man?

Another Woman: How can that be when the guy has no cane and walks as if nothing is wrong. Come, let's go near. He must be someone who looks like Chispa.

Woman: Are you Chispa, who's seen at the Water Gate every morning?

Chispa: The very same one my mother gave birth to! Yeah, I'm Chispa.

Woman: How come you can see me, or is this one of your tricks again, bandit?

Chispa: No, Lyna. Look how well I am now. I can even tell the number of hairs in your mustache.

Woman: Foul mouth! Damn you rascal!

Chispa: Please don't think I see unpleasant things alone, Lyna. I also see how pretty you are in that striped scarf of yours. What a sight to behold! Now I see everything! Everything! Except that teacher, whose name I don't know, the one who cured me. He told me to look for him. Where could he be?

Soon the news was all over the village.

A Man: How did it happen, Chispa? C'mon, tell us!

Chispa: This man, whose name I think is Jesus, rubbed my eyes with clay and told me to wash in the Pool of Siloam. I did, and presto! I was cured! That's it!

Man: And where's this man who cured you?

Chispa: I don't know. Right now, I'm looking for that teacher of the law with a shrill, crickety voice. I wonder where he's gone!

Finally Chispa found him.

Ezekias: What's with you, poor sinner?

Chispa: I can see! I can see!

Ezekias: You can see? What nonsense are you saying, rascal?

Chispa: That I can see with my eyes! That's what I'm telling you!

Ezekias: You can see? Do you see my hand?

Chispa: Of course! In fact, I see you've got dirty hands, teacher! Ha, ha, ha!

Ezekias: Let go of me, you fool! You're not Chispa, but an impostor. He sent you to confuse us.

Chispa: No, I'm the same one you saw at the Water Gate when you were telling the story of naked Eve!

Ezekias: So what happened to you?

Chispa: A man rubbed my eyes with clay and spittle and when I washed in the pool, presto, I could see!

Ezekias: And who is this man?

Chispa: The one who cured me. I was blind, so I couldn't see his face.

Ezekias: Today is a rest day! Nobody can heal on the Sabbath!

Chispa: But he cured me.

Ezekias: In whose name did he do it?

Chispa: He mentioned God's name when he cured me.

Ezekias: He couldn't have done that, because he who does not observe the Sabbath is a sinner!

Chispa: Well, I think he's a good man. And he cured me!

Ezekias: He is neither a good man nor has he cured you in God's name! Who was this man?

Chispa: They say he's God's prophet.

Ezekias: Liar! He who does not fulfill God's law cannot be a prophet!

Chispa: Well, prophet or not, I don't give a damn. He cured me.

Ezekias: Enough of this silly talk. You have never been blind, you brazen fool, impostor. Go fetch the parents of this man. I'm calling the priests right away.

Ezekias call the priests together and summoned the parents of Chispa.

A Priest: Be careful with what you are going to say. You are in the house of God and before his representatives. We shall take your statement in the name of the Almighty. Are you ready to tell the truth?

Mother: Yes, sir, we are.

Another Priest: Is this man here your son?

Father: Yes, teacher. He is our son Roboam. Some call him Chispa. He is the same one . . .

Priest: You are under oath in the name of God the Almighty! Is it true that this man was born blind?

Mother: Yes, it is true. Just as I am, right now, trembling with fear, I myself gave birth to him; he was born blind. That was quite a sad thing, teacher.

Priest: Well then, if he was born blind, why can he see now? In God's name, tell the truth.

Father: The truth is, we have no knowledge of how it happened.

Mother: Why don't you ask him? He is old enough to explain to you everything. Yes, ask him.

So they called Chispa.

Priest: Listen, rascal, and this is going to be the last time. You are before the books of the law and God's representatives. We know that the man whom you claim has cured you is a sinner. If you are a follower of his, then we declare you a sinner too. We cannot consent to the fact that this man has cured you on the day of the Sabbath.

Chispa: What if I was healed on a Monday?

Priest: You would commit a sin, just the same. We cannot tolerate a man who claims doing things in God's name. We are God's representatives, and only we can interpret the holy law! We declare that this man is a sinner.

Priest: C'mon, what can you say about him?

Chispa: Here you go again. I told you, I don't give a damn, whatever he is. I was blind, and now, I can see.

Priest: Who is this man, and where is he?

Chispa: Let's get this over with. I know what you want. You want to learn from him how to do marvelous things.

Priest: Damn, go away and join him. You're of the same stuff, anyway: you're both sinners with no breeding at all. Go ahead! We shall obey Moses, whom God has spoken to, and not this man, whom we know to be a charlatan from Galilee, who wears broken sandals and stinks of wine and whores.

Chispa: Exactly. This poor fellow has God on his side, because I couldn't imagine him giving sight to a blind man without having God on his side.

Priest: Are you lecturing us, the ministers of God? Get out of my sight! We can't allow a wretched man like you to tell us on whose side our Lord is and is not. That is our job. We can't allow anyone to do as he pleases. God's wrath befall you! Go away and don't you ever set foot in the house of the Lord.

The ministers of God drove Roboam out of the synagogue. When he went outside, he could see the color of the stones and the shapes of the clouds. Jesus had given him back his sight. Jesus did everything well: he opened the eyes of the blind man and left in the dark those who, full of pride, thought they could see.

•

The scribes, the doctors or teachers of the law, exercised a strong influence on the people. They were aware of it, and because of this, they considered themselves superior. On the other hand, by being "experts" in religion, those who "knew" felt they were exempt from sin. The superiority they displayed to the people was, therefore, intellectual and moral. Many people respected them and obeyed their instructions. They were consulted and were allowed to teach the people. It would be difficult for these teachers of the law, who had enjoyed the monopoly of God and religion, to give up this privilege that had brought them a lot of advantages. This explains their consistent opposition to Jesus, a layman with no special training in theology, who expounded on religious issues with total freedom and in a manner contrary to what was established by the official religion.

The question raised about Chispa's blindness responds to the mentality of the period. It was believed that all misfortunes were consequences of a sin committed and that God's punishment was in proportion to the gravity of the sin. God could also punish "out of love," in order to test a person. If these punishments were accepted in faith, then the misfortune was converted into a blessing, and people eventually acquired a more profound knowledge of the law, and received the pardon of their sins. But it was also believed that no punishment made "out of love" could prevent a person from studying the law. Since blindness prevented such study, it was believed that it could never be a test of love, but could only be an unredeemable curse. Some rabbis were of the belief that a boy could commit sin even in his mother's womb, but it was more common to think that congenital physical defects were due to the sins of the parents, in spite of the clarifications made by prophets on punishments inherited, insisting that sin was more an individual responsibility before God (Ezek. 18:1–32).

Against such intolerance and obstinacy, Jesus approaches the blind man as his equal, without accepting the judgment made by the religious authorities, much less the idea that God is behind this judgment. God is not monopolized by the theologians, and neither can people dictate God's actuations. God is free and wants all people to be free. All this indicates a sign to us, when Jesus opens the eyes of the man who was born blind. Those who claim they can see, that they know the truth and possess knowledge, are blind. And those who are despised, the last and the least ones, are those who actually see and get to know the truth about God.

Jesus rubs the eyes of the blind man with mud or clay mixed with spittle. This is a sign too: he is reenacting the scene in Genesis which describes God creating humans out of clay of the earth, mixed with his spittle. In Israel it was believed that saliva was a source of one's strength, of vital energy, and, therefore, it was used to cure certain illnesses. For example, it was a traditional belief that the spittle of the first born son could cure diseases of the eyes. The symbolic element of mixing spittle with clay in this manner is significant. The gospel of Jesus, his good news, is capable of creating a new man, who is truly free not only before his brothers, but also before the Lord. God does not put people in shackles, nor does God punish them with sufferings. God wants to relate to humans as his equal.

The Pool of Siloam was located outside of the walls of Jerusalem. Siloam means "the one sent." This makes reference to the origin of water that collected in the pool. The water reached Siloam from the spring of Gihon, situated in the eastern part of the city. The fountain of Gihon was the only fountain in Jerusalem from which water sprang forth throughout the year. This explains the authorities' concern to contain it as the source of the water supply for the whole city in times of drought and, above all, in times of war. That is why, seven hundred years before Christ, King Hezekiah ordered the construction of a tunnel from the springs of Gihon to Siloam, which was then situated inside the walls. This tunnel, excavated in bare rock, is an admirable feat of engineering. It is half a kilometer long, only half a meter wide, and with a height ranging from 1.5 to 4.5 meters. Today one can still pass through the tunnel in about three-quarters of an hour, with the use of a lamp and with the water below knee-high, until one gets to the ruins of the old Pool of Siloam.

What concerns the religious authorities here is not whether the blind man could see or not, but rather preserving their power and influence. What has taken place disturbs them because it spoils their theological schemes. They are not willing to accept the fact that a layman, who has also violated the law of the Sabbath, which is a rest day, can also manifest God's power. Their manner of condemnation is done by stages. First, they deny that what has happened is true, and they try to make it appear as a hoax. Then they aim to suppress the joy brought about by healing, and they do that by threatening and instilling fear, showing, with an authority arrogated upon themselves, that life (the blind can see) is something negative and perilous. They deny evidence and twist values: calling evil what is good, darkness what is light. Their false theology stops all arguments for everyone. Between humans and the law, they choose the law. The last phase becomes an act of violence: expulsion from the community.

(John 9:1–41)

80

The Pious Man and the Scoundrel

Ophel is a neighborhood right at the heart of Jerusalem where many people dwell and the houses pile over one another. Like it or not, one gets to know the entire life of his neighbor with this kind of set up. That Monday, as we passed by the front of the house of Ezekiel, a pious man . . .

Ezekiel: But of course, Rebecca, we left the temple covered with a cloud of incense. Master Josaphat was ahead, leading the procession, holding high the book of the law with his hands.

Son: Buaaaaa . . .

Ezekiel: Now, what's that noise, little boy?

Rebecca: It must be the chair's leg, Ezekiel. C'mon, continue with your story about the procession.

Ezekiel: Well, as I was saying, we left the temple with great fervor and . . .

Son: Buaaaaa . . .

Ezekiel: Hey, what's the matter with this boy?

Rebecca: Indigestion, perhaps.

Ezekiel: Or ill-breeding. My son, "A rude man is a disgrace to his family." You won't do that again, son, will you?

Son: Yes, Papa.

Ezekiel: Yes what?

Son: No, Papa.

Ezekiel: Yes or no? Answer me clearly.

Son: Yes and no, Papa.

Rebecca: Why don't you leave him alone, Ezekiel. He's just a kid. Stop pestering him. He doesn't know what he's talking about.

Ezekiel: "One's misdemeanors disturb the spirit. Good breeding, on the contrary, is like a balm that soothes it." Say, Rebecca, why don't you bring in some olives for us to munch?

Rebecca: Right away, Ezekiel.

Ezekiel: I know you love to eat black olives, don't you, son?

Son: I don't like them, Papa.

Ezekiel: And why not, son?

Son: Because they taste like shit to me.

Ezekiel: What? Rebecca! What manners have you been teaching our son?

Rebecca: He's learned that from his playmates.

Ezekiel: Son, do you know that what you said is sinful?

Son: But what did I say, Papa?

Ezekiel: What you said a while ago.

Son: Which one, Papa?

Ezekiel: You know what I mean. Anyway, I don't want to hear that word anymore in my house.

Son: Tell me, Papa, what word is that?

Meanwhile, in another house, where the scoundrel Philemon lived . . .

Philemon: Ha, ha, ha, I can't anymore . . .

Marthina: Hey, man, will you finish your story?

Philemon: Can you imagine the palace mayor telling the king, "My king, the prince is conspiring against you"? The king said: "Nonsense, this is all nonsense. The prince is still an innocent little boy." The palace mayor says: "Well, this innocent little boy has already set his two eyes on the throne." The king replies: "It's all right, as long as he does not lay his third eye on it." Ha, ha, ha. This one deserves a good laugh. Ha, ha, ha!

Marthina: Ha, ha, ha! Don't be so gross, Philemon.

Philemon: But the gross part is, when the queen came in and told the king . . . Ha, ha, ha! Oh, oh, I can't stand this anymore. My guts are going to explode!

The next day, Tuesday, in the house of Ezekiel, the pious man . . .

Ezekiel: My dear, today is Tuesday, and it is the day of the guardian angels.

Rebecca: What does that mean, Ezekiel?

Ezekiel: The angels are pure spirits. They don't eat or drink. We must emulate them, Rebecca. It's a day of fasting today.

Son: But Papa, I'm hungry.

Ezekiel: Shut up, you brat. Rebecca, why don't you just prepare light soup and some bread.

Rebecca: Is that all?

Ezekiel: Yes, that will be enough. "Our body is like a horse: You tighten his rein and he'll adjust to it."

Rebecca: But, Ezekiel, our child is a growing boy, and he needs sufficient food. I'm afraid he...

Ezekiel: No need to worry, Rebecca. He who fasts never fears the Lord. If you fast, you will appear before the Lord's tribunal with your head held high.

Rebecca: And at the rate we're going, that'll be soon!

At the same time, in the house of Philemon, the scoundrel...

Philemon: Damn, this chicken breast is better than yours, Marthina!

Marthina: But where does all the food you devour go, huh? There seems to be a hole in your stomach. Look, Philemon, you better stop now, or you might throw up everything.

Philemon: Who said so? I'm like those pelicans who swallow whatever gets into their beaks. Hey, lemme have more servings of those eggplants and lentils! And a sizable piece of that bacon too! Lalarooo!

Marthina: Well, as you wish. But if your belly explodes...

Philemon: You're a happy man when your tummy is full, so they say.

Marthina: Yeah, but people also die of overeating.

Philemon: Well, if Death comes and claims my life today, he'll drag me off a happy man.

The following day, Wednesday, in the house of Ezekiel, the pious one...

Ezekiel: "You will take one tenth of the yield from your fields, and you will take it to the Holy Temple of God, where you will offer as a pleasant sacrifice the tenth part of your wheat, the tenth part of your oil, the tenth part of your wine." It was thus commanded by Moses, as it is written in the Book of Deuteronomy. Thus, I will comply with it.

Rebecca: Today we shall offer our tithes and alms to the priests of God. Everything for the temple, for giving honor to the Lord, so that we shall all be included in the number of God's chosen people!

At that same moment, Philemon was gambling in the inn...

Philemon: This is the number! C'mon, count this! Four and six, then eight, and sixteen! I win again!

A Neighbor: Such luck you've got tonight, huh, Philemon? You've left me stark naked this time!

Philemon: Know why? I've got a twin brother, and the two of us started playing dice since we were in our mother's womb!

Neighbor: No, you've cheated me, that's why.

Philemon: I cheated you? Are you saying I'm a cheat? Hey, look, fellow, lemme give you another chance. I'm betting everything on seven! Everything, including the forty denarii I won last night, and what I won yesterday!

Neighbor: What else can I bet? I don't even have a cent left.

Philemon: Man, why don't you bet your tunic? No, no, your wife will be better. Right, your wife against my denarii. Is that okay with you?

Neighbor: Yeah. C'mon, cast the dice.

Philemon: In the name of the archangel of the seven clouds, of the cherubim with the seven wings, of the devil with the seven horns, gimme seven, c'mon! Here goes Seveennnnnn! By Jove! I won again! Your wife is mine now, neighbor!

Thursday evening, in the home of Ezekiel, the pious one . . .

Ezekiel: Rebecca, I'm telling you, just as the saintly Tobias told Sarah, Rachel's daughter: I'm not getting into bed without first invoking the name of the Almighty.

Rebecca: Hmmmm! Well, go ahead, invoke his name and get into bed at once, as I can't wait any longer.

Ezekiel: "Lord, you know fully well that I am not taking this sister of mine with impure desire, nor can I get close to her without the right intentions. The only reason I'm taking her is to procreate. A child, my Lord, who will not be the fruit of carnal desires, but of the hope of begetting the Messiah." My dear wife, let us procreate!

Rebecca: Ahuuuummmm! What a boring speech you gave, the Messiah has already fallen asleep.

Meanwhile, in the house of Philemon the scoundrel . . .

Philemon: Pssst, come over here, my sweet, chubby lady. Don't be a bore.

A Woman: Are you out of your mind, Philemon? What if my husband finds the two of us together?

Philemon: He wouldn't say anything. He'll have bitten his tongue out of shock.

Woman: And what do you suppose I should tell him, huh?

Philemon: Tell him you walk in your sleep, and while doing so, you ended up in my arms.

Woman: What if your wife finds out?

Philemon: She'll never find out. She's deaf and blind.

Woman: Then why did you marry her?

Philemon: Precisely because of that!

Woman: Oh, Philemon, you're a demon!

Philemon: Maybe, but you're the best.

Woman: Take that hand off me, you insolent...

Philemon: I'm cold, chubby dear.

It was a Friday in the pious man's house...

Son: Papa, Papa, I wanna go out. Let's go to the plaza, Papa!

Ezekiel: No, son. You'll only find several rude boys in the plaza. That's where you learn all those vulgar things.

Rebecca: Maybe we can go visit my cousin, Rose. Poor thing, she's all alone.

Ezekiel: She's not alone. She's divorced. I'll never set foot in the house of a divorced person. I look the other way when I walk down the street.

Son: Papa, let's go to the steps! That's where all the boys play "horsey-horsey"!

Ezekiel: The son of a good family does not mingle with street children. Wisdom means you maintain considerable distance from the rest. Don't you ever forget this, son.

Rebecca: Gosh, Ezekiel, let's go, if only to take a walk around the neighborhood.

Ezekiel: No, Rebecca. Very soon it will be late, and don't forget that tomorrow is a Saturday. We'll have to get up early to worship the Lord in the temple. Let's all go to bed now.

In Philemon's house, at bed time...

Marthina: C'mon, Philemon, it's time to sleep. Aren't you going to bed yet?

Philemon: Hik! Why the hurry? Is there a fire around here? The night is still long like a monkey's tail. Hik! Long live the monkey!

Marthina: You're drunk, Philemon.

Philemon: Who? Me? Drunk?

Marthina: Who else? Let's see: How many fingers do I have in my hand? Look at it very well.

Philemon: How many fingers? Lemme count them: two, four, six, eight, sixteen, twenty-four, forty-four...

Marthina: You're drunk. C'mon, go to sleep.

Philemon: Solomon was more loaded, but they didn't tuck him in bed. Hik! I'm King Solomon. Hik. I'm King Solomon! Hiiik!

Saturday came. It was a rest day, and all the children of Israel went up to the temple to pray.

Ezekiel: Lord, I thank you for giving me another week to live by your commandments. My family is different from the rest of the families in the city. We fast, we give alms, and we observe tithing. We observe all norms of your sacred law.

The pious Ezekiel, with his wife and son, was praying loudly before the altar of God. While he was doing this, a man entered the temple and stayed at the back. He knelt down and beat his forehead against the floor, and with his closed fist, beat his chest. He was Philemon, the scoundrel.

Philemon: Lord, please help me. I am a sinner, Lord!

Ezekiel: Thank you, God, because my family is not like those who are stained by sin. They are thieves, adulterers, drunkards, and full of vice. Ehem, like this one at my back.

Philemon: Lord, cast your eyes upon me. I am not King Solomon. I am, I am a shit. Help me, Lord, I want to reform my life. How I'd wished I could.

Jesus: And so it happened, my friends, that on that day, the scoundrel went home, having reconciled himself with God. But not the pious one, because, for the Lord, he who is last becomes first, and the first becomes last.

The pious man and the scoundrel are "the Pharisee and the publican," the decent man and the brazen one, the religious man and the sinner. In narrating this story, Jesus makes a harsh criticism of the arrogance that characterizes the pious men of his time and of all times. He also talks of his personal conduct: Jesus was usually surrounded by "scoundrels"; some of them became his disciples, to whom his good news was directed. These people sympathized with Jesus. His actions, his behavior, and his life reveal to us how God really is: a God who is

close to the suffering people who are discriminated against by those who consider
themselves perfect.

•

The organization of the Pharisees, composed of laymen, was very significant during Jesus' time. It was estimated to have about six thousand
members then. Although its leaders were educated and belonged to the
upper echelon of society, the movement had a number of supporters
among the lower class. Its communities were selective — like sects. They
thought of themselves as the good ones, the redeemed, and God's favored
people. In order to become part of this select group the candidates were
carefully chosen, after which they underwent training for one or two years.

The focal point of the pharisaic way of life was the scrupulous obser-
vance of the law, according to the interpretation they themselves made of
Scripture. In Jesus' time, they had formulated 613 precepts of the law. Out
of these, 248 were positive commandments, while 365 were prohibitions.
Thus they turned the will of God — the law — into a heavy and burden-
some yoke. Those who did not observe all these norms religiously were
damned. The Pharisees greatly despised the masses, and they were convinced that these people were beyond salvation. A considerable part of
the message of freedom and hope recovers its meaning by contraposing
it to the lifestyle of the Pharisees.

The Pharisees succeeded in getting the support of some layers of society, specially because they were anticlerical. They were against priestly
hierarchy, proclaiming that sanctity was not a monopoly of the priests but
could be attained by any faithful layperson. Nevertheless, this truth was
gravely distorted in the pharisaic interpretation of the practice of being
holy. It was reduced to a scrupulous compliance to a series of pious acts
like fasting, almsgiving, and prayers. The Pharisees were formalistic and rit-
ualistic. Salvation for them was a matter of earning more and more merits.
Every Monday and Thursday, they fasted (the law required only one day
of fasting a year); they observed tithing (even insignificant wild grass was
paid for); and they distanced themselves fanatically from the so-called sinners. These were precisely the gluttons, the drunkards, the gamblers (who
were frowned upon by the religious men), and the cheats. The latter were
the "scoundrels."

Jesus' constant message — as shown in his actions, in his words, in his
parables — is that God specially cares for the sinners, the brazen ones,

and consequently they become closer to God than the pious ones. This message always provoked an angry protest on the part of the Pharisees. This was something they could not accept since they were always sure of their piety. And this is what Jesus was rightfully telling to their faces. The gospel tells us that if there is anything that will alienate a person from God, it is self-righteousness. The self-righteous try to distance themselves from sinners, lest they become sinners too, without realizing that in reality, by doing so, they are alienating themselves from the Lord. The Pharisees believed that salvation was practically impossible for such sinners. Jesus reversed everything: by making salvation difficult for the "self-righteous," since what really separates them from God is that piety that leads to insolence and arrogance, and that attitude which is practically beyond conversion. The scoundrels, on the other hand, are more open to humility, in acknowledging their sins before the Lord.

This transcendental message is presented to us in this episode in a humorous and picaresque manner. The style is intended to enable us to recognize the caricature of our own attitudes, so that we may have the profound humility to learn to laugh at ourselves and not to take ourselves too seriously.

(Luke 18:9–14)

81

Beside Jacob's Well

When the feast of the tents was over, Jerusalem bade farewell with great sadness to the pilgrims who had filled up the streets during that week-long celebration. It was time for us Galileans to return to the north.

After two days' journeys on the road, we caught sight of Mount Gerizim. The dark plains of Samaria opened before our eyes.

James: Watch out! This area is full of thieves hiding even beneath the rocks.

John: But all the caravans have already passed. What will they rob from us?

Jesus: Maybe the lice we got from Jerusalem! That's all we got.

James: Say whatever you want, but I think this place is damned.

John: It's a barren place like the devil's belly.

James: Besides, it's empty and arid.

Philip: Damn it, James. Stop that silly talk. Can't you see I'm scared?

For about a hundred years, the Galileans of the north and the Jews of the south feared and hated the Samaritans, our countrymen who lived in the central part of the country. Stories spread all over Israel magnified those fears. For us, Samaritans were rebels to the traditions of our country, and therefore did not deserve our respect, to the extent that we would not even greet them. Obviously, the Samaritans hated us too.

John: What are these monsters saying, Jesus?

Jesus: They want to stop and rest for a while, John. Pff.

Philip: I would trade my cane and my sandals for a glass of water. I'm dying of thirst!

James: The sun in Samaria is as treacherous as her people, Philip.

John: Cool it, fellas. We shall be in Sychar any moment now. There we can have something to eat and drink.

James: In the meantime, you've got no choice but to swallow your own saliva, Philip.

When the sun reached its summit, a signal that it was noontime, we arrived at Sychar, a small village nestled between two mountains, Ebal and Gerizim, the latter being the sacred mountain of the Samaritans.

John: Hurry! Let's see who gets to the well first!

The well was located at the village entrance. It was this well that our father Jacob bought·from the Canaanites two thousand years ago, as a gift for his son Joseph before Jacob's death. It is a huge, deep well. The water that flows in abundance beneath the parched land nurtures the growth of date palm trees beside the well.

James: Come, let's go buy some olives and pieces of bread first! I'm already starved to death!

John: Let's go, Peter! And we'd better run! Are you coming, Judas? And you too, Philip?

Philip: Yeah, let's all go. And you, Jesus?

Jesus: No, I'm staying here by the well. I'm so tired. I think I'm running a fever. I'll just wait for you here.

Philip: Okay. Maybe you should take a nap, dark one. By the time you wake up, you'll have before you a good jug of wine! Let's go!

We started heading for Sychar. Then, Jesus leaned back on a piece of stone among the bamboo trees, and closed his eyes. After a while . . .

Abigail: Hello, anyone there?

Jesus: Hmm, I fell asleep.

Abigail: To hell with you, bearded man! You scared me, did you know that? I thought it was a rat.

Jesus: Well, as you can see, I've got no tail. I'm Galilean. That's worse than a rat, isn't it?

Beside Jacob's well was a Samaritan woman whose beautiful, sun-burned face was looking intently at Jesus. Her equally tanned arm that extended toward him was full of bracelets.

Abigail: I didn't say that. Look, I don't talk to anyone. I came here to fetch some water, and I'm going right away. I don't want any trouble, and I've got nothing to do with you, do you hear?

Jesus: Well, but I want something from you.

Abigail: Oh yeah? A Galilean dealing with a Samaritan woman. Now, now! That's quite amusing. I'm sorry, but you've got the wrong... Well, my friend, the water from "this fountain" belongs to someone else already.

Jesus: No, you're the one who's mistaken, woman.

Abigail: Mmmmm.

Jesus: What's that?

Abigail: Mmmmm. I mean I don't speak to Galileans, damn it! No way will I ever deal with them!

Jesus: Oh, but I talk to Samaritan women. I told you there's something I'd like from you.

Abigail: Mmmmm.

Jesus: Hey, will you stop purring like a kitten and give me some water. I'm dead thirsty! You don't have to talk to me if you don't want to, just give me something to drink, please.

Abigail: Oh so that was it? Look, I don't want to sound malicious, but is it only water that you wanted from me?

Jesus: Why, isn't that enough? It's less expensive, besides, it doesn't make you drunk.

Abigail: You're right, but I'd rather drink wine.

Jesus: So you're like a mosquito.

Abigail: I'm like a what?

Jesus: A mosquito. Don't you know what the mosquito said to the frog when he fell into the barrel of wine? "I'd rather perish in wine than live in water!" and splash! The mosquito plunged into the barrel and happily drowned himself in the wine!

Abigail: Ha, ha, ha! Mmmmm.

Jesus: What's the matter with you? Did you twist your tongue again?

Abigail: Look, country hick, once and for all, why don't you make your-self clear? What do you want? You don't convince me at all, you know. Who are you, anyway?

Jesus: Who do you think I am?

Abigail: I bet all my bracelets you're one of those bandits roaming the mountains, robbing the men and raping the women.

Jesus: Do I really look like one of them?

Abigail: No, you look more like a storyteller to me and a troublemaker. I'm a decent woman, and right now I'm messing up my life by talking to you, a Galilean, no less!

Jesus: There go your biases once more. Tell me, woman, what have the Galileans done to you?

Abigail: To me, nothing, but to my people, a lot. You Galileans think of yourselves as masters of the world; you despise us and you speak ill of us.

Jesus: You Samaritans think of yourselves as masters of the world; you despise us and you speak ill of us. So, why don't we stop this, and just give me water to drink. My throat is parched dry.

Abigail: Well, here's your water and stop messing up my life.

Jesus: Ahhh. This is nice!

Abigail: You're a Galilean all right. All you can do is beg. Did you hear what I said? All you can do is beg, and not even a word of thanks you utter.

Jesus: You didn't have to shout, woman. I heard you. Guess what, I'll give you something in return.

Abigail: What?

Jesus: Water.

Abigail: What water are you talking about?

Jesus: The same thing I asked from you. Do you want some water?

Abigail: The sun must have drained your brain. Tell me, how can you fetch water when I've got the bucket and the rope with me?

Jesus: I know of another well whose water is more refreshing.

Abigail: Another well? As far as I know, this is the only well we have here. That's why our great grandfather, Jacob, bought it, so that he and his children and their flocks could drink from it.

Jesus: But I know of a well that gives better water. You drink water from your well, and after a couple of hours, you become thirsty again. But once you drink the water from this well that I'm telling you about, your thirst will be gone forever.

Abigail: Hey, where's this marvelous well, huh?

Jesus: Ah, it's a secret.

Abigail: C'mon, tell me, so I wouldn't have to be coming here every now and then to fetch water.

Jesus: No, no, it's a secret.

Abigail: A secret? So it's a cock-and-bull-story, huh? Now I know who you are, a rumor-monger and a liar! A marvelous well, hah!

Jesus: Okay, okay, I'll tell you where it is, but first you've got to call your husband.

Abigail: My husband? What's he got to do with all this?

Jesus: So he'll know about it too.

Abigail: Well, I'm sorry, country hick, but I must tell you I haven't got a husband here. You see me as I am, single with no commitments.

Jesus: C'mon, woman, you know that's not true. Didn't you tell me a while ago that "the fountain" was already taken?

Abigail: Well, of course, I had to defend myself.

Jesus: Tell me, how many?

Abigail: How many what?

Jesus: How many husbands have you had?

Abigail: Hey, that's none of your business, meddler! How dare you ask me how many husbands I got. I never asked you if you went to jail or what not!

Jesus: All right, all right, don't get furious. C'mon, let me see your hand.

Abigail: Can you read the lines in my hand?

Jesus: One moment. Let me see it. Oh yes, I see five.

Abigail: How did you know? Yeah, you're right, I've had five husbands!

Jesus: No, I was saying I saw five fingers on your hand.

Abigail: Now I know who you are! You're a fortune-teller. A prophet! You're a prophet, aren't you?

Jesus: Well, I'm a Galilean, like you said before.

Abigail: No, you're a prophet! I've never seen a prophet before! But now, you can't get away from me! Lemme ask you a question. Yeah, you've got to solve this one question for me: look, you Galileans and Jews claim that God has his throne in the mountain of Jerusalem. We Samaritans say that is not true, because it is here in Mount Gerizim where the Lord lives. What do you think of that?

Jesus: Well, I think God rose from his throne and descended from the mountain, to put up his tent down here, among the people, among the poor.

Abigail: You're a prophet, I'm sure of it! And before I realize it, you might even be the Messiah himself.

As the Samaritan woman said this, Jesus bent over, took a white pebble from the ground, and began to play with it in his hands.

Jesus: And what if I were he?

Abigail: How's that?

Jesus: What would you do if I were the Messiah?

Abigail: That's what I'm asking you. What would you do?

Jesus: Look, the first thing I would do would be to buy a brush this big to clean out the barriers between Samaria and Galilee, between Galilee and Judea, between Israel and the rest of the countries in the world. Then, I would get a master key that would unlock all granaries so that there would be enough wheat for everyone. And with a big hammer, I would break the chains and shackles to set the slaves and the prisoners free. I would summon all the bricklayers of the land and tell them: Hey, friends, I want you to dismantle the temple of Jerusalem and that of Gerizim, and all other temples, because God lives there no longer, but in the streets and plazas. Those who are really seeking the Lord will find him here, among the people. I would likewise buy the best bleaching agent to wash away all those laws and norms, which for many years have been a burden on our shoulders, and I would have only one law engraved in the heart: the law of freedom. Yeah, I would do all these.

Abigail: Now I'm certain! You are the Messiah we've been waiting for! Come, come to my house and my people, so that they will hear you!

Jesus: All right, but let's wait for my friends who have gone to buy some food. They'll be back any moment now.

In a short while, we got back. We were surprised to see Jesus talking to that Samaritan woman. It was not customary for men to be talking to women alone. Neither was it acceptable behavior for a Jew to converse with a Samaritan on equal footing. But Jesus was never concerned about what people said about him. He was a free man, more free than the water gushing forth from the springs of Shechem. We who were getting to know him more and more didn't say anything; then we started to eat. It was noontime.

•

Samaria was the central region of Palestine. To go back from Jerusalem to Galilee, it was common to pass through the mountain road, crossing Samaria. About seven hundred years before Christ, the Assyrians had invaded this area of the country. They drove away the Jewish people residing in the place and settled as colonists. In the passage of time, the Assyrian colonists intermarried with native inhabitants who had stayed in Samaria. The result was the Samaritans: a race of mestizos, people with a hodgepodge of religious beliefs. The disdain the Israelites, the Galileans of the north, as well as the Jews of the south felt toward the Samaritans was a mixture of nationalism and racism. To be called a "Samaritan" was an insult; it was synonymous to being called a bastard.

About four hundred years before Christ, the Samaritan community definitely broke away from the Jewish community, and the Samaritans put up their own temple atop Mount Gerizim, a temple that rivaled that of Jerusalem. This formalized the religious schism between the two communities. After that, tension grew high, and in Jesus' time the enmity between them deepened. Intermarriage between the Jews and the Samaritans was explicitly prohibited, since the latter were regarded as impure to an extreme degree, and a cause for ritual impurities. They were even banned from entering the temple or offering sacrifices. They were referred to as "the stupid people residing in Shechem."

The Samaritans prided themselves in being descendants of the ancient patriarchs of Israel. In reality, they had Hebrew blood, but the rest of the Israelites considered them pagans and foreigners. The Samaritans likewise observed the Mosaic law with its many scruples, but this made them appear idolatrous because they worshiped God in Mount Gerizim. Gerizim, the sacred mountain of the Samaritans, was certainly significant in the history of the Israelites, because it was there that the blessings were given to the people before Joshua, as they entered the Promised Land (Josh. 8:30–35). The temple of the Samaritans erected there was destroyed in Jesus' time, but its summit continued to be a place of worship, where the Samaritans went up to pray and make some sacrifices.

The city of Shechem during Jesus' time corresponds to the present-day Nablus, one of the most genuine Arab cities in the Jewish territory. At present there is one neighborhood of the Samaritans in Nablus where the descendants of this rebellious race live. Actually, there are only about four hundred of them; they marry only among themselves, preserve their own dialect, their schools, and their literature. The leaders of the Samaritan community are always garbed with red turbans, signifying their rank of hierarchy. Today's Samaritans still keep their traditions zealously. They still ascend Mount Gerizim during Passover to offer a lamb as sacrifice, in accordance with their rite — which is different from that of the Jews. They keep a scroll of the law in the their synagogue, which, according to them, was written by a grandson of Aaron, Moses' brother, although this has no historical basis. It is a closed community, doomed to perish, due to the continuous intermarriage of cousins or relatives. Proofs of this biological deterioration are already evident in the large number of blind and abnormal people among them.

Sychar was a small village between Ebal and Gerizim, the twin sentinels of Samaria. Here was the land that Jacob had bought (Gen. 33:18–20), which he later gave as a present to his son (Gen. 48:21–22). There was a well in this land which, after almost two thousand years, the people persisted in calling — in Jesus' time — "Jacob's well." Wells are very significant in Palestine, as water is scarce in the country. These underground springs which are less abundant are easily located, even after centuries have lapsed. These were vital for the shepherds and the nomads since the life of their flocks, their only source of wealth, was dependent on them. These wells had a depth of as much as 20 meters. At present, after four thousand years, it is still possible to drink fresh water from Jacob's well — for the Christians, the well of the Samaritan woman. Very near the well is a burial mound which in the Arab tradition is venerated as the tomb of Joseph, the son of the patriarch Jacob, and heir of the lands of Shechem.

The narration in John's gospel about the conversation of Jesus with the Samaritan woman is a grand theological elaboration replete with symbols, similar to that of John 3 about Nicodemus. The basic element of this dialogue can be summed up in the word "freedom." Jesus, by talking to the Samaritan woman alone, is breaking once and for all two very deep forms of prejudice during his time: the sexual prejudice, which prevented a man from talking to any woman alone; and the national-racist form of prejudice, continuing the mortal enmity between the Israelites and the Samaritans. These are the yardsticks of Jesus' enormous sense of freedom and his great capacity for human relations. From the theological point of view, this episode likewise speaks of freedom, the freedom of God who does not want to be enclosed in temples — neither in Jerusalem nor in Gerizim — but prefers to relate with us as Father, in spirit and in truth. The new community that Jesus wants to inspire in us will not be known for the kind of worship it offers the Lord, but for the community through which it wants to bring God into our life.

(John 4:1–27)

82

In a Samaritan Village

Abigail, the Samaritan woman who had spoken with Jesus on the day we arrived in Sychar, insisted that we go to her village. She was walking ahead of us, telling all her neighbors that she had met a prophet beside Jacob's well.

Abigail: Hey, Nora! And you, Simeon! Come and see this man who read my palm and guessed everything I did. And what if he's indeed the Messiah, huh? Hey, neighbors, c'mon, hurry and don't miss this!

Abigail knocked at every door, inviting everyone to her house. We were following her, but not with enthusiasm. As usual, my brother James and I protested a lot.

James: But Jesus, how dare you do this? Are you sick or out of your mind?
John: I'd rather be tied to a post and be cooked alive than set foot in the house of these Samaritans.
James: They say whoever enters and sits in the house of a Samaritan loses his eyesight before the year ends.
Jesus: Well then, stay outside and look the other way.
James: If you do that, you'll turn into salt, like Lot's wife.
Jesus: It's okay, James and John. You don't have to go, if you don't want to. But I'm going into Abigail's house and greet her husband.
James: Abigail! What a sweet, little girl's name.
John: For a jug of water, you were taken in by the Samaritans, Jesus.
Jesus: No, it's you and your old ideas and biases against the Samaritans and our relationship with them that put us all in a fix. I'll drink from any well and visit any house. Do whatever you please.

So we went inside Sychar, Abigail's village. There was a small square along the road where a group of Samaritans wearing red turbans and gray tunics looked at us with hatred in their faces.

One Samaritan: Hey, hey, look who we have here.

Another Samaritan: Oh, the stinking Galileans! Why don't you just go to the Sea of Galilee and wash your armpits clean! Ha, ha, ha!

Jesus: Don't mind them, John. Can't you see they're trying to provoke us?

Samaritan: Galilee! Hail to you! Ha, ha, ha!

Another Samaritan: Hey, hey, what a scraggy-looking group of Galileans I see! I guess your mothers don't feed you very well! What's the matter with you, red head? Come, come over here, don't get scared. I simply want to beat your ass red! Ha, ha, ha!

Jesus: Cool it, James. They just want to get us into a fight.

James: Well, they'll get what they want, damn it! I won't allow any more insults from them! Listen well, you evil Samaritans, nephews of Lucifer! How I wish lightning would strike right now and split all of you into two!

Samaritan: And how I wish you'd lose all your teeth except one, that you may still suffer from pain!

John: May you swallow a handful of ticks that will suck the blood out of you!

Samaritan: Would that all your relatives be like onions whose heads are buried under the earth!

James: May fire and sulfur descend right now from heaven, as in Elijah's time, that all of you may burn, you sons of bitches!

Jesus: Stop it, James. You too, John. Damn those tongues of yours! They have more venom than a viper!

James: Do you hear that, Jesus? There's thunder coming!

John: God has answered our prayers! He'll send fire from heaven to kill the devil's Samaritans!

Jesus: Okay, okay. You stay here and wait for lightning and thunder to come. As for me, I won't allow myself to catch another cold!

Jesus ran toward Abigail's house. We followed him, too, but grudgingly. The rain had dampened all our enthusiasm. We had forgotten the curses previously uttered as we hastily crossed the small town plaza. In a short while, drenched by the rain, we arrived at the shabby little house of bamboo and adobe stones where Abigail and her husband, Jeroboam, lived.

Abigail: Come in, come in! This is my house, Jesus. Too small for such a big family, but... These are all my children and this is my husband.

Jeroboam: Welcome, Galileans! My house is like Noah's ark; it opens its doors to all kinds of animals!

Abigail: Don't be rude, Jeroboam.

James: So you and your wife were the first pair that slipped into the ark?

Jesus: Shut up, James.

Jeroboam: Abigail has told me that one of you is a witch who can read one's palm. Where is he?

John: The only witch here is your wife, who went to fetch water from the well at the wrong time!

Jesus: For God's sake, will you stop all those insults. Let's just talk to each other.

Abigail: Exactly! Say, Jesus, will you tell this stupid husband of mine what you have told me by the well, that this conflict between the Samaritans and the Galileans and the Jews is all over. C'mon, tell him.

We sat down and talked. After a while, the rain calmed down and the Samaritan neighbors started to arrive. Soon, Abigail's little house became full. Those who could, sat down on the wet ground, while the older ones remained standing, resting their chins on their canes.

A Samaritan: Who said that this thing between the Samaritans and the Galileans is all over. Who said such nonsense?

Jesus: I did.

Samaritan: So? and who are you?

Jesus: A brother of yours. You're my brother, too. We are all brothers and sisters, kneaded from the same dough, and we breathe the same air, the breath of God.

A bent-over old man with a long beard nodded his head.

Old Man: Yes. Baruch, the just man, says the same thing too.

A Woman: My aunt Loida says that the sheep must go with their own kind, in pairs! Well, stranger, our skin is not the same, you must remember that.

Jesus: But the blood that flows in you is as red as mine, cousin. Can't you see that? It's not the bark of a tree that matters, but the wood, and its fruit. Isn't that correct?

Old Man: Right. This is what Baruch, the just man, is saying too.

Samaritan: Hold it! Now this is getting tough! You Galileans have taken so much advantage of us, you have ruined our trade relations with Damascus!

John: Oh, yeah? Weren't you the ones who ruined the sale of wheat in the capital? Weren't you, Samaritans?

Another Samaritan: You set our forest in Ebal on fire.

A Woman: It was a Galilean who stole the scroll of the law of Aaron's grandson!

James: And who did the filthy thing of hurling those damned bones of the dead into the temple of Jerusalem?

Jesus: Damn it, will you stop it? Look, the rain has stopped. After the deluge, comes peace. What do we get by opening the wounds of our fathers? We are all one family with only one Father, who is in heaven. This is what matters more than anything else.

Old Man: Yes, yes, this is exactly what Baruch the just man is saying.

Woman: How can we be brothers when we don't speak the same language? When a Galilean says black, the Samaritan thinks white. When a Samaritan talks of Mount Gerizim, you think of Mount Zion.

Jesus: But when a Galilean says, "I'm hungry," and feels it, the Samaritan similarly feels the same thing. When a Samaritan cries for justice, the Galilean utters the same cry for justice! My friends from Samaria: we have been divided for many years now, ever since the Tower of Babel, I believe, when those ambitious men wanted to scale the heavens to rob the Lord of his place. Now, we have to put up another tower, not by the use of bricks this time but by joining our hands, crossing our arms, and those of the Galileans and the Samaritans, as well. Everyone is needed to be able to build this community of all one family, all brothers and sisters to each other.

Old Man: Baruch, the just man, said exactly the same thing.

James lost his cool when that old man mentioned for the fourth time the name of Baruch, the just man.

James: Wait a minute. Who the devil is this Baruch? It's Jesus talking and not any one else, not even Baruch!

Abigail: Baruch is a great prophet of ours. We owe him a lot. He has enlightened the minds of the people and defended our rights, the rights of the poor.

Old Man: Baruch, the just man, always says that . . .

James: What the hell do I care what Baruch says? It's Jesus who's carrying the staff of command here, the strong man of Israel!

Old Man: And what about Baruch?

James: I've got nothing to do with him!

Samaritan: Take back what you said, you red head from hell, or else!

My brother James and a Samaritan exchanged blows. Simon and Judas likewise engaged themselves in a fight with the other neighbors while the women were shouting menacingly. Abigail's little house shook and I thought it would have collapsed had it not been for Peter and Jesus who, after having yelled considerably, were able to get some little quiet.

Jesus: How many times do I have to tell you that we're all brothers and sisters and we must unite, instead of beating one another? If this Baruch is for justice, then he is with us, and we with him. What matters is that we are able to change things, not the person who changes them. Tell the just man, Baruch, that we would like to meet him and talk with him.

Night was already hovering over the village of Sychar when a tall and sturdy man entered the packed house of Abigail. He was dressed in a gray tunic with the red turban around his head, symbol of the Samaritan leadership.

Baruch: I'm Baruch. You were asking for me?

Jesus: We are just a handful of Galileans here. We're promoting the Kingdom of God in the north. I understand you and your group are doing the same in this part of Samaria. Can we be of any assistance to you?

Baruch: Of course. Look at the fields: the crops are already ripe for harvest. We need people. Can we be of any help to you?

Jesus: Certainly, Baruch. As they say, one sows and the other harvests. What is important is that things get done; who does the work is not an issue. In the end, both the sowers and the reapers are happy together.

Baruch: Let's be clear about this, Galilean. On whose side are you? the Zealots'? the rebels' of the desert? or the Sycharians' of Judea?

Jesus: We're on justice's side, Baruch. We're for the poor who, day in and day out, are clamoring for freedom.

Baruch: I'm pleased with your words. You can count on me. We are fighting for justice for our people.

Jesus: If you're not against us, then you're with us!

Baruch: Then this calls for a fraternal embrace, Galilean!

Jesus moved toward Baruch, the Samaritan leader. The two shook hands and hugged each other with much respect and excitement, like the two brothers, Esau and Jacob, when they met after so many years, beside the Yabbok River, near

Penuel. We stayed in the village for two more days, proclaiming the Kingdom of God among the Samaritans.

•

The enmity between the Samaritans, the Galileans, and the Jews was nurtured by a series of circumstances. One hundred twenty-nine years before Christ, the Jewish king John Hyrcanus destroyed the sacred temple of the Samaritans on Mount Gerizim. This sparked hatred in relationships between the two peoples. When Jesus was about ten years old, an incident happened that was horrifying to the Jews: During the feast of the Passover, the Samaritans, who had gone to Jerusalem, hurled bones of the dead into the temple. Such desecration of a holy place was an act of vengeance that the Jews could not forget. After that, tension mounted every now and then.

The Israelites took pride in their hospitality as a national virtue. But this was never manifested to the Samaritans. They refused to extend their greetings to them, and they shut their doors as proof of their total rejection. Every time Jews passed through Samaritan turf, it was not surprising to hear of serious incidents that would occasionally end up in killings. Jesus' disciples, specially James and John, mirror this hostility in an exchange of verbal invectives with the village people of Sychar. Jesus does not share in this narrow nationalistic spirit of his companions. He stays for two days with the Samaritans, a detail in John's gospel that highlights Jesus' breaking away from all sorts of racial nationalism and discrimination.

Baruch is not a historical character. In this episode, he appears as a leader of the Samaritans, loved and respected by his countrymen. As a just man in the service of the poor among his people, he easily relates to Jesus. The gospel is good news for the poor, transcending all barriers, notwithstanding one's being a Jew or a Samaritan, black or white, good or bad.

Ecumenism is one of the successes of the evolution of Christian thought in our day. Catholics, mainline Protestants, evangelicals, fundamentalists, and — far beyond — Muslims, Hindus, Buddhists, and so forth, are called to unite, not because we share the same ideas about God or immortality or the creation of the world, but rather because we are all called to construct a world of justice and peace.

Jesus said on one occasion: "He who is not with me is against me" (Luke 11:23). This phrase has been interpreted by some as a sign of intolerance or exclusivism. But the possible conflict arising from this is resolved with another phrase in the same gospel: "He who is not against you is for you" (Luke 9:50). Unfortunately, in the course of history, there has been an abundance of "religious wars," where thousands of persons have been tortured in the name of faith. Bloody crusades were organized, and tribunals were formed to excommunicate those who had a different way of thinking. None of this comes from the gospel. The gospel is not a call to intolerance, to discrimination, and to a rejection of those who think otherwise. In the face of such an unhappy historical legacy, Catholics must grow in humility, in repentance. As Jesus used to say — before they remove the mote in their neighbors' eyes, they must first remove the plank in their own.

(Luke 9:51–56; John 4:28–43)

83

The Banquet Guests

When we got back from the feast of the tents, Galilee was in great commotion. Rumors of what Jesus had done in the capital had reached Capernaum even before we got there. The talk about the new prophet was everywhere. Jacob and Simon, Jesus' cousins, returned from Jerusalem in the same caravan and spent the night in my father's house.

Simon: You're becoming famous, cousin, there's no doubt about it. Allow me to tell you this, though. It's true you've got the gift of gab and the knack for leadership, but you need people, and that's what Jacob and I are talking about. You've got to have popular support, which you haven't got.

Jesus: What about those who were at the wharf this afternoon? What are they, cousin Simon?

Simon: Nothing but a bunch of rotten rascals. Where the hell do you think you're heading for, with these paupers?

Jacob: And how! Just take a look at these people around you, Jesus. A handful of ignorant fishermen who know not where their right hand is.

Simon: Like Matthew, the despicable tax collector.

Jacob: And Mary, that prostitute who reeks of whore scent.

Simon: And Selenia, who's like her...

Jacob: Not to mention those stupid peasants and scoundrels.

Simon: What's gotten into your shell, Jesus? Listen to us, cousin, get other people, people with more training and with more, how shall I say it?, with more "influence." Those who can move the world at the snap of a finger. Haven't you got the idea yet? Open your eyes, Jesus, and wake up!

Jesus replied to their entreaties with a story.

Graziela: Open your eyes, Eliseus, wake up! Happy birthday! Did you sleep well?

Eliseus: Ahuuummm! Very well, Graziela, more than ever! Tralara, tralari, tralalalari!

Manolo: Happy anniversary, master! May the God of Israel bless you from head to foot!

Eliseus: And you too, Manolo! Blazes, I feel damned happy today. I want I just want to...

Graziela: What is it, Eliseus?

Eliseus: "I'd like to take you in my arms, my dear!" Tralara, tralari. Ha, ha, ha!

Graziela: Certainly you got up on the right side of the bed, yes siree! Happiness is man's best friend!

Eliseus: Today, I'd like all my neighbors to be happy with me!

Manolo: Then why don't you make it happen, master? It's been a long time since we had a party in the house!

Eliseus: You're right, Manolo. And this time, it won't be just an ordinary party. It's going to be something grand. A banquet! Damn! We've had bad times during the year and we need a break. Graziela and Manolo: we'll surprise the whole neighborhood. We'll treat them to a banquet, and all kinds of wine and drinks will flow. And there'll be music and dancing! Manolo, go to the farm right away and kill five of the best lambs that you can find.

Manolo: Five fattened lambs, and what else, sir?

Eliseus: Graziela, go and buy some boxes of olives.

Graziela: Which of them, the green ones or the black ones, master?

Eliseus: Two of each, and don't forget the figs!

Graziela: And a pot of good chick peas!

Manolo: As well as eggplants and cucumbers.

Eliseus: And almond sauce!

Graziela: Not to forget the nuts!

Eliseus: Manolo, start milking the goats, for today milk will overflow for all my friends!

Graziela: Milk and honey will flow!

Manolo: How many barrels of wine shall I bring in, master?

Eliseus: Two, no, make it four, four barrels of the best wine from the house of Carmelo! I want everyone to leave my house happy and contented!

Graziela: They'll be crawling on all fours, Eliseus, with all the wine before them!

Eliseus: Tralara, tralari!

Manolo: But the most important is missing, master.

Eliseus: What do you mean, Manolo?

Manolo: How about the guests, master? Whom are you going to invite?

Eliseus: The whole neighborhood! Everyone, yes sir! Send the word to Master Apolonius, to Doctor Onessimus, oh, and to Absalon and his beloved wife, Madam Eunice. I want you to invite everyone, Manolo; tell them I'm expecting them with open arms! I am expecting everyone at the banquet! I want my house to be filled with joy and with all my friends!

Manolo and Graziela worked feverishly and quickly, doing all that Eliseus had asked.

Eliseus: Is everything all set, Manolo?

Manolo: Yes, master, and don't be nervous.

Eliseus: Oh, I'm not nervous, Manolo. In fact, I'm happy. Graziela, Graziela, have you roasted the lambs?

Graziela: They're all well roasted, Eliseus! You've asked that question ten times.

Eliseus: You haven't forgotten the dates, I suppose.

Graziela: No, master. Everything is ready. Take it easy.

Eliseus: I'm just too happy, that's all! Tralara, tralari! Manolo, have the invitations been sent to all the neighbors?

Manolo: To everyone, master. Look at these corns on my feet. I got them from walking up and down the street I went to Master Apolonius's house, to Doctor Onessimus's, to Absalom's, and . . .

Graziela: And "his beloved wife, Madam Eunice."

Eliseus: Did you hear that? It's the first night watch.

Manolo: Well, the guests must be arriving by now.

Graziela: You know these people, Eliseus. The women have to braid their hair. The men have to oil their mustache. Well, anyway, they always come late.

The neighbors, however, felt superior to Eliseus, looking down on his invitation and hospitality.

Apolonius: But what has gotten into his head, that he should invite me? Why the heck should I, a very busy man, suck lamb's bones in his house? Hff, this guy Eliseus is crazy. Besides, he's a nobody; he hasn't got any fortune or business to talk about. Tell me, shall we talk about the birds in the sky? He's a crazy fool; that's what he is, penniless, without a single denarius in his pocket!

Messenger: Well, sir, what shall I tell him?

Apolonius: Whatever occurs to you. Tell him I'm not home; you don't know where I went. That's it: I went to purchase some lands, and I had to measure them, that he has to excuse me...

In a short while, the messenger was at Eliseus's door.

Eliseus: They're coming, they're coming! Graziela, run and open the door! Tralara, tralari.

Graziela: It's only the messenger, master.

Messenger: My master, Master Apolonius, cannot come because he is on a trip. He's sending his regrets.

Eliseus: Did you say he was on a trip?

Messenger: He purchased a piece of land, and he went to take its measurement. He wishes everyone to enjoy the food! Good-bye!

Eliseus: Too bad! I would have wanted to greet Master Apolonius.

Graziela: Don Apolonius is a very busy man, and he's got lots of money.

Manolo: They are now announcing the second watch, master.

Graziela: And still no one has come. The lambs and the chick peas are getting cold.

Eliseus: Well, don't get impatient, woman. They'll come. Tralara, tralari.

At the house of Doctor Onessimus, another invited guest...

Messenger: And what should I tell him, Doctor Onessimus?

Onessimus: Anything, man. After all, this Eliseus is so stupid he won't even know. My teacher, Jeconiah, used to say: "A man without culture is like a ball of excrement; he who touches it must clean his hand." You talk to him about the mysteries of science, he doesn't understand; you explain to him the subtleties of art, and he gets bored; you ask him: "Do you know philosophy?" and he replies: "Where does this woman live?" Ah, these ignorant fools!

Messenger: Well, so what do I tell him?

Onessimus: Tell this Mr. Nobody that I can't make it, that I just bought a couple of oxen, and that I still have to test them. Send him my regrets, of course.

Once again, there was a knock at the door.

Eliseus: At last, the guests are coming! Graziela, hurry up!

Messenger: Here's a message from my master, Doctor Onessimus: He wants me to inform Mr. Nobody, pardon me, Mr. Eliseus, that he cannot make it to the banquet, that he bought a couple of oxen, and that he wishes everyone a hearty dinner. Good-bye!

Eliseus: Good-bye.

Manolo: Such bad luck, master.

Graziela: Doctor Onessimus is a very cultured man.

Eliseus: Yeah, a brazen man, that's what he is. Say, Graziela, there goes the third watch and my house is still empty.

Graziela: Don't be sad, Eliseus, I tell you, they're coming.

Eliseus: Probably. Let's wait a little longer. Tararira lira . . .

At the house of another invited guest . . .

Eunice: What? We're going to the house of that common man? Oh, no, my dear, I'm sorry, I'm so sorry, but this Eliseus has no class, he's got no manners!

Husband: But what shall we tell him, my dear?

Eunice: For a swine like him, anything will do. Tell him that we have just gotten married and are still celebrating our wedding.

And the messenger reached the house of Eliseus.

Messenger: They have just gotten married and are still celebrating their wedding!

Eliseus: How's that?

Messenger: No, nothing. They are not coming.

Graziela: But these two were married more than a month ago.

Messenger: They are very much in love with each other and . . .

Eliseus: Yeah, they've got so much love, but no manners! Pff. What a flop. The cocks will crow in a short while, and yet, not even one of the guests has come.

Graziela: And the lambs are as cold as a dead man.

Manolo: And the barrels of wine are left untouched.

Graziela: Master Eliseus, could they possibly have lost their way, that's why they haven't come?

Eliseus: No, Graziela, it was I who made a mistake in inviting them. Manolo!

Manolo: Yes, master.

Eliseus: Manolo, put on your sandals fast, and go through the alleys and the marketplace right away, and bring me the beggars, the crippled ones, the blind, and all the poor people that you find in the street. Tell them to come to my house, to partake of the banquet that I have prepared for them.

Graziela: Are you out of your mind, Eliseus?

Eliseus: Of course not! I have never been saner in my life. Now I understand. Run, Manolo, and tell them at once, before the sun rises.

In a short while . . .

Manolo: Master, the whole neighborhood is excited! Many of them are coming over here! Shall I tell them that there is no more place?

Eliseus: On the contrary, Manolo, go back and tell them that those who are hungry may come, for there is enough place in my house, there are enough lambs and olives and wine for everyone!

Manolo: Yes, master, right away. Master, I also came across one of those prostitutes, you know, and she said that business was so bad, and if she could also come to partake of some food . . .

Eliseus: Of course, Manolo, tell her to come, as well as her friends.

Manolo: And those living on the other side of the river told me that . . .

Eliseus: Let them come too! Let all the tramps and the stinking men as well as the whores come too! They are all welcome in my house; this banquet is for them; the doors of my house are wide open for them!

Jesus: That night, Eliseus's house was filled to the brim with people. There was dancing, there was food, and there was fun. It was a great feast, the feast of the Lord.

Simon: What did you say, Jesus? the feast of the Lord?

Jesus: Yes, cousin Simon, the Kingdom of God is like the banquet given by Eliseus. God's true house does not smell like incense but the sweat and the perfume of a prostitute. God is one of us, don't forget that. God is with us, with the poor.

•

That Jesus, a man who was already popular, whom the people saw as a true prophet, was surrounded by the poor people of Capernaum and of Jerusalem was scandalous. To make the poor people the privileged beneficiaries of the good news and to trust in them that they might become the agents of change were intolerable. Jesus held on to this, and he even called "blessed ones or happy ones" those who were able to surpass a similar scandal (Matt. 11:5–6).

The gospels use various words to refer to Jesus' followers, but all the words refer to the same characteristic. One text talks of "the small ones" or of the "least ones" or of "the simple ones." Another word used is *nepis* (Greek), which is equivalent to *patit* in Hebrew and to *sabra* in Aramaic, a word which sums up the following: uncultured people with no breeding or religious formation. Jesus was surrounded by the *amha'ares* — as the Pharisees referred to them — men and women of ill reputation, slandered, and whom the self-righteous considered as doomed on account of their religious ignorance and bad moral behavior. Jesus simply referred to them as the "poor." They are those who have nothing, "those who are weary and overburdened," "the sheep without a shepherd." Jesus, who was from the same social class, an artisan and a peasant, proclaimed the good news of liberation to them.

A number of Jesus' parables try to "justify" God's conduct of addressing the good news to the most miserable. One of them is the parable of the "great banquet" where Jesus shows one of the reasons for this preference of God: the rich, the privileged, the wise, think highly of themselves, are so satisfied and so secure that they shut themselves out of the doors of the banquet. God has invited them, but they do not wish to attend the banquet. On the other hand, the poor, those who do not matter to anyone nor to anything, have their hearts open to the invitation. They have the capacity for excitement and surprises. They have hope in their hearts and they go. God counts on them for the realization of his historical plan, and they are the ones who will jampack his house and participate in the endless feast.

From the time of the prophets, Israel described the joy of the messianic times with the image of a banquet, where there was good food and, most of all, where drinks were in abundance (Isa. 25:6–8). In the minds of the people, the basic difference between ordinary food and a banquet was precisely in the amount of drink that was consumed. Wine was synonymous to celebration and happiness. It was the same with dancing. To mention the word feast meant dancing, to the point that the Hebrew word that corresponded to "feast" meant "dance" originally. The feast of the Messiah was likewise compared to a wedding feast. This is what Matthew's version adds to this parable. Even the last of the books of the New Testament, the Book of Revelation, preserves this imagery of the messianic wedding (Rev. 19:7–8). Within these solemn and brilliant allegories, Jesus puts in as a wedge the "scandal" of the gospel: the guests to that banquet are the tattered poor, the beggars, the least of the people, the rascals.

The scandal of the poor is the core of the gospel, a scandal that helps reveal the mystery of the Lord. After Jesus, the poor will be not only the privileged beneficiaries of the good news, but they will also be called to be a part of the kingdom. All this signifies that starting from Jesus, only those who grasp the real meaning of the poor know the real meaning of God.

The gospel is aimed at eradicating all types of differences among people, showing the way to a friendly and co-equal society. And, as it happened in Jesus' time, the only thing that can make us understand God's plan is to reiterate Jesus' example: by putting God within the hands of the poor.

(Matt. 22:1–10; Luke 14:15–24)

84

The Crafty Steward

After a hectic day of work at sea, battling it out with our nets and the waves, we would fasten our boats to the small wharf of Capernaum, and all of us fishermen would gather in the rambling tavern of one-eyed Joachim. There, we would gulp down a jug of wine as we protested the new taxes of King Herod and laugh at the antics of Phanuel's steward.

Pipo: This jug of wine is on me, pals! Hik! It's my treat, but first, you've got to shout "Long live Pipo!" C'mon one, two and three!

All: Long live Pipo!

Pipo: Yes sir, long live myself! Hey, one-eyed man, give more wine to all my fans, hik! Ha, ha, ha, ay! What a good life for a fattened cow like me! Ha, ha, hay!

Big Pipo was a special man. Being everyone's friend, with his three-edged beard and rotten teeth, Pipo hopped from one pub to another laughing at his own jokes and making us laugh at the same time. Because of his charm and his talent with numbers, he had landed a good job as steward of old Phanuel, one of the wealthiest proprietors of Capernaum. But Pipo was a spendthrift. All the money he earned, and did not earn, would be wasted, draining barrels and barrels of wine.

Peter: Well, Pipo, what a good life you have, you rascal! Your pocket has more money than the caravans of the Queen of Shebah could carry!

Pipo: It's my boss, Phanuel, who earns the money, hik! I just manage it.

John: Or better, you spend it, scoundrel!

Pipo: I'm just doing him a favor. Look, old Phanuel doesn't even know what to do with his money. Hik! He doesn't know how to enjoy it. Bah, if I don't help this miser, the moths will just eat up all his savings! Know something, pals? I'm just living up to a saying of Solomon: "The smart man lives on a fool and the fool lives on his work." Ha, ha, ha, hay!

James: Where did Solomon say that, Pipo?

Pipo: Search me! I dunno, and I don't care. But that's very well said, hik! Hey, guys, look at me, I'm the happiest man in Capernaum! Hik! C'mon everybody, get your empty glasses and let's all shout: "Cheers to Pipo!" Ready, one, two, hik! and three!

All: Cheers!

Phanuel: Long live Pipo!

It was something unexpected. There, at the door, was Phanuel, Pipo's employer, with his fine cane. His face was very serious. All of us remained motionless as the rich old man silently crossed the tavern. Pipo was as still as a statue, raising a glass of wine in one hand. He was unable to take the last gulp of wine.

Phanuel: Pipo!

Pipo: Yes, master.

Phanuel: You may collect all your things first thing in the morning, tomorrow.

Pipo: But, master.

Phanuel: I'm not your master anymore. I heard everything. You're fired.

Without further ado, Phanuel clasped the handle of his cane and left the tavern.

Pipo: Damn. Talk about good timing, huh? Why, he even cured my hiccups!

Peter: Your happy days are over, my friend!

James: Tomorrow at this time you'll be on the road begging!

Pipo: Old Phanuel should have let me explain.

Peter: What else is there to explain, rascal? You should be grateful he didn't send for two guards to have you arrested and kicked in jail!

Pipo: You're right, Peter. Now what am I to do, huh?

Peter: What the rest of us are doing — work!

Pipo: No, no, please, don't ever mention that to me. I get goose pimples just by hearing the word. I wasn't born for that. I don't have the strength for that.

John: Sure you've got it. The problem is you've got such a big belly that you can't even bend over!

James: You've got to do it, pal. I've seen you tending the pigs or gathering cucumbers.

Pipo: No, no, I'm no good for farm work. There's not a single laborer in my clan.

Peter: Well then, come with us, and let's go fishing in the lake. Do you know how to cast nets?

Pipo: All I know is that I get seasick, like a pregnant woman.

John: Learn something, damn it: be a potmaker, a tailor, or a tanner.

Pipo: At my age, John? Do you think I can still learn something? I'm forty, and I'm good for nothing!

James: Well then, my friend, Pipo, I guess there's nothing left for you to do but to beg at the door of the synagogue!

Pipo: Are you crazy? I'd rather die! I, Pipo, my mother's son, begging for alms? No way, do you hear? James, and everyone, you heard me, I'll never, never do that!

Peter: Okay, okay, you screaming fool! And what the hell do you plan to do?

Pipo: I've got one night to think about it. One night. I've got to clear my mind for it. Hey, one-eyed, give me another shot. I promise to pay you everything tomorrow, at this time. And this I swear!

That night, Pipo was restless and couldn't sleep.

Pipo: What shall I do? What shall I do? Oh Pythoness of King Saul, enlighten me! Almighty God, send me an angel who will whisper an idea in my ear! Damn it, I'm breaking my head thinking of something, and yet, nothing comes out of it. Pipo, think of something, fast, if you want to save your skin. Blazes, I've got it! I've got it! Oh, mother, what a smart son you brought into this world! Now, I must move and fast.

Pipo was on the move before it was dawn.

Lucius: But, who the devil is calling at this time?

Pipo: It's I, Pipo. Please open the door!

Lucius: What's the matter, man? Are you having nightmares? Are the police after you?

Pipo: They should be after me, but ...

Lucius: How's that?

Pipo: Nothing, good man. Tell me, how many barrels of oil do you owe my master, Phanuel?

Lucius: A hundred. You, yourself, made me sign the receipt, don't you remember? Is that what you came here for?

Pipo: You ask so many questions, old man. Look, here is your receipt: "I, Lucius, son of Luciano, am in debt of a hundred barrels of oil to Phanuel, in accordance with the Galilean measurement."

Lucius: What are you doing, you fool?

Pipo: I just tore the receipt that you had signed.

Lucius: So?

Pipo: And so, please sit down. Here, I'm giving you a new one, a blank one. Write: I, Lucius, son of Luciano, am in debt of fifty barrels of oil to Phanuel. Yes, yes, write that, fifty barrels.

Lucius: But Pipo...

Pipo: Ssshhh! Just shut up.

Lucius: What will your master say if he finds out?

Pipo: I don't care anymore what he'll say. What you'll say matters more to me, my friend, Lucius.

Lucius: I?

Pipo: Yes, you, my friend. Listen to me carefully. Now, you only owe Phanuel fifty barrels of oil, thanks to me, your friend, Pipo, who's helping you and who cares for you. Good-bye, old man, and go back to bed at once, that you may not catch cold!

Then he left and went and knocked at another door.

Urias: A hundred sacks of wheat, that's what I owe your master, Phanuel.

Pipo: A hundred sacks? Don't you think that's too much, my friend Urias?

Urias: That's what I say, Pipo. I'm but a poor man. I wonder how I shall finish paying what I owe your master.

Pipo: Don't talk anymore, Urias. I'm so touched and moved to tears. Here is your receipt. I just tore it. Sit down here and write another one. Just put eighty only. "I am in debt of eighty sacks of wheat to the miser, Phanuel." Well, strike out the word miser. And don't forget, I'm doing this for you because you're my friend.

Urias: Thank you, Pipo, thank you!

And so, Pipo spent the predawn hours knocking at every door, waking up the debtors of his master, Phanuel, and making them sign new receipts. When the sun peeped through the mountains of Bashan and the roosters of Caper-

naum began to shake their wings, Pipo, the crafty steward, had finished his mission.

Pipo: What a night! Now old Phanuel may kick me in the ass if he wants to. I'm ready for it!

At midmorning, he went to see his master.

Phanuel: There's nothing to talk about, Pipo. I don't believe your stories anymore.
Pipo: But master, Phanuel.
Phanuel: Let's get this over with, once and for all. You have been an immoral steward. I never want to see that disgusting beard of yours ever again.
Pipo: Well, master, if you say so. Look, here are the keys to the farm and here are the receipts of all your debtors.
Phanuel: Very well, leave them here. And now, you're dismissed.

Pipo then headed for Lucius's house.

Pipo: Oh, Lucius, oh!
Lucius: What happened? Tell me, my friend.
Pipo: Oh, Lucius, something unexpected happened, like the fire that burned Sodom. My master, Phanuel, just fired me.
Lucius: He fired you? But why?
Pipo: Because he did.
Lucius: What an injustice! Pipo, believe me, I understand your predicament.
Pipo: Believe me, Lucius. Nice words alone won't be of any help.
Lucius: Pipo, my house is your house. If you need shelter, if you need something warm to eat, some cash in advance, just let me know, I'm your friend!
Pipo: I wasn't expecting any less from you, Lucius!

Then Pipo proceeded to the other debtors of his former master.

Pipo: Urias, now I help you, tomorrow you help me.
Urias: What do you mean, Pipo?
Pipo: Yesterday was today and today will be tomorrow.
Urias: How's that?
Pipo: I was fired from work, man, and now I'm as poor as a rat.

Urias: Weep not, Pipo. What are friends for during these difficult times? You can count on me, my friend!

Pipo: Thank you, Urias, thank you.

That morning, Pipo took the same road he took the night before, knocking once again at the doors of his former master's debtors.

John: What the hell! Look how Pipo was able to get away with the devil!

Peter: Remember what I told you, Jesus? This guy, as always, is back on his two feet! He has a way with everything!

Jesus: Do you know what's on my mind, Peter? If only we were all smart enough to fight for the lives of other people, just as Pipo has been smart enough to save his own skin, then things would be different! If we were as crafty as he, then the Kingdom of God would move forward, don't you think so?

Pipo: Hey, what's up, fellas? I'm sure you're talking about me, is that right? Well, so you won't be talking behind my back, here I am. And do you know what? It's my treat tonight! Hey, one-eye, fill up their empty glasses with wine, and let them shout: Cheers to Pipo! Yeah, my friends, one, two, and three!

All: Cheers!

Jesus took up his glass too and gave a toast to Pipo, the astute steward. And so in between gulps of wine and jokes, we spent a hell of a time in Joachim's tavern beside the wharf. Jesus was laughing when we left, saying that in order to work for the Kingdom of God, one had to be as innocent as the doves but as clever as the serpents.

•

The landowners of Galilee usually hired an administrator or foreman (steward) who would oversee their lands and attend to their laborers or debtors. Many of these big landowners would not stay permanently on their farms. At any rate, the system of strict accountability as we know it in our countries did not exist in the Middle Eastern economy of that period. This explains the anomalous practices committed by Pipo.

Pipo is an astute and a tricky man. An opportunist. But he is capable, sagacious, shrewd, and resourceful when it comes to getting himself out of a difficult situation and saving his skin. Jesus does not criticize his behavior; instead, he gives it importance. More so, he finds in Pipo a model of astuteness that we must imitate. The parable about the "crafty steward" — which in this episode is told as a simply narrative — has always turned out to be something surprising. The fact that Jesus proposes a cheater to serve as a model of behavior is audacious. Jesus knows how to see beyond the indignant reaction resulting from the conduct of the steward. The mission of the kingdom is urgent and there are obstacles along the way. The moment is so crucial that the speed with which this Pipo knows how to solve his problem seems admirable to Jesus.

Jesus was never a moralist, a religious person, a puritan. He was a man in the midst of life, faced with a multitude of events, some of which were dramatic, others gray, and still others, amusing. Before such, he was a man with a sense of humor. He laughed, he knew how to laugh, he loved to laugh. We can't understand how Jesus is able to show his profound wisdom before life and people if we think of him as someone buried deep in his thoughts or uncaring. The ingenuity of a number of his parables and the ultimate surprise at the end of a number of them — this one, for example — are telling us about a born humorist.

The Bible is full of wit or bits of humor. It is impossible to read long stretches of it with an open mind and heart without smiling. One finds in them irony, ingenuity, mischief, all kinds of human wit. Humor is a sign of maturity and wisdom: the wisdom to take distance, to establish the relativity of things, not to give importance to one's self. Real humor always has some roots of true humility.

Those who do not know how to laugh at themselves, or who do not accept that others can laugh at them, may be suffering from pride and think too highly of themselves. Persons of authority who cannot take a joke, who get irked by the same, who censure humor, are afraid of losing something of their power, which probably hinges on impositions rather than on true moral authority. For a lot of people, what is religious is synonymous to seriousness, sadness, solemnity, and even bad humor. Something is wrong when Christian communities are made up of people who cannot afford to laugh.

Jesus suggested to his friends to become as "clever as the serpents and as innocent as doves" (Matt. 10:17). The serpent was considered in Israel — as in the majority of ancient cultures — as a highly dangerous animal, a symbol of the bad spirits. Jesus, who was a man of life, a positive man, saw values in the feared animal: it is shrewd, wary, wise, and knows how to get out of a difficult situation. The dove, the symbol of submission, will necessarily be the counterpoint of the serpent. Shrewdness is a Christian virtue, just as it is a human virtue. The equilibrium that is necessary so that shrewdness is not transformed into cynicism and innocence is not transformed into stupidity may be obtained by Christians in the constant confrontation of their actions with the word of God, with reality, and with the advice given by the Christian community.

(Luke 16:1–9)

85

The Master Went on a Journey

That afternoon, Rufina had gone to the market while her children played "horsey-horsey" in the street. Grandmother Rufa was alone, taking care of Tatico, the youngest of her grandchildren, when Jesus entered Peter's house.

Rufa: Go to sleep, my little baby. Ro, ro, ro, rorrito...

Jesus: Hello, grandma!

Rufa: Sshh! Hush, dark one, this creature has just gone to sleep. Poor child, with so much noise around, he can't even get a decent sleep.

Jesus: Okay, grandma, what's new around here?

Rufa: I gave him an egg to eat, but he wouldn't touch it. This little boy has lost his appetite.

Jesus: No, grandma, I mean, how are things going here?

Rufa: Oh, my son, speak louder, you know I'm hard of hearing!

Jesus: I said, how are things?

Rufa: All I can say is that this house is full of crazy men, the craziest of which is my son-in-law, Peter.

Jesus: Why do say that, grandma?

Rufa: You're asking me? Oh, my son, don't you know the kind of people you go with? Come. Just between the two of us I believe you've got the wrong company.

Jesus: D'ya think so, grandma?

Rufa: Like Matthew, for example. It's not because he's a tax collector, but because he's a jinx, a goner, Jesus. And Nathanael, the bald guy, is another one. I don't like him. Thomas, the stutterer, is another. Hmmm. It takes all kinds in your group!

Jesus: You think so, grandma? But people can be surprising at times.

Rufa: I don't want them to go to jail, but...

Jesus: I said people can do surprising things, grandma. A lot of people just need the chance to be able to do something worthwhile. Listen. There was once a wealthy man who had to go on a journey.

257

Master: Where are my stewards? I want the three of you to see me at sunset. There's something we'll talk about before I leave.

Jesus: So they went to see him.

Levi: What is it, master?

Master: Levi, you must have heard that I'll be away for some time. Here, take these five thousand denarii. Invest them in whatever business will be beneficial to you.

Levi: I don't want to brag, master, but rest assured that the money will be in good hands.

Jesus: Then the second steward came in.

Master: Come over, Jehu. Here, take these; they are for you.

Jehu: What's this, master?

Master: I'm leaving two thousand denarii for you to figure out what to do with. You'll report to me upon my return. Is that all right?

Jehu: Yes, master.

Master: Invest the money in any business and...

Jehu: Hold it, master! I know exactly what to do with the money. You'll see how much I'll earn with all this money!

Jesus: It was the third steward's turn.

Master: Here, Mattathias, take a thousand denarii. They are all yours.

Mattathias: A thousand denarii for me? But why?

Master: Yes, for you. Who else? Aren't you my third steward in the farm?

Mattathias: But, master, I...

Master: Aren't they enough?

Mattathias: On the contrary, master. Pff, now, what'll I do with so much money?

Master: Well, invest it! Make use of the money! While I'm gone, I want you to manage part of my money, as Levi and Jehu will do. Is that clear enough?

Mattathias: Well, yes, master, I mean, it's not so clear, but, pff, I'll try my best, master.

Jesus: In a few days, Levi, who received five thousand denarii, became a shrewd and great businessman.

Levi: I bought horses from you for three hundred denarii. That's it. Then you returned fifty for the horseshoes I had sold you, but since I paid you one hundred seventy-five in advance, now I only have to pay you half of the excess, that is...

A Man: Wait a minute, wait a minute, Levi. You gave me twenty-five yesterday.

Levi: And another twenty-five today, fifty all in all. Plus the other fifty from the horseshoes, less one hundred seventy-five included in the payment of one hundred, which you had discounted when I gave you five denarii for the nails.

Jesus: Jehu, the second steward, who received two thousand denarii, was posting a big sign at the door of his house.

Jehu: "Loans at 10 percent." Yeah, this is better. People know me well and soon they will all crowd here. To be a good lender, I must be smart and strict. I can be both. Well, come to think of it, I can be in any business of my choice. Ha, ha!

Jesus: Meanwhile, Mattathias, who received a thousand denarii, spent seven sleepless nights.

Mattathias: What if I invest in Don Celio's business? Yeah, but I don't like this fat man. No, I'd rather not ask him. Pff. What if I buy something, but what? Olives? If they get spoiled? No, no, forget it, Mattathias. If I buy, then I've got to sell, and I need the charm to do it, which I don't have. Ahuummm!

Jesus: Time went by and after many moons had passed, the master returned from his trip.

Master: Where are you, my servants? Come, come, I want to see you right away!

Jesus: Levi was the first to see him.

Levi: Master, how was your journey?
Master: Very well, Levi, very well. How did your business go?
Levi: Here it is, master. Count it, count it. You gave me five thousand. I earned another five thousand denarii.
Master: Good work, man!

Levi: I told you everything would be fine! Just like honey that passes through the throat. I knew exactly what was in my hands. I'm like a cat, you know, who can leap through any wall!

Jesus: Then Jehu came entered.

Master: What have you got, Jehu?

Jehu: Something better than I had imagined, master! Believe me, I've been very lucky. Look, you gave me two thousand denarii, didn't you? Here are your two thousand denarii. I was able to earn the same amount.

Master: Good work, man!

Jesus: Finally, Mattathias appeared.

Mattathias: Here is your money, master.

Master: Let's see, eight hundred, nine hundred, one thousand. But how much I did give you, Mattathias?

Mattathias: One thousand denarii, master. That's everything, up to the last penny. No more, no less.

Master: Didn't we agree that you were supposed to invest it in something that you might gain from it?

Mattathias: That's right, master, we had agreed on that. But, knowing how stupid I am, if I put this in business, I knew I would lose it in just two weeks. So I decided to keep it and, well, I dug a hole in the ground and there I kept it until now.

Jesus: His ears were red on account of his embarrassment, and he was trembling all over. Once again, he experienced the bitter pain of being a failure.

Mattathias: I am a worthless servant, master. The children in school used to ridicule me because I was always the last. My mother also said: "You were born dumb, Mattathias, and there's nothing we can do. You know better than anyone else, master, I'm a good for nothing servant.

Rufa: That's exactly what I meant to tell you. That guy was a worthless one, irresponsible, a weakling and a bum!

Jesus: That's all right, grandma, that's all right. Mattathias was a worthless man. The master was not. He was the generous type; he had a big heart. That's why the story didn't end there.

Master: "I'm good for nothing! I'm good for nothing." And the more you say it, the more you believe it, and the more it puts you down! Damn it, Mattathias! Listen to me very well: next time, I'll have your ears pulled if you don't come up with something.

Mattathias: Yes, next time, but will you give me another chance, master?

Master: Sure, because I know you can do it; you can do something worthwhile. Of course.

Jesus: Later, at one time, the master had to undertake another journey. He called for his three stewards again. To Levi, the shrewd businessman, he entrusted five thousand denarii again, and another two thousand to the able lender, Jehu. He gave poor Mattathias a thousand denarii.

Master: Invest this money until my return. Work hard and cheer up! Good-bye!

Jesus: The master's journey was shorter this time. After a couple of moons had passed, he was back to the farm. He summoned his three stewards at once.

Master: What do you say, Levi?

Levi: You see, master, this time I had wanted to take things easy. There is no hurry, I told myself. Anyway, I'm a very clever man and so . . .

Master: You did not do anything. You were too confident, weren't you? Levi, I can't believe that with all the things you could have done, you did nothing.

Jesus: Then, Jehu, the second steward entered.

Jehu: Ahuuummm! Here are the earnings.

Master: What's this? Only three coins? What's happened?

Jehu: Well, master, life is so difficult, you know. Ahuuumm! Things are not like before.

Master: You're not like before. You also got tired of it. You slept on your glory.

Jesus: Finally, Mattathias arrived, running, his hair in disarray.

Mattathias: Master, look, count this. You gave me a thousand denarii, and I've got another thousand! I earned it, look! I did it, master!

Master: I knew you would do it, Mattathias. I was sure of it.

Mattathias: That was what pushed me to do it, master. You had so much trust in me, I felt I had two wings at my back. I was afraid, yes, but I remembered what you had told me: you can do it, Mattathias, you can do it.

Master: And you did.

Mattathias: Yeah, I did! Pff! With my eyes closed, I went to purchase some tomatoes. Then I traded them for wool. I put up a shop. It was not that bad, after all, as you can see I earned a thousand denarii, master!

Master: You have worked very hard, Mattathias. With so little, you were enterprising. Now, I'll give you more denarii, and more responsibility. I know you will succeed. Because he who can be trusted with little things, can also be trusted with big things.

Jesus: So, you see, grandma, people can be amazing. Did you like my story?

Rufa: Sure I did. But the story, I suppose, does not end there.

Jesus: What do you mean, grandma?

Rufa: Well, if this master gave Mattathias a second chance, then he should also give the two sleepy-heads a third chance, don't you think?

Jesus: You're right, grandma. God always gives us another chance. Not only a third one. He always does.

•

The parable of the "talents" is — like that of the bridesmaids, that of the thief who arrives in the night, and that of the master who returns unexpectedly — a parable "of crisis." That is, these were parables told by Jesus basically to awaken the conscience of the leaders and the priests from whom God was to ask for a rigid accounting of what they had done, or better, what they had stopped doing for the people. After these series of stories, the first Christian communities sounded catechetical calls for Christian responsibility, that they would stay alert and wisely use their time, their lives, and their potentials, in preparation for the forthcoming judgment.

That's how the parable of the talents is generally understood: it is like a call to responsibility. Nevertheless, the society of technology and efficiency in which we live gives us, at present, a literal, yet dangerous, way of interpreting this parable. It would appear as if God had a preference for the smart people, the most intrepid, the most daring businessmen. In fact, that image of a prosperous businessman who accumulates as much wealth as he can is the one favored by capitalistic society, but linking that person with the parable of the talents totally distorts the authentic message of the gospel. Following such a literal interpretation, one could propose that those who have less, the indecisive, the inferior, are not acceptable to God. It is clear enough that a number of the poor, because they are the most exploited, find it difficult to face responsibilities, to be creative. Because of this, the one who is called to a task of responsibility, as the parable describes — to be active in negotiating — is given another important dimension of responsibility: not to rest in one's own security, nor to be satisfied with previous success. The talents referred to in the parable were a complex measurement, but suffice it to say here that each one was equivalent to about one thousand denarii. To be able to appreciate the approximate amount of money that a talent represented, one must take into account that the ordinary wage of a farmer or laborer was equivalent to one denarius for a whole day's work.

As regards Christian behavior, this parable is a call to responsibility. In relation to God, the story aims to highlight the infinite trust God puts in humans and, likewise, God's infinite patience with our failures and limitations. It is the trust shown by parents to their children which makes children believe, the affection/love given which teaches a child to live. Some orphans grow without the security of parental affection and love. Children grow, become mature, and become adults one day. They then live independently of their parents with the trust parents have put in them. They will someday acquire their own freedom. A similar thing happens with God. God empathizes with human weakness; God never condemns, but always opens a door, always gives us a chance. God wants us to live. If we can discover the profundity of this endless trust, then we shall keep on growing, and we shall become free even before God.

Only the trust born out of love can discover the sometimes hidden qualities of a person. This occurs not on the personal level only, but also structurally, within society. Only in a society organized on justice, on cooperation, can one discover one's worth, the mission he or she must undertake. This can be achieved in the same manner as the master has done in the parable, by giving opportunities to all. One of the major forms of injustice of the social organization in our countries is the tremendous inequality of opportunities among human beings. From the time of conception, and in all aspects — medical, nutritional, cultural, housing, recreational, labor — only a few enjoy everything, while the great majority are barely given the opportunity to surpass subhuman levels of existence. All this is contrary to God's plan, who wants equality for all humans. If there is a plan where equality among men and women can be and ought to be a reality, then it is precisely this: the equality of opportunities.

(Matt. 25:14–30; Luke 19:11–27)

86

The Blood of the Galileans

That winter, Jerusalem was garbed in white, the snow covering the walls and roofs of the houses. It was the month of Chisleu, and our town was festively commemorating with lighted lamps the dedication of the temple and the purification of the altar. Jesus and some of us went to the capital during the feast. As always, we stayed in the town near Bethany, at the inn of our friend Lazarus.

Lazarus: As you have heard, countrymen, it happened only yesterday, shortly before you came. Two Galilean men were in the temple, offering a lamb as sacrifice. Then two Roman soldiers entered and apprehended the two, who were then dragged into the Antonia Tower.

Martha: They were staying with us, the poor guys. In fact, their clothes and some of their things are still in the patio.

Lazarus: One of them is the son of a certain Reuben, of Bethsaida. They say the other one is called Nino. His mother is from Chorazin.

Jesus: What will they do to them, Lazarus?

Lazarus: Search me, Jesus! The life of these prisoners hangs on a spider's web. It depends on Pontius Pilate's whims. As you can see, the scoundrel didn't have any respect for the temple, nor for the sacrifice they were offering.

Judas: History repeats itself. Now the Romans are making fun of us, as they did with the Greeks before. Two hundred years back, during the time of the cruel Antiochus Epiphanes of the Greek domination, the foreigners had sacked the temple of Jerusalem and profaned the altar of the sacrifice. After the initial victories of the Maccabees brothers, our ancestors performed great ceremonies of atonement. Since then, in the winter of every year, we celebrate the feast of the dedication

Mary: Hey, Lazarus, Martha!

Lazarus: What's with you, Mary? Have you got any news?

Mary: Yeah. This cripple, Saul, told me that the two Galileans would be judged in the Antonia Tower. Pilate will present them before the people.

Judas: When will this be, Mary?

Mary: This morning, Judas. If we hurry, we'll get there on time.

Lazarus: C'mon, guys, let's all go there!

Lazarus, his two sisters, and we left the inn together. In a few minutes we reached the village of Bethphage, climbing over the slope of the Mount of Olives, crossing the Cedron River, which was slippery on account of the snow, until we got into the city of Jerusalem. Many people milled in the streets. Slowly, we shoved and pushed our way through to the front of the Antonia Tower. The black and yellow flags of Rome waved along the battlements. A giant bronze eagle on top of the flight of steps was a grim reminder that our country was under the domination of a foreign power.

A Man: That's where the trial is! Run, the governor is coming!

Below the tower was a small, paved patio, where Pontius Pilate, the Roman governor, tried the prisoners in public and meted out their sentence.

Pilate: When will you ever learn? How do you want me to say it? These clandestine meetings are never allowed!

A Woman: My son didn't do anything, governor. He was not meeting anyone!

Pilate: Your son and his friend were conspiring against Rome. Do you know what I do with conspirators? I crush them like bugs and fleas! Do you hear?

Pontius Pilate, the governor of Jerusalem and of the whole southern region, was a tall and robust man. He wore a white linen cape and a pair of braided sandals. His hair was short, according to the Roman style, and his face showed an eternal expression of contempt for us Jews.

Woman: Governor, my son is innocent! He was inside the temple!

A Man: And the temple is a sacred place!

Pilate: The temple is a mousetrap. It's the job of my men to catch the mice hiding in that hole.

Woman: Governor, they were not in conspiracy. They were offering a sacrifice, shedding the blood of a lamb on the altar of God.

Pilate: Oh yeah? So, that was what they were doing? Well then, the blood of your son and that of the other Galilean will be mixed with the lamb's! Soldiers, bring the rebels before me, now!

Soldier: Right away, governor.

There was tense silence while the Roman guards headed for the pits of the Antonia Tower, where the prisoners awaited their sentence. In a short while they were back, pushing with their lances the young Galileans who were caught inside the temple the other day. One of the men was tanned. His hair was disheveled, and his robe was torn into pieces. The other man was shorter, and he was covering his face with his tied hands. He was trembling, like he was suffering from fever. His back was smashed by lashings and beatings.

Woman: Have mercy on them, Pontius Pilate, and please pardon them! Where is your heart? Can't you find pity for a mother who is weeping? Please forgive my son, please!

Man: Clemency too for the other fellow!

Pilate: There's no forgiveness for rebels like them. Rome is an eagle, and no one can escape from her claws. You Jews are a stubborn people. After the feast, when you go back to your homes, tell them what you are now to witness with your own eyes.

Pontius Pilate looked at all of us in great contempt and raised his ringed hand for the fatal command.

Pilate: Behead them!

Woman: No, no!

Two soldiers from the governor's guards held the Galileans and lay them down on the humid tiling. Two other soldiers came close and unsheathed their swords and in one slash, the heads of the young men came rolling. We all gave out a terrifying cry. The mother of one of the victims screamed like mad, and a group of soldiers had to cordon the area in order to control the mob. But Pontius Pilate remained unperturbed.

Pilate: Bring me the victims' blood!

A soldier then took a jar, headed for the victims' bodies, filled the jar with the blood that gushed out of their necks, and presented it to the Roman governor who was standing by.

Pilate: This is going to be my sacrifice. I will pour the blood of these stubborn rebels on the altar of this more obstinate God of yours. Listen well, all you rebels: the only powerful god is seated in Rome. Emperor Tiberius is the only true God. He reigns over you all and mixes the blood of the sons of Israel with the blood of lambs and dogs. Long live Caesar!

A Man: Damn you, Pontius Pilate! May the blood of your own head be shed someday!

There was great bewilderment. Many of us had to close our eyes in horror as the governor, who was heavily guarded, crossed the hallway that joined the Roman fortress to the temple. Without any deference, Pilate proceeded to the altar of the holocausts and, amid the soldiers' laughter, poured the blood of the two young Galileans, which was still warm.

Another Man: This is desecration! Pontius Pilate has profaned our altar! Shake your robes, brothers!

Another Man: The governor is making a mockery of us. A while ago he brought Caesar's flags to the temple's atria. And now, this.

An Old Man: If the Maccabees had seen this, they would have taken up the sword of revenge.

Man: Revenge, yes, revenge! I swear there will be revenge!

Since then, more protests were mounted in Jerusalem, more people's uprisings were staged, and more assassinations occurred. A group of Zealots tried to dig a tunnel up to the Tower of Siloam, where the Romans kept their swords and other weapons. But the tower's foundation was already in a state of decay, and the tunnel caused the construction to suddenly collapse, claiming the lives of several Galilean families who had built their houses near the tower.

Lazarus: The situation is getting out of control, Jesus.

Jesus: There's a rumor that Pilate is increasing the surveillance.

Judas: Then I'm sure there'll be more prisoners and more to be crucified.

Martha: In that case, then why do they continue to get themselves into this mess? Why?

Judas: Because some of them can't stand it anymore, Mary. They have no right to trample on us, like these damned foreigners are doing.

Mary: But neither is it right to bring down a tower right on the heads of those eighteen innocent victims! They can break Pilate's bones if they wish to, but what good can they get out of it? The poor and innocent become victims of something they haven't done.

Lazarus: They're doing it to provoke Pilate.

Mary: That's right, and Pilate continues to kill to provoke them just the same. That's how it is now. We can never feel safe in the street, for anyone can just thrust a dagger at us at any street corner. No, no, no, I don't want to hear any more.

Jesus: Yeah, you're right, Mary. Pilate is a bloodthirsty man. And those who fight him become equally bloodthirsty. But who has taught them to be such? To be violent? This is basically the problem, don't you think so? Those in power sowed the wind, now they are reaping tempests from the poor. This will go on and on if we don't reform our ways, and soon we shall all drown in a bloody deluge.

The feast during that winter was embittered by crimes, by fear of the Romans and their surveillance. It was during that week of the dedication that a group of Jews gathered around Jesus in one of the arches of Solomon's Gate.

A Man: Hey, you, Nazarene, what's wrong with you? How long are you gonna keep us guessing?

Another Man: If you're the Messiah that we're waiting for, then say so, so we don't waste any more time.

An Old Man: What we need is someone with the gall to face up to Pilate's people.

All: That's it, that's it!

Jesus: No, my friend, no. What we need are a people who will know how to face up to themselves. When the babies are small, the mother leads them by the hand so they don't fall. When they grow up to be adult, they have to walk on their own two feet.

Judas: What boy are you talking about, Jesus?

Jesus: About us. Now is the time for us to strengthen our knees and lift our heads. Freedom is in our hands. We don't expect it from anyone. The Messiah is here, among us. He is there where two or three persons are fighting for justice. Yes, God breathed over dry bones, the bones were joined, and the people awoke and stood up. The Messiah is like a big body, with head, hands, and feet. All the members have the same spirit, and all parts are necessary. We've got to break the oppressive yoke among us, and together raise the flag of command. We've got to construct among us a new Jerusalem and write anew on her walls: "The House of God, the City of the Free." Here there will be no violence, neither the violence of the wolf who kills the lamb, nor the violence of the lamb who defends itself from the wolf. We shall convert our swords into hoes, and the bars of prison cells into plowing grills.

A Man: Now he's talking. Long live the Messiah of God!

All: Long live the Messiah, long live the Messiah!

A Soldier: Hey, you Galileans, disperse, all of you! Don't you know that such assembly is prohibited? C'mon, c'mon, beat it, if you don't wish to lose your heads like the two other Galileans!

The Roman soldiers tried to arrest Jesus, but we succeeded in hiding him. We mixed with the people who were assembled at Solomon's Gate. That same day we undertook the journey to Jericho, as the situation in Jerusalem made it more and more difficult for us.

•

There are only two seasons in Palestine: summer and winter, hot and cold, sowing time and harvest time. The month of Chisleu corresponds roughly to our mid-November to mid-December. Since Jerusalem is a desert city, the temperature goes very low in winter, and it snows unexpectedly.

The feast of the dedication of the temple was held in December and lasted for eight days. This feast, commemorating the consecration of the temple in Solomon's time, had been revived during the time of the Maccabees (about sixty years before Jesus was born). During the evangelical times, the people of Israel commemorated in this feast the victory of the Maccabees, who were nationalistic fighters, over the Greek Seleucids, the country's invaders. They also celebrated the purification of the temple and the construction of a new altar after the holy place was desecrated by the atrocious Seleucid king, Antiochus Epiphanes. The festival was also associated with the feast of light, as a reminder that the dedication of the temple brought back the custom of lighting the holy light with seven candles. In Jerusalem, the torches used during the feast of the tents were again lighted for this feast. Thus, the dedication was popularly known as the feast of the winter tents. The celebrations also bore a messianic flavor, like those of the harvest. At present, Jews solemnly light the hannukah (a candelabra with eight lights, each one corresponding to a day of the feast).

Rome ruled over its colonies in the provinces of the empire through the officials representing Caesar. These provinces were of three types: the senatorial (governed by the Roman proconsuls, who were annually replaced), the imperial (led by Roman governors, legates, and procurators), and other provincial territories, which were governed by the natives who served the economic and political interests of the empire. Galilee was the latter, which was governed by Herod. Judea — whose capital was Jerusalem — was definitely an "imperial" province, beginning the year after Jesus was born. Ruled by a governor, it was militarily occupied by Roman troops, and the administration was in the hands of Roman officials. Pontius Pilate was the governor of Judea from 26 to 36 C.E.. He used to stay in the coastal city of Caesarea — the official residence of the governors — and he would move with his special troops to Jerusalem for the feasts, as these were the most favorable occasions for uprisings and people's movements. The priestly class of Jerusalem, the highest religious-political authorities of Israel, was in total collusion with the Roman imperial power represented by Pilate. The image of Pilate as a man who was an intellectual, a man of stature, yet a coward has been projected by a certain Christian tradition, but such an image does not correspond to historical reality. All information provided by historians of the period — Philo, Josephus, and Tacitus, Jews and Romans as well — confirm the cruelty of that man who was detested by the Israelites for his continuous provocations and who occupied such a high position as a result of his intimate friendship with a military favorite of Emperor Tiberius. Aware of the religious aversion of Jews for images, Pontius Pilate paraded the images of Caesar Tiberius along the streets of Jerusalem and placed them in the ancient palace of Herod the Great. This caused an uproar on the part of the people. Pilate likewise desecrated the sanctuary on various occasions, by robbing the temple's treasury for his construction projects, and so on. Luke's text, the basis of this episode, most likely reflects one of these political vendettas and religious profanations pushed by the hated governor. Since Galilee was the principal focus of the country's anti-Roman movements, Pilate persecuted the Galileans with ferocity, suspecting that they were linked with the Zealots.

During the Roman domination, the Antonia Tower (Antonia Fortress), which was situated beside the temple and joined to the most sacred places of the sanctuary by interior stairways, was the seat of imperial garrisons. These were tasked to guard the whole city, especially the temple's open area, where the multitudes converged. In the tower was the tribunal — the praetorium — where Pilate would judge all cases of rebellion against Rome and its laws. This did not in any way resemble the present-day tribunals, as there was no justice to speak of. The sentences — which in the case of opposition to the empire could always be a death sentence — depended solely on the arbitrariness of the governor. Pilate's cruelty and profanity unleashed the people's protest movements and violent retaliations by the Zealots, the most organized group for the purpose. The Roman rule, oppressive both politically and militarily, and economically exploitative, generated strong resistance in Israel. Indeed, in the entire empire, Israel was the seat of the most constant, angry rebellion against the Roman power; the last uprising took place in the year 70 c.e. Jerusalem was destroyed; this caused the start of the long Jewish exile that has lasted up to our time. Jesus' time was rife with the violence of the oppressors and the counterviolence of the oppressed, leading to the inevitable deaths of innocent persons as in the case of the collapse of the Tower of Siloam, the subject of this episode.

Violence is generated by unjust structures of power. This is found in laws, in courts, in economic inequality, in the lack of opportunities. It comes in the form of hunger, labor exploitation, ignorance, lack of good hygiene, and so on. It comes also in the bloodier forms of torture and assassination. There is another type of violence. It is resorted to by those who because they have grown weary of injustice resist, attack, and fight. From the Christian point of view, it is not fair to judge these different forms of violence with the same measure. How can one resort to counterviolence without feeling hatred, which is blinding and dehumanizing? How to avoid the risk of using counterviolence as a form of retaliation or revenge is one of the major challenges before us.

Solomon's Gate was situated in the eastern facade of the large outer court of the temple. Jesus' words to the people who were gathered to listen to him refer to the prophetic texts about the idea of a "collective Messiah" (Ezek. 37:1–14; Isa. 2:3–5; 9:2–4; 11:6; on the same theme see also 1 Cor. 12:1–29; etc.). Using the prophet Micah (Mic. 2:12–13), Jesus began to open the minds of the Israelites to the idea of the capacity of the poor to liberate themselves, a liberation that originates from "the least" of the people, or from the entire people of Israel who had been captive in Babylon but had become the bearers of messianic promises of the kingdom (Zeph. 3:11–13). Jesus, faithful to this theological tradition, never wished to monopolize messianic action. He was more his real self when he assumed the role of leadership among the poor and awakened them to their own strength (in contrast to accepting the role of a self-glorifying triumphant Messiah).

(Luke 13:1–5; John 10:22–40)

87

In a Sycamore Branch

From Jerusalem, we journeyed to Jericho, the city of the roses, which Joshua had conquered with the sounding of his trumpet. That winter, Jesus was already known all over the country, from the lands of the tribe of Dan, to the desert of Idumea, from the sea of the Phoenicians to the barren mountains of Moab. When we arrived in Jericho, the people were excited, and they all came out to receive us.

A Woman: He's coming! The prophet is coming!
A Man: Long live the Nazarene! Down with the Romans!

The people pushed us on all sides. We could hardly move along the tree-lined street that joined the old walls of the city to the square-shaped plaza. The synagogue was there, and also the Roman headquarters and the customs house.

Zacchaeus: Damn it, what is this mob? People can't even do their work well when they gather. Hey, you, what the hell is going on? Is there a fire, a wedding, or a funeral?
A Young Man: A prophet! The prophet of the Galileans is here! A man called Jesus of Nazareth!
Zacchaeus: This is too much. As if we hadn't had enough of John, that long-haired guy who drowned the people in the river.
Young Man: This man has got long hair too, Mr. Zacchaeus.
Zacchaeus: He'll suffer the same fate, too, young man. Israel produces a lot of prophets on one hand, and crucifies them with the other hand!
Young Man: Take a look at the crowd, Mr. Zacchaeus. The people are milling around like ants. Look!
Zacchaeus: Hey, are you making fun of me?

Zacchaeus would have needed a stool to see Jesus. Zacchaeus was plump and balding. He was a short man. For years he had devoted himself to the despicable job of collecting taxes for the Roman government. His ability with numbers and

273

other money matters had made him the chief of all the tax collectors in the area. Everyone in Jericho hated Zacchaeus. People made fun of his short stature, as a way of getting even with him, on account of his abuses.

A Man: Shorty, shorty, traitor! You're done with and your trade, too! The new prophet will drive away the Romans and all those who lick their asses, like you!

The entire city was out in the street. As Zacchaeus left his office, all kinds of insults rained on him.

A Man: The prophet from Galilee is out to squeeze the eagle's neck of Rome, you hear that, shorty? Like this, look, grrr!
Zacchaeus: He'd better do it before Saturday! You owe me fifty denarii, and if you don't pay me soon, you'll end up in jail.
Another Man: It's you who'll pay for all this, you leech! You can't get away with it, even if you hide yourself in a latrine. The Nazarene will get you out of there and he'll drag you through the street.
Zacchaeus: Eat your hearts out imbeciles.

The people continued to swarm the plaza, shouting and applauding Jesus, who could hardly be seen because of the multitude. Zacchaeus elbowed his way among the crowd. Underneath his arm was the leather roll where he kept the receipts, listed all debts and tax payments. Gradually he succeeded in getting away from the place, took a shortcut through some of the huts, and headed for his comfortable house at the other end of the town.

Zacchaeus: The prophet from Galilee. Well, well. This country is dying of hunger, but we never run out of prophets. There's so much talk everywhere, but nothing happens. Everything is the same. Things can't change with words. Such beautiful words, but they could spell danger.

Before entering his house, Zacchaeus looked at his reflection in the water in the ditch that crossed through the city. He saw that he was small, ridiculously small. Once again, he was filled with bitterness.

Zacchaeus: Nothing has changed, damn it, nothing! What a disgusting life!

He went inside his house, kissed his wife, as always, and sat at the table to eat. Then, he lay down to get some sleep. But the noise persisted and . . .

Zacchaeus: What the hell! Can't I even sleep in my own house?

Sarah: It's the prophet who is in town. Everyone is so excited about him.

Zacchaeus: That man again! I don't want to have anything to do with that prophet. Close the window, woman.

Sarah: It's already closed, Zacchaeus. The noise outside is very loud.

Zacchaeus: Open it then. Who can sleep with that noise? Pff! Ahuu-ummm! How disgusting!

Zacchaeus grudgingly got up from the bed, climbed on a stool, and peeped through the window.

Sarah: Can you see, Zacchaeus?

Zacchaeus: Whom?

Sarah: Who else? The prophet?

Zacchaeus: What the heck do I want to see him for?

Sarah: I don't know, but since you peeped through the window…

Zacchaeus: Do you, too, want to go see him? Go ahead, see him. It's not my business prying into other people's lives!

Zacchaeus's wife opened the door, headed for the street until she was lost amid the screaming and admiring crowd.

Zacchaeus: What a man! What bait has he got in his hook? Even Sarah has fallen for it. Who would ever think of it — my wife is also following that Galilean. Well, well. There must be something special in this fellow. All these rascals are mesmerized by him. I think I'm getting curious too.

The noise and uproar in the street had heightened.

A Man: Tell us, Jesus, when will you drive the Romans out of the country?

Another Man: Tell us what happened in Jerusalem, prophet!

A Woman: Hey, little girl, watch where you're going. You're stepping on my corn.

Another Woman: Neighbors, look over there, and don't lose sight of him! Ha, ha!

All of us turned to where that woman with long, braided hair was pointing. Perched in one of the sycamore trees in the patio of his house was Zacchaeus, his short legs balancing from one side to another.

A Man: How in the world could the dwarf climb that tree? Blazes! The devil is coiled like the serpent in paradise!

An Old Man: So, Zacchaeus, you too wanted to see the prophet, huh?

Man: Don't you know that the Nazarene is out to pluck your tongue shorty?

Another Man: Get down from there, scoundrel! Hey, guys, let's pull him down!

The people forgot about us as they hurried toward the patio of the publican's house. A group of men surrounded the sycamore tree and began to shake its branches with all their strength. We also started to run toward the place.

Jesus: Who's that guy?

A Woman: Zacchaeus, the chief of the tax collectors of the area. He's a cheat and a thief.

A Man: A treacherous dwarf.

Another Man: Down with the traitors! Down with the traitors!

Jesus: Zacchaeus, come down fast, or these people will pull you down faster than you imagine.

Finally the crowd from Jericho, amid shoutings and laughter, succeeded in bringing Zacchaeus down. His little body fell down in the middle of the patio.

Man: Beat it, go away, you traitor! Dwarf!

Zacchaeus: Get out of my yard, all of you! Go to hell, all of you!

Woman: After you!

Jesus forced his way through the people to be able to get to Zacchaeus, whose face was red with rage and shame. He was exchanging barbs with his neighbors.

Woman: Crush him like you would a roach, prophet!

All: Yeah, crush him, crush him!

Jesus: Hey, Zacchaeus, how much will you collect from us?

The neighbors exchanged surprised glances when Jesus said this. Zacchaeus, likewise, looked at Jesus with amazement.

Zacchaeus: What did you say?

Jesus: I said, how much are you going to collect from us? But first let's break bread in your house. If it gets too late, we may even have to sleep there as well.

After a while, we all went inside Zacchaeus's house. No one in Jericho understood it, and everyone criticized Jesus. Everyone was indignant that Jesus had chosen to go into the house of that man who was hated by all. We, too, who had great contempt for publicans (tax collectors), and much difficulty in accepting into our group Matthew, the tax collector from Capernaum, could not easily force ourselves to be seated at the table of the chief of tax collectors.

Zacchaeus: Be my guests. Ask whatever you want, eat whatever you want. This house is never wanting for anything!

James: Naturally, since you steal everything.

Zacchaeus: How's that?

James: No, nothing. I was talking about carob beans. In Galilee there are many.

Zacchaeus was happy. Seated on one end of the table beside Jesus, his eyes were glowing with joy. For the first time, after so many years, he had guests in his house.

Zacchaeus: Well, yes. What I least expected was having the prophet here in my house and breaking bread for all of you, my friends from Galilee!

Peter: And they almost broke your legs, shorty!

Zacchaeus: Pardon, what did you say?

Peter: That the meat is so tender, countryman!

Zacchaeus: But of course. These are lambs from my flock from the other side of the river. We have direct transaction with the Moabite shepherds, and we get a very good price.

John: Plus the taxes you've been collecting, you can't complain, rascal!

Zacchaeus: Were you saying something?

John: Oh, nothing, I was saying that it's Monday today! Ha, ha!

James: And tomorrow is Tuesday! Ha, ha, ha!

Peter: And after tomorrow is Wednesday! Ha, ha, ha!

The laughter spread among everyone as if an invisible hand had tickled us pink. Peter and I were laughing over a plate of lamb. Zacchaeus was all red, laughing to his heart's content. Suddenly he stood from the table.

Zacchaeus: Ha, ha, ha! Ay ha! I'd like to say that because I'm a short man, you don't really have to break my legs. I'm short, but I'm not deaf. Yeah, the carob beans of Galilee...I know these hands of mine have robbed a lot. It's true. My neighbors are right: I'm a leech, and I've sucked so much blood...

We looked at each other, not knowing what to do or say until Jesus broke the silence.

Jesus: Forgive us, Zacchaeus. We didn't mean to offend you.
Zacchaeus: Save the nice words, prophet. Things won't change with words.

Then Zacchaeus went near the shelf where he kept his receipts and list of accounts. He put them on the table where everyone could see them.

Zacchaeus: I won't talk much. I'd like to do it this way. My debtors are free. Those whom I cheated, I shall return four times what I've stolen. I'm getting half of the money from my chest: it's no longer mine, it's yours.

Zacchaeus's words stunned all of us. Jesus was filled with joy.

Jesus: Know what, Zacchaeus? I believe that today you've been the prophet in Jericho. Look, a just deed is worth more than a thousand words. Yes, things do change if people change. And the truth is that salvation has come to your house today.
Zacchaeus: What did you say? Do you want some more wine? Why, sure, Jesus! Come, give me that cup! And all of you too!

Once again, Zacchaeus filled all the pitchers with wine. We continued eating and drinking in the house of the chief of the publicans. Without knowing it, we were proclaiming the great banquet of the Kingdom of God, where the most downtrodden were to occupy the seats of honor.

•

Jericho is a city partly situated in the desert of Judea, in the middle of a fertile plain with tropical climate. It is 250 meters below sea level and about seven kilometers from the bank of the Jordan River. After excavations done in 1952, a conclusion was made that Jericho is the oldest known city in the world, the remaining wall dating back to the Stone Age. Jericho was the first city conquered by the Israelites when they entered the Promised Land under the leadership of Joshua (Josh. 6:1–27). These very significant ruins are found about two kilometers from the present Jericho.

In Jesus' time, Jericho became important because it provided a passageway for the trade caravans crossing the desert. On account of this, an important office was set up to attend to the collection of taxes. Heading this office was the chief of the publicans or tax collectors, Zacchaeus.

The taxes collected in Jericho enriched the Roman coffers, since the city was in Judea, a province administratively dominated by Rome. (The taxes collected by Matthew in Capernaum were intended for King Herod.) The post of tax collector was auctioned off by the Roman authorities, leasing it to the highest bidder. Then the publicans (tax collectors) had to pay Rome for the lease and other expenses. Rome set the fixed amount to be collected in the form of taxes. The publicans would earn very little if they were honest with the collection. That is why they arbitrarily increased the rate of collection, so they could get rich from the remaining amount. Their continuous dishonesty and their collaboration with the Roman powers earned for them the hatred and contempt of their own people.

The sycamore is a large tree that originated from Egypt from the fig family, and grows along the coasts of Palestine and the entire plains of the Jordan. It is also known as the "crazy fig tree." Its trunk is the source of durable wood, which was used in Egypt for coffins of the mummies. Its roots are very strong, and its thick leaves are heart-shaped. Its fruits, which resemble small figs, are abundant.

Zacchaeus is one of the few rich men — together with Nicodemus and Joseph of Arimathea — converted by Jesus. His conversion, a result of his curiosity to take a look at the prophet and the kind of welcome he gets from Jesus, could not be sheer sentimentalism or the result of a vague desire to be good. His conversion does not remain in words or in remorse of conscience: it is something that involves his pocket. He pledges to return to the people he has cheated four times the amount he has taken from them. Half of what would be left shall be given to the poor. It is a well-concretized conversion, and even an "exaggerated" one. Zacchaeus will apply not the Jewish law but the Roman law (which requires the return of four times the amount stolen) to himself as a form of "penitence" for his fraudulent acts. The Jewish law is less severe. He will also do away with the Jewish norm which prohibits the use of more than one-fifth of one's fortune to help the poor. Instead, he shall donate half of it. Jesus contextualizes this authentic conversion of Zacchaeus with a gesture that shows a profound theological meaning. Generally it is believed the sinner should be welcomed with affection, but only after his repentance. We even believe God works in that manner. Jesus shows a new religious attitude. Jesus accepts Zacchaeus even before he begins his penitence. The fact that he wants to go to his house — even to eat with him, a great indication of friendship — seems inconceivable to Zacchaeus. That gesture is so amazing that it overwhelms him, as it obviously lets him see and admit to who he is, and what he has done to the people he has cheated. What his neighbors' reproaches of Zacchaeus have failed to do Jesus succeeds in doing by risking this gesture of unconditional welcome. That man, despised by everyone, within himself suddenly recovers his lost dignity, and so his life becomes transformed.

The rich are not excluded from the Kingdom of God. What happens is that for them, conversion must necessarily involve giving up their wealth, precisely because they keep on selfishly storing their wealth for themselves. When he discovers his lost dignity through Jesus' gesture of welcome, Zacchaeus likewise discovers why he has lost that dignity. He realizes that he has acquired his wealth while oppressing the poor people of his town. He not only realizes this, he takes positive action as a result of this: the giving up of his ill-gotten wealth.

(Luke 19:1–10)

88

At the Gateway of Jericho

In the middle of the desert of Judea, in the valley of the Jordan, Jericho lies like a green, circular tapestry, the city of roses and palm trees, the oldest city in our country.

Bartimaeus: Thank you, countrywoman! God give you joy for this denarius!

A Woman: Say that again! We all need to be happy! Go home, Bartimaeus, and buy yourself something to eat.

Bartimaeus: No, madam. I'd rather stay here. There's nothing in my house. A lot of people pass this way. I don't get to see their faces, but I smell their joys and sorrows and that's living! Please, please, I'd like to stay here.

At the gateway of Jericho, along the wide and dusty road that leads to Jerusalem, blind Bartimaeus was seated, begging alms for many years. Although his beard was spattered with white hair, he was not yet old. His nervous hands clasped a greasy well-worn cane.

Woman: Well, countryman, God bless you!

Bartimaeus: May God's twelve angels guide you, madam. May God reward you!

Bartimaeus held the denarius carefully and kept it in his pocket. Then he closed his unseeing eyes and began to journey in the valley of memories.

Ruth: Uff! Here is the leather, Bartimaeus. It weighs more than a whale.

Bartimaeus: What do you know about whales, when you've never been out to sea, you dense woman? Ha, ha! But I do know that you're getting stouter than Jonah's whale! Ha, ha! I can't even carry you in my arms anymore!

Ruth: Hey, you're tickling me! Ha, ha! C'mon, stop that ribbing now, you've got to cut the leather. A lot of orders are pending.

Bartimaeus: Okay, okay. C'mon, woman, give me a hand. Bring me the razor.

Bartimaeus had his small tanning shop in one of the long streets of Jericho. He lived with his wife, Ruth, a cheerful and resolute woman, whom he loved even in his dreams. Months and years had passed, and Bartimaeus's life was filled with joy, thanks to his work, the love he had, and his friends.

Bartimaeus: Ruth, bring me the needle.

Ruth: The needle? I haven't got it.

Bartimaeus: Neither have I.

Ruth: Let's see, Bartimaeus, let's see. How disorganized you are. Where the hell? But it's right there on the coffee table, my gosh! Had it been a snake, it could've bitten you!

Bartimaeus: Where do you say it was?

Ruth: There, stupid, don't you see?

Bartimaeus reached out his arm to the table, and groped until he found the long and thick needle he was using to sew the pieces of leather.

Bartimaeus: Okay, okay, now I've got it.

Ruth: You didn't see it before?

Bartimaeus: No, no, woman. I couldn't see it.

The disease spread rapidly, and in a few months Bartimaeus's dark eyes were deprived of light forever. He couldn't use the needle or cut with a razor. He had to stop working in the shop. Anguish and sorrow filled his house. Like two unwelcome guests, they became his constant companions when he was seated at the table during the day, and at night when lying beside his wife.

Bartimaeus: Ruth, oh Ruth, where are you? Woman, where've you been? Ruth, Ruth!

A Woman Neighbor: May I come in, son?

Bartimaeus: Who are you?

Neighbor: I'm Lydia, Ruth's friend.

Bartimaeus: Where is she? When I woke up, she wasn't here. Where is she?

Lydia: She's gone, my son.

Bartimaeus: What do you mean?

Neighbor: Try to understand, son. You can't see and you can't work. She's still young. She has the right to be happy.

Bartimaeus: What silly things are you saying?

Neighbor: She wanted me to tell you that she was going to Bethany, to her parents' house.

Bartimaeus: With another man? She went with another man? With someone who's not blind like me? Tell me! Tell me!

Neighbor: Look, son, since you haven't had any children.

Bartimaeus: But we love each other! Unless it doesn't matter anymore.

Neighbor: Bartimaeus, try to understand. Life has been okay with you but not with her.

Soon enough, Bartimaeus had to close down his shop. His blindness had left him in anguish, without his work and the love of his wife. Little by little, his friends, showing him no compassion, had abandoned him.

Bartimaeus: This was not the life she wanted. Not this kind of life... What about me? All my little savings are gone. What can a blind man do? Beg? But I'm still young and strong enough to work and how stupid of me! The blind are a good for nothing lot! They must be led by the hand. If they forget their canes, then they're no better than children. They are useless. There's no choice but to beg for alms, like beggars do. I curse the day I was born! Is this why I came out of my mother's womb? God! Why did you make me see the light, and then deprive me of it?

A few days later Bartimaeus was groping his way, with the help of a cane, through the street where the residents of Jericho and the traders from other cities passed. Seated along the edge of the road, he began to beg for alms. Later, when it was dark, he would go back to his old and solitary house. Feeling weak from not having eaten or talked to anyone, he would just lie down on the mat and press his dead eyes with his closed fists.

Bartimaeus: It's always night for me, always! It'll always be so forever! How was the face of Ruth? How did she look? I can't remember anymore how her eyes looked, her lips. I'll never see her again. What am I living for? Nothing! Nobody needs me and I need no one. I just want to get out of this nightmare.

With much effort, Bartimaeus stood up from his mat and began to rummage around his empty shop.

Bartimaeus: The sycamore tree in the patio . . . Yes. A rope will do. It will be difficult, but it will only be for a moment. It's more difficult to live like this, expecting nothing, only death, which doesn't have to come after me since I'll go seek death myself. Yes, yes, that'll only take a while and everything will be over! But where the hell is that rope? Where? Damn it! And everyone will say: "He has gone mad." I couldn't care less. No, no, I didn't go crazy, I just became blind, which is worse. The rope was somewhere here . . . The rope. Where's the rope? God, where the hell is that rope? Did you hide it from me, God? Or was it the devil? Damn the two of you! Can't I even choose to hang myself?

Bartimaeus was crawling all over the shop, looking for the thick rope with which he used to bundle the bales of leather. He looked in all corners for the rope, in vain.

Bartimaeus: Damn, damn! Where's the rope? Where? I want to die! I want to die! I want, I want . . . to live. I, I want to live. I want to live!

Bartimaeus: Why didn't I kill myself that day? No, it was not the devil. It was God who hid the rope from me. It was God who gave me the desire to live. I don't know how you got here, Bartimaeus, old lazy bones, after all these years of pitfalls and frustrations. But here you are, stronger than the sturdy sycamore in the patio, appreciating the fragrance of the most beautiful roses in the world. This is life, I say, and life is worth living, good Lord!

Boy: Goodbye, Bartimaeus! We'll talk again next time!

Bartimaeus: Hold it, little boy. Why the hurry?

Boy: The prophet of Galilee is leaving Jericho.

Bartimaeus: Who, Jesus of Nazareth?

Boy: Yeah! He's heading this way, with lots of people! I'm gonna go get my friend so he can see him.

As we were leaving Jericho, many men and women of the city went out to the street to see us off.

A Woman: Long live the prophet of Galilee!

A Man: Down with the Romans and the people's oppressors!

Bartimaeus: Hey, give way and let me pass, damn it! I haven't seen the prophet yet, and I wish to see him.

An Old Woman: Jesus, when are you coming back to Jericho?

Man: We hope to see you next Passover!

Bartimaeus: I want to see the prophet!

Man: Stop yelling, you idiot!

Bartimaeus: I want to see him!

Woman: Shut up, will you, Bartimaeus!

Bartimaeus: I want to see him! I want to see him!

Man: How can you see him, when you're blind?

Bartimaeus: Then let him see me. Prophet Jesus! Jesus!

Jesus: Who's that guy screaming, grandma?

Old Woman: This blind troublemaker here, the one in the middle.

Jesus: Give way, please, and tell him to come over.

Man: So, you got away with it, Bartimaeus. C'mon, slip through the crowd. The prophet is asking about you.

Blind Bartimaeus, his face radiant with joy, cast his beggar's cloak in the air, threw his cane away, and suddenly stood up, and made his way through the crowd till he was facing Jesus.

Bartimaeus: Jesus, the prophet!

Jesus: Here I am. What's your name?

Bartimaeus: Bartimaeus. I'm blind.

Jesus: Why were you shouting? Did you want something?

Bartimaeus: Yes, if you would allow me to touch your face.

Jesus paused and closed his eyes for a moment. Bartimaeus stretched his arms toward him and touched his wide forehead, his cheeks, his nose, the shape of his lips, his thick beard.

Bartimaeus: Thank you, prophet. They've been telling me a lot about you. Some say you're ugly. Others say you're a good man. Still others say you're this and that. Now I know.

Jesus: How long have you been blind?

Bartimaeus: Oh, for many moons now. It's been ten years since . . .

Jesus: So, you've been waiting for ten years.

Bartimaeus: Well, hoping and despairing. Once, I wanted to take my life. But God hid the rope from me.

Jesus: And now?

Bartimaeus: Now, I've learned to accept it. Life is beautiful until the hour of death. Don't you think so? Well, so . . .

Jesus: Wait, Bartimaeus, don't go. Will you let me touch your face?

Bartimaeus: You touch my face? But you're not blind.

Jesus drew near and placed his hand on the eyes of that man who never stopped smiling.

Jesus: Your hope served as your cane through all these years. You had the vision to see what matters most, Bartimaeus, and you saw it with your heart.

Bartimaeus: And now I can see you! No this can't be! I can see your face, prophet! I only knew about you through hearsay, but now, I can see you with my own eyes!

The city folks of Jericho pushed us, and they shouted with all their enthusiasm. They were saying that Jesus was the Messiah, the one our people had been awaiting for many years. Bartimaeus was weeping with joy. He was with us for a long while, as we undertook our journey back to Galilee. At the gateway of Jericho, along that dusty road, lay the dirty beggar's cloak and his old cane . . .

•

In the middle of the desert of Judea, Jericho appears as an oasis, fertile and green. It is also known as the "city of palm trees." The roses of Jericho were famous (Sir. 24:14), although we are not sure if these are the same flowers that we know as such at present. Some people believe that these flowers are the adelfas, which are typical in a tropical climate. Nevertheless, Jericho is an authentic green land. The so-called Fount of Elisha, watering the whole of the land, accounts for its fertility. Tradition has it that it was Elisha, the disciple prophet of the great Elijah, who had purified and enriched its otherwise saline waters (2 Kings 2:14–22).

The gospel gives us scant information about the person of Bartimaeus, although it does preserve his name (a detail that is less common in the scriptural/biblical history of miracles), the cause of his blindness, and so on. In this episode, Bartimaeus gives us a picture of a man about to commit suicide. His failure in life — in his work, his marital life, with his friends — has been unbearable. Having been in extreme desperation and having descended to the darkest pit of helplessness, he learned to hope. The miracle performed by Jesus on his dead eyes teaches us that life always has a meaning, in spite of everything. The meaning is sometimes too obscure to discover, too difficult to comprehend. Those who have suffered a lot are aware of this — but this can only be appreciated if we give life a chance to show us what it has in store for us.

The act of suicide is very rare in the Bible. It appears only once in the entire Old Testament (2 Sam. 17:23). Other cases would be those of the warriors who would rather die than fall into the hands of their enemies, like what happened to Saul, the first king of Israel (1 Sam. 31:1– 6), although these deaths are different from a "dispassionate" suicide. In the New Testament, the only case of suicide would be that of Judas. This absence of suicide reveals the great respect for life that characterized the whole people of Israel. For the Israelites, life came from God and belonged to him solely. The human being was destined to live, and life was always better than death. Some books of the Old Testament, marked by a certain pessimism, related that death was better than a life of sickness (Sir. 30:14–17). In any case, Israel's people prioritized life.

There is not a single word in the Bible orienting Christian reflection on suicide. However, after knowing the attitude of Jesus and his words, it can be said that in a Christian context, there should not be any condemnation for the suicidal person. (Sometimes, especially in past years, a church burial was denied a suicide victim, as a form of posthumous punishment.) Suicide is resorted to as a consequence of desperation, fear, an extreme psychological maladjustment, and so on. None of these, which can be the basis of such a dramatic decision, should be a cause for rejection or condemnation because this whole gamut of human flaws always finds compassion and understanding in Jesus.

In this episode, Bartimaeus has something in common with Job, that biblical character who rebelled before God because he thought he was not deserving of his misfortunes: sickness, destruction, abandonment by friends (Job 3:1–4, 20–23; 6:2–4). At the end of the book, Job utters to God the same words that come from Bartimaeus's lips: "I knew you only by hearsay, but now, I can see you with my own eyes" (Job 42:5). Although we must stay away from sorrow and pain, try to avoid it, minimize it, and fight it in order to become faithful to the will of the God of life, sometimes we cannot escape from it. We have to accept our own limitations. In this case, the positive acceptance of pain and sorrow can make us more mature, more tolerant, and more understanding. In other words, we become wiser in the face of life and before God's mystery. Pain can be a passageway to a new way of facing the reality of God. Like what happened to Job and to Bartimaeus.

(Mark 10:46–52; Luke 18:35–43)

89

The Lepers of Jenin

Male Leper: Lord God! I come to you on bended knees, with my face lying prostrate on the ground! Take pity on this unfortunate creature. I've got nothing but bumps all over my body. I pray you, Lord, I beg you, and I trust in you. I pray, I beg, and I trust in you.

Female Leper: What are you saying, chatterbox? Do you think you'll impress the Lord with your silly talk? Oh Lord, you know fully well I'm worse than he is. Look, the wounds in my body outnumber the hairs on my head.

Another Leper: Shut up, scabby, I came here first! I started praying before you.

Male Leper: I pray, I beg, and I trust in you!

Female Leper: Lord, have mercy, Lord, have mercy!

There in the caves of Jenin, near the mountains of Gilboa, lived several men and women suffering from the worst of all known diseases at that time: leprosy. The lepers were not allowed to enter any town, nor knock at any door, much less to enter the synagogue. That is why, every Saturday, some of them would gather in the big cave to pray for healing. They would scream and burn incense so that their prayers would reach God through his ears and nose.

Male Leper: If you heal me, I swear I'll never cut my hair nor taste a drop of wine for the rest of my life!

Female Leper: Every month I'll walk barefoot to the Sanctuary of Shiloh!

Another Leper: I'll consecrate my life in service to you! If you cure me, Lord, I'll go the Monastery of the Dead Sea to study the Holy Scriptures day and night!

While the rest of the lepers prayed, Demetrius, the Samaritan, entered the cave. He was also a leper.

Demetrius: If someday you get cured, rascal, go get yourself a twin brother and let him fulfill your oath! Hey, folks, stop praying and listen to me! The Lord in heaven must've strained his ears with your stories. Why don't we give him a chance to rest? Listen, do you know what I've discovered?

Male Leper: How would we know unless you tell us?

Demetrius: If you don't shut up, how can I tell you? Listen. Haven't you heard of Jesus of Nazareth?

Female Leper: Who's he?

Demetrius: He's a prophet. He's God-sent. They say the angels are with him.

Male Leper: Prophets make me laugh, more so if they come from Galilee.

Female Leper: Me too! And I won't lift a finger for them.

Demetrius: What you should move are your feet. I heard that he and his friends are taking the road to Capernaum. And so they will have to pass by Jenin.

Male Leper: Well, let them pass where the road is good. What the hell do we care, Demetrius?

Demetrius: They say he has healed many sick people. He simply touched them and presto! they were cured.

Male Leper: Well, as for me presto! I'm not moving from here.

Another Leper: Neither am I. Look, Demetrius, I understand how things are. You come out of the cave, walk four miles, the heat, the exhaustion, the blisters on your feet and what for?

Demetrius: What for? To see the prophet, to talk to him! Maybe he can help us.

Female Leper: Help us! Ha! You are a Samaritan, and that's why you're stupid enough not to understand that the only thing we can do is to accept our fate. We're all doomed.

Demetrius: That's right, we're doomed, but we don't lose anything by trying. So, my friends of ill omen, stop lamenting. Let's all go and see the prophet.

Male Leper: No, Demetrius, we're not going.

Demetrius: Why not?

Male Leper: The prophet is not passing through Jenin.

Demetrius: Don't tell me. How did you know?

Male Leper: Because I know. I'm sure they'll take the road to Dothan. People like us are jinxed; we are never lucky. We'll just be wasting our time.

Female Leper: I think our friend, Ptolemius, is right. They'll take the road to Dothan.

Demetrius: You know something? I think with a band like you, even Nebuchadnezzar would fall from his horse! It's all right. Just burn your incense here, while I go and wait for him along the road of Jenin. But don't tell me I didn't inform you.

Some Lepers: Wait, Demetrius, don't go, wait.

Amid grumblings and protests directed against Demetrius the Samaritan, the rest of the lepers put on their black and dirty rags to cover their bodies. The little bell hanging on their clothes was a reminder for people to stay away. After walking four miles, they took their place along the road coming from Jerusalem and leading to the entrance of Jenin.

Male Leper: We came at the wrong time, Demetrius! Look, we've been waiting here for quite some time and what for?

Female Leper: So we'll know they have taken a detour to Dothan, that's it.

Another Leper: I bet nine against one, we'll never get to see even the shadow of that roving prophet.

Demetrius: Well, I'm taking the bet. You'd better start paying, my friend, because I swear they're those people coming along the bend! Look! Can't you see? It's they, I'm sure!

Male Leper: My grandfather's name was "Sure" and he's dead now.

Demetrius: Can't you see them? The prophet of Galilee is coming!

Male Leper: Okay, okay, so what?

Demetrius: Now we'll tell the prophet our problem, and maybe he can help us.

Male Leper: Do you think he'll waste his time on us? C'mon, Demetrius, don't aim so high. If you fall, it could even be worse. The prophet will pass by this road, all right, without even getting a glimpse of us.

Female Leper: I agree with Ptolemius. We've got the jinx, you know.

Demetrius: Okay, okay, but I want to see the Galilean. Hey, Jesus, help us. Do something for us. Hey, Jesus, over here, even for a minute, please!

Demetrius the Samaritan signaled to us with his two arms. He was shouting and jumping, so we would see. Behind him, the other lepers were looking at us suspiciously.

Demetrius: They have seen us! And they're coming over! Hey, Jesus, prophet! But what's wrong with you? Will you just stay there like wet chickens? C'mon guys. Move, do something!

Female Leper: What do you want us to do, Demetrius? C'mon, tell us. What can the prophet do for us, huh? How can he help us? Don't be too excited. You might only be disappointed.

Male Leper: I agree with her. C'mon, Demetrius.

Demetrius: Go to hell, all of you! Even patient Job couldn't put up with you!

Jesus, Peter, and I were walking ahead of the rest, and when we saw the group of lepers at a stone's throw, we came to a halt.

Jesus: Hello, my friends, who are you? Where did you come from?

Female Leper: Now, he'll ask us to go away.

Demetrius: We came from the caves of Jenin. We're lepers. Can you help us?

Jesus: Well, the truth is, we didn't bring anything, not even food or money.

Male Leper: I told you! It's all just a waste of time, plus a bonus of blisters on our feet.

Jesus: Why don't you see the priest and tell him your problem? Who knows, you might be lucky! Goodbye!

Male Leper: "Who knows, who knows." This prophet knows nothing and passes it on to the priests.

Female Leper: "Go to where the priest is and tell him your problems!" Great!

Another Leper: Well, a man forewarned is worth two men. I brought some dates with me for the long walk back to the caves. Goodbye!

Demetrius: Come back, you bunch of idiots! If the prophet had told us to go barefoot to the Sanctuary of Shiloh or to go up to the Monastery of the Dead Sea, wouldn't we have done that?

Male Leper: Well, in that case . . .

Demetrius: Well, he's asking us to do something easier: to go to the priests of Jenin. C'mon, let's all go there and see what happens.

Male Leper: See what happens! I'm sick and tired of this "come and see what happens" thing! I pray, I beg, I trust, but nothing happens!

Demetrius: If the prophet said this, then it must be for something.

Male Leper: Of course it's for something. It's to make fun of us. Didn't you see his expression? I'm not going anywhere.

Another Leper: Neither am I.

Another Leper: Nor I.

Another Leper: Look, Demetrius, do you think with these wounds in my leg I can show myself to the priest for examination?

When Ptolemius, one of the lepers, took off the rag that covered his legs, everyone was aghast.

Male Leper: Look, look, my skin has become so smooth, like a child's!
Female Leper: How can it be possible? Let me see.
Another Leper: Yours too, Marthina! And yours, Godolias!
Another Leper: And mine! And yours too, Demetrius!

The lepers of Jenin wept and shouted with joy when they realized that their wounds had disappeared without any traces at all.

Male Leper: Something fantastic has happened here.
Female Leper: It has never happened before! It's a bunch of miracles!
Demetrius: See, I told you, killjoy! The prophet of Galilee has cured us, without even lifting a finger! C'mon, guys, hurry up! Run!
Male Leper: Where to, Demetrius? Where do you want to bring us now?
Demetrius: To where the prophet is! Whether he is still in Jenin or if he has arrived in Capernaum, we'll go see him!
Female Leper: Are you out of your mind, Demetrius? Why are we going to look for him?
Demetrius: What for? To thank him, damn it!
Male Leper: Forget it, Demetrius. We won't see him anyway.
Female Leper: Of course not! Don't you see he's a prophet?
Demetrius: So?
Female Leper: Prophets just disappear. Remember Elijah, who went up into the air in a chariot? We won't see him anyway.
Another Leper: Right. He'll just disappear.
Another Leper: Well, you may go on with bickerings if you want, but I'm heading right now for Bartholo's inn, since my throat hasn't had a taste of wine for three years!
Another Leper: I'm doing the same tonight!
Female Leper: I'll go greet my family in Bethulia!
Another Leper: I'm seeing Martha and Filomena, the good one and the bad one! Hahay!

But Demetrius had left them and started to run along the streets.

Demetrius: Hey, have you seen a brown, bearded man pass by? His name is Jesus of Nazareth!

A Man: No, my friend. Wait a minute, but aren't you Demetrius, the leper?

Demetrius: Excuse me, madam, did you see a group of Galileans pass by? One of them is Jesus, the prophet.

An Old Woman: No, my son, I haven't seen anyone. I'm also looking for my lost grandson.

Finally, after a lot of running and asking, Demetrius caught up with us.

Demetrius: Jesus, thank you, Jesus!
Jesus: Hey, and where are the rest of your friends?
Demetrius: Well, they, they only think of God during rainy days.

Demetrius the Samaritan stayed with us for quite sometime in Jarod's inn. There we all drank a toast to him and to his nine companions who stayed behind; and for God, who makes the rain fall over the good and bad, and the sun shine on the grateful as well as the ungrateful.

•

The original word in Hebrew for leprosy is *sara'at,* which is derived from the expression "to be punished by God." Leprosy was always considered a horrible divine punishment. The religious "impurity" was thus contracted by the sick person, which made him repudiated by the rest of the community. So the lepers had to live in segregated places; they were strictly prohibited from entering the cities; and they had to announce their presence in the streets for everyone to avoid them. Since the disease was also perceived to be incurable, the only hope of the patients was a miracle. In any case, if the disease was cured, it had to be confirmed and certified by the priest (Lev. 14:1–32).

Dothan and Jenin are two small cities about eight kilometers apart, situated along the road ascending to Galilee from Judea, passing through the Samaritan mountains. Of the ten lepers praying and suffering in the cave of Jenin, Demetrius is the only Samaritan. There is an interesting symbolism here: the most despised of all (for being a leper and a Samaritan) shall be the only one who will keep alive the trust of the group (because of his faith, the miracle will work for everyone) and the only one who will express his gratitude for what was done for him.

A fatalistic attitude toward life paralyzes us. If everything is indeed "written," if destiny (fate) is something that cannot be contradicted, then nothing can be done but to wait for the time of its fulfillment, for good or for bad. Demetrius fights against his companions' pessimism and mobilizes them. This brings him near Jesus and opens possibilities in his life. A false religion has taken over the hearts of many men and women, fatalistic beliefs about life. These ideas, however, are not supportable: we are free men and women. The direction that our life takes depends on us. If it seems that we are not free, if ours is a life that is crushed by suffering and oppression, a fatalistic attitude (it has always been so, it will always be like this) will only perpetuate the situation. It is not destiny that perpetuates it, but our attitude.

In this episode we see how, reluctantly, the lepers go in search of Jesus; how they distrust him, criticize him, and finally, how ungrateful they are. In spite of all this, Jesus heals all of them. This miracle is, therefore, a sign that God's gifts are free. God grants us life, good health, and opportunities not because we are more grateful or less grateful or in order for us to be good, but because God loves us. God's love is unselfish, disinterested, and doesn't expect any incense burning or applause in return.

Luke, the only evangelist who wrote about this picturesque and "incredible" account of the ten lepers who were healed, wished to elaborate a catechetical scheme about how our attitude toward God should be, and he did it by way of this parable on gratitude. This attitude is important not because God "needs" it to help us, but because being grateful helps us to be truly humble and to be more brotherly/sisterly with one another. There are people who only remember the Lord during bad times. They also follow the rest of the pattern: they are good only when they have reason to be. They never express their gratitude. Such behavior obviously implies a certain egoism, while to be grateful makes us aware of our limitations and gives us a certain joy which egoists will never experience. To be grateful is closely linked to human solidarity, to sharing, and to the knowledge that we support one another and are responsible for each other as we involve ourselves in the performance of the common task.

(Luke 17:11–19)

90

Jonah's Miracle

The rumors of what Jesus had done in Jerusalem and in the cities of Judea spread like an avalanche of stones from a mountain. The stories spread by word of mouth, were magnified, and were interspersed with legends. They became the topic of discussion in the markets and in the caravans. People said a lot about Jesus. They said lightning rays came out of his head, like Moses; that Elijah had lent him his chariot so that he could travel faster from one place to another; that miracles came out of his hand like butterflies.

Old Woman: Hurry up, friend. I was told how the sick get healed just by passing through the shadow of the prophet! Let's go!

Jesus' fame grew and grew. The multitude that followed the new prophet of Israel soon doubled.

A Man: Bend your head a little, sweet thing. With that hairdo of yours, we can't see anything.
A Woman: Here you go again with your needling!

That winter on our way back to Capernaum, the townsfolk waited at the entrance of the neighborhood, near the Gate of Consolation.

Old Woman: Hey, Jesus, how's everything in the capital? What did you do this time?
Jesus: The usual thing: we announced the Kingdom of God.
Old Woman: Yeah, yeah, I know. What else did you do?
Jesus: That's it, grandma. We talked to the people, opened the eyes of the small fish, that the big fish may not gobble them up.
A Man: What the old woman wants to know is if you made the blind see.
A Woman: Precisely. How many miracles did you perform this time, Jesus?

When the woman spoke of miracles, the multitude pushed around even harder. Many sick people had come, on crutches or carried in improvised stretchers of intertwined branches. Others had rags tied around the sores on their arms or legs.

A Man: Bah, what really matters now is not what you did in Jerusalem but what you will do at the moment, is that right? Look at all these unfortunate people. They're waiting for you to do something for them.

The sick looked at Jesus with pleading eyes, stretching their arms to touch his tunic. Then, Rebecca, the weaver, forced her way through the crowd until she was facing him. Her right leg was thin and twisted; a cane was her only means of support.

Woman: Heal me, please. Make me walk again! Heal me, prophet, heal me!

Jesus looked at the woman, then he remained silent.

Woman: Heal me! You can do it! Yes, yes, I feel better now. I feel a certain warmth in my body.

The woman suddenly raised her hands toward heaven, hurled the cane serving as her crutch, and shouted to the top of her voice.

Woman: I'm healed, I'm healed!
A Man: Oh, yeah? You might break your other leg with that excitement of yours!
Another Man: Jesus, heal me too. I've been ill longer than she was. Clear the way and let me pass!

Julius, the blacksmith, was giving hand blows to the air to be able to get to Jesus and ask for a miracle. He had a hunchback like a camel's.

Julius: C'mon, make a miracle, straighten my back. C'mon, what're you waiting for? Heal me!

Jesus looked at him sadly, without saying a word.

Julius: What's the matter? Have you lost your healing power? Why don't you do something? Why don't you heal me?
Woman: You gave back the eyesight of a certain Barnaby in Bethsaida. I'm blind, too, and I want to see again. Or is he better than I am?
A Man: You can do it. You cured Seraphim in Chorazin. He was deaf and dumb.

The sick people were getting impatient with Jesus, who remained silent, with his eyes downcast. The noise was getting louder and louder. It was at this time that Rabbi Eliab appeared.

Eliab: Our paths have crossed again, Nazarene, this time not in the synagogue, but right here in broad daylight.

Jesus: Are you sick too, rabbi?

Eliab: No, the Almighty has blessed me with good health. He has likewise given me intelligence, that I may catch the wolves hiding in sheepskin.

Jesus: Then take a good look at me, rabbi. Have I got wolf's ears?

Eliab: That's why I came. I'm tired of hearing so many stories. All of Israel is talking about you. Some crazy men call you prophet. The more brazen ones even refer to you as the Messiah, for whom our people have been waiting for centuries. Very well. What can you say? Are you the Messiah or not? Speak up! Silence means an admission.

Jesus: The tree is known by its fruit. You will know me by my deeds.

Eliab: Let's put things in order, Nazarene. The Scriptures say that when God sends a prophet, he gives him the power to make miracles.

A Man: And Jesus has that power!

A Woman: Jesus has done a lot of miracles, rabbi! Have you forgotten what he did to Floro, the crippled one? He was brought down from the roof, and he came out running with his legs stronger than a mule's.

Eliab: Yes, I've heard of it, but I didn't see it. The heart can't believe what the eye doesn't see.

A Man: What about the fruit vendor with a withered hand, rabbi? Jesus cured his hand right in front of you in the synagogue.

Eliab: It's no use crying over spilt milk. Leave the fruit vendor and Floro alone, and stop talking of things in the past. We're all here, and I want to see a sign today. Am I asking too much, Nazarene? Look at all these sick people. You can choose from them. Heal whoever you want, but give us one clear proof. Perform a miracle before us, and we shall all believe in you. I'll be the first to believe.

Jesus remained still, his eyes fixed on the ground. Suddenly, he bent over and plucked a few leaves from the ground. He put them in his palm and blew on them. The breeze from the lake carried the leaves on the air.

Jesus: Man's life is like a plant. One day it grows, and with just one last breath, it dies. Our life is in God's hands. Only God has the power to heal us.

A Woman: God and you, because you are his prophet.

Some People: We want a miracle! Make a miracle!

Jesus: Okay. There will be one miracle for all of you, just one.

A Man: Yes, yes, just one. C'mon, do it now!

Some People: Do it on me! Cure me!

Woman: I was here first! Do it on me, Jesus!

The sick milled around Jesus. Rabbi Eliab stayed a little distance away and waited, suspiciously, for the miracle that Jesus was about to make.

Jesus: Just one miracle, my friends. Jonah's miracle. Just this one.

Man: What's happening to Jesus?

Jesus: What's happening now happened before, when God called for Jonah and sent him to preach in the great city of Nineveh. The story is this:

> *Voice of God:* Jonah, son of Amittai, get up and go to Nineveh. The Ninevites are violent people. They trample the weak, abuse the orphans, and drag the widows to court. Go and shout through the streets of Nineveh that if things don't change, I will make them change. I'll raise my hand and defend the cause of the poor. I shall be firm with those who abuse my people.
>
> *Jonah in Nineveh:* Change your ways! Change your ways, everyone! This city is built on injustice. If you don't change your ways, Nineveh will be destroyed within forty days. Reform your ways!
>
> *King:* An order from the King of Nineveh: all from the first to the last, men and women, young and old, must change their ways. Each of us must cleanse our hands which have been stained with blood and violence. Let us all repent before God and practice justice. Who knows? God might also relent from the punishment that we deserve, who knows?

A Man: Jonah was a great man all right.

Another Man: Greater than the whale that swallowed him.

Old Woman: And you are greater than Jonah, Jesus?

Man: Then heal me. C'mon Jesus, let's stop all this talk and just heal me. What's keeping you?

Woman: Make a miracle for us to see.

Jesus: Jonah did not perform any miracle in the city of Nineveh. It was the Ninevites who made the miracle themselves, by changing their ways and living a life of rectitude. The city, which was sick before, healed itself.

Old Woman: My son is sick too. Heal him, like you healed Jairus's daughter.

Woman: Heal me, too! Don't I have the right to be healed?

Jesus: Woman, one gets healed by faith, and not by right.

Woman: I have faith and I believe in God. What more do you want?

Jesus: It is God who has faith in us, and hopes that we ourselves perform the miracle, the miracle of Jonah.

Eliab: I've had enough of this talk, and please stop pushing around. Will you make a miracle or not? Can you do it or not?

Jesus: Why don't you do it yourself, rabbi? I'm sure you can. Look, do you know how this poor creature got sick? By bending his back day and night on the loom. That's how he broke his bones! Do you know how this man twisted his neck? By carrying sacks and sacks of flour on his head to earn that measly denarius. You make the miracle, yourself, Pharisee! It does not consist of bringing back the eyesight of the blind, but offering your pocket and sharing your food with the hungry. It is not cleansing the skin of lepers, but purging the country of the stink caused by the abuses of some people. This woman is crippled on one leg because our country is crippled on two. Let us not ask God for more miracles! They should come from us. The miracle of justice.

Eliab: Now you're talking politics. This is the only thing you can do, Nazarene. Stir up the minds of this bunch of rascals. You're a charlatan, that's what you are. And an agitator. Go away and preach all this nonsense somewhere else.

Another Woman: The rabbi is right. This guy is a fake, that's all. Let's get out of here, c'mon.

A Man: Go to hell, Jesus. You and your good for nothing stories.

The sick people began to leave, each one going his or her own way. Some were supported by canes, others by crutches. Still others were carried on stretchers, or in their neighbors' arms. Soon no one was left in the place except our group. It was getting dark in Capernaum. The cities adorning the shore like a pearl necklace began to light their white lamps. Jesus looked sad, his gaze lost in the water's reflection.

Jesus: Poor Chorazin! After all that preaching in the square and in the streets you still haven't changed. You're still an adulterous city, worse than Nineveh and Sodom. I pity you, Bethsaida, as you lie in your warm bed in the company of big businessmen, while your people agonize in hunger and suffer in the open cold. You continue to coddle usurers and the gods of violence. You never hear the cries of the dying innocent. And you, Capernaum, you want to scale the heavens to rob the Lord of his miracles, but you never make an effort to change your ways on earth. You refuse to perform the only miracle that God asks of you: that of doing justice.

•

People's religiosity that is poorly oriented and nurtured under a situation of misery easily converts into "fantastic tales" of miracles. Religion and faith become identified with something marvelous, amazing, and exceptional. God is reduced to a powerful doctor or to a circus magician. Faith becomes adulterated, its acts simplified into one sole purpose: to be able to believe in a miracle. Yet what is even worse is that when people succumb into this frenzy, they miss what is most important: the reality of each day that is full of injustice and "sicknesses," clamoring for changes that should originate from us.

In an effort to explain who Jesus is, how he did good by performing miracles, healing the people possessed by the devil because God was with him (Acts 10:38), a number of miracle stories have been transmitted to us by the evangelists, and the gospel texts are spattered with marvelous accounts. All these narrations should not be read as such. A strict, literary criticism of the same will show how some of these miracle accounts are duplicated (compare Mark 10:46–52 with Matt. 20:29–34); others are magnified; still others are loosely elaborated; and so on. All this simply tells us that although there is a certain historical nucleus in the stories about Jesus' healings, we cannot convert the gospel into something like a catalog of miracles performed by a powerful superman. This idea is common in many people with poor theological formation. In order to overcome this obstacle, which may be a setback in our quest for Jesus and his good news, we might have to start with a differentiation of the terms "miracle" and "sign." The gospel of John, which brings down to seven the number of miracles performed by Jesus, gives us a reason for this. In referring to these acts, John always uses the Greek word *semeion* (= sign). A sign has no value in itself. It points in a certain direction; it indicates a road, a way. It is not the goal but the means to attain it. In this sense, the "miracles" of Jesus would not be isolated and marvelous acts instigated by his compassion for suffering individuals. If that were so, they would not mean anything at all, and would simply vanish. On the other hand, if we take them as signs that will lead us to an understanding of Jesus' mission, we expand considerably the theology of the miracle. What can it mean for us today that Jesus of Nazareth healed a paralytic in the first century? The fact that Jesus, the messenger of God's plan of justice for history, has raised a man from his downtrodden position is a sign that his good news is capable of lifting us from our passivity. A broader and more profound reading of the miracles is therefore necessary if we want to be faithful to the full content of the gospels. This is so because, for every person healed by Jesus, the evangelists are actually giving us a picture of the "prototypes" of people, in which case the picture could perhaps be of us.

Just as there is a difference between a miracle and a sign, there is a difference between faith and religion. Religion "reunites" humans with God, making the former dependent on the latter. This may be good, but it may also be risky. Sometimes religious consciousness makes us expect from God what we may achieve through our own efforts or through everyone's unity or organization. It might make us fear God's punishments for our evil deeds and shortcomings. Likewise, it might make us feel that God's benevolence may be bought by good deeds: prayers, sacrifices, vows. These feelings have been entrenched in the hearts of men and women ever since the creation of the world. Nevertheless, if we want to grow as free individuals, then we must be able to overcome them. In fact, God wants us to overcome them. The proof of this desire is Jesus, who with his word and attitude lifts up people and takes away from them the fear of the Lord, making them responsible for their own lives and for history, making them grow in freedom. Our authentic attitude toward faith is anchored in freedom, historical commitment, equality, triumph over fear, and so on; it is not grounded on religious feelings which may revert people to a childish status if they give in to them unquestioningly.

People or certain groups hiding in the shadow of these fantastic tales of miracles may be concealing an enormous degree of materialism, thus reducing the act of God to a palpable and provable proof of his supposed power over humans. We must realize that healing a number of diseases may be done—in fact this has been proven in history—by way of a strong psychological impact, by suggestion, and through "faith" in a manner of psychic power, letting loose hidden potentials in our being. Naturally, God is present at this moment, just as God is there when nothing of this sort happens. That is why it is highly perilous to attribute to God's direct intervention what can be explained as the body's means to overcome, during specific moments of exaltation. God's involvement in our life, in history, is revealed in other "miracles." We just need to open our eyes to realize this. Jonah's miracle did not consist of his having been swallowed by a whale and spewed out later on, safe and sound. The miracle was that Nineveh, a city wallowing in corruption and injustice, was transformed and the people realized the wrong they had committed, so they changed their ways. We can undertake at this moment the miracle that God wants of us. The Spirit of God will sustain us in our struggle, keep our commitment alive, and grant us hope that will transcend even death.

(Matt. 11:20–24; 12:38–42; Mark 8:11–13;
Luke 10:13–15; 11:29–32)

91

The Time to Go to Jerusalem

That winter passed swiftly, like a comet in the sky. The branches of the almond trees showed signs of their first fruits. The fields began to spread their mantle of flowers, and the fresh air of spring diffused its fragrance over the plains of Esdraelon. That day, while we were having lunch in Peter's house...

Peter: Anything wrong, Jesus? Why don't you eat?

Rufina: Looks like the dark one hasn't slept a wink.

Jesus: That's right, Rufina, but that's nothing. The truth is, I had to see very clearly...As a matter fact, I've been praying for months, asking the Lord to show us the way and...

Peter: And what?

Jesus: I think the time has come.

James: For what?

Jesus: For us to go to Jerusalem. This is also the time when the poor flock to the heart of the city to share what they have and thus confront this old weary world that is about to end. Yes, what we have been saying over and over again in all corners of Galilee, we shall be repeating all over the city.

Peter: Hey, Rufi, did you put a lot of spices in the soup? I think it's gotten into Jesus' head.

Judas: Well, then, Jesus, when do we start?

Jesus: As soon as possible, Judas. God is in a hurry. There's so much misery in the country. Herod is committing terrible abuses in the north, and the Romans are getting more atrocious in the south. Meanwhile, Caiaphas and the priests of Israel are talking about patience. Friends, we can't be patient anymore. It's time to put an end to all these, to expose the atrocities of these wolves, like Samson did when he set everything on fire.

Judas: Yes, sir! We should not be afraid to burn them. Ash is the best fertilizer.

Rufina: All of you will be the ashes. Are you all out of your mind? You were almost arrested last time, and now you still want to go back to Jerusalem? You're courting death.

Jesus: Of course, Rufina. That is indeed what we'll be doing. Samson also risked his life, but God gave him the strength to face his enemy. God will not fail us, either, I'm sure of that.

Thomas: I'm s...s...sure o...our enemies have de...deadly fangs, b...b...but we have to go.

Peter: And fast! The Passover is near!

Judas: We'll have to take advantage of the time. It's during this time when more and more people mill around the city.

Peter: And all the wolves come out of their dens. Pontius Pilate will be coming from Caesarea. Herod, from Tiberias. They all get together in Jerusalem for the Passover.

Jesus: We, too, shall go, but not only to remember our ancestors' freedom when they left Egypt, but also to start a new liberation. We continue to be slaves, because the Pharaohs are still well entrenched in their palaces in Jerusalem. We'll go there to expose their abuses to their faces, like Moses did.

All: That's right, Jesus! Very well said!

Jesus: Go, tell everyone, all those who want to join us. We're all going up to Jerusalem to set fire to all of them!

In a few days we incited the whole fishermen's barrio to go with us to Jerusalem. A lot of men and women from the neighboring villages of Sepphoris said they would join us. The city of Capernaum was virtually converted into a beehive. Nothing else was talked about except the journey to the capital in that month of Nisan.

Peter: Join us everyone! The time has come to go to Jerusalem! Hey, guy, are you coming or not?

A Man: Of course! I wouldn't miss the action for anything in this world!

Peter: And you, ma'am, what's keeping you? C'mon, make up your mind!

A Woman: You better make yourself clear, Peter, and stop talking nonsense. Tell me, what are you up to in the capital? What the hell are you going there for? To look for trouble, to pray, or to have fun?

Peter: Oh, ma'am, I haven't had the time to think about that yet. But not to worry, because Jesus knows what he's doing. We're going with him, and we'll cross the bridge when we get there. Believe me, neighbor, you

will see, this dark one is the Messiah that our ancestors have been waiting for.

Woman: Hey, what nonsense are you talking about?

Peter: What everyone else is saying, that Jesus will free Israel, and he
will smash the faces of these scoundrels who have been making a mockery
of us. With Jesus on the front-line, we shall capture the capital and all the
cities of the country.

Woman: Oh, yeah? If indeed this Jesus is the Messiah, where's his sword?

Peter: He's hiding it, damn! If he shows it now, the Romans will make
him swallow it. Long live the Messiah!

All: Long live the Messiah!

Peter: So, what now, ma'am? Are you going or not?

Woman: No, no. I'm not going. I'm sick.

Peter: What an alibi! You've got a pair of strong legs to walk to
Jerusalem!

Woman: Are you crazy, Peter? You'll have to carry me then like a sack
of flour. No, count me out. I'm sick.

Peter: No, you're not. You're just scared, that's all. Ma'am, remember
that cowards never have a place in history.

Woman: Right, and the valiant ones are all stiff dead.

Jesus: Hey, Simeon, c'mon and join us. We need courageous people like
you!

Simeon: I'd like to, Jesus, but . . .

Jesus: But what?

Simeon: My family. You know how it is at home. My mother worries a
lot about me.

Jesus: And you worry a lot about your mom. Hey, you're almost thirty
years old, man, and you haven't cut that cord yet?

Simeon: Listen, Jesus. Let me tell my folks about this, so they will
understand. Give me time, will you?

Jesus: Look, Simeon, let me tell you what happened to a neighbor of
mine in Nazareth who went to plow. While he was plowing the soil, he
would turn his head here and there in order to greet everyone passing by
the road, and, of course, in the end, he got a twisted neck and the furrows
were even more twisted.

Jesus then turned to the others who were gathering about.

Jesus: Listen, my friends: if a bricklayer were to construct a tower, wouldn't he count the bricks first to see if he had enough, so that he would not be left unfinished in the middle of the wall? Or if a king declared war against another king, wouldn't he count his soldiers first? If he had ten thousand soldiers and he found out that his enemy had twenty thousand before the battle started, wouldn't he send a peace emissary first? Yes, we are going to Jerusalem, but how many soldiers can we count on?

A Neighbor: Here, count me in! All I need is a uniform!

Jesus: All you need is a pair of sandals and a cane, brother!

Neighbor: Well, then, I'm ready. To Jerusalem I go!

Jesus: And after that, what?

Neighbor: What do you mean?

Jesus: Jerusalem is just the beginning.

Neighbor: I'll go where you go, don't worry.

Jesus: Are you ready to leave your nest?

Neighbor: What nest?

Jesus: Your nest. Everything that gives you warmth and comfort.

Neighbor: Oh, that's another thing. I'm sleeping on a mat.

Jesus: What if we haven't got a mat?

Neighbor: There ought to be something, a stone, perhaps, to sleep on!

Jesus: And if they take the stone from you?

Neighbor: Then I sleep on my two feet, damn it! Even horses do it, and how!

Jesus: In that case, you're one of us. Yes sir! We can count on you!

Julius: Hey, Jesus, I wanna go with you too.

Jesus: Well, then, come. Who told you not to?

Julius: No one, but I'm scared, that's the truth. You know, my father was killed when I was a little boy. My mom remained a widow, penniless, and with five mouths to feed. Yes, my father was a brave man, but what did he get? That was a long time ago, and yet, as you can see, things haven't changed ever since . . .

Jesus: Your father lost his life, but you haven't. That's why you shouldn't lose hope. Otherwise, you're dead like your father.

Julius: Yeah, that's it, probably. But, honestly, I'm scared. I know what'll happen. The closer you are to the fire, the easier you end up burning yourself.

Jesus: But fire gives you light. Indeed, Julius, you gain life by losing it. My father, Joseph, also lost his life when he helped the unfortunate ones fleeing from an unjust murder. His life was short, but it was worth more than that of those who protect themselves. They end up smelling like moths. Have courage, man!

Peter: You can't trust this guy, Jesus. He looks scared to death.

Jesus: Aren't you scared, Peter?

Peter: Who, me? I've never been afraid in my life. Look, Jesus, you know how deeply involved we are in this matter of the Kingdom of God. We've given up everything, even our fears! These guys who join the bandwagon at the last minute just make me laugh. At first, they looked at us like a bunch of crazy guys. Now, everyone wants to join us in Jerusalem.

Jesus: The more, the better. Don't you think so, Peter?

Peter: Of course, but they shouldn't break ranks. We've been rowing the boat for quite sometime now, haven't we? And when we finally conquer Jerusalem and sing our victory something special must be awaiting us, right, Jesus?

Jesus: Something special, Peter?

Peter: You know what I mean, Jesus, not that I'm interested, but . . .

Jesus: Oh, I understand. Don't worry. For every problem that you had before, you'll have a hundred more. A hundred troubles more and a hundred persecutions more.

Peter: Well, Jesus, there'll no doubt be rough and smooth sailing. I know that. What I mean, though, is that, you know, everybody loves to sit at the place of honor. Right?

Jesus: Peter, where have you seen a servant seated at the master's place?

Peter: I haven't, but . . .

Jesus: No talk. All of us, when we accomplish the task entrusted to us by God, will say just one thing: the task is finished, I complied with my duty. Nothing more.

During the week of going to and from Capernaum informing the people, Jesus never grew tired talking to the people.

Jesus: They will accuse us of dividing and inciting the people. Well, it's true. From now on, there will be division even in the family: if there are five, they will be divided, three against two and two against three, the son against the father, and the daughter against the mother, and the mother-in-law against the daughter-in-law. No one can any longer just wave their arms around. Whoever does not reap, scatters. Whoever does not fight for the poor is against the poor and plays the game of the those who are oppressing the poor.

All: Very well said, Jesus!

Jesus: Onward, my friends. Jerusalem is awaiting us! God will be with us in Jerusalem and will deliver us from bondage just as he freed our ancestors from the Pharaoh's yoke! We, too, shall cross the Red Sea, and we shall all be free.

We had never seen Jesus speak so ardently as during those days. His eyes glowed like those of John's, when the prophet cried out in the desert. Like John, Jesus spoke rapidly, as if words were being pressed up his throat, as if time was too short for him to say everything he wanted our people to hear.

•

The topic about the "time" of Jesus is of utmost significance in the fourth gospel. With this word "time," John designates the culminating moment of Jesus' life, initiated by his last journey to Jerusalem. The "time" for John's theology is the moment when God will intervene in a definitive manner, that of the fulfillment of the mission of the Messiah (the final, eschatological hour). It is the moment of the glorification of Jesus and the emergence of the Kingdom of God in history. All this grand eloquence may be expressed in this manner: Jesus' commitment at the time he was baptized in the Jordan will reach its ultimate consequence — the offering of his life. We must not see any tinge of fatalism in this, as if Jesus had prepared himself for this moment and had taken the death road, knowing beforehand what was going to happen to him. No, Jesus had thought of a plan of action and other activities, one of which is seen in this episode, and which eventually would be his ultimate plan: to jolt the foundations of Jerusalem with the good news of the kingdom. Jerusalem, the city of contentment and injustice, was the center of religious and socio-political power of that time.

One continuously discovers in the person of Jesus, in his psychology, in his words and actions, a dominant factor: haste, urgency. From a purely historical point of view, Jesus is presented to us as a man who believed in the imminent coming of the Kingdom of God. He was convinced that God's definitive intervention in favor of the poor would be immediately realized, that the final hour was at hand. That is why, for him, every minute was precious. It was this sense of urgency that inspired him to speak the way he did: about the war, the sword, and the fire. He tried to awaken the people from their lethargy, those who believed there was plenty of time. A lot of Jesus' words and parables ought to be situated within this context of crisis which he lived historically. The future and ultimate crisis he saw were imminent and necessary in order for God's justice to come. This should not make us think of Jesus as an enlightened fanatic, like the prophets of doom roaming our streets and cities, driving our people out of their wits. Nevertheless, one should not forget this vision of Jesus during this period, if we indeed want to remain faithful to the truth transmitted to us through the gospel.

At the time Jesus undertook his last journey to Jerusalem he was already known as a prophet, not only in Galilee but in the capital as well. Jesus had popular support, and the leaders hated him and persecuted him. His going to Jerusalem hinged on two given factors: he knew the risks he was taking; yet he also knew the importance of bringing his prophetic message to Jerusalem, to the temple. He was anticipating death, yet he was convinced it would be a triumph for the Lord. He knew that the kingdom would be won through pain and risks, and he was ready to pay the price, trusting fully in his Father's power. Obviously, this is not fatalism, but a full understanding of the forces at play: courage in the face of perils; blind — but not fanciful — faith in the power of God, who is the most powerful of all.

Within this atmosphere of urgency are found the "vocations" of the three compatriots of Jesus. Of the first, Jesus gives an analogy of the plow. The primitive system of plowing in Palestine demanded full attention of the farmer to his work, since any form of distraction would be adverse to the task. It is a sign of what is expected of a vocation for the kingdom: constant commitment regardless of consequences. A frivolous attitude is useless in a risky task. The second vocation demands austerity. There is "no place for one to stay." One is expected to give up everything: one's own comfort and tranquillity. Finally, one must be willing to give his or her life (Matt. 16:24–26) to overcome the fear of death. Nothing makes one more free. Vocation is a lot more than a vague desire to be good (to be "perfect" as expected at times). It is adjusting one's life radically to a direction which turns out to be difficult, conflicting and disturbing. Jesus came to bring the sword, not peace (Matt. 10:34). The way entails a lot of tension, self-denial, firm decisions, and intelligent strategies (Luke 14:28–33). Neither should one give much credit to what he or she does (Luke 17:5–10).

Sometimes, "vocation" is perceived to be only a matter for priests and nuns. This is incorrect. A greater part of the evangelical texts makes reference to those called by Jesus — including those of this episode in relation to the matter of "one hundred for every one" (Matt. 19:27-29) — as being people from every social status. All are called to work for the kingdom. Each one should do it in accordance with his/her family, social, or professional status. Perfection is not greater in the monastery than in the street, nor is there more Christianity in the priest than in a layperson. All gospel texts referring to vocations are about God's call to all people, from whom Jesus demands the same commitment. This commitment — and Jesus knew this fully well — would bring sorrows and sufferings. There is no need to pursue them; they will be provided by those who are opposed to God's plan.

When we say that Jesus is a sign of contradiction, this must be taken seriously. That he belongs to the world of the poor, making them the beneficiaries of God's message of love, makes him the object of scandal. In Jesus' time he had to clash with the learned and the powerful who could not tolerate what he said and did, especially — and this was the height of it all — his demand that God's name be put in the center, making God's will ultimately responsible for all. Jesus was fully aware of the enmity engendered as a consequence of his actions (Matt. 10:34-35).

(Matt. 8:18-22; Luke 9:57-62)

92

Through the Eye of a Needle

Reuben: But, Nivio, are you really serious?

Nivio: Of course, my friends. Don't you believe me?

Titus: What happened? Did you have a spat with your girl? Did your father disown you?

Nivio: Neither of the two.

Reuben: You must be sick, then.

Nivio: No, nothing of that sort. I'm perfectly all right. But I'll feel better if I go and tell him: "Hey, prophet, count me in! I'd like to join your group, too, and travel to Jerusalem, and spend the Passover in the city of David."

Titus: I bet you won't dare.

Nivio: I won't dare what?

Titus: Say that to the prophet.

Nivio: You don't know me then. Right now I'm gonna tell him.

Reuben: Wanna make a bet, Nivio?

Nivio: Sure. How much? Twenty denarii?

Reuben: Make it forty.

Titus: Nah, a barrel of wine would be better. When you lose, we can all drink to our hearts' desire, as you drown these out-of-this-world ideas of yours in the sweetness of wine.

Reuben: Ha, ha. C'mon, there's no turning back. You'd better swear.

Nivio: I swear and I promise, and this bet is on, for a barrel of wine.

Titus: All of Capernaum is going nuts! Nelson, the son of a rich man, took the bait and fell into the Nazarene's mousetrap.

Reuben: What'll your dad say when he finds out?

Nivio: What the heck do I care? He lives his own life. I live mine.

Reuben: What'll people say, Nivio? The landlord's son wants to be in the service of a farmer who is half-witch and half-agitator.

Nivio: I don't care what you say, but this guy, Jesus, is different. He's gutsy. All it takes is to listen to him.

Titus: Or better, to smell him! He reeks of onions and whore's perfume!

Reuben: Birds of a feather...

Titus: So, the Nazarene has given you the itch?

Nivio: I think you're all envious.

Reuben: What? We, envious? Ha, ha, ha. No way! Hey, I'm happy with my life. I've got lots of servants, and I don't have to work hard.

Titus: Same here.

Nivio: I'm not, and I've decided to change my life. I'd like to do something great. I'll go see the prophet this afternoon, and go with him to the capital and then...

Reuben: And then, go bathe yourself to remove the lice that you will have picked up from that miserable prophet.

Titus: Look, Nivio, don't you understand? Oil will never mix with water. Jesus is not of our kind. You're not of his kind either. If you join him, what good will come of it?

Reuben: I don't know what's gotten into you, Nivio, but this much I can tell you: wait till he picks on your father and the rich. That'll be the time to say goodbye!

Nivio: This is what you think of him. But I do believe that Jesus has an open mind. I'm sure he'll be delighted to see me. I can be useful to him. I've got money, education...

Titus: And most of all, don't forget our bet!

Reuben: Right, and it's been decided: a barrel of wine. Do you agree, Nivio?

Nivio: You bet, friends.

Nivio was the youngest son of Phanuel, one of the wealthy landlords in Capernaum. He was tall and strong, never wanting in good food and elegant clothes, and he went to the best school. He helped his father in the management of their land, and he had plenty of time to spend with his friends. That afternoon, he left his luxurious house and headed for the fishermen's barrio, to a street by the sea.

Little Simon: C'mon, stupid, Jump!

Canilla: Tacatan, tacatan, tacatan, hiyahh, horsey!

Little Simon: My little horsey jumps better than yours, look! Ha, ha, ha!

Canilla: Now it's my turn!

Nivio: Hey, kids, could you tell me where Jesus of Nazareth lives?

Little Simon: Pff! Yeah, he's inside, fixing a door. Hey, Jesus, someone's looking for you!

Jesus: Here I am! Who is it?

Little Simon: A young man!

Jesus was alone when Nivio came to the house. My mother was mending nets on the wharf, and old Zebedee, my brother James, and I were fishing in the middle of the lake, as always.

Jesus: Say, aren't you one of Phanuel's sons, the landlord?

Nivio: Exactly! How did you know me?

Jesus: You know, in Capernaum one gets to know everyone. Well, this door is fixed. Not even a hurricane can bring it down! What's your name?

Nivio: Nivio. I've been called by that name for eighteen years.

Jesus: Fine, Nivio. They say you're a good person, in spite of your father.

Nivio: Nonsense. The only good person in this city at the moment is you.

Jesus: Me? Why do you say that?

Nivio: Because you are. You and your group are the only ones doing something so that things may change in our country.

Jesus: Well, the truth is, you wouldn't want things to change in the country. They wouldn't suit you.

Nivio: You're a great man, Jesus. I have always said so.

Jesus: I have always said that the only great one is the Lord. All of us push a nail here and there, put bricks one over the other, and we simply do what we can.

Nivio: That's why I came to talk to you. I also want to put my own brick on the wall and do my share in building it up.

Jesus: You?

Nivio: Yes. You're surprised, aren't you? Of course, I understand. Imagine, the son of Phanuel! Please don't be misled by appearances, Nazarene. You and I will get to understand each other, you will see.

Jesus: I hope so. Come, sit over here and let's talk.

Jesus put the hammer and nails away and sat down on the floor. The landlord's son did the same.

Nivio: Everyone in the city talks of nothing except the journey to Jerusalem.

Jesus: What journey?

Nivio: What else? Your journey.

Jesus: Ah, of course...

Nivio: I also thought about it and made a decision: count me in, Jesus.

Jesus: Don't tell me, you've got the sting too?

Nivio: Can't I go with you?

Jesus: But of course. You're welcome. Indeed, I'm glad. I'm sure everyone will be pleased too.

Nivio: I hope so. Okay, Jesus, let's go to the point. Exactly what are we gonna do in Jerusalem? What are your plans? Tell me.

Jesus: Well the plan is to change everything.

Nivio: What everything?

Jesus:. We're going to build a new heaven and earth where everyone gives a hand, that all of us may smile and live in happiness. What do you think of this plan?

Nivio: I like it. It seems like a beautiful plan.

Jesus: Exactly, but in order to do it, there'll be a little problem, because we're trying to make a world in which "those who have less have more, and those who have more have less."

Nivio: What was that you said? Seems like a tongue twister.

Jesus: No, it's something very simple. Listen. Why do some people in Israel experience hunger? Because others eat twice as much. Why do some children walk barefoot and half-naked in the street? Because others have seven tunics and fourteen pairs of sandals kept in their chests. Some of us carry only a grain of wheat in our pockets while others have their barns filled to the brim. Do you understand, Nivio?

Nivio: Understand what?

Jesus: That the only way to fill up a ravine is to reduce a hill. God's plan is to equalize, do you understand? What do you think of that?

Nivio: Sure, of course. Okay, going back to the trip... Tell me, how many are we going to Jerusalem? Many? Few? Whom have you invited?

Jesus: Look, we've invited everyone, but you know how people are. First, they say "yes, yes"; then, later, they say "I forgot."

Nivio: That's right. People talk a lot, but that's all. Right, Jesus?

Jesus: Precisely. We need people who are willing to work hard and to push forward the Kingdom of God.

Nivio: Well, here I am ready to put my shoulder to the wheel. As a matter of fact, and I'm not bragging, but since I was a child, I was taught the commandments of God, which I complied with. I have never stolen in my life.

Jesus: Neither were you ever hungry.

Nivio: I have never killed anyone. Neither have I wished to do it.

Jesus: And neither have you felt the steward's lashing on your own back.

Nivio: What? You don't believe me? Seriously, Jesus, I swear I have never done wrong to anyone.

Jesus: You don't have to swear. I believe you. Of course, even the drones do nothing bad in the beehive.

Nivio: Ah, now I see what you're up to. Well, in that case, why don't you go out to the street and find out who in Capernaum has given more alms than I?

Jesus: Who do you think can do that here, when everyone has a hole in his own pocket?

Nivio: Well, yes, but going back to our trip. Have you decided on what we shall bring for the trip? I guess we'll have to bring something, won't we?

Jesus: You don't have to worry about that, Nivio.

Nivio: If we have to buy something, feel free to tell me.

Jesus: To buy, no, but to sell, yes.

Nivio: To sell? To sell what?

Jesus: Everything. You've got to leave everything, to set your hands free.

Jesus stared at the hands of Phanuel's son. They were so smooth, unlike the callused and chapped hands of the poor. Then he lifted his eyes and looked at him with sympathy.

Jesus: Listen, Nivio. Moses, too, grew up in a rich house. The Pharaoh's daughter fed him well, gave him the best clothes, and sent him to the best school in Egypt. But one day, Moses went down to visit his brothers and saw an Egyptian foreman beating a Hebrew slave. Moses got so furious, he killed the foreman. He lost everything — his house and his comfortable life. Left with nothing, he was persecuted by the Pharaoh's guards. Thus, he became worthy of his people. Then he was able to draw close to the slave, like his equal, and call him brother, and help him to be free. C'mon, Nivio, think about this, and come back later, so we can discuss our trip.

Nivio: Sure, I'll think about it, Jesus. I'll think about it...

Nivio looked at Jesus, not knowing what to say. Then he stood up from the floor, shook his new tunic that became soiled, and left the house. He was very sad.

Peter: Hey, dark one, why did Phanuel's son come over?

Jesus: To teach me a game, Peter.

Peter: A game?

Jesus: Yeah. Hey, Little Simon, come here, run.

Jesus peeped through the door and called Peter's son who was playing in the street with a group of children.

Jesus: Say, little Simon, what game are you playing?

Little Simon: Horsey-horsey. Tacatan, tacatan, tacatan!

Jesus: Do you want to learn a new game?

Little Simon: Sure, sure, how is it?

Jesus: Listen. It's a camel's game. You are the camel. Let's see. Get down on your fours like this. See, you have a big hump on your back. Do you see this needle?

Jesus joined his fingers to form a small circle.

Little Simon: So, what do I do now?

Jesus: Do you see this small hole? The camel should try to pass through the needle's eye. If he succeeds, he wins. If not, he loses.

Little Simon remained staring at Jesus' hand. Then he stood up from the floor.

Little Simon: I don't like this game, Jesus. Bye! Tacatan, tacatan!

Jesus: That was the game that Phanuel's son wanted to play. But the camel will never pass through the needle's eye. Even children know that, Peter.

In the richer part of the city, Nivio met again with his friends.

Reuben: I've got this feeling, Nivio, that today we'll drown our sorrows in sweet wine!

Titus: "I swear, I promise, I declare . . . "

Reuben: And your bet was a barrel of wine! Ha, ha!

Titus: Hey, Nivio, cheer up, and let's all of us toast to your silly head! Ha, ha, ha!

Nivio's friends went inside his house, opened a barrel of wine, and started to drink and play jokes on him. The landlord's son, between gulps and laughter, eventually forgot about the trip to Jerusalem.

•

This text, oftentimes used to illustrate the theme of vocation, has disturbing ideas for the rich. We might say that this is an account in which Jesus appears to be a "demagogue." The primitive Christian tradition was faithful to Jesus' harsh criticism of wealth, and he never found any possible justification for those who had accumulated wealth. The Holy Fathers of the Church were also "demagogues" when dealing with this topic: the gospel rightfully refers to excessive wealth as "unjust," since it springs from no other source than injustice, and one cannot possess it unless others lose what they need. As St. Jerome put it, four hundred years after Christ: "The rich are rich on account of their own injustice or their inheritance of properties unjustly acquired" (Epistle 120.1).

Nivio is what we would call today a "coffee table revolutionary." What he feels is what is sometimes justly understood to be a "vocation": an undefined restlessness to become a better person, to be of help to others. In him, there is also some sort of a warped/malformed conscience, on one hand, and, on the other, a desire to hobnob with Jesus, a leader who wins people over and becomes important in the eyes of his followers.

It is good to demythify the "rich young man." Sometimes he is pictured as a good man, pure, honest, one who obeys all the commandments, but is "not fit for the religious life" because he is not courageous enough to heed the "advice" of Jesus to sell everything and give it to the poor. This is not the focus of the gospel. Jesus is not giving "advice" to those who seek perfection. Jesus shows the rich young man the only valid way to enter the kingdom: through the experience of the poor — by putting one's self in their place, sharing in their life, taking as one's own the cause of their liberation. Jesus' advice deals not with an isolated slice of life but with the whole project of life itself. The rich young man has not committed great wrongs, but he has not done much good either. His is a sin of omission. And when Jesus shows him where he has gone wrong — in his lack of sensitivity to the poor — he continues to be blind, to be obstinate in his own individualism, satisfied with his comfortable, "decent" life.

This callousness of the rich brought about by money, a callousness constantly in evidence, is what brought Jesus to make his exaggerated analogy of the camel and the needle. This phrase about the needle has nothing to do with the shape of the opening of a Middle Eastern door, as has often been claimed, in order to soften the comparison made by Jesus. (It has been argued that the "eye" of Middle Eastern doors was very narrow, but if the camel lowered his hump and bent a little, then he could pass.) No, this comparison is about a sewing needle and a camel, the biggest known animal in Palestine. A camel can never pass through this eye. Never. With this exaggerated analogy, Jesus simply wants to say this: it is impossible, unless God performs a miracle. These extreme analogies are, on the other hand, typical of Middle Eastern expressions, and Jesus frequently uses them to be sure that the radical character of his message is not distorted.

Nivio's "decency," his good deeds, are being questioned by Jesus, because he was well-fed, well-educated, with a sure future. He had all the conveniences to be good, had no need to steal or to feel constrained to violence. The "morality" of some persons is no more than a luxury. Their economic status allows them not only to live a good life, but also to be good, besides being considered such by society. Meanwhile, for many people living in misery, cheating, aggression, and sometimes prostitution or other forms of "sin" are not vices, but the logical consequence of their desperate situation or their only way of survival.

(Matt. 19:16–24; Mark 10:17–25; Luke 18:18–25)

93

Those Who Kill the Body

James: The hour has come, the hour of victory!

Simeon: Within three days we'll be heading for Jerusalem, and in three days the capital will be ours!

Julius: So the traitors to the country had better be ready! Down with the traitors!

Simeon: And with the Romans!

Julius: And the Herodians, too!

James: And the Sadducees!

Neighbor: Who'll be left in the city then?

James: Silly man, we'll all be seated on twelve thrones with the scepter on our knees.

Neighbor: Really, James? Do you think we'll go this far?

James: I'm certain of it. That's why I'm going with the Nazarene and with all these people. Cheer up, man. The end of it will be something great. Later you'll regret not having come.

Anne: You heard it, Rufina. Jesus said there would be trouble in Jerusalem, and no stone in the temple would be left unturned.

Rufina: And then what?

Anne: What else but the sharing of the loot, after the battle! I've been setting my eyes on the atrium's drapes. And the tablecloths, too.

Rufina: Well, I'd settle for one of those candleholders with seven golden angels.

A Woman Neighbor: And what'll be left for me, huh? The seven little candles?

Every day, more and more neighbors in Capernaum were deciding to go with us to Jerusalem to celebrate the feast of the Passover that year. I guess everyone had a distinct idea of what was to take place during the holidays. Each one was holding on to a different kind of expectation. But everyone was dreaming of the grand day of liberation of our people.

320

Julius: Listen, Clete: the heavens will open wide. God will stick out his finger through the clouds and say: Jesus is the Messiah. Follow whatever he tells you. Do you understand, Clete? He'll be in the forefront. And we'll be behind him.

Clete: Behind us are the guards with their cudgels, right? No, no, just leave me in peace. I'm not going anywhere.

Julius: Why not? What if the Lord sticks out his finger?

Clete: Then let him lick it, I wouldn't care! Even if you tie me up, I'm not going with you, even if you drag me.

The news of our journey to Jerusalem spread beyond Capernaum, through the valley, from village to village, from door to door, until it reached Nazareth and sneaked into the hut of Mary, the mother of Jesus.

Susana: Mary, Mary! Haven't you heard? Haven't your cousins told you anything?

Mary: Yes, Susana. I know it already. Jacob came a while ago, to tell me.

Susana: Jesus has finally gone crazy! Tell me, Mary, why can't this dark-skinned son of yours just stay put? Did you nurse him with milk or with hot sauce?

Mary: They say about seven hundred, eight hundred, a thousand men are joining him. That's an entire army!

Susana: Of course, an army of ants versus a giant.

Mary: Well, David fought against Goliath and he won.

Susana: Oh, really? Are you changing your mind now? This is the height of it, friend! I'd say I'm smelling something different in this trip.

Mary: What do you mean?

Susana: Politics, revolution…

Mary: Well, if he is in danger, I can't be at peace here in Nazareth. I'm leaving right away for Capernaum.

Susana: What nonsense are you saying, Mary? Don't you remember anymore? The last time you went to see him, he sent you away. Jesus won't listen to you anymore.

Mary: This time, I won't quarrel with him, Susana, but I'll be on his side. I'll help him in any way I can. If necessary, I'll go to Jerusalem with him, anywhere!

Susana: But, Mary, wait, let me explain…

Mary: Tell me on the road, Susana. You're coming with me, aren't you?

Susana: Who, me? But, Mary!

Mary: C'mon, Susana, hurry up. We've got to be on our way before nightfall.

Susana: Holy God, what malady has gotten into me?

Mary and Susana walked to Capernaum to join Jesus, surprising Mary's son.

Jesus: But mother and you too, Susana, what are you two doing in Capernaum?

Susana: We're going with you and your shaggy followers to celebrate the Passover in Jerusalem.

Jesus: Are you out of your minds?

Susana: The only crazy creature here is you, Jesus, but that's another matter.

Mary: Jesus, son, this seems to be a hot topic. People talk of nothing else but the trip to the capital.

Jesus: Yeah, they just talk and talk. When the moment of truth comes, how many of them will remain?

Susana: Well, here you have two more ants coming out of the anthill.

Jesus: So I see. But it'll be better for you to go back to Nazareth. Things are getting more and more complicated, and we don't know how it'll all come out.

Mary: Precisely, son, which is why we won't budge from here. If you go to Jerusalem, we go with you. If you go back to Galilee, to Galilee we return.

Jesus: But mother, don't you realize that . . . ?

Mary: You're just wasting your time, Jesus. You didn't listen to me when I asked you to return to Nazareth, remember? This time, I won't listen to you either. We'll all go to Jerusalem together. Come, Susana, let's talk to Salome, Zebedee's wife, so she can tuck us in some corner of her house.

It was two weeks before the feast of the Passover, but the townsfolk of Capernaum were already preparing their provisions. Everyone was excited about the trip. That day, when I saw Jesus talking with Peter, I realized he had something else in mind.

Peter: But, Jesus, how am I gonna say that?

Jesus: Listen to me, Peter. It'll be better this way.

Peter: But it's like scaring the horse away even before he crosses the river.

Jesus: It'll be worse if he gets scared in the middle of the current. We might have the same fate as the Pharaoh's horsemen.

Peter: Okay, okay, if you say so, then I'll do it. But don't blame me later. I warned you beforehand.

That night the moon seemed like a big piece of round cake. The barrio folks were gathered with us on the wharf, asking Jesus what we would do when we got to Jerusalem.

Julius: Tell us, Jesus, where do we begin? Shall we start from the Antonia Tower or from Herod's palace?

Simeon: I say we should first give the fat Caiaphas a nice good kick on his ass!

Anne: They will find out how we Galileans are if we are all united.

Neighbor: Last night, I dreamed of the moment we entered Jerusalem, with the banner of the Messiah in our hands! Long live Jesus, Hosanna!

As we became more and more excited, Jesus gave a signal to Peter.

Peter: Well, I dreamed of something else, fellas.

Anne: What was your dream, Peter? C'mon, tell us. A good dream is worth a bowl of nice, hot soup.

Peter: I'd rather not tell you anyway, it's just a dream.

Some: C'mon, tell us! Speak up, man!

Peter: Okay. This was my dream. We were all walking, walking along a huge valley when, suddenly, as we looked up we saw a vulture hovering in the sky, above us. And every time he finished doing one circle, another vulture came to join him, and together they flew until another vulture came and another . . . until finally, there were many of them, a flock of black and ugly birds hovering over our heads, waiting.

As Peter said that, all of us swallowed hard. The women looked at each other out of the corner of their eyes. Some of us bit our nails, not daring to say anything. It was Julito, a young man, and a little stupid, who broke the silence.

Julito: Hey, Peter, that dream of yours, does it mean anything? C'mon, explain it to us.

Peter: Why don't you explain it, Jesus? I'm sure you know what it means better than I do.

Jesus: All right, Peter, I think everyone here understands what it means. Friends, let us not be disillusioned here. The Kingdom of God has its price, which is blood. The powerful men of Jerusalem will make us pay the price. They will never forgive us for what we have done here in Galilee. Neither will they pardon us for what we shall say to their faces as soon as we get to the capital. The wolves roam in the night in search of the flock, and they hide and wait for the right moment to pounce on the sheep and devour them. They'll do the same thing to us. Then, they'll offer us to the vultures.

Julius: Golly, Jesus, don't be a killjoy! First it was Peter, and now, it's you!

Jesus: Look, we're not going to a party, but to a fight. The enemy is a lot stronger than all of us. Today we're here. Tomorrow, we might be in jail. We're all in danger, and a lot of us will be pursued from town to town. We'll be dragged before Herod and Pilate, and the high priests will beat us in the synagogues and then many of us will lose our lives.

Clete: Don't talk that way, Jesus. We shall all be the victors, with you at the forefront.

Jesus: Precisely, I'll be the first one to fall. The prophets always perish in Jerusalem.

We all looked at each other restlessly and felt the cold air of the night, like a knife penetrating our flesh and bones. Jesus continued speaking.

Jesus: But don't be scared, my friends. You don't have to fear those who kill the body, but not our spirit. God is on our side. God knows even the last strand of our hair and will not allow our struggle to be in vain. Maybe we shall fall in that struggle. But then, we shall bear fruit, like the seed when it falls on the soil.

I was seated on the floor, my head cupped in my hands. When I looked up, I saw Ishmael and his friend, Nephtali, leaving the wharf. The barrio folks, old Simeon, Mam Anne, and the twins were quietly slipping away, too. Then, the biggest group of men and women, as if responding to a silent command, suddenly stood up, and disappeared in the night.

Peter: Cowards! May they swallow the devil's embers for being charlatans!

James: The soldiers retreated before they could put on their uniforms!

Peter: I warned you, Jesus. We Galileans are all chickens. Look how many of us are left behind, twelve, as always!

James: Plus your mother and your neighbor, Susana.

Magdalene: Count me in, of course! Or aren't the Magdalenes people too?

James: What's this cheap woman doing here?

Magdalene: Like what're your doing, stuffy. I told Jesus I was coming, so here I am. I'm going to Jerusalem with you.

Peter: No one is going with anyone, Mary. There won't be any trip.

Jesus: Why do say that, Peter?

Peter: Open your eyes, Jesus. Everyone has gone. Only a handful of nothing is left.

Jesus: So what, Peter? Remember Gideon? He went to war with thirty thousand men, but only three hundred went forth. The rest had left. They were scared and they surrendered. But the Lord granted victory to that small group. Yeah, we're only a small flock, but the Lord will raise the shepherd's staff and protect us from the wolves. Let us not fear: God will be with us in Jerusalem.

James: Are you serious, Jesus?

Jesus: Of course, James. Tomorrow, we'll be leaving for the capital.

Peter: But it's still two weeks before the Passover.

Jesus: We've got to hurry. We can delay no longer. There are too many spies and surveillance teams around. Hey, fellas, cheer up! God'll be with us. Jerusalem is awaiting us!

Peter: And the vultures, too!

That night, we all went to sleep startled. After a few hours, when the sun had barely risen, having stretched our arms and legs, we took our walking sticks and knapsacks and headed for the route of the caravans. Capernaum was left behind. The fishermen's boats were already in the middle of the lake. Ahead of us was a three-day journey; Jerusalem awaited us.

•

Jesus' idea of the imminent coming of the Kingdom of God is not the same as that of his disciples, nor that of his neighbors in Capernaum. Although everyone awaits it, some give it individual considerations; others take it as an opportunity for revenge against the Romans. Some know not where they are heading; there are others who have a deeper understanding of it. The moment of screening comes, generally, when people begin to see the risks, the dangers, and the price to pay. Then the prudent ones, the less convinced, the comfort-loving, and the cowards back out of it. Commitment to the gospel is extremely demanding. By the time Christians grow in it, they discover the consequences of such commitment in their life, just as they begin to discover the strength given them by God as God accepts them.

Mary lived this process of growing in faith. Her "yes" to the Lord was an everyday thing, with every new situation she was in. She would not have been a model of our faith or of our hope had she not doubted, had she not taken the risk even if things were not clear to her. At this point of the episode, aware of the risk that Jesus was undertaking in his trip to Jerusalem, she wanted to share this risk with him. She was no longer opposing – as she used to, during the initial activities of Jesus – neither did she passively await what was going to happen. Now she wanted to collaborate. Her faith had matured and reached the decisive point of the process: solidarity in the face of danger.

As he undertook this trip to Jerusalem, Jesus had to consider the possibility of a violent death. His confrontations with the religious authorities in deliberate violation of the law (specially the law of the Sabbath, the apex of the social and religious system of the time) had exposed his life to danger. He was fully aware of this. In Galilee, Herod had the authority to have him killed. In fact, he had wanted him killed (Luke 13:31). In Judea, where Jesus went, only the Romans could mete out the sentence, but his decision to perform a prophetic act in the temple had put him in the most grievous danger before the civil authorities, who were very close to the priests.

In Jesus' time, the people considered the prophets as martyrs, because they were persecuted by the kings of the country. Besides, many of them were killed on account of their accusations against the oppressive rulers. Isaiah, Jeremiah, Ezekiel, Amos, Micah, and Zechariah, were, for the people of Israel, national martyrs. Jesus knew he was to become heir to the prophetic tradition which began with Elijah and continued with John the Baptist. By this time he knew he was a prophet. That is why, without directly seeking death, he could not expect for himself a destiny better than that of the great men of his country.

The gospel tells us that Jesus "predicted" his passion. He makes three predictions of his passion as more evidence shows that the days of his death are nearing. Caution must be taken in reading these texts, in order not to come to a conclusion that Jesus predicted his own life and death; that he knew beforehand what would happen to him and, therefore,

suffered "less," knowing the beautiful denouement of his story. That interpretation dehumanizes Jesus, converting his death and resurrection into
a theatrical play. Being fully human, he was aware of the risks, though
he would not know the exact circumstances. And being fully human, he
was amazed at the circumstances, and would try to modify them. Everything seemed to indicate, for example, that Jesus thought he would be
stoned to death (Matt. 23:37); that he would be buried as an offender in
a common pit (Mark 14:8); that immediately after his death, his disciples
would also suffer violent persecution and death (Luke 22:35–38). At other
times, he thought that God would not allow his downfall, that God would
not abandon him. Had he not thought that way, then his anguish on the
cross could not have been explained. But things did not happen as he had
imagined: Jesus died, though not by stoning, was interred in a dignified
sepulcher, and the Jewish authorities left his group in peace. All this tells
us that Jesus, indeed, considered the possibility of a violent end, nothing
more. His awareness of danger cannot be construed as an infallible pre-
diction of everything that was to happen to him. Jesus' death happened in
history, subject to actual, historical circumstances, which could have been
otherwise. The passion and death of Jesus are historical events. They are
not the fatal fulfillment of the design of a God detached from history, nor
the result of predetermined "prophecies." These events are the fruit of
human freedom. Jesus was free when he risked his life, deliberately en-
gaging in his awareness-raising activities for months, especially his actions
in the temple. The people who killed him were free. In the passion, no
one is God's puppet; rather, human freedom, including murderers and
the murdered victim for the sake of justice, is put at play.

(Matt. 10:16–33; Mark 11:9–13; Luke 12:4–12; 21:12–19)

94

The Right and the Left Seats

The sun was already high when we left Capernaum for Jerusalem. We were twelve in the group, with the addition of Mary, Jesus' mother; Susana, their neighbor; my mother, Salome; and Mary, from Magdala. Jesus led the trek. He walked fast. The spring, with its colors, clothed the fields of Galilee. It was already dark when we reached Jenin, and we decided to spend the night in one of the fields surrounding the small city, at the border between Samaria and Galilee.

Salome: With these chicken bones I brought, I can make some delicious soup. What do you think?

Susana: That's a good idea, Salome. This is going to be a cold night. These rascals will sleep well with a warm stomach. Hey, young lady, go and bring me a handful of thyme for the soup flavoring.

The woman from Magdala went to get some thyme, while Susana, Salome, and Mary stayed by the fire, preparing the dinner that first night of the trip.

Salome: Look at this Magdalene: how she walks and steals glances...

Susana: And how, Salome. Jesus says she has changed a lot, although my grandmother used to say that the leopard cannot change his spots.

Magdalene: Here's the thyme.

Salome: Here, give it to me. Hey, what grass is this, young woman? This is not thyme.

Magdalene: Yes it is, M'am Salome, smell it. It's thyme.

Salome: Okay, okay, drop it in the pot. If it doesn't kill us, then it will only make us fat.

Mary: Shall we get some cheese, too?

Salome: No, Mary, with this soup and some olives, we already have enough.

Magdalene: Peter says he's starved!

Salome: He always is. He's never satisfied. He's always hungry.

Magdalene: But the man is quite strong! He's not Jesus' right hand man for nothing.

Salome: Right hand for what?

Magdalene: Well, he's the second man, after Jesus.

Salome: Tell me, where did you get that idea, Magdalene?

Magdalene: Everyone knows about it. Didn't you know that, M'am Mary. You're Jesus' mother. Hasn't he told you about it?

Mary: No, but...

Salome: You're a gossip, Magdalene. Such a malicious tongue you've got!

Magdalene: Who, me, a gossip? But isn't it true that Jesus is close to Peter?

Mary: I don't know. I think he's close to everyone, Magdalene. The truth is, I haven't noticed that.

Magdalene: Look, either I'm a gossip or Salome is a distrustful person, my goodness! I heard somewhere, precisely from James and John, these good sons of yours, that should anything happen to Jesus, heaven forbid, the guy to man the helm of the ship is Peter.

Susana: Hey, young woman, stop talking of misfortunes now!

Magdalene: Okay, I'll shut up, but the truth is, this trip to Jerusalem is putting us in such a big mess. Yeah, Jesus is in charge now, but if anything happens to him, then it will be Peter.

Salome: Here you go again! Why does it have to be Peter, tell me. Why?

Magdalene: Look, m'am, Jesus has got a sure eye, and among these rascals he would choose someone a little more decent, of course. For all his defects, Peter has word of honor unlike the "others."

Salome: Are you referring to someone in particular?

Magdalene: No, no one.

Mary: Okay, will you stop that silly talk. C'mon, young woman, tell those men that the soup is ready.

Magdalene: Hey, Jesus! Everybody, come over! It's dinner time! C'mon!

Salome: Have you noticed, Mary and Susana, how this woman defends Peter? How insolent! She wouldn't be a whore for nothing. What nerve she's got.

Mary: Forget it, Salome. I don't think she said it with malice.

Salome: Stop defending her, Mary. This woman doesn't waste time maligning my children, the whore.

Susana: If she wants to malign them, then she should say something to their faces.

Mary: Shut up, Susana, don't make matters worse.

Salome: I don't know, Mary, but I don't trust her being with our men.

Philip: This soup is marvelous, yes siree!

Nathanael: It's so good, I almost forget about the corns on my feet!

Peter: I find the taste rather strange.

John: It's your weird ideas, Peter.

James: What we need now is wine!

Mary: Tomorrow we'll buy some in Shechem, where they sell good wine.

James: Puah! The Samaritan wine tastes like castor oil.

Philip: There goes James with his idiosyncrasies again! Why don't we leave the Samaritans in peace and play dice instead. Are you gonna play, Jesus?

Jesus: Wait till I finish licking this bone, Philip. Just go ahead.

Jesus remained seated near the fire, while the women collected the leftovers and put away the pieces of bread for the following day. The twelve of us went a little distance away, where the light of the half-moon could shine over us, so that not one of us could cheat with our dice.

Jesus: Are you tired, mother?

Mary: No, son. It's been quite sometime since I have walked this far, but as you can see, I can still manage.

Susana: You know something, Jesus? Your mom may be old, but she's got strong legs like a young woman's. On the other hand, look at me, I'm too darn sleepy. Ahuuumm!

Philip: Number eight! This time I win! Boy, am I lucky!

James: To hell with you, Philip! C'mon, Peter, open up, it's your turn.

Peter: No let somebody else do it. I I've got to go.

James: Hey, what's bugging you, man?

Peter: Uff! After having felt too much hunger for hours and then zas! It's the soup with the weird taste.

Philip: But it was very good; it really warmed my stomach.

Peter: It has upset mine, just like a turbulence on the Sea of Galilee. Look, I'd better do something about it, somewhere over there or else. Uff!

John: Better do it far from here, naughty man!

Philip: Be back soon, will ya?

Peter headed for a small olive grove till he got lost among the trees.

Salome: Look at these three women. They're already snoring.

Jesus: Yeah, they're dead tired; they couldn't even say a word.

Salome: Say, Jesus, now that we're alone, I'd like to tell you something.

Jesus: What is it, Salome?

Salome: Let's go over there so we don't wake the sleepy-heads up. Come.

Jesus and my mother went toward the grove and sat beside a tree.

Salome: It's about that Magdalene, Jesus. To hell with that "girl"!

Jesus: What happened? Have you been quarreling?

Salome: I hate to say this, but that woman and Peter! I don't want to be malicious, but either it's Peter who's flirting with her or the other way around. Something seems odd around here.

Jesus: Don't say that, M'am Salome.

Salome: Oh, if only Rufina had come along! Right, the problem is with Peter. Magdalene thinks Peter is everything. He's strong, most courageous, the best. It's too obvious, Jesus. She can't deny it. Of course she should know, having been in the business for years. Well, I don't want to malign her, but that woman is dangerous.

Jesus: Are you sure?

Salome: That's not the worst of it. She's been telling everyone what you said, that this delinquent is your right hand man. That Peter is second to you. I say that can't be, and I can't believe it. Everyone knows Peter too much. He barks but never bites. He's a little scatterbrained, all right. And she says he's courageous. A simple sneeze can scare the wits out of him. Oh, pardon me for being catty.

Jesus: No, no, go ahead.

Salome: Look, Jesus, they say there's nothing like the old horse for the hard road. Look at my white hair, dark one. You want some advice?

Jesus: Go ahead. What is it?

Salome: With Peter as your right hand you had better be a one-handed person! Jesus, you need a right arm and a left arm. Two strong arms that are willing to help and defend you.

Jesus: Who do you have in mind?

Salome: My two sons. It's not because they are my children, but because they deserve it. James and John are willing to give the last drop of their blood for you, Jesus, believe me. Forget about that dirty old man, Peter, and count on my sons, who'll be by your side. One on your right and the other one on your left.

Peter: You treacherous witch, I want to strangle you. Damn you, Salome. Hey, all of you, come over here!

Peter's thunderous voice shook the entire olive grove. We all stood up from our game, while the three women roused from their sleep. Everyone ran toward Peter, who was calling to us at the top of his voice.

Jesus: Peter, where've you been?

Peter: I was behind that tree and I heard everything.

Salome: And what were you doing there, you wretch?

Peter: Something more decent than what you were doing. Over here everyone! Hurry and pull out the tongue of this old hag!

James: What's going on here, damn it? What's all this shouting about, Peter?

Peter: Why don't you ask your mother about all the intrigues she's making up? Do you know what she said? That there's "something" between me and the Magdalene.

Magdalene: What? How did I get into this mess? Hell, what have I done? Tell me, Salome, what have I done to be dragged into this muddle?

James: You better shut up, Mary, you're just making things worse!

Peter: Your beloved mother started all this, do you hear? You too, redhead, and you, John, hypocrite! Scoundrels!

It took us a great deal of effort to appease Peter and convince him to explain what he had heard behind those trees. While he was talking, my mother Salome barely looked up.

Philip: Really? Your mother could say that?

Peter: You bet! This old hag should be hanged.

James: Wait a minute, Peter. If the cap fits, then wear it. The truth hurts, after all.

Peter: Are you insinuating something?

James: It's you who's insinuating a lot of weird things. Tell me, who the devil told you that you were somebody else's right hand man?

Peter: Jesus said so during our trip to the north. Don't you remember anymore?

John: He didn't say that. That's what you wanted to be, big nose. But he didn't say that.

Peter: You see? They're just like their mother, scheming fools! You sent her here in order to speak ill of me.

James: One more mention of my mother, Peter, and I'll tear you to pieces!

Peter: You just dare, James, and you'll be dead before the night ends!

Magdalene: Okay, so it's all my fault, isn't it? If that's it, I'm leaving right now. I'm going back to Capernaum!

Jesus: No, Mary, you're not going anywhere.

Peter: If there's anyone who should leave, it's that old gossip-monger and her two sons.

Jesus: No one is leaving, Peter. Neither Salome, nor Mary, nor the two of you. Damn it, that's enough! It's only our first night together and we're already fighting like angry cocks. We're going to Jerusalem, and things will be very difficult for us. We've got to be united. When the most trying moment comes, we shall all have to drink from the same cup. Everyone. Let's forget about this right arm and left arm stuff. Here no one is better than anyone else. We're all in the same boat, and everyone must help in order to go on. Either we all come out afloat or we all end up sinking and drowning.

John: We're all coming out alive, dark one! Guys, Jesus is right. And now why don't we get out of here; this place stinks like hell!

That night, we could not sleep. Peter's grumbling seemed to have no end. My mother, Salome, tossed and turned often before she fell asleep. We were all very tired. We had to wake up early the next morning to resume our journey to Jerusalem.

•

The gospel puts on record that some women formed part of Jesus' group that followed him from town to town in proclaiming the Kingdom of God (Mark 15:40 – 41). There is great novelty in the fact that Jesus was followed by these women in the company of his disciples. Salome, Susana, Mary Magdalene — and still others who probably formed part of the group — thus become a symbol of the revolutionary character of the gospel in a totally male chauvinistic society. Jesus' words and his attitude toward the women deeply clashed with the customs of his time. The Christian church, in order to be faithful to Jesus, ought to be a venue for authentic equality among men and women, where no one feels discriminated against because of gender while rendering service to the community.

In Jesus' group, as in any other human group, not everything turned out smoothly. There probably were ambitions, bickerings, suspicions, distrust, and dishonesty. These were not always dramatic. They were everyday conflicts, full of ups and downs. This is true of all human relationships. Magdalene's presence in the group would surely result in clashes because of the implication of her job. Jesus did not evade such conflicts. In gathering such a diverse group, he even provoked them. Such crises within the community may sometimes be healthy if the members confront them, thus helping them grow in the knowledge of their capabilities as well as their limitations.

Jesus does not intend to avoid all these conflicts. What he expects of his group is that no one should be above anyone else. No one should appear to be favored or oppressed in the community; no one should be different because of having greater intelligence, more ability, or for any other reason. The gospel offers itself as an alternative to the "master-slave model" which the world powers are trying to preserve — not only in Jesus' time but also in our days. This alternative tries to create communities where this system of dependency will be totally wiped out, where all its members will live in equality, where the only authority is God, where the only competition is geared toward better service to others. The Christian communities should be the critical conscience of societies founded on power, favors, and inequality.

This episode attempts to focus on a daily life situation, rather than on a plot to "take power" or a significant intrigue with political overtones. The focus is simply a problem arising from Salome's envious attitude. The typical moral prejudice (against prostitutes), the maternal ambition to see her sons honored, and that obvious feeling of envy are the causes of the conflict. The comic scene, as played out by Peter, is inspired from a text in the Old Testament where David experiences a similar situation when he is pursued by Saul (1 Sam. 24:1–8). The Bible has many picturesque scenes of everyday life which are anything but insipid, colorless, and odorless.

(Matt. 20:20–28; Mark 10:35–45)

95

Seventy Times Seven

Before dawn, before the first cocks of Samaria began to crow, we got up and resumed our trip to the south, toward Jerusalem. It was a cool morning. The clouds in the east were tinged with red, announcing a radiant day.

Magdalene: Ahemmmmm! What's the matter, Peter? Did you sleep well?

Peter: Not a wink. What does it matter to you, Magdalene? Who told you to meddle in my life?

Magdalene: What a creep! Look, I am what I am, and I'm concerned with people.

Peter: Hey, look, don't deny it anymore. Those two, James and John, must have told you to talk to me asking me to forget and forgive, right?

Magdalene: Man, will you stop being angry?

Peter: I'll do whatever pleases me, do you hear? And tell those damned sons of Zebedee I'm not called a "rock" for nothing. No way will I relent because of their sweet words.

During that long morning walk, Peter didn't utter a single word. What transpired the night before in Jenin with my mother, Salome, had got the better of him. The rest of us didn't talk much, either. We arrived in Shechem at noon, and there we had lunch.

Philip: Hey, M'am Salome, where are those dates you brought along? The worms must be feasting on them by now.

Magdalene: Peter's tongue has died. Don't you see how quiet that big nose has become?

Nathanael: Young lady, will you stop provoking? Something terrible might happen here.

Magdalene: Ha! Nothing will happen. I assure you. I know this won't go too far.

James: Isn't this fish really delicious? You salted it just right, momma. Here, have some more, Peter. Peter?

Peter: Eat it yourself, James, and may the devil make a fish bone get stuck in your throat.

James: But Peter, why don't you open your eyes so that you will undestand?

Peter: What is it that I should understand, you red-headed devil?

James: I've explained it to you already.

Magdalene: Oh, here we go again. What happened last night is all over. Are we going to start again?

Simon: You'd better shut up, Magdalene. If you weren't what you are, things wouldn't have become so muddled up.

Magdalene: Oh really? So I'm the one to blame for all your squabbles, is that it?

Andrew: Simon, you mean you believe the stories of M'am Salome? You should know her better. Those stupid stories should be ignored.

John: Wait a minute, Andrew, don't you ever call my mother stupid, do you hear? No one here should call her stupid, do you hear?

Matthew: You talk like a brave man. Later you'll run for your life like a rabbit, John, and you know what I mean! Ha!

John: Don't push me to the wall, Matthew, you wouldn't like what you'd hear, you leech!

Thomas: G-g-guys, stop b-b-blaming each other. W-w-we sh-shouldn't be th-th-throwing stones at one another!

Simon: Just shut up, will you, Thomas, and don't dip your finger into this mess!

Judas: Damn it, I'm sick and tired of all these gossips and intrigues!

John: Are you saying I'm a rumor-monger, Judas?

Judas: Yeah, that's what you are, John! Remember our trip to the north? You made up stories like Nathanael was a coward, that Philip was more stubborn than an ass.

Philip: You said that about me, John? You should be ashamed of yourself. Say that again to my face, I dare you.

Nathanael: Shut up, Philip, leave everything to Judas. C'mon, Judas, out with it. Things should not go on like this. Let's get things clear.

James: Don't be silly, Nathanael. Isn't it obvious that Judas is accusing my brother to win Peter's sympathy? Can't you see the plan?

Judas: What the hell are you talking about, you idiot? Why should I try to win over Peter? Do you think all of us are like you, rubbing elbows, to win the sympathy of important people?

James: Then you're worse, Judas Iscariot, because you lick their asses to get what you want!

Jesus: Stop it everyone, damn it! Can't we have at least a moment of peace to eat our dates? We're killing each other here. We don't even need Herod's soldiers nor those Romans to do it.

James: You, too, shut up, Jesus. There's no use defending Judas.

Peter: You shut your mouth, James! This is all your fault, big mouth!

James: No, no, you're the only one to blame for this, Peter, no one else.

Peter: You're right, red head. I want to strangle you.

Peter leaped over Matthew and Thomas, pounced on my brother James, and grabbed him by the neck. He unleashed all the fury raging quietly inside him since the previous night.

Magdalene: They're killing each other! They're killing each other!

John: For God's sake, keep them apart!

Some of us pulled Peter away, while the others worked on James. Since they were already enraged, soon enough we were all caught in the fight, and everyone, no more, no less, got his share of the blows in that sea of fury. The storm lasted long enough. Finally we got back to our senses. That was not the first time we had a squabble, and we knew damned well it wouldn't be the last. Anyway, we resumed our trip, and by the time we reached the elevation of Shiloh, everything was forgotten, and we were laughing again and teasing one another. Only Peter continued with his grumbling.

Peter: No, no, no! Never will I look at his face again, ever. For me, he's dead and should be buried.

Jesus: Peter, please, listen to me: if among ourselves we continue to kill each other and remain divided, then what can we expect from the ones on top?

Peter: Look, Jesus, this wasn't the first time it happened. Remember the incident on the wharf a month ago? It's the same old thing, you know. I can't stand this red head and the little squirt anymore!

Jesus: It's all over, Peter.

Peter: Yeah, it's all over, but it'll happen again. I forgave him once, all right, but . . .

Jesus: You'll have to forgive him again, and again, for even seventy times seven. Always.

Peter: And may I know why I should tolerate the stupidity of this rascal?

Jesus: Because a grain of sand is nothing compared to a mountain. Let me tell you a story, to try to get this into your thick skull.

Jesus: The kingdom of King Shaddai was enormous, like the Great Sea. One had to undertake a hundred journeys to go from one end of the territory to another. In order to manage the affairs of the kingdom, he had assigned officials all over the provinces who were tasked to distribute the money of the kingdom. Some of these officials, however, were crooks, as in the case of Neriah.

Neriah: Here, cross-eyed, take it.

Cross-eyed man: But, Neriah, this is too much dough. What if they find out?

Neriah: C'mon, take it. And don't get yourself caught. I'll come back tomorrow.

Jesus: Neriah came back the next day, and the succeeding days. He always left his office with a sackful of money under his tunic and gave it to his accomplice, the man with the crossed eyes.

Neriah: At last, the days of poverty are over! Soon, you'll be a millionaire, Neriah, you'll be richer than the king!

A soldier: You're under arrest, Neriah!

Neriah: Wh-wh-why?

Soldier: You're a thief, a smuggler, damn you! I'll bring you before the king, and when he finds out what you have stolen, he'll have you beheaded, scoundrel! C'mon!

King: What? One hundred million denarii! Do you realize what you have stolen, Neriah? Even if you work like a beast all your life, you won't be able to pay me back. Summon the executioner and have this devil beheaded!

Neriah: No, no, no! Take pity on me, King Shaddai! Have compassion and forgive me! I'm asking your forgiveness, please pardon me!

King: Very well. You will not die. But tomorrow, before dawn, you will be sold as a slave; your wife and your children too. That's the least that you deserve for being such a thief!

Neriah: No, no! Have pity on me, King Shaddai! I, I didn't know what I was doing.

King: You didn't know what you were doing?

Neriah: Well, I knew, but forgive me just the same!

Jesus: Since the king was a good man and had a heart bigger than his immense kingdom, even bigger than the debt of his official, he pardoned him.

King: Well, then, Neriah, I forgive you. Go back to your post. Your debt has been written off, and I'll forget all about it.

Cross-eyed man: How fortunate can you get, Neriah! You were born with a lucky star, wretch!

Neriah: Boy, am I lucky, but penniless, with not even a single cent to buy me some dates.

Cross-eyed man: Man, you should be happy. You could have lost your neck. Money is the least of your problems.

Neriah: Oh yeah? So, it's the least problem, huh? Then, pay what you owe me. If I remember right, I lent you a hundred denarii.

Cross-eyed: Bah, that was a long time ago, long before my eyes got twisted like this!

Neriah: They'll get all the more cross-eyed if you don't pay me back!

Cross-eyed: Okay, Neriah, I'll pay you when I get my wages.

Neriah: No way. I need that money now, do you hear? Right now!

Cross-eyed: But wait, man. It can't be now . . . Ahhggg!

Jesus: Neriah rushed toward this fellow and grabbed him by the neck with all his strength.

Cross-eyed: Ahhgg! I ain't got the money now. Wait, please listen to me.

Neriah: I can't wait, damn it! Either you pay me now or you go to jail!

Cross-eyed: Please have pity on me. Have pity on me!

Jesus: But Neriah had no compassion for the guy and had him sent to jail.

A soldier: And that's the story, my king. First, he dragged the cross-eyed man to the city and had him imprisoned.

King: Go get Neriah and bring him back here. Now he will know who I am. He owed me a hundred million denarii and yet I pardoned him. Why couldn't he do the same to one who owed him only a hundred denarii?

Peter: How did the story end, Jesus?

Jesus: Well, the king got so furious he sent Neriah to jail.

Peter: Right. If I had been the king, I would've grabbed this man and torn him to pieces!

Jesus: Really? But that man is you, Peter. You've become like Neriah.

Peter: Me? Oh, of course, I know where that leads to...

Jesus: Look. You and James and all of us owe the Lord a lot of debts, and he forgives us all of them. Yet we can't forgive the small things that other people do to us.

Peter snorted, then quickened his pace. For some time, he continued to sulk. But later, before sunset, he approached my brother James and started talking to him, and they ended up making peace with one another. The truth is that, with Jesus, we learned to overlook each other's mistakes, so that the Lord would also forget our own mistakes.

•

In our day-to-day interaction with each other, a little argument may easily accelerate into a quarrel, where long time grudges and misunderstandings may surface. This is perfectly logical. This is part of human interaction. And Jesus' disciples were not spared these conflicts. On account of the social class they belonged to, their varied personalities, the situation they found themselves in, ever since they joined Jesus — perilous and uncertain — and the very testimony of the gospel (Matt. 20:24; Luke 22:24), it was most likely that the disciples would get entangled in arguments similar to what appear in this episode.

The number seven was a very important number in the world of the Israelites. Its origin can be traced to the observation of the four phases of the moon, each of which lasted seven days. Thus, the Israelites began to associate the number seven with a complete cycle. The number seven became synonymous with plenitude, with something complete and finished. For Israel, the number seven signified totality, and given a theological context, the totality desired by God. Thus, the order of time was based on seven (the Sabbath, the sacred day, would come every seven days). The temple's candleholder had seven arms, and so on. To forgive "seven" times meant to forgive "everything" completely. It's like saying "Let's wipe the slate clean and let's start anew." To drive home this point, Jesus tells Peter to forgive "seventy times seven." Seventy, obviously, equals seven times ten. If the number seven meant plenitude and totality, the number ten (its origin is traced to the ten fingers of the hand) likewise had the nature of a round and complete number, although to a lesser degree. "Seventy times seven" means always, in all occasions, without exception, and so on.

The parable of "the unmerciful servant" is typically Middle Eastern in its exaggeration about the use of figures representing one's debts. Ten thousand talents is equivalent to one hundred million denarii – that is, the salary of a hundred million work sessions. It is a gigantic amount, unrealistic and unimaginable. This intensely emphasizes the contrast with the measly sum of a hundred denarii, the small amount owed by one of the characters in the episode. Rather than present an incident in Palestine, Jesus, in this parable, refers to a foreign king in the style of those great sovereigns of the Middle East. This foreign quality is seen, for example, in the order given by the king to sell the wife and children of the debtor, a custom that was not Israelite, or in the act of sending him to prison as payment for his debts, a law that did not exist in the Jewish legal system.

In Jesus' time, the writings of the rabbis about the final judgment always referred to the two measures employed by the Lord in ruling the world: one, the use of mercy; the other, that of justice. In the end the rabbis would claim "mercy vanishes, compassion appears too remote, and benevolence just fades away." Only pure justice remains. Jesus totally transformed this theological idea prevalent in his time. He showed us that even mercy, God's forgiveness, can be valid at the final hour of reckoning, though he added one decisive factor. It shall only be granted to those who have learned to forgive, who, knowing they have been forgiven, have had compassion for the others. And they who have underestimated God's pardon shall be meted full justice. Such measure is what we set for ourselves as we pray the Lord's prayer: "Forgive us our sins as we forgive those who sin against us."

Forgiveness among men and women is basic in the gospel. When we forgive, we undertake a risk. Jesus, in the act of forgiving, risked his trust in someone, hoping this gesture would be a call to his conscience, that he might reform his ways. That was what he did to Matthew, to Magdalene, to Zacchaeus, and to Nicodemus. He created a new relationship with them, setting aside all prejudices, forgiving the past to attain a different future. His was a positive attitude toward men and women, something that is profoundly optimistic: evil will never have the last word, and humans are capable of transformation. This is forgiveness in the Christian sense, completely trusting others – but never naively – and entrusting in them the hope of the community.

It is not easy to talk about forgiveness and reconciliation if we leave the community of our brothers and sisters and situate ourselves in a society where inequality and injustice exist. Those who have power in unjust societies have often used the message of Christian reconciliation to alienate the poor from their task of struggle, telling them they should "forgive" those who wrong them rather than working to achieve real justice. Christian love is struggle, denunciation, and criticism, but we must know how to overcome the vicious circle of bitter revenge and retaliation. Through our capacity to forgive, we must set forth a new era of justice in a new society.

(Matt. 18:21–35)

96

The Prostitutes Shall Be First

It was the month of Nisan, the spring month. The plains of Esdraelon woke up, garbed in yellow daisies and wild lilies. The whole field smelled of humid earth in anticipation of the fresh blooms. In two days, we left Galilee and Samaria behind. We were heading for Judea, the barren land.

On the third day of our journey, we could see Jerusalem's silhouette in the distance. The Holy City was already preparing for the feast of the Passover.

Mary: Jesus, my son, I'm scared.

Jesus: Of what, mother?

Mary: Of Jerusalem. There were times when, looking at the walled city from afar, I thought it was the crown of a queen. I don't know. Now, it seems to me that the walls are like teeth of stone, of a huge mouth, wide open and threatening.

Jesus: Jerusalem is a queen, all right, but a murderous queen. When a great prophet lifts his head and denounces it, the giant mouth tears at him.

Mary: My God, don't talk that way, son. You scare me all the more.

It was already getting dark. We were very tired and our feet had become callused. We passed through the Fish Gate and entered Jerusalem. We had to pass through the wall of the Ammonites where, every night, the heavily made up prostitutes of Jerusalem lined up, exhibiting their wares.

Salome: Listen to those hookers sing! Aren't they ashamed of themselves?

Philip: Well, M'am Salome, if they don't advertise, then they don't sell. I used to do the same when I had my cart.

Salome: Stop being vulgar, Philip.

Philip: Besides, these women are an unfortunate lot.

Salome: It takes one to know one. Just look at our "Magdalene" here. She's got her eyes fixed on the group.

Filomena: Mary, hey Mary!

Before we knew it, Mary of Magdala was already rushing to greet a friend stationed by the wall.

Salome: See, I told you, Philip. What's bred in the bone will come out in the flesh!

Filomena: My gosh, Mary dear, what brought you here, young lady?

Magdalene: Filomena, what are you doing here in Jerusalem? Have you lost something in this mad city?

Filomena: Yeah, my dignity. That's all. Oh, Mary, you're still young, but I've already turned thirty. Before, my customers used to go after me. Now, it's the other way around. Do you understand?

Magdalene: And you came as far as Jerusalem, is that right?

Filomena: You bet, my friend. But, obviously, you've changed your turf too. Are things that bad in Capernaum?

Magdalene: Nope. I just decided to leave the trade.

Filomena: What? Did I hear you right? You mean you've betrayed us? I don't believe you, Mary!

Magdalene: You'd better believe me, Filo. I've not been lighting the lamp for a couple of months now.

Filomena: Tell me, what's occupying your time now, young lady?

Magdalene: I'm involved in something else, Filo.

Filomena: What? Are you into textiles smuggling? Or crocodile charms?

Magdalene: Nothing of that sort. It's the Kingdom of God.

Filomena: Kingdom of God? Can you eat that, or what?

Magdalene: God must've grown so weary of everything, he showed his angry face through the clouds and said: "Those who don't know must now learn how to swim, for another deluge worse than the first is forthcoming!"

Filomena: What nonsense are you talking about?

Magdalene: Sshh! There's big trouble coming, Filomena. Those who are up will be down, and those who are down will be up! At any rate, I'd go for the Kingdom of God.

Filomena: For God's sake, are you into politics, Mary? That would be the height of it! Oh, this is funny! Well, if you come to think of it, politics and our trade have a lot in common. But, tell me, on whose side are you, the Zealots' or the Sadducees' or somebody else's?

Magdalene: I don't know, Filomena. As far as I'm concerned, I understand nothing, although where he goes, I go.

Filomena: Who are you talking about?

Magdalene: Jesus.

Filomena: Who's that?

Magdalene: The best guy I've ever met in my life.

Filomena: Now I get it! This guy is in love with you and brought you here.

Magdalene: No, Filo. It's not that.

Filomena: Okay. You're in love with him, which is the same thing.

Magdalene: No, it's something else. Jesus is different. He's a little nuts, you see, but he's a prophet. No, not a prophet. Do you know what, Filo? Jesus is no less than the Messiah!

Filomena: I'm not surprised. Every night a dozen messiahs with their swords and everything pass through this wall.

Magdalene: I tell you, Filo, this dark-skinned man is different. When he speaks, he looks at you straight in the eyes, like this!

Filomena: You're acting strange, Mary.

Magdalene: You would be too, if you knew him. Come and greet him, Filo. C'mon!

Filomena: Wait a minute, Mary. If I go, they go too. Hey, girls, why don't you conceal your wares for a while, so we can take a glimpse at a prophet. Let's not miss this for anything. C'mon!

Soon, we were surrounded by sloppily dressed women, with heavily painted faces and reeking of jasmine perfume.

Magdalene: Friends, this dark one here is Jesus, the guy I was telling you about. And these are all his friends. This lady here is Filomena, a colleague of mine in Magdala, and all these are her friends and . . .

Filomena: That's all right. C'mon, you guys, out with it. What's all this about the Kingdom of God? Mary has been telling me about it.

A Prostitute: I'm more interested in the king than in the kingdom. Who knows, I might even like him! Tell me, Galilean, will you be sitting on the throne at the moment of victory?

Jesus: No. In the Kingdom of God, there won't be any thrones, nor kings nor chiefs who will oppress the poor. No one shall be above anyone. Everyone shall be brothers and sisters.

Filomena: Gosh, I love to hear that. Maybe I could free myself from those who drool over me! Hell they sure can be oppressing!

My mother, Salome, could not contain herself . . .

Salome: Hey, look lady, aren't you ashamed of yourself? You need not wait for the Kingdom of God to cleanse yourself of that slime. All it takes is to repent and to give up your bad life.

Filomena: Oh yeah? How easily you picture it? I didn't know that repentance could make for survival. Tell me, lady, how many children have you got? Please pardon my indiscretion.

Salome: I have two sons, thank God.

Filomena: Well, I've got eight, and thank the devil for that, and for my husband too, who must've been Satan's first cousin. He made me pregnant eight times and now he's deserted me without having left a single cent to support my eight children. So what do you expect me to do, madam? You consider yourself decent enough for not displaying your body in the street. Eve didn't show herself either, but she did something worse.

Magdalene: C'mon, Filomena, you're messing up your make-up

Filomena: She's getting on my nerves, Mary! To hell with that woman!

A Prostitute: Well, I'm excited about this Kingdom of God, who knows this could be our hope for a better situation. At the rate we're going, with or without our trade!

Another Prostitute: Yeah, let them shake off the bush at once so that all the parasites will fall off from the branches.

Philip: Pshh! Don't shout, filthy woman, the guards might hear you!

Filomena: That's it, precisely! Listen, Galileans, and you, Jesus. You must be the brains of all this: if they begin to pursue you, this is the safest place for you to hide. No one looks for the Messiah in Filomena's brothel!

A Prostitute: They say a colleague of ours saved the life of our ancestors when they first stepped on this land. So now you know where to go when the going gets rough.

Jesus: When the Kingdom of God comes, there will be a place reserved for all of you, Filomena. I promise.

A Prostitute: Well, well, let's not be sentimental now, for God created night that we might relax and be happy. Hey, you, with the mole, why don't you sing a song to welcome our comrades? After all, they're still Galileans, first and foremost! Can't you see, they haven't even washed their feet?

Another Prostitute: Okay, here goes my song: I dedicate this song / to all of you Galileans / if someone sings better here / then he should reply and let us see him.

Filomena: C'mon, c'mon, now it's your turn.

Jesus: Philip, it's your turn, now.

Philip: You're a pretty lady / but your head is crazy / you're like a bell / any time it peals.

Filomena: Oh yeah? What bell are you talking about? Hey, big sis, will you answer him?

Prostitute: They say that the smallest chili / is hotter than pepper spice / but not your evil tongue / that always tells lies sweet and nice.

Filomena: More, more, and let's see who comes out the winner!

Peter: Here's one to add more excitement to the game: If I were a singer / all my life I would sing to you with grace / all because of those moles / that you've got on your face.

Salome: Don't be impudent, Peter. Wait till Rufina hears this!

Although we were very tired after the trip, the playful mood of those women had infected us, so we started to clap and responded to their songs. We were oblivious of what was happening behind us.

A Pharisee: Look who's here! Jesus, the Galilean. This was how I was expecting to see him — drawn to whores.

Another Pharisee: This is unbelievable, he who calls himself the Lord's prophet. How immoral!

Jesus: Hey, you guys, why don't you come sing and dance with us?

Jesus looked straight into the faces of the Pharisees, the followers of the law.

Jesus: Let's continue with our songs. I'm dedicating this song to all of you. Listen: A father had two sons / whom he invited / to work on his farm / beginning at sunrise. / The first said no / but later relented / and went to the farm to work. / The second said yes / but finally didn't go / he never did budge.

Philip: Hey, that's a weird song, isn't it, Jesus? I didn't understand it, and it didn't even rhyme.

Jesus: Well, it seems that the Pharisees understood, because they left. They are the ones who say much but do nothing. Hypocrites! All these women here are a lot more worthy than the Pharisees, and they shall be the first to enter the Kingdom of God.

Philip: Don't mind them, Jesus.

Magdalene: Right, let them go. Hey, Filomena, sing us another song. The atmosphere is getting gloomy.

Filomena: Okay, here's one: Hear ye well, Pharisees who think you're so great: / in the Kingdom of God / the prostitutes will leave you in their wake.
All: Very well said! More, more!

We stayed for quite some time singing by the wall of the Ammonites. Jesus was very happy, like David when he danced with the maids of Jerusalem in the presence of the Lord, the day he brought the Ark of the Covenant to the holy city.

•

In Jerusalem, the city where businessmen converge, where caravans, pilgrims, and "tourists" converge, there was an abundance of prostitutes. During the holidays, possibilities of work for these women increased considerably. Most of them came — as is still generally true — from the lowest rungs of the social ladder. These were women deserted by their husbands, oftentimes with children to feed. Or they were young ladies — like Magdalene — who got stuck in the trade at an early age due to economic considerations, with no chances of recovery, as they got so accustomed to the job.

Jesus had a soft heart for the prostitutes. This ought to be interpreted as a sign of theological profundity. This was not a paternalistic predilection of a pure master who approached lost women out of compassion. It was a deeper sympathy, which made him see in these women — who were among the poorest in the social strata of his time, and therefore who were in greater need of liberation and hope — the people preferred by the Lord. Being women and prostitutes, they were perhaps the most marginalized of the groups in Israel. Jesus, sensitive to their situation, said something that was authentically scandalous: they, the whores, would be the first to enter the Kingdom of God, together with the thieves and ill-reputed tax collectors. That was a subversion of the whole morality of his time and therefore elicited a scandalous reaction, not only among the leaders but also among common people like Salome and some of his disciples.

It is pure fiction to make of Mary Magdalene a woman in love with Jesus. This notion is just a cheap way of explaining the conversion of the poor lady. Jesus related to her as an equal. Admitting her into the group of his friends and trusting her, he gave back her lost dignity. He made her rise again and be reformed, and she sensed the justice that Jesus was announcing when he spoke of the kingdom. Because she had been one of the poorest among the poor, such dignity had never been accessible to her before, and, with Jesus' words, that dignity would now also be available to the women of her class who never had had a place in their society except that of complete dependence on the whims of the men. Because of Jesus' attitude toward these women and the hope he had given them, Magdalene understood who God was and began to glimpse his kingdom. All this sufficed to explain Mary's enthusiasm for the cause of Jesus and her affection for him, without giving it any romantic tinge.

Filomena, Mary's friend, in inviting Jesus to hide in her brothel, is recalling the act of Rahab, the prostitute from Jericho who hid the Israelite spies as they prepared the road for the chosen people to the Promised Land (Josh. 2:1-24). The Letter to the Hebrews praises the faith of this prostitute (Heb. 11:31), and Matthew mentions her in the genealogy of Jesus, more for her gesture of solidarity than for historical fidelity, as a sign of the closeness to God of these women who were ostracized by everyone. Jesus' song evokes the parable of "the two sons." He reiterates this idea throughout the gospel, in order to show that those who are sure of themselves, those who are happy because they are good — those learned men listening to him and the leaders of Israel — shall be the ones left behind. The others, the poor, those reputed to be immoral, shall be present in the banquet of the Lord.

The scene with Jesus singing along with the prostitutes of Jerusalem was inspired from the gesture of King David as he entered Jerusalem with the Ark of the Covenant, dancing with the maids and the women of the town (2 Sam. 6:1-23). On that occasion, the free behavior of the king caused a scandal, and he was told that he acted like "a nobody." Similar criticisms were made against Jesus. That a prophet should mingle with this type of people constituted a scandal, more so if he felt so at home with these prostitutes. David's gesture, as well as Jesus', points to a sign revealing the identity of God: the One who becomes "one of them," one of his most despised of children.

(Matt. 21:28-32)

97

The Flames of Gehenna Moloch

Beside the city of Jerusalem, beneath the south walls, was a rocky cliff known during our time as Gehenna. Here, offerings had been made to the pagan god Moloch. It was cursed by the prophet Jeremiah. After that, it was utilized as a dump site. At dusk, the residents of Jerusalem would pass through the Ravine Gate, carrying their trash, leftovers, dried branches, and dead animals, to be thrown off the cliff. Then, sulfur would be sprinkled over the rubbish, and it was set on fire.

Peter: I wonder where all this filth comes from! Look at that blaze!

Philip: Damn, I hope the wind doesn't blow toward this direction. We might all burn!

Susana: Cover your noses. This stinks like the devil!

Leaving behind the huge flames of Gehenna, we crossed the other valley, called Cedron, by way of Bethany. It was already dark when we reached our friend's tavern where we stayed.

Lazarus: At last they're here! Martha, Mary, our Galilean friends are here! I'm sure they're starved. But that's no problem. Here at Beautiful Palm Tree they'll be treated to the specialty of the house: lamb's head broiled on low fire.

Peter: Look, Lazarus, don't remind us of fire or dead animals — we just passed through the Gehenna, where they have the same specialty as you do!

Mary: C'mon, guys, go wash yourselves first; dinner is ready. C'mon, c'mon.

Peter: I tell you, Lazarus, I almost burned my face! I won't ever pass through that wall again, especially when they burn all that trash!

Lazarus: So what'll you do, Peter, when you're burning in hell and the devil grabs you by the hair and hurls you into the Dump Site of Eternity?

Peter: Ha! That won't ever happen. By then, I'll have lost all my hair like Nathanael. Being bald could also be a blessing. . . .

We, the whole group, with Jesus and the women, plus the other Galileans who were staying with Lazarus and his sisters, were all seated around a dilapidated and greasy table. It was placed in the inn's patio, and it reeked of rancid wine. Nothing was left of the lamb's head. A couple of oil lamps hanging on the walls formed mysterious shadows on the faces of everyone gathered that evening.

Peter: Believe me, guys, while watching the flames in the Gehenna, I became scared stiff, like those crabs when you put an ember on their eyes. Then I felt I was having some cramps here in my back.

Philip: I felt worse when I saw what they did to a friend of mine.

Mary: What did they do to him, Philip?

Philip: That was horrible. They tied up his hands and feet and gagged him to silence him. Then they took him to the topmost part of the wall at the Gehenna. There was a candle below. Four men swung him like a sack of flour, and at the count of four — plash! It was horrible. After some time, the candle went out.

Nathanael: Don't be a liar, Philip. You just made up that story.

Philip: I made it up, Nat? Okay. Why don't you go down to the dumpsite and collect his charred bones?

Lazarus: At least, in the Gehenna, the candle gets extinguished. They say that in hell, the flames just continue to burn and burn and burn — it's like sticking a smoldering ember on your chest which never dies out.

Susana: May God Almighty protect us, amen and amen!

Mary: My goodness, Philip and Lazarus, can't you talk of something else? Has the food upset you or something?

Lazarus: I liked the food very much. How about you, Philip?

Philip: So did I. Of course it wasn't good for some.

Mary: For whom?

Philip: For these poor lambs that we've eaten. If only they could speak, then we would have known how it felt to be hit on the bones and get roasted over fire!

Lazarus: Well I don't mean to rub it in, but they say that even the devil has a fork this big, which he uses to hook the damned ones and roast them over low fire.

Philip: No, man, that's not so. What he has is a pot, forty feet high, where he cooks his friends in boiling oil.

Nathanael: Either you all go to hell or you shut up once and for all! I'm having goose pimples even underneath my armpit!

Mary: My teeth are gnashing too!

Sadducee: Ha, ha, haaaa!

The boisterous laughter came from a corpulent man whose face was covered with warts.

Mary: Hey, you, what's so funny?

Sadducee: Ha! I'm laughing at all your stupidities. I don't believe in anything you're saying at all.

Mary: You don't say! You mean, you don't believe in hell, compatriot?

Sadducee: No. Let the dead bury the dead. The rest are stories to scare the children. When you die, that's the end of everything.

Philip: Oh, I see you're a Sadducee.

Sadducee: And so? I meditate on things, and I think a lot.

Mary: And what is it that you have so much thought about?

Sadducee: What another fellow has said: "Eat, drink, and be happy, for tomorrow you die." The rest is all nonsense.

Lazarus: But how can you speak that way?

Sadducee: I can prove it. Listen: I knew of a woman who got married and shortly after, her husband died. Then she married again, and the husband died again. Again she married, and again and again and again. That woman was widowed seven times, after which she too died.

Mary: And what does that mean?

Sadducee: That there can't be another life after this. Otherwise, tell me, which of the seven husbands should she stay with for eternity? C'mon, tell me. You can't, and that proves that there's no resurrection from the dead.

Peter: No, man, that's not the point here. It only shows how unfortunate that woman has become!

Sadducee: Well, I insist that that is an overwhelming proof.

Peter: I'd say that's sheer stupidity!

Sadducee: There's neither heaven nor hell, fellows, nothing at all. No one believes in them anymore.

Tobias: I do. How can I say there's no hell? I've just been there myself.

We all turned to look at Tobias, the old cameleer, who had not uttered a single word the whole night. He was a thin but brawny man, with sun-burned skin. He seemed to be made of strong stuff.

Tobias: That's right, guys, I just came from hell. For four days I was there, and I hope never to go back.

Nathanael: What happened? C'mon, tell us.

Tobias: You know, I always take the route through the desert, from Bethshittah to Hebron. This is what happened:

One night, the cold wind was blowing from Teman. I had not slept for many days, and so I got off the camel, rolled myself in my woolen blanket, and fell asleep on the sand. While I was sleeping, the camel was frightened by the whistling wind, and got lost in the night.

Tobias: Where the devil are you, beast? Camelllll Camelll! Damn, wait till you come back. I'll have your hump cut off!

But the camel never came back. The only companion I had in that interminable road had deserted me. So went my jug of water, my food, and my lamp.

Tobias: Camelll! Camelll!

I felt so helpless in that immense darkness. I could not even see the palm of my hand. Then I began to walk, not knowing where to go, sinking in those mounds of desert sand, inhabited by scorpions.

Tobias: Camelll! Camelll!

I was thirsty, hungry, and tired. But that was not the worst part of it. The most terrible thing was that I was all alone. Dawn came, but there was no one nor anything around me. I continued walking. Night came. The moonless night was like a tombstone to me. I ran, I screamed, there was no response from anyone. I was a completely lost, lonely soul.

Tobias: So I was in hell for four days and four nights.

Peter: How did you get out of it, friend?

Tobias: I was saved by the stars. The most faithful friends a cameleer can ever have. Gradually, I was guided by them, until I could make out, from afar, a small village called Gerar. I swear, my friends, that when I finally saw a person, I rushed to him, threw myself down at his feet, and kissed them. I was shouting with joy. I was no longer alone. Believe me, I'd rather be burned in the Gehenna with somebody than be in that place again with no one beside me. Because that's what hell is: to be alone.

When Tobias, the cameleer, finished his story, all of us heaved a deep breath, as if we had just come out of the desert too. The oil lamps continued sizzling on the walls of the inn.

Peter: Pff! Hey, guys, why don't we talk of something else, huh? I still feel the lamb's eyes somersaulting here in my tummy.

Susana: No wonder, Peter, what with our talking about hell so much. Say, why don't we go up to heaven for a little while? At least no one will ever feel alone in that place, I'd say.

Philip: I don't know, ma'am, but the widow with seven husbands sure won't be alone. Isn't that right, Sadducee?

Sadducee: Leave me out of your nonsense! What I said was if there was heaven, then I don't know how she'd choose. That's what I said, you imbecile.

Lazarus: If indeed there is no heaven at all, then what do we do with all these angels, huh? And where do we put the little angels, tell me?

Philip: Yeah, remember, there are male and female angels too. So, where do we put all of them?

Mary: There you go again, Philip. Big head, in heaven there's nothing of that sort of thing.

Philip: Oh, really? So what does one do, simply lick his fingers?

Susana: He must kneel before the Lord and worship him. That's it.

Philip: Then what?

Susana: You go on worshiping him because the Lord is thrice holy, and in heaven we shall all be such, with our hands joined in prayer before God's throne, as we ceaselessly utter "Holy, holy, holy" forever and ever.

Lazarus: Amen! Ahuuumm! Pardon me, Salome, but just the thought of eternity and uttering "holy, holy, holy" makes me sleepy already.

Philip: Say, fellas, isn't there any better place to go? Frankly speaking, this place called heaven is a little boring.

Mary: There's no other place, Philip. Either you go to heaven or to hell. Make your choice.

Philip: Well, in that case then when you bury me, will one of you put dice inside my pocket? Maybe, if I find somebody, a cherubim or a saint who is willing to play, then we can have a little session. What do you think?

Jesus: I've got a better idea, Philip.

Philip: Damn, Jesus, it's high time you spoke up! C'mon, out with it!

Jesus: Why don't you get the dice now so we can start heaven right away. You don't have to wait to die, man!

Peter: I agree with Jesus! Where are the dice?

Philip: Here they are, guys! C'mon, who's playing?

Lazarus: I am!

Nathanael: So am I!

Jesus: Hey, Lazarus, why don't you fetch some jugs of good wine? Mary, oil the lamps so these rascals can't cheat in the dark! Martha, add more fuel to the fire, to keep us all from getting cold to the bones! C'mon, c'mon!

Jesus cast the dice. All of us joined the game, from the Sadducee to the cameleer.

Philip: I bet five to one that heaven is exactly like this: a happy gathering of friends!

Jesus: Well, I bet fifty to one that it is something much better!

That night in Bethany, Jesus taught us that heaven was something like a big feast, an endless one. From then on, we just played dice, enjoying ourselves, something no one could take away from us.

•

The valley of Gehenna surrounds Jerusalem in the west. It is joined in the south by the valley of Cedron. "Gehenna" is the Greek form of the Hebrew word "Ge-Hinnom" (Valley of Hinnom). In the early times, human sacrifices were offered to the pagan god Moloch in this valley, and for this reason the prophets had cursed it (Jer. 7:30–33). About two hundred years before Christ, it was the popular belief that in this place was found a hell of fire for those condemned for their evil deed, and this hell received the same name as the valley: Gehenna.

Since the place was cursed, Gehenna became a public dumpsite for Jerusalem. Along the southeastern side of the walls was the so-called Ravine Gate, facing the valley. Through this gate passed all the garbage of the city. There were streetsweepers in Jerusalem who apparently cleaned the streets of the capital every day, and all trash ended up in the valley, where it was burned. The job of the garbage collector was included in the list of "despised" occupations on account of its repugnant character.

For many centuries, the people of Israel believed that after life on earth, the dead went down to Sheol, a place in the depths of the earth or underneath the seas, where the good and the bad languished together, with

no feeling of joy or pain. Sheol is mentioned sixty-five times in the Old
Testament, always as a gloomy place, offering no hope whatsoever. Other
people — like the Babylonians — likewise believed in a similar place (Job
10:20–22; Ps. 88:11–13; Sir. 9:5, 10). Even Revelation, the last book in
the Bible, manifests this idea, stating that it is Christ who keeps the keys
to this abyss (Rev. 1:18). It is only in the last part of the Old Testament
that the Israelites come to realize that after death, the good deeds shall
be rewarded and the bad deeds punished. The Book of Wisdom, written
about fifty years before Christ, speaks of this idea (Wisd. 3:1–10; 4:7–
19; 5:1–22), by way of reflections which are spiritual and moral in nature.
From the historical point of view, however, the anticipation of individual
immortality of those who have died is found in the books of the Maccabees (see, e.g., 2 Macc. 12:41–46). The most interesting contribution
of these books insofar as this aspect is concerned is the following: when
the Israelite warriors were confronted by death in their struggle for freedom from foreign troops, the people began to feel that these martyrs of
national liberation would be resuscitated by God; that the just who were
victims of death would continue to live and be rewarded by God for their
gesture of solidarity with the people and their cause. Those martyrs could
not die. First Maccabees does not mention the resurrection of all people —
only that of those who have died in battle. That is, the idea of resurrection
in Israel springs from its history of insurrection, just as the Israelites came
to know God as their "liberator" who saved them from their continued
slavery in Egypt. Much later, about a hundred years before Christ, the Israelites came to know God as their "resuscitator," realizing that the best
of their men, who died in their struggle, were "the very ones who would
never die."

What will become of all persons after death is something that has concerned every culture and all peoples up to our days. The gospels were
written by persons who were heirs of a series of ideas — some of which
were more ancient, others more recent — about this matter. Therefore,
there is no consensus as to what the life beyond is. We are simply not
given this data. Besides, the historical fact of Jesus' resurrection completely
changed the ideas of those who called themselves Christians after converting from Judaism. Jesus spoke of the fire and the "gnashing of teeth"
because he was the son of his time. He did not "dogmatize" on the matter
though. He spoke in the manner of his time, influenced by the garbage
men of Gehenna. If there is one clear thing in Jesus' mind as he thinks

of the death of the children of the kingdom, it is this: for those who are just, who fight for justice and who love their neighbor, their destiny is in God's hands, just as is the fate of the sparrows (Matt. 10:29). There is no reason to fear. Faith in God, Jesus' Father, encompasses the certainty that we shall conquer death. In summary, the gospels make "life after death" the object of hope. In the face of insurmountable death and God's silence before it, Jesus' word is: hope. The liberation that he is proclaiming will also triumph over the "ultimate enemy," which is death (1 Cor. 15:26).

Jesus spoke of the "full" realization of the Kingdom of God, without calling it heaven. From experience, we know, however, that such plenitude is not of this life, since death and suffering always lurk behind.

A number of points stand out when we examine Jesus' ideas about this full realization of the kingdom. First, there will be no distinction between "nationalities"; there will be no barriers or discrimination. There will be full equality, regardless of biological differences (Matt. 22:3). One must take note of this apparent — at first glance — "spiritualization" as pointed out by Jesus, in opposition to the ideas represented during his time by the Sadducees. These were influential and powerful people who did not believe at all in life after death, for they had it so good in this life. Since they were close to the Roman authorities and enjoyed economic benefits from the situation, they had to defend in their "theology" that the reward could only be given here on earth, precisely in the form of good position, money, and privileges. Their lack of "hope" in life after death was, therefore, understandable. That is why the Sadducees were ardent defenders of the established system and brazen collaborators with the Romans. Jesus rejected the Sadducees' materialistic view as a yardstick to the plenitude of the Kingdom of God (Mark 12:18–27).

Second, Jesus utilizes symbols when he speaks of the "new world": people will come face to face with God, the inheritance shall be handed out, there shall be laughter, the family of God shall sit around the table of God, there shall be breaking of bread, and so on. Everything shall change: the last shall be first, the poor shall become rich, the hungry shall be satiated. Obviously, this must begin here on earth, and only thus shall we have a glimpse of what will be experienced after the fullness of life is reached.

Third, Jesus promises the fulfillment of the Kingdom of God, the salvation of the community. Within this perspective, the image of the banquet and the house filled to the brim (Matt. 22:1–14) synthesizes Jesus' words about the kingdom. "Heaven" shall be an endless feast for the poor.

The images given of heaven and hell by some preachers pose a grave hazard to an authentic maturing of faith. Hell is pictured as a horrible place and God as a sadist who rejoices at the sufferings of the damned who were sent to burning torture chambers. On the other hand, heaven is too often pictured as a boring place where a proud God remains solemn and distant, wishing only to be contemplated, revered, and praised on a majestic throne. Jesus is not presented as having spoken of a Father God who is filled with kindness, revealing his compassion for all weaknesses, mingling with everyone as one of us, enjoying himself in the feasts, and suffering with us in our pain. Heaven and hell are so near to us. Heaven is in the community that shares and rejoices in genuine love among all, in coexistence, in relationships, in being together and knowing that everyone loves each other, where no one aims to dominate anyone. Heaven is creativity, humor, good health, the willingness to live, a game. Hell is being alone. Whoever denies being a brother or sister, fails to treat others equally, does not serve or share may possess money, fame, and power, yet they are digging their own grave.

(Matt. 22:23–33; Mark 12:18–27; Luke 20:27–40)

98

With Dirty Hands

Just two days after we arrived in Jerusalem, Magistrate Nicodemus, whom we had met on one of our trips, came early in the morning to Lazarus's inn in Bethany. He wanted to see Jesus.

Nicodemus: Believe me, Jesus, this guy has an open mind. He has heard a lot of things about you and he wants to meet you. He asked me to invite you to have lunch in his house.

Jesus: Fine. Tell your friend that if he really wishes to meet us, then he must invite all of us.

Nicodemus: Of course Manasseh is also inviting your friends, Jesus, but I'm not sure about this Matthew, the tax collector, and that woman...

Jesus: Who, Magdalene?

Nicodemus: Yes. Maybe she won't feel comfortable with the group.

Jesus: That doesn't speak well of your friend with an "open mind." Look, Nicodemus, we're like ants, you know: where one goes, everyone goes.

Nicodemus: Yeah, I know. I just wanted to keep you out of trouble. You should go easy with these people. I hope you understand, Jesus.

Jesus: They should understand, too, Nicodemus: all or no one.

So everybody went, the thirteen of us, including the women. That afternoon, we left Bethany at dusk, entered the city through the Gate of Siloh and climbed the long street until we reached Manasseh's house. The Pharisees and Nicodemus's friends were there, in the upper neighborhood of Jerusalem.

Nathanael: Hey, your sandals are full of holes, Philip, and there are decent people in this house.

Philip: And what did you expect, Nat? You don't want me to come barefoot, do you? It's the only pair I got!

Nathanael: You should've asked Lazarus. He's got the same size as you.

Philip: That would've been worse! His sandals stink, didn't you notice?

Magdalene: Well, I'm okay here. See my new scarf! These men can't say I'm not properly attired!

Peter: Look who's talking! Listen here, lady, you'd better shut up, and just wait to be served so you don't make a boo-boo of any sort.

In Manasseh's house friends of Nicodemus were waiting for us: three Pharisees and their wives. The Pharisees were regarded as the most ardent followers of God's laws and the ways of our ancestors. The word "Pharisee" means "separated." They felt they were chosen by God, and were the best in the world.

Manasseh: Welcome to my house, my friends! Come in, come in. Servants, please attend to the guests.

Nathanael: Brace yourself, Philip! Wait till they see the holes in your shoes!

Philip: Sshh! Quiet, Nat.

Three servants waiting at the door removed our shoes and washed our feet. That was a sign of the hospitality with which the master of the house welcomed his visitors. Inside the hall where the food was to be served, there were six big jars of water for the initial washing of hands. The Pharisees were very scrupulous with cleansing rites. Since we were not used to these, however, not one of us washed our hands when we got inside.

Persius: Well, gentlemen, I think an introduction is proper here. Before we all gather ourselves to eat, it is good manners that we acknowledge each other's presence.

Manasseh: Well, Nicodemus must have already told you about me, Jesus. This is Sarah, my wife.

Sarah: It's a pleasure to meet all of you.

Nehemiah: I am Nehemiah, the magistrate from the Sanhedrin.

Persius: He's also in charge of the textile trade with Tyre. That's where you see him. He's the fifth man in the whole of Jerusalem, starting from the top. He's got half of the city in his pocket!

Nehemiah: This is Melita, my wife.

Melita: My pleasure! I've long wanted to see a prophet at close distance.

Manasseh: And this is Persius here, a doctor of the law. He studied the Holy Scriptures since he was twelve years old, and he knows them by heart, from top to bottom and vice versa. He's quite a man, you know, he can recite the laws of Moses even in his sleep!

Magdalene: Well, I sympathize with his wife.

Peter: Sshh! Hush, Mary!

Manasseh: Well, Jesus, we would like to meet your, er, your friends.

Peter: It's easy to know us. I'm Simon. I'm known as the troublemaker. This skinny guy here is my brother, Andrew. Those two, the red head and the other one, are James and John. We're fishermen, and, well, I guess that's all.

Philip: I'm Philip, a junk dealer. I sell things in my cart and with my horn. Starting from the bottom, I'm the first man of Bethsaida! This bald-headed guy here is Nathanael, a friend of mine. He owns a shop with woolen fabrics: business is not so good! Sometimes he gets some profit and sometimes he loses.

Nathanael: For God's sake, Philip!

Melita: That's funny indeed.

When the introduction was over, the servants proceeded to prepare the table, while the Pharisees' wives whispered among themselves, looking at us with disdain, and giggling occasionally.

Melita: Well, isn't it obvious that she's the hooker? The nerve! She seems to have no qualms about coming here!

Sarah: They say her name is Mary.

Melita: No, my dear, the prophet's mother is called Mary.

Sarah: Then she must be another hooker because her name is also Mary! Hey, be careful, if you don't watch out, she might hook your husband.

Melita: Nonsense, she's already hooked to her prophet. They say that Jesus brings the whore everywhere. I'd say there's something going on there.

Persius: Hey, gossip bespeaks poor manners.

Sarah: Not to worry, Persius. We're talking about the prophet and the hooker and the long-haired guys with him. They'll be famous for the lice they carry on their heads, ha!

Persius: You bet! What were you telling me about the tax collector who looks drunk? I'm so disgusted, really.

Manasseh: Friends, the table is ready!

Persius: Well, but first, our custom...

Manasseh: Of course, you may now wash your hands.

Since we were so starved, we did not hear Manasseh, the master of the house, invite us to wash our hands, according to the rite of purification of the Pharisees.

They sat at the table only after washing their hands. In a short while, we became so agog at the sight of the wine and the good food that we forgot about the cold welcome we received initially. Peter was so excited he licked the spare ribs one by one. Philip, who was beside him, thoroughly searched the tray for the pieces of meat that were left.

Philip: ...and I changed the wick from the oil lamp. Then the guy said: an oil lamp without a wick, of what use is it? Ho, ho, ho! What do you think?

Nathanael: Could you pass the gravy, Mary, it's very good!

Peter: This lamb is fantastic, I tell you. Rufa, my mother-in-law, says that when you eat good meat, you must be ready for the consequences.

Melita: Well, well, can't we talk of something else beside the lamb? Since the prophet is here with us, I'd like to know what he thinks of the things that are happening around the city. This is Babylon, Jesus, I tell you. You don't have to go far — take the case of the family of Ptolemy. What do you think of what they have done to the daughter of Benisabe?

Jesus: I don't know. I don't know this family, Madam Melita.

Melita: Oh, if you only knew. Poor girl. Well, poor, no, but she's a lost girl, to tell you frankly. She's like a rolling stone. She can't stay put. This is between you and me, as I don't wish to poke my nose in somebody else's life, but a reliable source told me she is pregnant, by no less than her first cousin! The father, naturally, is distraught!

Sarah: Distraught? Is he really? What a creep! Why, it runs in the family! Like father, like daughter!

Melita: So that's what's going around here, Jesus, but...

Sarah: But that's not even half of the story. There's more to it. Well, I don't really want to talk about anybody else's life, but there are some things that have gone too far already.

Melita: Did you know that his wife tried to leave him by passing through the window? That was a great scandal through all of Jerusalem! It turned out that...

After a while, two servants appeared with a jug of water for the purification rite, a custom observed by the Pharisees during meal time. The servants were at one end of the table, where Philip was seated.

Nathanael: C'mon, Philip, pour it, man.

Philip: What? Hik! More wine? Oh man, this is cool! Okay, here goes!

Philip grabbed the jug with his greasy hands and gulped the water for the cleansing rites down his throat.

Persius: What obscenity is this?

Sarah: He's drunk. Just look at that hooker beside him. She thinks it's funny!

Nehemiah: This is the last straw!

When Philip put down the jug and wiped his drenched face with the sleeve of his tunic, Nehemiah, the magistrate, stood from the table and left the dining room with an air of outraged dignity.

Magdalene: Say, what's bugging that man now?

Philip: How should I know? The hot sauce must have upset his tummy.

Nathanael: No, Philip, I think it's you.

Philip: Why me? No, Nat. He went to relieve himself in the latrine. I'm sure of that.

Then Persius, the other Pharisee, stood up.

Persius: I'm sorry, gentlemen, but I can't stand it anymore. I tried to keep silent during the meal, but this is too much. My friend Nehemiah felt the same. No, he did not go to the washroom as one of you has hinted. The doctor left because he could no longer tolerate what's going on here. And he is right. Not one of you has observed the rite of washing the hands before you came inside. Neither have you washed yourselves while we were eating. And now, this guy did the most vulgar thing we have seen in our lives.

Philip: Don't you point at me with that finger of yours! Okay, okay, I'm a swine. Well, I'm sorry, damn it!

Magdalene: Hey man, forgive him now so we can continue eating! Okay, so you're forgiven. Or if you wish, I can sing to you a song to cheer you all up!

Nathanael: Shut up, Mary, you'll just make matters worse.

Melita: What a disgrace! I'm leaving too. So these are "the prophet and his friends." Ha!

As Madam Melita arrogantly left the dining room, Manasseh, the master of the house, looked at Jesus despisingly.

Manasseh: A while ago, I would have wanted to ask you, Nazarene, whom they call God's prophet, I would have wanted to ask you, I said, why your friends did not wash their hands before sitting at the table. I see that you have not done it, either. I see that you, their master, who is supposed to teach them the way of the law, also don't comply with the law.

Jesus: And you, my friend, overdid it.

Jesus stood up, resting his two hands on the table.

Jesus: Please excuse us, Manasseh. It's the lack of practice in us. We farmers don't know much about good manners. Our hands are always dirty.

Manasseh: I'm glad you're aware of it, Jesus.

Jesus: But maybe our tongues are purer than your wife's, who, while eating, did nothing but gossip about the entire neighborhood.

Manasseh: Pardon me, did I hear you right, or . . . ?

Jesus: Yeah, you heard me right. If you wanted to, you could even hear better. Listen, Pharisee: What makes the person unclean is not what enters through his mouth, but what comes out of it. What goes inside passes through the stomach and then out of the body. But what comes out of the mouth comes from the heart, and from her heart came gossip, lies, and the belief that she's better than the rest. This is what makes the person unclean.

Jesus: So this friend of yours has an open mind, huh, Nicodemus?

Nicodemus: Fine, Jesus, but next time, be a little more careful.

Nicodemus went with us as far as Bethany, at the other side of the Mount of Olives, where our friend Lazarus was waiting for us with the warmth of his smile. There, in his inn, we could sit around the table with dirty hands.

•

In Jerusalem, the wealthiest and the most influential group was the priests. Alongside this powerful circle of priestly families was the lay aristocracy composed of land owners and big-time businessmen — especially those who engaged in the trade of wheat, wine, oil, and timber. They were represented in the Sanhedrin (the judicial and administrative tribunal of Israel). Nicodemus, being a counsel to the Sanhedrin, belonged to this social class, and his friends would naturally come from this group.

Jerusalem — like other capital cities — dictated the ways of the wealthy class all over the country. The rich men of Jerusalem loved anything luxurious in their homes, in their manner of dressing, in their food. Their banquets — sometimes catered to impress their guests — were occasions to flaunt the wealth of this privileged social class. They were very particular about how their guests were invited, and their customs in this respect were rigorously followed: the sending of invitations through their messengers. In this episode, it was curiosity which motivated the wealthy friends of Nicodemus to invite Jesus, whom they were cautious of but from whom they anticipated something original, interesting, and novel that would have compensated for the "sacrifice" they had made by going to Nicodemus's house.

The arrogant people in this episode, aside from being wealthy, were Pharisees. Not all Pharisees were rich, but the leaders of this religious group belonged to the upper class of society. They were accustomed to washing their hands before and after meals. Washing is not only a hygienic measure. The priests were originally obliged to observe it as a ritual symbol of their "sanctity." Later, the Pharisees had used it to show that they were God's chosen people, since they believed in their "holiness." Jesus and his group never had this scrupulous habit.

Basically, the conflict as seen in this episode is more of a clash of different religious perceptions in the face of ritual purity, a clash that is common among the social classes. Many times, it has been desired that good manners be identified or associated with Christian virtue, though they have nothing to do with each other. A person may be "foul-mouthed," but this is not considered a virtue or a defect from the Christian point of view. It is simply a consequence of the environment where one has been brought up. Besides, we must bear in mind that the gospel emerged from among the simple folks. Jesus, who was part of this group, was certainly not particular about these social manners.

Jesus counteracts the false purity of the rich Pharisees, manifested only in the washing of the hands, with the purity of the mouth, which helps avoid making judgments about other people. Behind those whispers and gossip among the "elite" women of Jerusalem there is pride, spite for others, and false moralism. Above all, their purpose was to stress their difference from the rest, as the superior people. This is what Jesus tells them to their face. There is an interesting text in the Letter of James (James 3:1–18) regarding the offenses of the mouth — which, obviously, are not a patrimony of only the upper crust of society.

(Matt. 15:1–20; Mark 7:1–23)

99

The Vineyard of the Lord

At spring time, Jerusalem opened its twelve doors to thousands and thousands of Israelites from all parts of the country. Everyone wanted to take shelter within its walls to celebrate the great feast of the Passover. The caravans of pilgrims also included junk dealers pushing their carts, vendors selling their wares of sweets in baskets on their heads, roving teachers, prostitutes from the neighboring towns, the Bedouins who were experts in buying and selling sheep, professional beggars, and the old zither players seated at the street corners who earned their money by playing old songs.

Zither Player: Let me sing to my friend / the song of his love for his vineyard. / My friend had a vineyard / on a fertile hillside. / He dug the soil, cleared it of stones, / and planted choice vines in it. / In the middle he built a tower, / he dug a press there too. / He expected it to yield grapes. . . .

As we entered the city through the Water Gate, a lot of people recognized Jesus and followed us. By this time, he was already known in the whole of Jerusalem.

Jesus: That's a beautiful song, grandpa.
Zither Player: Beautiful and old, my son. It's seven times older than I. They say the prophet Isaiah used to sing it right here, beside the temple.
A Man: Now Israel has her prophet and Messiah!
A Woman: Yes, sir! Long live Jesus of Nazareth!
All: Long live Jesus! Long live Jesus!
Zither Player: You mean, the great prophet is here? Where is he? Where?
Peter: Don't turn around, old man. It's this bearded guy before you who was praising your song.
Zither Player: How's that? You? Oh, my son, I'm almost blind, you know . . .
Another Man: Long live the prophet from Galilee?

The uproar of those around us was getting louder and louder. Soon, a group of priests and magistrates from the Sanhedrin was seen coming out of one of the doors of the temple in their elegant tunics and tiaras. From the steps of the temple, they continued watching us. They despised Jesus, yet they also feared him; most especially, they feared the great mass of people who were gathered around us. Jesus, who saw them at once, raised his voice.

Jesus: Hey, grandpa, why don't you sing more songs about the vineyard? I'm sure the people will listen to you, and surely, you'll be earning some denarii.

Zither Player: Oh, my son, I don't remember the lines anymore. How about you? Maybe you're a singing prophet, like Isaiah, or like our king David.

Jesus: Nah, I sing worse than a toad, but let me tell you a story without music. I think the people up there want to hear it. Listen, all of you:

Jesus: There was a master who owned a vineyard. His name was Michael. He loved his land very much. Since it was good land for grapes, he planted a vineyard. He cleaned his land very well, put a fence around it, put up a wine press beside it, and built a tower from which he could see his entire land.

Michael: Look, son. What do you think? Isn't this the most beautiful land of all?

Jesus: Michael had a son. He loved him very much, more than anything else, more than his vineyard, so to speak.

Michael: This is your inheritance, son. Take good care of her. The land is like a woman. You have to attend to her, pamper her, and watch over her. In time, she will give her best fruit.

Jesus: Michael and his son had to go on an urgent trip. So they decided to lease the land to a group of tenants.

Michael: My friends, I trust in you. Take out the bad weeds, sprinkle some fertilizer, water the vineyard, prune the shoots, and then at harvest time gather the grapes and press them in the winepress. On that day, we shall have a grand celebration! So long, I leave everything in your hands. Okay?

A Tenant: All right, master. Don't worry, we shall take care of the land like it was our own child.

Michael: Thank you, my friends. So long! Horse, let's move, c'mon! Hiyaah!

Jesus: A month passed and another and another. Then came harvest time.

A Tenant: Look how beautiful the grapes are, guys! They're as big as melons!

Another Tenant: Yeah, let's cut the bunches and have them made into wine!

Another Tenant: Then let's all drink and have fun! Yippee! I'll get drunk tonight like old Noah! And let the deluge come, for all I care!

Jesus: The harvest was abundant. The clusters of big sparkling grapes were pressed, filling the buckets with sweet and foamy wine.

A Tenant: Hik! Hey, you, Acaz, there's a guy looking for you. He wants to see the foreman of the vine growers. Hik!

Another Tenant: I'm the foreman here. Hik! Let him in, and let him stuff himself with all the grapes he wants. There's enough for everyone here. Hik!

A Messenger: Good morning. Michael, the owner, sent me. He sends you his greetings.

Another Tenant: Well, send him our greetings too.

Messenger: And he wants me to tell you to collect your salaries as agreed upon, since the grapes must have been sold already, and that the rest of the harvest must be given to me.

Tenant: How's that again? Hik! I didn't quite hear you!

Messenger: Since the grapes have already been sold, and . . .

Tenant: Sold? We have drunk and eaten them, that's it, but nothing has been sold! Ha, ha, ha!

Another Tenant: Hey, don't be a killjoy. Go away and leave us in peace.

Messenger: But I, what shall I tell my master?

Tenant: Master or no master! Tell him not to bother us, please, for we're too busy and sleepy and too . . .

Jesus: So the messenger told his master about it.

Michael: It's my fault. I sent you without a letter signed by me, and, of course, they must have thought that you were a smooth talker or spy.

Messenger: Maybe, sir, they have a story to tell.

Michael: Okay, don't worry. I'll send another messenger next week, to collect the money from the harvest.

Jesus: And the other messenger arrived in the vineyard.

Messenger: Michael, the owner has sent me. He's sending you his regards. You may look at his signature on this tablet.

A Tenant: Well, send him our greetings too.

Messenger: And he asks me to collect the proceeds from the sale of the harvest.

Another Tenant: There goes the same old story again! Pff! What a bore! Doesn't he have any other story to tell?

Messenger: Well, since the land is his, he wants...

Tenant: His? Did you say "his"? Ha, ha, ha! Did you hear, fellas? This is his! Ha, ha!

Messenger: Wait a minute! Ahggg! Wait! Look at his signature here...

Tenant: Eat that tablet, yourself! and enjoy it too!

Jesus: The owner of the vineyard could not believe what happened.

Michael: But how could that be possible?

Messenger: But it happened. Look at my bruises, sir.

Michael: I don't get it! There must be some confusion. I'll send another messenger, and the third time will be lucky, as they say.

Jesus: So another messenger went.

Messenger: I came on behalf of my master, Michael, the owner of this farm and he says that...

Tenant: Hey, fellas, here's another one! Come, let's give him a nice beating! Ha, ha, ah!

Messenger: But, I...

Another Tenant: No buts. Here take it, snoopy! Don't pity him!

Jesus: Soon enough Michael learned about it.

Michael: What the hell is happening here? Who do these tenants think they are? We made a pact, but they broke it.

Messenger: It's my ribs, sir, they have broken them.

Michael: I've had enough of it. Right now I'm sending my son to put things right.

Messenger: Be careful, sir, these men are not only thieves; they are also murderers.

Michael: Don't worry, they will respect my son. They have to.

A Tenant: Hey, look, isn't that the master's son coming?

Another Tenant: This is the height of it! Either the master is stupid or he's nuts! Ha!

Another Tenant: Wait, wait a minute. Let's all be rational. He's the heir of all this land. If we are not nice to him, then we lose all this food and our work.

Tenant: Ha, ha, ha! What an imbecile you are, blondy! Hasn't it occurred to you yet? This is our chance! He's the heir. If we get rid of him, then no one will remain in this land except us! Do you get the point, idiots? We shall be the owners of the land! So, fellas, let's do it fast and clean!

Jesus: So the tenants lay hands on the owner's son, who was insulted and spat upon, beaten and kicked out of the vineyard. After inflicting such brutalities on him, they cut off his head with a sharpened knife, like they do to lambs.

A Woman: Has this thing ever happened before? Where? In the north?

Jesus: In the north and in the south. It's happening right here. C'mon, grandpa, try to remember the last line of your song. It's something like this: "Hear the end of my sad song" . . .

Zither Player: Oh, yes, now I remember! Wait a minute, prophet, it's now coming back.

Hear the last part / of my sad song. / God entrusted his vineyard / to the leaders of Israel. / He expected justice / but reaped only abuses. / So I'm suing them / and taking the vineyard from them / to be given to the poor / because the others have been corrupt tenants / and now they will know who I am!

Jesus: Very good, grandpa, very good. So there goes the end of the story. Yes, God is the owner of the land and will demand an accounting from this band of robbers, the leaders of our country; and the vineyard shall be handed over to us, the poor people of Israel.

A Priest: Are you insinuating something, you cheating Nazarene?

Jesus: Nothing new, my friend. The old songs of our country are as clear as the morning sun. You know the song we sing during these holidays. The stone rejected by the builders was chosen by God to strengthen the corners in the topmost part of the building. The builders did not see the value of the stone. The tenants did not listen to the messages of the owner of the vineyard. You, leaders of Israel, are like them: blind and deaf. You don't forgive those who criticize you. When the prophets came, you beat them and persecuted them, and even ridiculed them. John came and you silenced him, until finally, you had him beheaded. And now . . .

Another Priest: And now what?

Jesus: And now you want to do the same with the son: you want to kill him.

The silence that ensued was broken by a shout of one of the priests.

Priest: Did you hear him? He says he is the son of God! Everyone has heard the blasphemy! That's blasphemy! That's blasphemy!

The priests rushed toward us, screaming like mad. They picked up stones in the street and began to hurl them at Jesus, who was covered by the crowd as it retaliated against the Sanhedrin leaders and members. Stones rained on all sides. It was a moment of great confusion. Finally, we were able to mingle with the swarm of foreigners who were beginning to engulf the streets, and left the city. Inside its walls, in the Street of Doves beside the temple, the old zither player with the white beard continued with his song.

Zither Player: People of Jerusalem / inhabitants of Judah / come and tell me: / what else could I do / for the vineyard that I sowed? / what more could I offer it?

•

In the Old Testament, the vineyard was a symbol used oftentimes to represent Israel, the people of God (Isa. 27:1–6; Ps. 80:9–17). The song sung by the old zither player in this episode is the "song of the vineyard" (Isa. 5:1–7), a poem composed by the prophet Isaiah before he started his preaching, probably on the occasion of the harvest. It is one of the major literary texts in the entire Old Testament. Grape planting, which is typical of Palestine and the neighboring countries along the Mediterranean Sea, demands special care. Isaiah speaks of this special care in his poem. The clearing of the land, the construction of the watchtower and the winepress, and so on, are symbolic of God's care and affection for his people.

Aside from the official singers and musicians serving in the temple of Jerusalem, who were from the religious class (Levites) and were experts in various instruments (flute, harp, drum, trumpet, etc.), there were also street singers in Jerusalem, like the old man in this episode. Even to this day, this group still exists in many towns and villages. The songs and poems eventually become the collective memory of the people. Through these verses, they transmit from one generation to another the life and sentiments of the people. Before these were written, a number of great literary works in the ancient times were sung and orally transmitted by roving minstrels.

The parable of "the evil tenants" may be read as an allegory where each of the elements of the story has a meaning. God is the owner of the vineyard, which is Israel. The messengers sent by the master to collect the fruits of the harvest are the prophets. Jesus is the son of the owner. The tenants who reject the messengers are the religious leaders of Israel, who seek to defend their sole interests, under the guise of false fidelity to religion. In order to attain this, they vilify, defame, and even murder the prophets who expose their misbehavior.

Jesus often stressed the difficult mission that the messengers of the kingdom had to face. He said they would be like "lambs among wolves" (Matt. 10:16). He warned them of doors being shut in their faces, of their being accused as heretics, of their being charged in tribunals, and of their being killed. This had been the fate of the ancient prophets, and will continue to be so for the artisans of justice of the kingdom. Not all persons vilified and persecuted are prophets, but all true prophets are always vilified and persecuted. Such persecution is a guaranteed sign of the authenticity of working for justice's sake. The contrary — a road full of roses and comfort — would mean a betrayal of the gospel, no matter if proclaimed in the Lord's name (Luke 6:26). Up to this day, the prophets are still being persecuted, tortured, and murdered. This unjust world rejected by them is "not worthy of them" (Heb. 11:35 – 38), and the hope in the new world which they are fighting for sustains them amid all their sufferings (2 Cor. 4:7-15).

This parable speaks of the inconceivable patience of God, which is due to end. The time has come — Jesus says in this story — when the limit has been reached and God will seize the vineyard from the leaders of the country and give it to "others." These "others" are the poor, despised by the religious institution, those who matter only because they are many in numbers, those who pay their tithes and comply with oppressive laws. They will be the heirs of the vineyard. Isaiah's song is a sad one, something that reflects betrayal. The religious leaders of Israel have been unjust, have oppressed the handicapped, resorted to violence, and monopolized the harvest. So the Lord had to decide: the leaders are out and the heirs shall be the poor.

The title "son of God" attributed to Jesus marks the continuity of his mission with that of the other great prophets of Israel. He presents himself before his people and before the religious as God's final messenger — the son of the owner, who fully knows the owner's will — who likewise affirms, in a definite manner, the plan of the Father. God's patience is over: God shall relinquish the vineyard to the poor, who in turn will sow and collect the harvest, so that they may live.

In talking about the stone chosen by God to become the cornerstone of the building, Jesus makes reference to some verses of the solemn psalm of the Passover (Psalm 118). The psalm tells us how God is able to change things: the stone rejected by the builders is given the most important place by God. Jesus, the poor man, is the cornerstone. The poor are the stones for the building (1 Pet. 2:5). The psalm ends with an expression of marvel: "This is the work of God, and we marvel at it." God's decision is amazing. It is the very essence of the gospel: the last shall be the first, the outcasts shall be the chosen ones.

(Matt. 21:33 – 46; Mark 12:1–12; Luke 20: 9 -19)

Suggestions for Using This Book

Just Jesus can be used in many ways. It is ideal for catechetical and liturgical dramatization. Here are listed liturgical and biblical references.

Volume 1, Chaps. 1–51
Volume 2, Chaps. 52–99
Volume 3, Chaps. 100–144

LITURGICAL REFERENCES

Cycle A

1 Sunday of Advent	Mt 24:37–44	Chap. 105
2 Sunday of Advent	Mt 3:1–12	Chap. 2, 6
3 Sunday of Advent	Mt 11:2–11	Chap. 45, 136
4 Sunday of Advent	Mt 1:18–24	Chap. 133
Christmas	Lk 2:1–14	Chap. 134, 135
Holy Family	Mt 2:13–15, 19–23	Chap. 137
2 Sunday After Christmas	Jn 1:1–18	Chap. 131
Epiphany	Mt 2:1–12	Chap. 135
Baptism of the Lord	Mt 3:13–17	Chap. 7, 8
Ash Wednesday	Mt 6:1–6, 16–18	Chap. 49
1 Sunday of Lent	Mt 4:1–11	Chap. 9
2 Sunday of Lent	Mt 17:1–9	Chap. 68
3 Sunday of Lent	Jn 4:5–42	Chap. 81, 82
4 Sunday of Lent	Jn 9:1–41	Chap. 79
5 Sunday of Lent	Jn 11:1–45	Chap. 102
Passion Sunday	Mt 26:14–27:66	Chap. 108–9, 111–16, 118–23
Good Friday	Jn 18:1–19:42	Chap. 113–14, 116, 118–23
Holy Saturday	Mt 28:1–10	Chap. 125
Easter Sunday	Jn 20:1–9	Chap. 125, 126
2 Sunday of Easter	Jn 20:19–31	Chap. 128
3 Sunday of Easter	Lk 24:13–35	Chap. 127
4 Sunday of Easter	Jn 10:1–10	Chap. 104
5 Sunday of Easter	Jn 14:1–12	
6 Sunday of Easter	Jn 14:15–21	
Ascension	Mt 28:16–20	Chap. 130
7 Sunday of Easter	Jn 17:1–11	
Pentecost	Jn 20:19–23	Chap. 128
Trinity Sunday	Jn 3:16–18	Chap. 56

Cycle B

Baptism of the Lord	Mk 1:7–11	Chap. 7, 8
Ash Wednesday	Mt 6:1–6, 16–18	Chap. 49
1 Sunday of Lent	Mk 1:12–15	Chap. 9
2 Sunday of Lent	Mk 9:2–10	Chap. 68
3 Sunday of Lent	Jn 2:13–25	Chap. 107
4 Sunday of Lent	Jn 3:14–21	Chap. 56
5 Sunday of Lent	Jn 12:20–30	
Passion Sunday	Mk 14:1–15, 47	Chap. 103, 108–9, 111–16
Good Friday	Jn 18:1–19:42	Chap. 113–14, 116, 118–23
Holy Saturday	Mk 16:1–7	Chap. 125
Easter Sunday	Jn 20:1–9	Chap. 125–26
2 Sunday of Easter	Jn 20:19–31	Chap. 128
3 Sunday of Easter	Lk 24:35–48	Chap. 128
4 Sunday of Easter	Jn 10:11–18	Chap. 104
5 Sunday of Easter	Jn 15:1–8	Chap. 111
6 Sunday of Easter	Jn 15:9–17	Chap. 111
Ascension	Mk 16:15–20	Chap. 128–30
7 Sunday of Easter	Jn 17:11–19	
Pentecost	Acts 2:1–11	Chap. 142
Trinity Sunday	Mt 28:16–20	Chap. 130
Body and Blood of Christ	Mk 14:12–16, 22–26	Chap. 109, 111
2 Sunday Ord. Time	Jn 1:35–42	Chap. 5
3 Sunday Ord. Time	Mk 1:14–20	Chap. 14
4 Sunday Ord. Time	Mk 1:21–28	Chap. 18
5 Sunday Ord. Time	Mk 1:29–39	Chap. 19
6 Sunday Ord. Time	Mk 1:40–45	Chap. 20
7 Sunday Ord. Time	Mk 2:1–12	Chap. 35
8 Sunday Ord. Time	Mk 2:18–22	Chap. 46
9 Sunday Ord. Time	Mk 2:23–3:6	Chap. 29, 30
10 Sunday Ord. Time	Mk 3:20–35	Chap. 32, 66
11 Sunday Ord. Time	Mk 4:26–34	Chap. 24, 46
12 Sunday Ord. Time	Mk 4:35–41	Chap. 39
13 Sunday Ord. Time	Mk 5:21–43	Chap. 44
14 Sunday Ord. Time	Mk 6:1–6	Chap. 22
15 Sunday Ord. Time	Mk 6:7–13	Chap. 60
16 Sunday Ord. Time	Mk 6:30–34	Chap. 57
17 Sunday Ord. Time	Jn 6:1–15	Chap. 57
18 Sunday Ord. Time	Jn 6:24–35	Chap. 58
19 Sunday Ord. Time	Jn 6:41–52	Chap. 58
20 Sunday Ord. Time	Jn 6:51–58	Chap. 58
21 Sunday Ord. Time	Jn 6:60–69	Chap. 58
22 Sunday Ord. Time	Mk 7:1–8, 14–15, 21–23	Chap. 98
23 Sunday Ord. Time	Mk 7:31–37	
24 Sunday Ord. Time	Mk 8:27–35	Chap. 67
25 Sunday Ord. Time	Mk 9:30–37	Chap. 36
26 Sunday Ord. Time	Mk 9:38–43, 45, 47–48	Chap. 63
27 Sunday Ord. Time	Mk 10:2–16	Chap. 36, 71
28 Sunday Ord. Time	Mk 10:17–30	Chap. 92

Cycle C

9 Sunday Ord. Time	Lk 7:1–10	Chap. 42
10 Sunday Ord. Time	Lk 7:11–17	Chap. 38
11 Sunday Ord. Time	Lk 7:36–8:3	Chap. 41, 62
12 Sunday Ord. Time	Lk 9:18–24	Chap. 67
13 Sunday Ord. Time	Lk 9:51–62	Chap. 82, 91
14 Sunday Ord. Time	Lk 10:1–12, 17–20	Chap. 57, 60
15 Sunday Ord. Time	Lk 10:25–37	Chap. 78
16 Sunday Ord. Time	Lk 10:38–42	Chap. 50
17 Sunday Ord. Time	Lk 11:1–13	Chap. 47
18 Sunday Ord. Time	Lk 12:13–21	Chap. 73
19 Sunday Ord. Time	Lk 12:32–48	Chap. 33, 105
20 Sunday Ord. Time	Lk 12:49–53	
21 Sunday Ord. Time	Lk 13:22–30	Chap. 105
22 Sunday Ord. Time	Lk 14:1, 7–14	
23 Sunday Ord. Time	Lk 14:25–33	Chap. 111
24 Sunday Ord. Time	Lk 15:1–32	Chap. 27, 34, 52
25 Sunday Ord. Time	Lk 16:1–13	Chap. 84
26 Sunday Ord. Time	Lk 16:19–31	Chap. 37
27 Sunday Ord. Time	Lk 17:5–10	
28 Sunday Ord. Time	Lk 17:11–19	Chap. 89
29 Sunday Ord. Time	Lk 18:1–8	Chap. 74
30 Sunday Ord. Time	Lk 18:9–14	Chap. 80
31 Sunday Ord. Time	Lk 19:1–10	Chap. 87
32 Sunday Ord. Time	Lk 20:27–38	Chap. 97
33 Sunday Ord. Time	Lk 21:5–19	Chap. 93
Christ the King	Lk 23:35–43	Chap. 122
Assumption	Lk 1:39–44	Chap. 132
All Saints	Mt 5:1–12	Chap. 28
Immaculate Conception	Lk 1:26–38	Chap. 131

BIBLICAL REFERENCES

Matthew

Mt 1:18–24	Chap. 133
Mt 2:13–18	Chap. 137
Mt 3:5–6	Chap. 2
Mt 3:7–12	Chap. 6
Mt 3:13–17	Chap. 7
Mt 3:16	Chap. 3
Mt 4:1–2	Chap. 63
Mt 4:1–11	Chap. 9
Mt 4:12–17	Chap. 11
Mt 4:13	Chap. 13
Mt 4:18–22	Chap. 14
Mt 5:1–12	Chap. 28
Mt 5:38–48	Chap. 55
Mt 6:1–18	Chap. 49
Mt 6:5–15	Chap. 47
Mt 6:25–34	Chap. 33
Mt 8:1–4	Chap. 20
Mt 8:5–13	Chap. 42
Mt 8:14–15	Chap. 19
Mt 8:18–22	Chap. 31
Mt 8:23–27	Chap. 39
Mt 8:28–34	Chap. 40
Mt 9:1–8	Chap. 35
Mt 9:9	Chap. 25
Mt 9:10–13	Chap. 26
Mt 9:14–17	Chap. 46
Mt 9:18–26	Chap. 44
Mt 10:1–4	Chap. 48
Mt 10:5–15	Chap. 60
Mt 10:16–33	Chap. 93
Mt 11:1–17	Chap. 136
Mt 11:2–6	Chap. 45
Mt 11:7–19	Chap. 62
Mt 11:14	Chap. 116
Mt 11:20–24	Chap. 90
Mt 11:25–27	Chap. 60
Mt 12:1–8	Chap. 29
Mt 12:9–14	Chap. 30
Mt 12:38–42	Chap. 90
Mt 12:46–50	Chap. 32
Mt 13:1–23	Chap. 31
Mt 13:22–29	Chap. 66
Mt 13:24–30	Chap. 43

Mt 13:31–32	Chap. 24
Mt 13:33	Chap. 52
Mt 13:53–58	Chap. 22
Mt 14	Chap. 10
Mt 14:3–12	Chap. 54
Mt 14:13–21	Chap. 57
Mt 14:24–33	Chap. 59
Mt 15:1–20	Chap. 98
Mt 15:21–28	Chap. 65
Mt 15:32–39	Chap. 57
Mt 16:1–12	Chap. 62
Mt 16:13–24	Chap. 67
Mt 17:1–13	Chap. 68
Mt 17:14–21	Chap. 69
Mt 18:1–5	Chap. 36
Mt 18:6–9	Chap. 63
Mt 18:12–14	Chap. 27
Mt 18:21-35	Chap. 95
Mt 19:1–9	Chap. 71
Mt 19:10–12	Chap. 72
Mt 19:13–15	Chap. 36
Mt 19:16–24	Chap. 92
Mt 20:1–16	Chap. 61
Mt 20:20–28	Chap. 94
Mt 21:1–11	Chap. 106
Mt 21:12–17	Chap. 107
Mt 21:28–32	Chap. 96
Mt 21:33–46	Chap. 99
Mt 22:1–10	Chap. 83
Mt 22:15–22	Chap. 101
Mt 22:23–33	Chap. 97
Mt 23:1–36	Chap. 107
Mt 23:37–39	Chap. 106
Mt 24:3–51	Chap. 105
Mt 25:1–13	Chap. 70
Mt 25:14–30	Chap. 85
Mt 25:31–46	Chap. 100
Mt 26:6–13	Chap. 103
Mt 26:14–16	Chap. 108
Mt 26:17–19	Chap. 109
Mt 26:26–35	Chap. 111
Mt 26:36–44	Chap. 112
Mt 26:45–56	Chap. 113
Mt 26:57–68	Chap. 115
Mt 26:69–75	Chap. 114

Mark

Luke

John

Acts